10/2002 /

Virgil Thomson

Other Books Edited by Richard Kostelanetz

Virgil Thomson

A READER

SELECTED WRITINGS 1924–1984

EDITED BY

RICHARD KOSTELANETZ

Routledge
New York and London

Published in 2002 by
Routledge
29 West 35th Street
New York, NY 10001

Published in Great Britain by
Routledge
11 New Fetter Lane
London EC4P 4EE

Routledge is an imprint of the Taylor & Francis Group.

Printed in the United States of America on acid-free paper.

10 9 8 7 6 5 4 3 2 1

Cataloging-in-Publication Data is available from the Library of Congress

ISBN 0-415-93795-7

To the memory of S. Foster Damon,
Thomson's teacher and friend.

It was during those first two years [at Harvard in the 1920s] that I came to know S. Foster Damon, . . . a composer as well as a poet and a scholar. . . . I do not remember how I first knew him; but I do remember long walks and talks; and I remember his bringing me music and books that he thought I should know. Some of these, such as the critical writings of T. S. Eliot and the Irish tales of James Stephens, I found merely informative or charming. Others changed my life. Among the last were the piano works of Erik Satie, a pile of them four inches high, and a thin small volume called *Tender Buttons* by Gertrude Stein. I returned these favors by introducing him to peyote, which we would take together, sometimes with another poet and English instructor, Robert Hillyer. Foster has often reappeared in my life and almost always with gifts in hand, the most remarkable of these being a facsimile collection, with Damon's notes, issued in 1937 at Brown University, of one hundred American popular songs from before the Civil War, a source that has helped me ever since to evoke early times in composing for films and dramatic spectacles.

—Virgil Thomson, *Virgil Thomson* (1966)

My peyote adventures are recounted in my autobiog on pages 42 & 43, also page 46, which involves Damon and Hillyer. There were others too, but not poets or famous; no musicians, I think.

I do not remember whether Damon or Hillyer wrote poetry under the influence, though they may have. I did.

Some exercises were incidental to the "trip" itself, as it would now be called. The vast parade of visions in color, many with meanings attached, that are specific to peyote. You should try it sometime, but the real, not the synthetic "mescaline." Yrs, Virgil T.

—Handwritten postcard to Richard Kostelanetz, 20 January 1972

Acknowledgments

"Life Among the Natives," "How Composers Eat," "Why Composers Write How," reprinted from *The State of Music* (1939) by permission the Virgil Thomson Foundation, Ltd., copyright owner. "Age Without Honor," "Masterpieces," "Conducting Modern Music," "The Intellectual Audience," "Bigger than Baseball," "Conservative Institution," "English at the Met," "Mozart's Leftism," "Acquaintance with Wagner," "Fairy Tale About Music," "French Music Here," "Reactionary Critic," "Great Music," "Pipe-Organ Obsession," "Master of Distortion and Exaggeration," "Gian-Carlo Menotti," "Silk-Underwear Music," "The Toscanini Case," "The Koussevitzky Case," "In Spite of Conducting," "Sacred Swing," "La Môme Piaf," "Olivier Messiaen," "Star Dust and Spun Steel," "Expressive Percussion," reprinted from the *New York Herald Tribune* by the Virgil Thomson Foundation, Ltd., copyright owner. "Gertrude Stein [I & III]," "Music Does Not Flow," "The Genius Type," "On Being Discovered," reprinted from the *New York Review of Books* by permission of the Virgil Thomson Foundation, Ltd., copyright owner. "Carl Ruggles," "Aaron Copland [1971]," and short notes on composers, reprinted from *American Music Since 1910* (1971) by permission of the Virgil Thomson Foundation, Ltd., copyright owner. "Jazz," reprinted from *American Mercury* (August 1924) by permission of the Virgil Thomson Foundation, Ltd., copyright owner. "Aaron Copland [1932]," "Swing Music," "Swing Again," "George Gershwin," "Most Melodious Tears," reprinted from *Modern Music* (January 1932, November 1935, May 1936, March 1938) by permission of the Virgil Thomson Foundation, Ltd., copyright owner. "The New Grove...," reprinted from *MLA Notes*, September 1981, by permission of the Virgil Thomson Foundation, Ltd., copyright owner. "On, Donald Sutherland," reprinted from *Denver Review*, by permission of the publisher. "The Paper," "Europe in America," "All Roads Lead to Paris," reprinted from *Virgil Thomson* (1966) by permission of the Virgil Thomson Foundation, Ltd., copyright owner. "Possibilities: V.T. Questioned by 8 Composers," reprinted from *Possibilities* (1947) by permission of the Virgil Thomson Foundation, Ltd., copyright owner. "The Music Reviewer and His Assignment (1953)," "Music Now (1961)," "Aaron Copland (1957)," "Edgard Varèse (1966)," "Eugene Berman (1974)," "Leonid Berman (1978)," reprinted from the *Proceedings of the American Academy and Institute of Arts and Letters* (New York) by permission of the American Academy of Arts and Letters. Copyright © 1953, 1961, 1957, 1966, 1974, 1978 by the American Academy of Arts and Letters. "Personal Statement," "About Four Saints," "Synopsis," "A Note on Lou Harrison," "Background of the Opera," Notes to *The Feast of Love, Sea Piece with Birds, The Seine at Night*, reprinted from various sources by permission of the Virgil Thomson Foundation, Ltd., copyright owner. "On Writing Operas and Staging Them" reprinted from *Paranassus: Poetry in Review* X/1 (1982) by permission of the Virgil Thomson Foundation, Ltd., copyright owner. "Edwin Denby," reprinted from *Ballet Review* XII/1 (1984), by permission of Francis Mason and the Virgil Thomson Foundation, Ltd., copyright owner. "Remembering Gertrude," reprinted from *Columbia Literary Columns* (February 1982), by permission of the Virgil Thomson Foundation, Ltd., copyright owner.

CONTENTS

III CONTEMPORARIES—PERFORMERS

IV CONTEMPORARIES—COMPOSERS

V CONTEMPORARIES—PUBLISHERS, ARTISTS, WRITERS, AND A MUSEUM DIRECTOR

VI Successors

VII Autobiography

VIII His Own Works

To expose the philanthropic persons in control of our musical institutions for the amateurs they are, to reveal the manipulators of our musical distribution for the culturally retarded profit makers that indeed they are, and to support with all the power of my praise every artist, composer, group, or impresario whose relation to music was straightforward.

—Virgil Thomson (1966)

Virgil was always a model for me, and his music criticism was the greatest pleasure in New York. It was so unexpected to find anything like that in a newspaper.

—Edwin Denby, quoted by John Gruen, The Party's Over Now *(1972)*

This book was originally intended to be the initial volume in a series that still may happen. Collectively titled "American Composers in Their Own Words," the editorial proposal assumed that many of our best composers have also been skillful writers whose most important essays should be collected in individual volumes. It seemed appropriate to begin with Virgil Thomson, who in the middle of the last century epitomized the ideal of the composer-writer who didn't resist publishing and publishing widely, even if it was often said that "his writing is better than his music."

This book differs from the previous, now out-of-print *Virgil Thomson Reader* (1981) in being shorter and more focused. Though Thomson in his dotage seemed at times a harmless, avuncular chatterbox, I wanted to restore an image of the intellectual in his prime: a gritty critic who didn't fear deflating august institutions or exposing publicly his professional friends or the world he knew.

As a fan, I regret that Thomson did not broach two subjects that deserved his toughest critical scrutiny. One was his conflicts of interest as a New York City newspaper music critic whose works were often performed in his hometown. Usually these performances were reviewed by his assistants, none of whom ever submitted a negative notice. Nonetheless, it was not for nothing that his music was more widely performed and honored during his tenure at the *Tribune* than afterwards, for as the publisher/editor Minna Lederman (Daniel) reportedly quipped at the time about Thomson retiring from the *Trib*, "How would he get his music played?" The second, more obvious to us now, is homosexuality in a music world at the time when differences in musical style corresponded to differences in sexual persuasion. Though Thomson publicly acknowledged his modest drug use, he scarcely mentioned his homosexuality, which was in fact scarcely modest. Incidentally, as Arnold Schönberg changed the spelling of his name to Schoenberg when he moved to America in the 1930s, I've asked the publisher to keep Thomson's orthography as it originally appeared.

This book is dedicated to S. Foster Damon (1893–1971), Thomson's friend and sometime teacher. It was on the occasion of Damon's 75th birthday in 1968 that I first met Thomson. As Damon's student in the early '60s (and being more than 40 years younger than Thomson), I too was influenced in more ways than I can remember. Unable to offer drugs in return (which are scarcely equal to Damon's taste-changing advice to Thomson on what to read and hear), I have been dedicating books to Damon's memory. One predecessor was *AnOther E. E. Cummings* (1998), because Cummings too has acknowledged Damon's influence in print. The image of Damon as an ideal teacher/intellectual companion should not be forgotten.

I'm grateful to Richard Carlin for commissiong this book; to my intern Jaime K. Lee for functioning as assistant editor for a while; to David Sachs, Noah Creshevsky, Michael Ochs, and other colleagues for their advice in making selections; and to James M. Kendrick, Esq., for representing the Thomson Estate (and the V. T. Foundation).

Richard Kostelanetz

VIRGIL THOMSON AS WRITER

My starting point is always a feeling of partisanship, a sense of injustice. When I sit down to write a book, I do not say to myself, "I am going to produce a work of art." I write because there is some lie that I want to expose, some fact to which I want to draw attention, and my initial concern is to get a hearing.

—*George Orwell, "Why I Write" (1947)*

Virgil Thomson (1896–1989) functioned best as a composer with an outside stimulus, such as a poetic text, a libretto, a film requiring a score, or early American folk songs. Likewise as a writer, he functioned best not with texts imagined from scratch, such as poetry and stories, but with essays about things, beginning with the previous night's concerts, then including certain issues, his colleagues, and finally himself. "I can describe things and persons, narrate facts," he once wrote. "Language, for me, is merely for telling the truth about something."

No other American composer wrote as well: sentence by sentence, paragraph by paragraph, essay by essay. It was not for nothing that Edmund Wilson, his near-contemporary, once identified Thomson as the only "first-rate critical journalist [who] has appeared since [Alexander] Woollcott's time"—which was a generation before. As a very professional essayist, Thomson was skilled at various expository forms from the short review to the extended essay, and at many tones from the puffy to the severe. His style reflected the influence of two English masters of the previous century: Oscar Wilde and the historian Thomas Babington Macauley. Thomson wrote directly with clean sentences scrupulously free of emotional language, obscure formulations, irrelevant metaphors, and intimidating jargon, all of which have been at times as prevalent in musicology as other academic disciplines. His writing resembled his music composition first in the exploration of possibilities of various lengths, including very short forms, whose musical genre Thomson called "portraits," and then in his striving for simplicity and thus accessibility (which has made his music "postmodernist" for some).

Not unlike other newspaper reviewers, he had to write well about subjects barely interesting to him, beginning with the previous day's concert. Only in his longer "Sunday" pieces could he choose his own subjects and write more considered criticism. He wrote by hand, even in the age of the typewriter. His short reviews are no less strong than his extended essays; nor are the latter organized, as sometimes happens when newspaper reviewers write at length, as a series of short reviews. He made music criticism seem so fluent that you wonder why few others in America have done as well.

He was the master of the negative notice, knowing well that no reviewer is taken seriously unless he rejects as well as promotes. The simplest test of the professional integrity of any critic, as well as any reviewing medium, is the publication of negative judgments, particularly about prominent subjects. Those avoiding severe criticism know that they are merely publicists.

Thomson had a taste for exposing the nitty-gritty of his profession: how careers were made and unmade, how prominent institutions killed an art, how the manager of a prominent talent agency was also influencing an institution's hiring selections. As a gossip with critical intelligence, he told readers what they wanted to know: better, what they *had to know* if they were to be discriminating spectators. The fact that there is no one like him in this respect among music critics today merely underlines his uniqueness. One would measure a change in Thomson's position when he no longer published gritty pieces: when he became a defender of establishments rather than their critic. My sense is that this happened in the early '70s, after he turned 75, even though his last essay in this vein, his snippy portrait of Aaron Copland in *American Music Since 1910* (1971), ranks among the best of this rare kind.

Thomson began as a protegee of S. Foster Damon, a Harvard English instructor who had previously majored in music. In addition to writing the first American book on the poet William Blake, *William Blake* (1924), Damon in the 1920s was initiating his studies of American vernacular culture that led eventually to publications on square dancing and a pioneering collection of *100 American Songs* (1937). The latter became a favorite Thomson source that, he wrote, "helped me ever since to evoke earlier times in composing for films and dramatic spectacles." Given this background, it is scarcely surprising that Thomson's first publication in 1924 dealt with jazz. It was written for *The American Mercury*, edited by H. L. Mencken, who was likewise concerned with studying popular Americana. When Thomson reprinted the essay in 1981, he claimed it was "to my knowledge the first published effort submitting jazz to the procedures of musical analysis." Even in the 1940s, reviewing for a New York newspaper, he wrote respectfully about gospel music and the French cabaret singer Edith Piaf.

The style of his literacy was more American than European. It is hard to imagine a French writer producing this insightful paragraph:

Chopin's prescription for rubato playing, which is almost word for word Mozart's prescription for playing an accompanied melody, is that the right hand should take liberties with the time values, while the left hand remains rhythmically unaltered. This is exactly the effect you get when a good blues singer is accompanied by a good swing band. It is known to the modern world as *le style hot*.

My sense is that the reason Thomson stayed in New York, even after retiring from daily newspaper work, was that he knew that not just his cultural roots but his best audience were American. His countrymen were more likely that the French to understand this paragraph, notwithstanding Thomson concluding with a French epithet.

After publishing mostly in *Modern Music*, Minna Lederman's quarterly periodical featuring well-edited writing by American composers, Thomson wrote the short book upon which his literary reputation is based. *The State of Music* (1939) was a general essay about the musical world and its relation to the other arts. Painters and writers loved it for situating music in a larger cultural universe; emerging musicians treasured it for practical insight into a society that they hoped to join. One of its chapters, "Why Composers Write How," subtitled "The Economic Determinants of Musical Style," remains more than 60 years later a model for tracing the relationships between social position and artistic style in clearly persuasive prose. (Later attempts at musical sociology, such as, say, those by Marxists and by those influenced by Marxists, seem clumsy and evasive in comparison.) The success of that book established Thomson's credentials as a courageous critic.

So it was scarcely surprising that Thomson began his American newspaper career with a spiky test balloon: a comprehensively negative review of not just a Philharmonic concert but its typical repertoire. "The Philharmonic Symphony Society of New York opened its ninety-ninth season last evening in Carnegie Hall," he wrote in the *New York Herald-Tribune* on October 11, 1940. "There was little that could be called festive about the occasion. The menu was routine, the playing ditto. Beethoven's Overture to Egmont is a classic hors d'oeuvre. Nobody's digestion was ever spoiled by it, and no late comer has ever lost much by missing it." Not yet done, he continued that the concert itself "was anything but a memorable experience. The music itself was soggy, the playing dull and brutal. As a friend remarked, who had never been to one of these concerts before, 'I understand now why the Philharmonic is not a part of New York's intellectual life.'" If only because it is easy to imagine a beginning critic at a lesser outlet being fired for such an opening-day salvo, consider it a tribute to the *Herald-Tribune* and his editor Geoffrey Parsons that Thomson was retained. (Remember this was a time when more than one New York city newspaper was competing for an elite audience.) It was not for nothing that "The Paper," as Thomson called it, merited an entire, memorable chapter in his autobiography.

Thomson had no patience with the European-born conductors who were so prominent in America at the time. His favorite bête noir was Arturo Toscanini

(1867-1957), whose reputation at the time seemed impregnable. "Publicly you couldn't say anything against him," Thomson recalled many years later. "I was allowed to because I was able to write with a certain brilliance." He became one of those radical characters who was tolerated because he was read. (Consider him in this respect in a pantheon with G. B. Shaw, Gore Vidal, and H. L. Mencken.) He said what no one else dared say; audacity was a key component of his critical style, as in the following assessment of Gertrude Stein's Jewish sentiment (which is rarely discussed in other Stein literature):

> She held certain Jews in attachment for their family-like warmth, though she felt no solidarity with Jewry. Tristan Tzara—French-language poet from Rumania, Dada pioneer, early surrealist, and battler for the Communist party—she said was "like a cousin." Miss Etta and Dr. Claribel Cone, picture buyers and friends from Baltimore days, she handled almost as if they were her sisters. The sculptors Jo Davidson and Jacques Lipschitz, the painter Man Ray she accepted as though they had a second cousin's right to be part of her life. About men or goyim, even about her oldest man friend, Picasso, she could feel unsure; but a woman or a Jew she could size up quickly.

Having known Stein in France, Thomson could account for why she and Toklas were buried in a Jewish section of the great Parisian cemetery: Père Lachaise.

It is commonly said that Thomson was a Francophile who, when he returned to the U.S. at the beginning of World War II, advocated French music over German. While that impression is true, I think his principal bias was toward American music and American composers and thus against those oblivious to native work, such as Toscanini. In this respect, he created the preconditions for the acceptance of Charles Ives as a great American composer and for Leonard Bernstein as the first native-born conductor of the New York Philharmonic. It was this partisanship that made him stay on his job.

During his years at the *Tribune* he arranged for the paper to hire at various times Paul Bowles (who subsequently became known as a novelist), Peggy Glanville-Hicks, Arthur Berger, Elliott Carter, and Lou Harrison. The composer Eric Salzman (b. 1933) once told me that even though Thomson had retired from the *Herald-Tribune* in 1954, his policy influenced Salzman's being hired there in 1956. As Thomson's first biographer Anthony Tommasini put it:

> Thomson thought that it was essential for musicians, especially composers, to take charge of the institutions and organizations that propagated music. Composers should write the reviews, run the orchestras, program the radio stations, release the recordings, reform the copyright laws. To the charge that this would represent a conflict of interest, Thomson was withering in his rebuke. Who would be better qualified to handle these tasks, he asked. Businessmen? Lawyers? Advertising executives?

II

No writer contributed more toward the sophistication of musical life in the United States than Virgil Thomson.

—Robert Craft, **New York Review of Books** *(June 16, 1988)*

Virgil, who spoke as he wrote, economically and to the point, in whole sentences and paragraphs, had the wittiest English language repartee of anyone around.

—*Ned Rorem, "Virgil (1944)" (1994)*

Adopting the tone of a brilliant raconteur, a Kansas City boy who needed to impress the New Englanders at Harvard, Thomson became in time the awesomely sharp fellow portrayed in his pages: a legendary conversationalist, the closest American semblance to Cyril Connolly or Oscar Wilde. His classic lines are remembered to this day, more than a decade after his death. They appear not only in his own writings but also in biographies about other people. For instance, in his *City Poet* (1993), about the well-liked writer Frank O'Hara (1926–66), Brad Gooch writes: "There had indeed been much discussion over who was to speak at the grave. According to the composer Virgil Thomson, 'After his death a dozen of his lovers turned up looking for the glory of being the chief widow.'" Elsewhere in the biography, Gooch quotes Thomson on O'Hara's working at the Museum of Modern Art and writing about contemporary artists:

> It was like those French poets. They all wrote blurbs about modern painters and got paid off in pictures. The Picasso gang were all plugged by poets. I don't say incorrectly, but they were. Poets write the best advertising copy in the world. Now the Museum of Modern Art was very busy keeping up the price of the pictures in its trustees' collections. They were back and forth to Paris all the time. As a matter of fact, they used to get Paris writers to do catalogues for them for a while. And then they found Frank, this flexible Irishman, who could push the opinions they wanted.

In The *Importance of Being Oscar* (1968), the pianist Oscar Levant, himself once a celebrated raconteur, tells the following story:

> Stravinsky was commissioned by the Venice Festival to write them an original work. His contribution turned out to be fifteen minutes long. The officials of the festival complained to Stravinsky that this was too short. "Well then," Stravinsky replied calmly, "play it again." Since that time, Virgil Thomson christened him "the Merchant of Venice."

In his memoir of New York in the 1950s, *The Party's Over Now* (1972), John Gruen likewise quotes Thomson:

> People often ask me whether I would have preferred working for the *New York Times*. The answer is no, because the *Times* is prissy. The *Times* never liked distinction, you know; they don't like intellectually oriented reporters or critics. The *Tribune* did. The *Tribune* was the only paper on which an educated, intellectual man had no shame of being there.

Thomson continues to Gruen, who incidentally studied music orchestration with Thomson:

> Leonard Bernstein and I have always been terribly friendly. But we didn't seek each other out. We kind of operated on two sides of a fence. I didn't throw enough balls to him, and he didn't throw enough balls to me.

Thomson, to Calvin Tomkins on his testy relationship with John Cage:

> John and I have always been friends in a real sense, but we're also enemies. He could never understand why I wasn't as far out as he was. He felt that, since I was bright, and gifted, and had done things in music he liked, then why the hell wasn't I? And did my not being so far out imply a possible error on his part?

In Gruen's *Close-Up* (1968), Thomson reflects on different ways of responding to negative criticism:

> Whether you clash with your critics or not depends upon on how accustomed you are to being famous yourself. In general, the people who have been famous from their youth, like Koussevitzky or Toscanini, do not deign, no matter how angry they are, to dispute openly with the press.

And on celebrity:

> The price of fame, as I observe in my friends like that, seems to be that being a celebrity takes lots of time....And I hear them complaining a great deal that they are so successful that they have no time for themselves, and nobody ever loves them for themselves alone. Well, they have got themselves where they have got by wanting it and working very hard at it, and now if they wish to indulge in a little self-pity because they are rich and famous, well, I find myself slightly lacking in sympathy.

In his biography of Natalie Barney, *The Amazon of Letters* (1976), George Wickes quotes Thomson on the Parisian visits of Edith Sitwell and her literary brothers:

If the Sitwells came over and were around Gertrude's [Stein's], she'd probably take them to Natalie for some soirée. If you've got Edith Sitwell on your hands, you don't want to see her every day. You get somebody else to see her, which amuses her, too, you get her around, distribute her.

Ned Rorem recalls in *Other Entertainments* (1996) that Thomson emerged from an operation three years before his death asking the doctor, "Will I live?" Assured that he would survive, he added, "In that case I'll need my glasses." Anthony Tommasini's otherwise informative biography (1996) fails to do what James Boswell did for Samuel Johnson—memorialize his conversation—because one quality not shared by biographer and subject is a sense of humor.

It must be said that not all of Thomson's writing was equally successful. I find his autobiography, *Virgil Thomson* (1966), to lack the wit and mischievousness that marked his best writing, notwithstanding its audaciously eponymous title. By the time he turned seventy he had lived securely in New York for a quarter-century; he was no longer the bouncing, pugnacious young man (and could not persuasively pose as one). Ned Rorem recently charged that Thomson excluded him from this book because Rorem had earlier revealed in print the homosexuality that Thomson could not so publicly acknowledge for himself. In general, the essays written in the last 25 years of his life are inferior to those written before that milestone. My hunch is that once Thomson retired from the *New York Herald-Tribune* in 1956, he didn't work as hard on his writing as before; he may not have felt the need to do so.

Thomson belongs to that great modern tradition of composers who knew they had to write, and write often, if their music were to find its maximal audience: a tradition that includes Arnold Schoenberg, Béla Bartók, and Roger Sessions among the moderns; Pierre Boulez and Karlheinz Stockhausen among the younger Europeans; and both Milton Babbitt and John Cage among many younger Americans. Thomson's writing made him famous to a level that could not have been reached by his music alone. He wrote perhaps one million words in sum, or 20,000 per year for 50 years, which means he was perhaps twice as prolific, or promiscuous, as, say, Bartók or Schoenberg. In America, only Ned Rorem and Eric Salzman, among writing composers, could rival Thomson for sheer volume. His music is remembered, to be sure, but his writing is remembered better. While he was a good composer, he was a great writer, one of the few composers whose best writings belong in every literary anthology of American criticism or American exposition.

*The richest brief (auto)biography of Thomson, containing nearly all the impor-
tant facts, appears in his entry on himself in his book* American Music Since
1910 *(1971).*

THOMSON, VIRGIL GARNETT born Kansas City, Missouri 25 November 1896;
A.B. Harvard 1922; honorary degrees from Syracuse, Rutgers, Park, Fairfield,
Roosevelt; Academic Medal New York University; studied piano with G.
Lichtenwalter, H. Gebhard; organ with Clarence D. Sears, Wallace Goodrich,
Nadia Boulanger; conducting (choral) with A. T. Davison, (orchestral) Chalmers
Clifton; composition with E. B. Hill, Rosario Scalero, Nadia Boulanger.
Fellowships (Harvard) J. K. Paine, Naumburg; (Paris) Ecole Normale de
Musique; (New York) Juilliard, Guggenheim, Fulbright. Assistant instructor
Harvard 1920–21, 1922–23, 1924–25; organist and choirmaster King's Chapel,
Boston 1922–23; lived in Paris 1925–40. Pulitzer Prize in music; gold medal
National Institute of Arts and Letters; Brandeis University award; David
Bispham medal for American opera; special citation New York Music Critics'
Circle (of which he was founder and first chairman).

Has conducted major orchestras in United States, Latin America, and
Europe; opera in Chicago, New York, Paris. Visiting professorships Colorado
College, State University of Buffalo, University of California in Los Angeles,
Carnegie-Mellon, Trinity (Hartford); lectureships University of Southern
California, Stanford, Smith, Emory. Commissions: Louisville, Dallas, Kansas
City, New York Philharmonic orchestras; Ballet Caravan; Alice M. Ditson; Kansas
City Festival; Library of Congress; New York State College (Potsdam); Goucher
College; Smithsonian Institution; Koussevitzky and Ford foundations (for
Metropolitan Opera). Was associated 1935–36 in federal theatre projects with
John Houseman, Orson Welles, and Joseph Losey; from 1932–38 with A. E.
Austin, Jr., in Hartford (opera, concerts, ballet, plays), also with Lincoln Kirstein,
L. Christensen, G. Balanchine (ballet); Sir Frederick Ashton (opera). Fellow
American Academy of Arts and Sciences, member American Academy of Arts and
Letters, Honorable Order of Kentucky Colonels, officier Légion d'Honneur.

Chief works: operas: *Four Saints in Three Acts*, 1928 (produced 1934) and
The Mother of Us All, 1947 (librettos by Gertrude Stein); *Lord Byron* (Jack

Larson) 1968; ballet: *Filling Station*, 1937; films: *The Plough that Broke the Plains*, 1936 and *The River*, 1937 (both by Pare Lorentz); *Tuesday in November*, 1945 (by J. Houseman and N. Ray); *Louisiana Story*, 1949 (by Robert Flaherty); *The Goddess*, 1957 (by Paddy Chayevsky); *Power Among Men*, 1958 (United Nations film by Thorold Dickinson); *Journey to America*, 1964 (by John Houseman); incidental music for plays by Shakespeare, Sophocles, Euripides, Giraudoux, Truman Capote, directed by or starring Leslie Howard, Orson Welles, Joseph Losey, Tallulah Bankhead, Peter Brook, Alfred Lunt, Audrey Hepburn, Alfred Drake, Katherine Hepburn, collaborating frequently with John Houseman (opera, plays, films, TV); orchestral: two symphonies; six suites from films; twelve portraits; three landscapes—*The Seine at Night, Wheat Feld at Noon, Sea Piece with Birds*; three concertos (cello, flute, harp); suite *In Homage to an Earlier England; A Solemn Music and a Joyful Fugue; The Feast of Love* (with baritone); Storm and Love Scene from Byron's *Don Juan* (with tenor); Five Songs to Poems of William Blake (with baritone); Mass for Solo Voice (mezzo) or union choir with orchestra or piano; Eleven Chorale-Preludes by Brahms orchestrated by V.T.; band: *Ode to the Wonders of Nature* (brasses); *At the Beach* (trumpet solo); *A Solemn Music*; divers fanfares and portraits; chamber: Sonata da Chiesa for five instruments; two string quartets; one violin sonata; Sonata for Flute Alone; Serenade for flute and violin; Three Portraits for Four Clarinets; eight portraits for violin alone, four for violin and piano, forty for piano; three arranged for violin and piano (S. Dushkin), four for cello and piano (L. Silva); choral: Missa Brevis (with percussion): *Dance in Praise* (with orchestra); *The Nativity* (with orchestra); Missa Pro Defunctis (with large orchestra); *Crossing Brooklyn Ferry* (Whitman) orchestra or piano; *Seven Choruses from the Medea of Euripides* (with percussion); *Scenes from the Holy Infancy*; and many shorter pieces; organ: Variations and Fugues on Sunday School Tunes (four sets); *Pange Lingua* (for large organ); also smaller pieces: (voice with instruments) Four Poems of Thomas Campion for mezzo with clarinet, viola, harp; *Stabat Mater* in French for soprano with string quartet; *Five Phrases from the Song of Solomon* for soprano or mezzo with percussion; *Capital Capitals* (Gertrude Stein) for four male soloists with piano; *Collected Poems* (Kenneth Koch) duet for soprano and baritone with small orchestra; piano: four short sonatas; two books of études; many portraits (forty published); *Ten Easy Pieces and a Coda; Synthetic Waltzes* (two pianos); and *Walking Song* (two pianos); a large number of songs in English and French, one group in Spanish, two extended vocal works in French—*Air de Phèdre* (Racine) and *Oraison Funèbre* (Bossuet).

Has written on music for *Vanity Fair, Boston Transcript, Modern Music, New York Review of Books*; chief critic *New York Herald Tribune*, 1940–54. Books: *The State of Music*, 1939 and 1961; *The Musical Scene*, 1945; *The Art of Judging Music*, 1948; *Music Right and Left*, 1951; *Virgil Thomson* (autobiography), 1966; *Music Reviews, 1940–1954*, 1967; and *American Music Since 1910*, 1971.

I

THE LIFE OF MUSIC

or
Musical Habits and Customs (1939)

Though written more than sixty years ago, Thomson's book, The State of Music *(1939; rev. 1961), remains a masterpiece of musical sociology, with persuasive distinctions and insights, for instance shrewdly regarding stylistic characteristics as reflections of social factors. The fact that Thomson lived and worked in the world he was writing about, caring for it passionately, accounts for his acerbic wit. The versions reproduced here include Thomson's comments made several decades later, placed in brackets, sometimes updating and amending what he originally wrote.*

Musical society consists of musicians who compose and musicians who do not. Those who do not are called "musical artists," "interpreters," executants, or merely "musicians." Those who do compose have all been executants at one time or another. One only learns to create performable works of music by first learning to perform. The longevity of musical works, however, is dependent on their being performable by executants other than the composer. This particular relation between design and execution is peculiar to music.

There is no such thing today as a serious painter who doesn't execute his own canvases. In the great days of Italian painting there was a tradition of workmanship that envisaged and even required the use of apprentice help. Veronese, for example, was a factory of which the large-scale execution and quantity production were only made possible, at that level of excellence, by the existence of such a tradition. The movie studios today produce as they do by means of a not dissimilar organization. Such formulas of collaboration are indispensable whenever a laborious art has to meet a heavy public demand. Even still the "mural" painters use assistants. But without an apprentice system of education, it is not possible to train assistants in a brush technique similar to the master's, or to depend on them for quick comprehension of his wishes. Hence the co-operation is not very efficient, and little important work can be delegated. Art-painting is really a one-man job today.

Poetry too is nowadays a one-man job. It neither derives from declamatory execution nor contemplates its necessity. Poets don't begin life as actors or elocutionists, and certainly actors and elocutionists do not commonly or normally take up poetic composition. Poetry, like prose writing, is not even recited at all for the most part. It is merely printed. Such reading of it as still goes on takes place privately, silently, in the breast; and although many efforts have been made to reinvigorate the art by bringing it out of the library and back to the stage and to the barrel-house (there is also a certain market for *viva voce* "readings" at women's clubs and on the radio and for recordings of the poet's voice), on the whole your enlightened poetry-fancier still prefers his poetry in a book. There are advantages and disadvantages in the situation, but discussion of them would be academic. The facts are the facts. And one of the cardinal facts about the poetic art today is that declamation is not essential to it.

Music is different from both poetry and painting in this respect. A musical manuscript is not music in the way that a written poem is poetry. It is merely a project for execution. It can correctly be said to consist of "notes" and to require "interpretation." It has about the same relation to real music that an architect's plan has to a real building. It is not a finished product. Auditive execution is the only possible test of its value.

Architects seem to get on perfectly well without having to pass their youth in the building trades. The successful composers of the past (and of the present) have all been musical artists, frequently virtuosos. The celebrated exceptions of Berlioz and Wagner are not exceptions at all. Because Berlioz was master of the difficult Spanish guitar, and Wagner was a thoroughly trained conductor. (He could also play the piano well enough to compose quite difficult music at it, though not well enough to perform that music effectively after it was written.) Conducting, as we know it, was at least half his invention (Mendelssohn was partly responsible too), and he wrote the first treatise on the subject. He was one of the most competent executants of his century, unbeatable in an opera-pit.

A further special fact about music writing is that it is not only a matter of planning for execution but also of planning for execution by another, practically any other, musician. It may not be better so, but it is so. Interesting and authoritative as the composer's "interpretation" of his own work always is, necessary as it is frequently for the composer, in order to avoid misreading of his intentions, to perform or conduct his own piece the first time or two it is played in public, still a work has no real life of its own till it has been conducted or performed by persons other than the composer. Only in that collaborative form is it ripe, and ready to be assimilated by the whole body of music-consumers. A musical page must be translated into sound and, yes, interpreted, before it is much good to anybody.

At this point criticism enters. It used to amuse me in Spain that it should take three children to play bull-fight. One plays bull and another plays torero, while the third stands on the side-lines and cries "ole!" Music is like that. It takes three people to make music properly, one man to write it, another to play it, and a third to criticize it. Anything else is just a rehearsal.

The third man, if he plays his rôle adequately, must analyze the audition into its two main components. He must separate in his own mind the personal charm or brilliance of the executant from the composer's material and construction. This separation is a critical act, and it is necessary to the comprehension of any collaborative art-work.

Criticism of the solitary arts is possible but never necessary. In the collaborative arts it is part of the assimilation-process. It is not surprising, therefore, that the criticism of music and of the theater should be vigorously practiced in the daily press, and widely read, and that architectural criticism, which occupies whole magazines to itself, should be exercised by reputable scholars as well as by the most celebrated architects of our time, whereas the daily reporting of painting shows turns out to be almost nothing but merchants' blurbs and museum advertising. Poetry-reviewing, on account of poetry's small public, is pretty well limited to the advance-guard literary magazines. When verse is covered by the daily and weekly press, the reviewing of it is done by definitely minor poets, who fill up their columns with log-rolling.

The separateness of design and execution in the collaborative arts is not necessarily to the esthetic disadvantage of these, as the poets like to pretend. It is, on the whole, rather an advantage, I think; but we shall speak of that another time. Music's particular version of that duality, in any case, is what makes composers the kind of men they are. The necessity of being a good executant in order to compose effectively makes their education long and expensive. Of all the professional trainings, music is the most demanding. Even medicine, law, and scholarship, though they often delay a man's entry into married life, do not interfere with his childhood or adolescence.

Music does. No musician ever passes an average or normal infancy, with all that that means of abundant physical exercise and a certain mental passivity. He must work very hard indeed to learn his musical matters and to train his hand, all in addition to his school-work and his play-life. I do not think he is necessarily overworked. I think rather that he is just more elaborately educated than his neighbors. But he does have a different life from theirs, an extra life; and he grows up, as I mentioned some time back, to feel different from them on account of it. Sending music students to special public schools like New York's High School of Music and Art or the European municipal conservatories, where musical training is complemented by general studies, does not diminish the amount of real work to be got through. It merely trains the musician a little more harmoniously and keeps him from feeling inferior to his little friends because of his musical interests. In any case, musical training is long, elaborate, difficult, and intense. Nobody who has had it ever regrets it or forgets it. And it builds up in the heart of every musician a conviction that those who have had it are not only different from everybody else but definitely superior to most and that all musicians together somehow form an idealistic society in the midst of a tawdry world.

For all this idealism and feeling of superiority, there is nevertheless a rift in the society. The executant and the composer are mutually jealous.

The executant musician is a straight craftsman. His life consists of keeping his hand in, and caring for his tools. His relation to the composer is that of any skilled workman in industry to the engineer whose designs he executes. He often makes more money than the composer, and he refuses to be treated as a servant. He is a hard-working man who practices, performs, gives lessons, and travels. He not infrequently possesses literary cultivation. He is impressed by composers but handles them firmly and tries to understand their work. His secret ambition is to achieve enough leisure to indulge in musical composition himself. Failing that, to become an orchestral conductor. He doesn't mind teaching but on the whole prefers to play. He doesn't become a confirmed pedagogue except under economic pressure, when he can't earn a living by execution. He enjoys excellent health, can't afford to waste time being ill, in fact, and often lives to an advanced age. He pretends to a certain bohemianism, is really a petty bourgeois. His professional solidarity is complete. His trade-unions are terrifyingly powerful and not unenlightened. Economically, humanly, and politically the workman he most resembles is the printer.

The composer is a transmuted executant. He practices execution as little as possible, but he hasn't forgotten a thing. It is his business to know everything there is to know about executants, because he is dependent on them for the execution of his work. Executants, being embarrassed by the composer's broader knowledge, try to avoid the composer. Composers, on the other hand, fearing to be cut off from communication with the executant world, are always running after executants and paying them compliments and begging to be allowed to play chamber-music with them, in the hope of picking up some practical hints about instrumental technique. On the whole, composers and their interpreters get on politely but not too well. Composers find executants mean, vain, and petty. Executants find composers vain, petty, and mean. I suspect the executant's potential income level, which is much higher than the composer's, is at the bottom of all this jealousy and high-hatting.

Composers by themselves don't get on too badly either, but they don't like one another really. They are jovial, witty, back-biting. When young they keep up a courteous familiarity with one another's works. After thirty they preserve an equally courteous ignorance of one another's works. Their professional solidarity is nil. Even in the well-organized and very effective European societies for the collection of performing-rights fees, they are likely to let a few semi-racketeers do the work. They grumble no end about how they are robbed by managers, by performers, and by their own protective associations; but they don't do anything to change matters. Politely gregarious but really very little interested in one another, they are without any of that huddling tendency that poets have, without the simple camaraderie of the painters, and with none of that solid fraternalism that is so impressive among the musical executants. [Enormous advances in composer solidarity have taken place since 1940.]

The island of music is laid out in four concentric circles:

1. The outer one defines the requirements of Minimum Musicianship. These are musical literacy and an ability to play some instrument otherwise than by ear. Singing doesn't count in the literacy test. The basic instrumental skill usually turns out to be piano-playing. There are some exceptions; but roughly speaking, our musical state can be said to consist of fourth-grade pianists.
2. The next circle includes everybody who can play any instrument properly. Call this the region of Special Skills. It is divided into pie-shaped sections, each representing an instrument. The pianoforte has its section here just as the other instruments do, and there is a small terrain allotted to singers. The singers who have a right to inhabit the region of Special Skills are more often than not those who have had operatic experience. Although the pie-shaped sections are pretty well walled off one from another, they are open at both ends. There is free access to them from the surrounding suburbs of Minimum Musicianship, and through any of them it is possible to pass into the higher circles.
3. The third region is Orchestral Conducting. Its altitude and climate are salubrious; the good things of life, including high public honor, abound. The superiority of conducting as a professional status over mere instrumental virtuosity is due to the fact that its practice requires a broader understanding of both technique and style than playing an instrument does. Its practitioners have a happy life, not only on account of the attendant honors and general prosperity, but also because it is technically the easiest specialty in all music. Residence in this region is usually limited, however, to persons who have migrated into it from the region of Special Skills. There is no other access normally.
4. The inner circle and summit of our mountain-city is Musical Composition. One does not have to go through Orchestral Conducting to get there; one can jump right over from Special Skills. It is a little difficult to get there directly from Minimum Musicianship. It is the summit of music because extended composition requires some understanding of all musical problems. Composers are the superior class in a musical society for the simple reason that they know more than anybody else does about music. This superiority is not necessarily reflected in their income-level.

The opera singer is a special form of singer and a special form of musician. He is the only kind of singer, for instance, who has to know something about music, though he doesn't have to know much. He bears the prestige of a great art-form and dresses handsomely for the rôle. His glamour in the nineteenth century was equal to that of conductors and movie-stars today, and he is still not badly paid when he has work.

The way he lives is the way all other executants would like to live; his house is the type-habitation of the Musical Artist. Not plain slummy like the poet's narrow hole, or barn-like and messy like the painter's, the musical artist's house or flat can best be described, I think, as comfortable but crowded. No doubt the model is, unconsciously, a star's dressing-room. It is full of professional souvenirs and objects of daily utility all mixed up together. It resembles at once a junk-shop, a photographer's vestibule, a one-man museum, and a German kitchen. There is always food around. The furniture is luxurious-looking but nondescript. No matter how spacious the rooms, the inhabitants are always too big for them.

Any musician has a tendency to fill up whatever room he is in, but the opera singer is especially permeating. He just naturally acts at all times as if he were singing a solo on a two-hundred-foot stage. His gestures are large and simple; and he moves about a great deal, never looking at anybody else and never addressing a word to anybody privately, but always speaking to the whole room. He has a way of remaining quiet, motionless almost, when not speaking, but alert, like a soloist between cues. He is hard-working, handsome, healthy (though somewhat hypochondriac). When hope is gone he drinks. Till then he cares for his health and is cheerful. He knows entertaining anecdotes and loves to do imitations of his colleagues. He lives embedded among scores and photographs and seldom moves his residence.

Composers, on the other hand, are always moving. A painter I know calls them "neat little men who live in hotel-rooms." They are frequently unmarried; but unmarried or not, they are super-old-maids about order. [Bachelor composers, to mention only the dead, include Handel, Beethoven, Schubert, Liszt, Chopin, Brahms, Moussorgsky, Rossini, and Ravel.] The papers on their desks are arranged in exact and equidistant piles. Their clothes are hung up in closets on hangers. Their shirts and ties are out of sight, and their towels are neatly folded. There is no food around. There isn't even much music around. It is all put away on shelves or in trunks. Ink and pencil are in evidence and some very efficient rulers. It looks as if everything were ready for work, but that work hadn't quite yet begun.

Living in hotels and temporary lodgings, and frequently being unmarried, your composer is a great diner-out. Of all the artist-workers, he is the most consistently social. Those painters who live in touch with the world of decorating and fashion are not infrequently snobs, for all their camaraderie and democratic ways. The composer is not a snob at all. He is simply a man of the world who dresses well, converses with some brilliance, and has charming manners. He is gracious in any house, however humble or grand; and he rarely makes love to the hostess. He eats and drinks everything but is a bit careful about alcohol, as sedentary workers have to be.

He has small illnesses often and gets over them. His diseases of a chronic nature are likely to be seated in the digestive organs. He rarely lives to a great age unless he keeps up his career as an executant. After all, the child who practices an instrument properly usually learns to live on what muscular exercise is involved in musical practice and in the ordinary errands of education. If he continues throughout his adult life some regular instrumental activity, he keeps well and lives to be old. If he gives up that minimum of muscular movement and alternates heavy eating with the introspective and sedentary practice of musical composition, he is likely to crack up in the fifties, no matter how strong his digestive system or his inherited organic constitution.

If he can survive the crack-up, he is good for another twenty years, frequently his finest and most productive. Your aged poet is rarely as vigorous a poet as your young poet. Your aged painter is tired, and his work is repetitive. The grandest monuments of musical art are not seldom the work of senescence. *Parsifal* was written at seventy, *Falstaff* after eighty. Brahms published his first symphony at forty. Rameau's whole operatic career took place after fifty. Beethoven's last quartets, Bach's *Art of the Fugue*, César Franck's entire remembered repertory, were all composed by men long past their physical prime.

The composer does not have a turbulent life, even in youth, as artists are commonly supposed to. He is too busy working at his trade. He leads, I should say, the quietest of all the art-lives. Because music study takes time, music writing is laborious, and manuscript-work cannot often be delegated to a secretary. In middle life your composer takes rather elaborate care of his health.

His professional prestige and social charm, moreover, can bring him opportunities for wealthy marriage. His behavior in such a marriage will be described in another chapter.

How Composers Eat

or
Who does what to whom and who gets paid (1939)

It is not necessary here to go into the incomes of musical executants. They have engagements or they don't. If they don't, they take pupils. If they can't get pupils they starve. If they get tired of starving they can go on relief. Unemployed musicians of high ability and experience are shockingly numerous in America. The development of sound-films and the radio has thrown thousands of them into technological unemployment. The musicians' union has a very large relief budget, however, and the W.P.A. formerly gave musical work to many. Eventually their situation is that of all artisan wage-workers in crowded crafts. Their large numbers and their powerful union organization have made it advisable to handle the problem of large-scale indigence among them by means of a definite social policy. This policy is operated in part directly by the union itself (plus some freelance philanthropic organizations like the Musicians' Emergency Relief Committee) and partly by the state and federal governments through unemployment insurance and Social Security.

Composers, being professional men and none too well organized either, have not yet found themselves the object of public concern. They do have, however, their little financial problems, I assure you, not the least of which is bare existence.

The poet of thirty works, whenever possible, at something not connected with literature. The composer practically always works at music, unless he can manage to get himself kept. He plays in cafés and concerts. He conducts. He writes criticism. He sings in church choirs. He reads manuscripts for music publishers. He acts as music librarian to institutions. He becomes a professor. He writes books. He lectures on the Appreciation of Music. Only occasionally does he hold down a job that is not connected with music.

A surprisingly large number of composers are men of private fortune. Some of these have it from papa, but the number of those who have married their money is not small. The composer, in fact, is rather in demand as a husband. Boston and New England generally are noted for the high position there allotted to musicians in the social hierarchy and for the number of gifted composers who have in consequence married into flowery beds of ease. I don't know why so many composers marry well, but they do. It is a fact. I don't suppose their sexuality is any more impressive than anybody else's, though certainly, as intellectuals go, the musician yields to none in that domain. After all, if a lady of means really wants an artistic husband, a composer is about the best bet, I imagine. Painters are notoriously unfaithful, and they don't age gracefully. They dry up and sour. Sculptors are of an incredible stupidity. Poets are either too violent or too tame, and terrifyingly expensive. Also, due to the exhausting nature of their early lives, they are likely to be impotent after forty. Pianists and singers are megalomaniacs; conductors worse. Besides, executants don't stay home enough. The composer, of all art-workers in the vineyard, has the prettiest manners and ripens the most satisfactorily. His intellectual and his amorous powers seldom give completely out before death. His musical powers not uncommonly increase. Anyway, lots of composers marry money, and a few have it already. Private fortune is a not unusual source of income for musicians. It is not as difficult for a rich man to write music as it is for him to write poetry. The class censorship is not so strict. The only trouble about wealth is that spending it takes time. The musician who runs all over town giving lessons and playing accompaniments has often just as much leisure to write music as does the ornamental husband of a well-to-do lady living in five elegant houses.

Many composers are able to live for years on gifts and doles. Include among these all prizes and private commissions. I don't suppose anybody believes nowadays that money one has earned is any more ennobling than money one hasn't.

Money is money, and its lack of odor has often been remarked. Gifts sometimes have strings, of course; but so has any job its inconveniences. Equally punctured, I take it, is the superstition formerly current that struggle and poverty are good for the artist, who is a lazy man and who only works when destitute. Quite the contrary, I assure you. Composers work better and faster when they have a bit of comfort. Too much money, with its attendant obligations, is a nuisance to any busy man. But poverty, illness, hunger, and cold never did any good to anybody. And don't let anyone tell you differently.

The number of composers who live on the receipts from their compositions is very small, even in Europe, though on both of the northwestern continents that number is larger in the field of light music than it is in the domain of massive instrumentation and extended form. We owe it indeed to the composers of light music that we get paid at all for our performing rights, since it is they who have always organized the societies for exacting such payment and furnished the funds for fighting infringers in the courts.

Royalties and performing-rights fees are to any composer a sweetly solemn thought. They are comparatively rare, however, in America, since composers, even composers of popular music, are nothing like as powerfully organized there for collecting them as the electrical and banking interests (whose shadow darkens our prospects of profit in all musical usages) are for preventing their being collected. So that when every now and then some composer actually makes enough money off his music to sleep and eat for a while, that is a gala day for the musical art. He feels like a birthday-child, of course, and fancies himself no end. Let him. His distinction carries no security. And he had better keep his hand in at performing and teaching and writing and at all the other little ways he knows of turning a not too dishonest extra penny. He had better seize on the first flush of fame too to "guest-conduct" his own works. This brings in two fees at once, one for his conducting and one for his performing rights. Invariably the composer who has enough composer-income to live on can pick up quite decent supplementary sums, as well as keep his contacts fresh, by not giving up entirely traffic in the by-products of his musical education. [Since this was written both ASCAP and BMI have developed vastly as collectors and distributors of performance-rights in "serious" music. And the foundations are commissioning composers.]

I have been running on in this wandering fashion because I wanted to show how flexible is the composer's economic life and how many strings he has to his bow. Briefly, the composer's possible income-sources are:

1. Non-Musical Jobs, or Earned Income from Non-Musical Sources
2. Unearned Income from All Sources
   a. Money from home
      (x.) His own
      (y.) His wife's

   b. Other people's money
     (x.) Personal patronage
       i. Impersonal subsidy
       ii. Commissions
     (y.) Prizes
     (z.) Doles
3. Other Men's Music, or Selling the By-products of His Musical Education
   a. Execution
   b. Organizing musical performances
   c. Publishing and editing
   d. Pedagogy
   e. Lecturing
   f. Criticism and musical journalism
   g. The Appreciation-racket
4. The Just Rewards of His Labor
   a. Royalties
     (x.) From music published
     (y.) From gramophone-recordings
   b. Performing-rights fees

Every composer receives the money he lives on from one of these sources. Most have received money from several. I have lived on nearly all of them at one time or another.

Between the extremes of being too rich for comfort and being really poor, the amount of money composers have doesn't seem to affect them very much. Photogenic poverty and ostentatious spending are equally repugnant to their habits. The source of their money has, however, a certain effect on their work. We have noted that the composer, being a member of the Professional Classes, enjoys all the rights and is subject to the obligations of what is known as Professional Integrity. This does not mean that he enjoys complete intellectual freedom. He has that only with regard to the formal, or structural, aspects of his art. His musical material and style would seem to be a function, at any given moment, of his chief income-source.

WHY COMPOSERS WRITE HOW

or
The economic determinism of musical style (1939; revised, 1962)

Before I go on to explain how a composer's chief income-source affects his musical style, I think I had better say what is ordinarily meant by style in music. It is not the same thing as style in literature, for instance, which is mostly considered nowadays to be personal. The word style is employed in four ways with regard to music.

Its most precise usage is a technical one. The phrases "fugal style," "canonic style," "modal style," and the like are all descriptions of syntactic devices. They are methods of achieving coherence. More recent devices of similar nature are the "chromatic" style, the "atonal" style, the "dissonant tonal" style, even the "jazz" or "swing" style. These last two refer, of course, to rhythmic texture within a given tonal syntax; but the rhythmic texture of jazz is just as much a technical device for achieving coherence as the twelve-tone-row system of atonality is.

The ensemble of technical procedures plus personal mannerisms that marks the work of any given composer or period of composition is also referred to as the style of that composer or period. One can say that a piece is written in the style of Schumann or in the style of Handel or in the style of Debussy. Writing "in the style of" is taught at some music schools. It is used in musical practice chiefly for the "faking" (improvisation from a figured bass) of harpsichord accompaniments to pre-nineteenth-century music and for the composition of Roman Catholic masses, the "style of Palestrina" having been firmly recommended to modern composers by Pope Pius X's encyclical of 1903 known as *De Motu Proprio.*

Pianistic, violinistic, vocal, and similar adjectives, when they qualify the word "style," indicate a manner of writing that is convenient to the instruments so referred to, that is "grateful" to execute upon them, or that suggests their characteristics.

The word is used sometimes also in a qualitative sense. An artist is said to perform with "good" or "bad" style. A piece may not be said to be written in good or bad style, but if it is well written it may be said to have "style."

For the present discussion I shall try to limit the word to its first associations, to the divers syntactic devices that are available to any composer. This is the commonest usage of the word as applicable to musical composition. A composer's choice among these devices I shall call his stylistic orientation. It will not be necessary, I think, to employ the executional and qualitative meanings at all. It will be necessary, however, to distinguish between style and subject-matter.

The subject-matter of vocal music is its verbal text. The subject-matter of theater-music is whatever the stage-directions say it is. The subject-matter of an instrumental concert piece is not necessarily what the composer says it is. If he calls it *The Rustle of Spring* or *Also Sprach Zarathustra,* we can take him at his word. But if he calls it *Fifth Nocturne* or *Symphony in F,* we can never be sure. Sometimes it is an objective piece that was written to illustrate some program that he isn't telling us, and sometimes it is a depiction of non-verbalized visceral feelings. In the latter case, the subject-matter is pretty hard to describe verbally. "Absolute" was the nineteenth-century term the Germans used for such music.

That meant that no matter how the composer wrote it or what he was thinking about, the piece could be satisfactorily enjoyed without verbal aids. The term "absolute" being now superannuated, I propose to substitute "introspective"; and I think we can apply it as "absolute" was applied, to all music that has no verbal text, no specific usage, and no evocative title.

Let us now return to the four sources of income and examine their relation to the composer's work in general and to his stylistic orientation in particular.

1. Non-Musical Jobs, or Earned Income from Non-Musical Sources

The composer who lives by non-musical work is rare; but still there are some. The chief mark of his work is its absence of professionalism. It is essentially naïve. It breaks through professional categories, despises professional conventions. The familiarity with instrumental limitations and current interpretative traditions that composers have who are constantly working with the executant world is of great practical advantage in most respects. Your naïve composer has no such mastery of well-known methods, no such traditional esthetic. The professional makes esthetic advance slowly, if at all, progressing step by step, in touch at all times with the music world. The naïf makes up his music out of whole cloth at home. He invents his own esthetic. When his work turns out to be not unplayable technically, it often gives a useful kick in the pants to the professional tradition. The music of Modest Moussorgsky, of Erik Satie, and of Charles Ives did that very vigorously indeed.

The naïfs show no common tendency in stylistic orientation. Their repertory of syntactical device is limited to what they can imitate plus what they make up for themselves. They are like children playing alone. Their subject-matter is likely to be the great literary classics, their comprehension of these atavistic and profoundly racial. They put Dante to music, and Shakespeare, Dialogues of Plato, the Book of Revelation. They interpret these in terms of familiar folklore, remembered classics, and street-noises. They derive their melodic material from hymns and canticles, from jazz-ways and darn-fool ditties. They quote when they feel like it. They misquote if they prefer. They have none of the professional's prejudices about "noble" material or about stylistic unity. They make music the way they like it, for fun. The naïfs are rare whose technique is ample enough to enable them to compete at all with Big Time. They mostly flower unknown and unheard. Those whom we do encounter are angles of refreshment and light, and their music is no small scandal. Its clarity is a shock to the professional mind. It doesn't hesitate about being lengthy or about being brief, and it neglects completely to calculate audience-psychology. It is not made for audiences. As Tristan Tzara said of Dada, it is a "private bell for inexplicable needs." It is beyond mode and fashion. It is completely personal and gratuitous.

2. Unearned Income from All Sources

a. Money from home

(x.) His own

The composer whose chief revenue comes from invested capital shows the following marks of his economic class:

His subject-matter reflects the preoccupations of his kind. In the present age it reflects that avoidance of serious remarks that is practiced in capitalist circles today. He tends to write playful music, to seek charm at the expense of emphasis. He abounds in witty ingenuities. He is not given much just now to writing introspective music. Before World War I, when refined Europeans with incomes gave up most of their time to introspection, both sentimental and analytic, the financially independent composer wrote a great many symphonies and reveries. Ernest Chausson and Albéric Magnard should serve to fix the pre-war type for us. Francis Poulenc will do for the European post-war capitalists. In America there is John Alden Carpenter.

The stylistic orientation of the rich composer is toward the French salon-school. He goes in for imagistic evocation, witty juxtapositions, imprecise melodic contours, delicacy of harmonic texture and of instrumentation, meditative sensuality, tenderness about children, evanescence, the light touch, discontinuity, elegance. Debussy is his ideal and model, though Debussy himself was not financially independent till after his second marriage.

(y.) His wife's

The composers who have married their incomes are not so likely to be Debussyans as they were in 1920. If they marry too young they don't get much time to write music anyway. They are put through the paces of upper-class life pretty much all day long. [Or else forced into films and TV and teaching, to prove to the family that they *can* earn money.] If they marry in middle life, their working habits are already formed. Also their stylistic orientation. Sometimes nothing changes at all, especially if there isn't too much wealth around. If there is a lot of it, class pressure is pretty strong. The composer subjected to this is likely to turn toward capitalistic proletarianism. There are two common forms of this. One is the exploitation of ornamental folklore (somebody else's folklore). The other is a cult of urban populistic theatrical jazz (jazz by evocation) and of pseudo-Viennese waltzes.

The relation of music-writing to unearned income is about like this. Unquestionably children get the best preparation for professional life in families that are well enough off to have access to good instruction. In families where there is big money around, the children are always kept so busy learning how to live like rich people that serious musical instruction is usually out of the question. The families of professional men, of school teachers, of civil service employees, and of shopkeepers continue to supply the bulk of talent to the artistic professions. [Skilled union labor is rising now as a favorable background for urbane leisure and educational access.] The musician rarely inherits from such a family enough to live on once he is grown and educated. In richer families he seldom learns much music. When he does, or when, having mastered his art in less disturbing circumstances, he insures his future income by marriage, there is nothing to prevent his achieving the highest distinction as a composer. He does, however, tend to write the kind of music I describe.

The sources of contributory income are without effect on the gentleman composer (or on any other for that matter), unless they provide what would be enough money to live on if he were not independent, and unless, of course, the professional experience entailed may give him a bias toward the pianoforte or the violin or some other instrument. He has class bias about both subject-matter and style, but he does not have any of the occupational conditionings of the musical journalist, of the pedagogue, or of the executant concert artist.

b. Other people's money

Let us take for granted that every professional composer has had access by one means and another to adequate instruction. It is necessary to assume this, because if he hasn't by the age of twenty-five come into contact with all the chief techniques, he must count as a naïve composer. The naïfs, like the composers of popular music, can achieve high distinction; but their music is never influenced by the source of the money they live on. If it were, they would not be naïve. Naïfs exist in all classes of society. Professional musicians are mostly bourgeois, indeed mostly petty bourgeois.

It is not certain that this is the necessary class situation of the composer, as we have just seen. It is simply that the rich are mostly too busy and the poor too poor to get educated in musical technique. Musical instruction is so expensive, even in slum music schools, that only the bourgeoisie has complete access to it; and only those families who live in the more modest economic levels of the bourgeoisie have sufficient leisure to oversee a proper musical upbringing. This is why, although there is some ruling-class art-music, there is no proletarian art-music at all except what is written at the proletariat from somewhere above. The poor farmer and the mountaineer, the slum child and the segregated Negro, have open to them only the simple popular ways, the folk-ways. They make beautiful music, very beautiful music indeed. Jazz, swing, ho-downs, chanties, hymn-lore from the Southern uplands, work-songs, dance-ditties, cowboy laments, fiddle-jigs, torch songs, blues, ballads from the barrack-room and barrel-house, children's games, prison wails, collegiate comics, sentimental love-songs, country waltzes, mambos, sambas, Lindy hops, and the syncopated Scotch-African spirituals—nine-tenths of all these are made up and brought to their definitive shape by poor people. It isn't musical vigor or inspiration that the poor lack. They have everything for making music but access to the written tradition. Massive instrumentation and the structural devices that make possible the writing of long pieces are the property of the trained musician, and he comes mostly from the lower levels of the bourgeoisie.

(x.) Personal patronage

Let us now tell how a composer (we have already got him educated) gets hold of money to live on when he hasn't a rich papa or wife. It is extraordinary the amounts of money, just plain gift money, that a composer with some social charm (and they all have that) can put his fingers on, especially in early manhood. Some go on getting it till they die.

There seem to be two formulas for giving money to composers. One is direct subsidy. The other is the commissioning of works. The latter is really a kind of subsidy, because the ordering of musical works is practically never an expression of a patron's or of a foundation's musical needs. Half the time they don't even have the work performed once it is delivered. In cases where they do, there is always an air of philanthropy around, and a careful disclaiming of any responsibility on the patron's part for the nature and content of the piece. The piece is usually an orchestral or chamber-work called *Symphony* or *Sonata* or something equally non-committal on the composer's part.

I. IMPERSONAL SUBSIDY

Composers living on subsidies personal or impersonal tend to write introspective music of strained harmonic texture and emphatic instrumental style. They occasionally write very long pieces. They are not much bothered about charm, elegance, sentiment, or comprehensibility, though they are seldom deliberately hermetic. They go in for high-flown lyricism and dynamic punch, less for contrapuntal texture, unless that seems to heighten lyrical expansiveness. They are revolters against convention. At least, that is their pose. Beethoven is their ideal; and they think of themselves as prophets in a wilderness, as martyrs unappreciated, as persecuted men. Appearing to be persecuted is, of course, their way of earning their living. The minute they lose the air of being brave men downed by circumstances, they cease to get free money. Because people with money to give away don't like giving it to serene or successful characters, no matter how poor the latter may be. When a composer who has been living for some years on patronage and gifts starts earning money, there is always a noticeable change in his music. His subject-matter becomes less egocentric. His musical style becomes less emphatic and a good deal easier to follow. He eventually stops over-writing the brass in his orchestral scores.

II. COMMISSIONS

Composers are rare who can pull down commission all their lives. But my theories about economic determinism do not demand that the composer live from any given source for a long time before his music begins to reflect that source. On the contrary, I maintain that composers vary their manner from piece to piece in direct conformity with their income-source of the moment, the subject-matter and the stylistic orientation of any musical work being largely determined by the source of the money the composer is living on while writing that piece.

Privately commissioned works, therefore, should show some kind of uniformity. Which they do. Less Beethovenesque than the works of the steadily subsidized, less violent, and less animated by personal dynamism, they lean toward an abstract style. I am not even certain that the international neo-classic style was not invented as a sort of *lingua franca* that could be addressed to any possible patron or patroness anywhere in the Western world. [The 1960 international style is similarly functional, but it is chromatic and twelve-tonish instead of diatonic.] During the 1920s there were just about enough available patronesses in America, France, Belgium, Germany, England, Switzerland, and Hungary, all put together, to enable a clever composer to get hold of with luck about one of these commissions a year. This gave him a basic income of from one to two thousand dollars.

What was the international style for commissioned works? It was a dissonant contrapuntal manner welded out of the following heterogeneous elements, all chosen for their prestige value:

A. The animated contrapuntalism of J. S. Bach,
B. The unresolved dissonances of Debussy and Richard Strauss, and
C. The Berlioz tradition of instrumentation.

   This is the instrumentation of Berlioz, Bizet, Saint-Saëns, Rimsky-Korsakov, Chabrier, Debussy, Ravel, and Stravinsky. It is differential instrumentation. Clarity and brilliance are achieved by keeping the different instruments at all times recognizably separate. A thin and reed-like fiddle-tone is presupposed.

   The rival tradition is that of Meyerbeer, Wagner, Brahms, Tchaikovsky, Mahler, Strauss, and Puccini. This is absorptive instrumentation. Emotional power and tonal weight are achieved by lots of doubling at the unison, which is to say by the building up of composite instrumental timbres, all sounding somewhat alike but differing greatly in weight and carrying power. It pre-supposes a husky and vibrant fiddle tone. The German tradition is a perfectly good one, as you can see from the big names connected with it. It has not enjoyed the same international prestige, however, since World War I, as the Franco-Russian.

D. To these elements were added frequently a fourth, the reconstructed or modern French sonata-form—a device practiced originally by the pupils of César Franck and expounded at Vincent d'Indy's Schola Cantorum.

The sonata-form was invented in Berlin by K. P. E. Bach; and it flowered in Vienna as the favored continuity device of Haydn, Mozart, Beethoven, Schubert, Schumann, Brahms, and Mahler. It was introduced into France by Reyer in 1845, practiced and fought for by Camille Saint-Saëns, and finally domesticated by César Franck. Since the death of Johannes Brahms it has been very little practiced in Vienna. What is practiced today in Paris (and internationally) is not the Viennese sonata-form at all. It is a French reconstruction for pedagogical purposes. D'Indy is largely its inventor. It is based on certain practices of Haydn and Beethoven. It has not yet been successfully introduced into Vienna. It enjoys worldwide prestige, however, a prestige borrowed from that of the Viennese masters and based on the extreme simplicity of the reconstruction, all of which makes it just fine for the Appreciation books. The Viennese form, when it was alive, was never very teachable, because no two examples of it were ever near enough alike to make standardization possible. The good ones all seem to be exceptions to some rule of which nobody has ever seen a typical case in point. [Neither Haydn, Mozart, nor Beethoven ever spoke of sonata-form. The first reference to it in print occurs, according to Paul Henry Lang, in 1828.]

The French orchestral palette presents no especial difficulties. Any good student can handle it. And the writing of animated counterpoint in the dissonant style is easy as falling off a log. The real difficulty about any contrapuntal style is length and always has been. Now the modern-music fan likes his pieces fairly long. Nothing under twenty minutes will impress him very much. And twenty minutes of wiggly counterpoint are too much (because too vague) for anybody. [This applies equally to today's pulverized (or one-note-at-a-time) counterpoint.] Bach had the same problem to face. Fugal construction helped him over many a bad moment. But modern audiences won't listen to fugues very long or very often. They lack punch. Sonata-form, even in its rather static reconstructed version, is about the only dependable device (outside of literary texts and verbal programs) that will enable a composer to give continuity to a long and varied movement. [Today's involvement with canonic textures and rhythmic permutations, though inevitable to an atonal style, makes for even less variety.]

It offers free play to sustained lyricism, to stormy drama, and to emphatic orchestration. But there are two musical styles it cannot digest very well, the animated contrapuntal and the stricly dissonant. The first is inimical to it because that kind of counterpoint, whether practiced in a Brandenburg concerto or in an improvised jazz session, being a cerebral manifestation, is viscerally static. And sonata-form is only good for dramatizing visceral states, which are never static, which, quite to the contrary, are constantly varying in intensity, constantly moving about over the pleasure-pain and the tranquillity-anxiety scales. Systematic dissonance is inimical to the essential virtues of sonata-form for a similar reason, those virtues being all of a dramatic nature. The sonata is abstract musical theater, a dramatization of non-verbalized emotions. There is no sonata without drama, struggle, the interplay of tensions. Systematic dissonance, like systematic consonance, is the contrary of any such interplay. It too is viscerally static.

For the bright young composers of the world, who knew all this long ago, to have gone in as thoroughly as they did, between the years of 1920 and 1935, for such an indigestible mixture, such a cocktail of culture as the international neo-classic style, leaves us no out but to ascribe to them a strong non-musical motivation. The sharing of the available private commissions of the Western world among a smallish but well-united group of these composers I maintain to have been the motivation. That and the corollary activities of winning prizes and foundational awards and eventually, when all the prizes and all the possible commissions have been had, of grabbing off one of the fancier institutional teaching jobs. [The adoption after World War II of another international style (this one chromatic) and its triumph in all the European modernistic festivals, as well as over the German publishers' cartel and over the commissioning of music by European radio establishments, make it fairly clear that I was right about the earlier one.]

In any case, all international styles are God's gift to pedagogy. That we shall go into in another place, perhaps. Here just let me mention the slight but interesting differences possible within the internationalist conception.

For commissions and festivals, a long piece is indicated in dissonant contrapuntal style, neutral in emotional content and hermetic in expression. It should be a bit difficult to listen to and very difficult to comprehend, yet withal skillful enough in instrumentation that nobody could call the work incompetent. A maximum of impressiveness and a minimum of direct significance are the desiderata.

(y.) Prizes

For prize-competitions the above strict formula needs a little alleviation. Sometimes the injection of a lush tune here and there will satisfy the judges of the candidate's fitness for eventually pleasing a large public. More respectable, however, is the substitution of folklore for original melodic material. Folklore, as you can easily see, adds popular charm without the loss of cultural prestige. [Today folklore is out, Indian or Japanese influence very much in.] A high dosage of dissonance proves the candidate's modernism. A bit of counterpoint will show his good will toward pedagogy. And brilliant orchestration guarantees musicianship. Prize committees, mark you, never judge musical mastery on anything but orchestration. They can't. Because counterpoint is too easy to write; anyone can do it; everything sounds well enough; no judgment of its merits is possible. And harmony is difficult to judge; the gulf is of but a hairsbreadth between superb and lousy. Melodic material, tunes, can only be judged by the way they stand up under usage. Formalized construction is not one of the essential elements of music, but that too can only be judged from usage. Instrumentation is the one element of musical composition that is capable of being judged objectively today, because it is the one element that is taught, learned, and practiced according to a tradition that has been unbroken for a hundred years, and that is accepted intact, especially the French version of it, by all educated musicians.

The international-style music world used to be a well-organized going concern, with its own magazines, its "contemporary music" societies, its subsidies, its conspiracies, and its festivals. Of late years business has not been so good. Private commissions are scarce, institutional funds diminished, the societies defunct or moribund, the public fed-up. The high-pressure salesmanship that forced into the big orchestral concerts (by pretending that an international movement should be supported on nationalistic grounds) music that was never intended for anything but prize-winning and the impressing of other musicians, has given a black eye to all music written since 1918. The general music public and the trustee class have both revolted. The conductors have seized the occasion to pull all the cover over to their side of the bed, thus leaving quite out in the cold the problem of contemporary composition in large form (which presupposes as an essential factor in the equation the presence of a large general public). I know there still appear new pieces periodically on the orchestral programs, though less frequently than before 1932, the year in which the trustees of the Philadelphia Symphony Society formally warned Leopold Stokowski to lay off modern music. Everywhere the preceding decade's chief offender (the international style) is taboo. Boston is an exception in this, because one of the movement's chief survivors, Walter Piston, is head of the Department of Music at Harvard; and his works must of course be performed. The new pieces most orchestras play nowadays are in the vein of pre-war post-Romanticism. They are chiefly by schoolteachers and children just out of the conservatories. They are often tuneful and pleasing. They seldom get a second performance, however, even when the first goes over big, as it does not infrequently. I don't think the conductors quite want any composer to have a very steady public success. They consider success their domain. And their success depends on keeping orchestral performance a luxury product, a miraculously smooth, fabulously expensive, and quite unnecessary frame for sure-fire classics.

[This paragraph describes the end of the Depression decade. In 1960, at the end of a boom decade, an internationally subsidized contemporary-music combine is prospering again, with trustees and general public again resisting it.]

(z.) Doles

A special category of patronage is the government dole. When home-relief is a composer's chief source of income, he isn't likely to write music at all. Life is too difficult, too desolate. When, as in Europe, it is less than minimum sustenance, he tends to become proletarian class-conscious, to tie up with a Marxian party (usually the Communist), and to produce angry music of exaggerated simplicity and a certain deliberate vulgarity.

The W.P.A., America's work-relief organization, never had a Composers' Project. A number of composers were engaged, however, to write music for theatrical productions; and quite a few more were placed on the regular Music Project as executants. The W.P.A. theater people did quite well by music. They showed as good taste in their choice of composers as they did in their choice of plays and directors. The Federal Theater was for the years 1935 and 1936 the most vigorous new art movement in the whole West. The music written for its productions varied greatly in style and subject-matter, as all music must that is ordered with a specific art purpose in view. The composers who wrote music for the Federal Theater are not classifiable as dole-subjects or charity-cases. They were earning their living by musical composition, and their music bears all the marks of music that has paid its way.

[Today, in 1960, there is no work-relief, only temporary unemployment insurance. Commissions designed, however, for a specific sort of performance (and paying for that performance), such as The Ford Foundation orchestra and opera commissions, are not dissimilar to work-relief, though they are aimed less at helping composers than at creating repertory.]

3. Other Men's Music, or Selling the By-Products of His Musical Education

a. Execution

People who earn their bread by playing the piano or playing the organ or playing the violin or conducting, by musical interpretation in short, are the most timid of all when they start writing music. They have only one idea in their heads and that is to write "gratefully" for the instrument in question. They often succeed in doing so. Their subject-matter is likely to be pale, wan, and derivative.

This was not always so. Exploring the musical possibilities of any new instrument or medium is a job for persons who play that instrument. The history of violin-composition in the seventeenth century, of writing for the harpsichord and for the organ clear up to the death of J. S. Bach, of piano music in the nineteenth century, of jazz music in our own, is the history of performing virtuosos who composed. From the time of Corelli and Domenico Scarlatti to Chopin and Franz Liszt, all the solo instruments were the springboards of musical art; and many of the greatest masters of musical composition earned their living by instrumental virtuosity, even by the interpretation of other men's work. Richard Wagner was about the last of the great interpreter-composers in the non-popular tradition. [Strauss and Mahler were also conductor-composers. Today we have Manuel Rosenthal, Leonard Bernstein, Juan José Castro, and Carlos Chavez.]

Today all composers can play an instrument still, and most can conduct if they have to, but they avoid doing either steadily. Instrumental virtuosity and the interpretation of "classical" music have both reached the point of diminishing artistic returns to the composer. The expansion of techniques has so slowed down that regular practice is no longer a source of constant revelation to him. Rather it stupefies his imagination and limits his musical horizon.

This is not true in the jazz-world, where technique is still expanding. Duke Ellington has been a number-one jazz-pianist and a number-one jazz-composer. But the music of Ignaz Paderewski, of Ferruccio Busoni, of Charles-Marie Widor, and of Fritz Kreisler (even including his clever fakings of early violin-writers) cannot possibly be considered to be anything like so high-class as their respective instrumental performances were.

A bit of concert work is good for composers in their youth. The organ and the kettledrums seem to be especially useful for amplifying the musical conceptions of people brought up on the pianoforte or the violin. The first introduces them to quantitative meter. The second sharpens their sense of pitch. Both are invaluable trainings in rhythmic exactitude and in notation.

b. and c. Organizing, publishing, and editing

The organizing of concerts and the publishing business are both bad for composition. They are businesses, not crafts. They contribute nothing to a composer's musical experience. The composers who get involved with them write music less and less. Arranging and editing are all right. The trouble with them is that they don't pay enough. It is rare that a composer can exist on their proceeds for any length of time. They are best done by performers and conductors as a side-line.

d. Pedagogy

I sometimes think the worst mischief a composer can get into is teaching. I mean as a main source of income. As a supplementary source a little of it doesn't hurt, is rather good, in fact, for clarifying and refreshing the mind. A little criticism or musical journalism is good too. A lot of either is not so good, because they both get you worried about other men's music. Whenever the by-products of his musical education become for any length of time the main source of a composer's income, occupational diseases and deformities set in.

As everybody knows, school-teachers tend to be bossy, pompous, vain, opinionated, and hard-boiled. This is merely their front, their advertising. Inside they are timid and over-scrupulous. Their music, in consequence, comes out looking obscure and complex. Its subject-matter, on the other hand, and its musical material are likely to be over-subtle and dilute. When we say nowadays that a work is "academic" we mean all this and more. We mean that the means employed are elaborate out of all proportion to the end achieved.

When I speak of pedagogues I mean teachers who live by their teaching, whether they teach privately or in institutions. All teachers who live by teaching are alike. The holders of sinecure posts are an exception. The director of any French conservatory, for instance, is always an elderly composer of distinction. He is not expected to do anything but an overseer's job, to protect, from the vantage point of his years and experience, the preservation intact, with all necessary renewals, of whatever tradition of musical instruction that institution represents. He is not expected to bother with administrative detail or to drum up trade for his institution or to have anything whatsoever to do with trustees. He may dine occasionally with the Minister of Public Instruction and the Secretary for the Fine Arts. An hour a day will cover all his duties. His job lasts till he dies, short of public moral turpitude on his part. A smaller sinecure sometimes available to young composers is the librarianship of a conservatory. The rarity of sinecures in the United States is one-half the trouble with music-teaching. Save for the occasional composer-in-residence who teaches part-time, almost any young person's college job ends by taking about fifty hours a week to accomplish and to keep. The other half is what is the matter with music-teaching anywhere, with living off any of what I have called the by-products of a musical education. It is the constant association with dead men's music that they entail. Only in vacation time, if there is any money left to take a vacation, does the school-teacher get a chance to forget all that, to put the classics out of reach at the bottom of his mind, well out of the way of the creative act. Daily dealing with the music of the past is probably all right after fifty. It never fails to produce in a younger man a derivative manner of writing that no amount of surface-complexity can conceal.

Teachers tend to form opinions about music, and these are always getting in the way of creation. The teacher, like the parent, must always have an answer for everything. If he doesn't he loses prestige. He must make up a story about music and stick to it. Nothing is more sterilizing. Because no one can make any statement three times without starting to believe it himself. One ends by being full of definite ideas about music; and one's mind, which for creative purposes should remain as vague and unprejudiced as possible, is corseted with opinions and *partis pris*. Not the least dangerous of these *partis pris* is the assumption that since the finest examples of musical skill and stylization from the past (the so-called "classics") are the best models to expose before the young, they are necessarily the best models for a mature composer to follow in his work. This is very nearly the opposite of the real truth. As Juan Gris used to say about painting, "the way to become a classic is by not resembling the classics in any way."

When I speak of teaching, I mean teaching for money; and I deplore it, for composers, as a habit-forming vice. I would not wish, however, that the young composer be denied access to professional advice. He is, in fact, not denied it. Professional composers are only too delighted to read over the works of the young and to give practical advice where needed. They enjoy the homage implied; they like the chance to steal a good trick; they like seeing their own tricks stolen and advertised. All this can take place without any exchange of money. It is free graduate-instruction. Elementary instruction (which is a bore to give) must always be paid for, and usually the student gets his best money's worth from regular pedagogues who are not composers.

Allow me, please, at this point to digress a little further on the subject of how people learn to write music. You never learn anything technical except from somebody who possesses technique. You can only learn singing from someone who has sung, piano-playing from a reasonably competent pianist, conducting from a conductor; and you can only acquire so much of these techniques as the instructor himself has mastered. There are, however, elementary subjects which are so conventional that their mastery requires no personalized skill and implies no higher achievement. It is not necessary, for example, or even very desirable to try to learn grammar from a poet. Any school-teacher is better, can show you better how to parse, decline, and diagram according to accepted convention. So with solfeggio, counterpoint, fugue. They are stylized drills, not living skills. Harmony is the difficult branch to learn, because it is neither really stylized nor really free. I doubt if anybody can teach it satisfactorily; but even still a routine pedagogue is usually quicker and more effective about it than a composer is. Orchestration is different. It can only be learned from a composer or from a professional orchestrator. The subject is a completely practical one and requires a practical man. All the text-books are by practical men like Berlioz and Strauss and Rimsky-Korsakov and Widor. Musical form is also a practical matter. It is scarcely a subject at all and can only be advised about after the fact. There is no text-book on the subject, no formal instruction available.

How then can musical education be organized so that the instructor's as well as the student's interest may be respected? Singing and playing must be taught, as they are now, by singers and players or by ex-singers and ex-players. The elements of musical theory (that is to say harmony, counterpoint, fugue, and musical analysis) should be taught, as they are not always now, by trained seals, which is to say by persons especially prepared for that drill-work, by pure pedagogues. Instrumentation must be taught by composers; there is no way around it. But since the composer is not much benefited musically by teaching, some arrangement must be reached that will serve his interests as well as the student's. One of the best is to use as professors of instrumentation only men over fifty. These can teach an hour a day something they know without getting vicious about it. Also, the whole system of musical instruction must be co-ordinated and watched over by a composer, an elderly one preferably, and one for whom the job is either a sinecure or else a quite negligible source of income. It should never be full-time work.

As for the actual composition of music in the early stages of a student's career, he had better keep that as separate as possible from his life as a student.

Let him show his efforts to other composers, to friends, to anybody but to his professors. Unless the teacher in question is or has been a successful composer, the student will only get confusion and discouragement out of him.

e. and f. Lecturing, criticism, and musical journalism

Turning an odd penny here and there by lecturing doesn't count. Earning one's bread by lecturing does. But lecturing is not a trade in itself; it is always something else. Either it is teaching, or it is criticism, or it is the Appreciation-racket, or it is musical interpretation. Sometimes it is all four. I mention it separately, merely because it is a common way of earning money.

Criticism and musical journalism are also frequent sources of contributive income to composers. They seldom provide a full living. The only kind of written musical criticism that really feeds its writer is a permanent post on a metropolitan daily. Musical composition seems to be quite impossible to combine with such a full-time job. [I managed it, all the same, as music critic of the *New York Herald Tribune* from 1940 to 1954.] In any case, these "major" critics never seem to write much music, not the way dramatic critics write plays. Writing occasional articles, however, is an inveterate habit of composers. The profession is incurably literate. Such writing is interesting to the musical public, because it is both authoritative and passionately prejudiced. It is interesting to the composer because he can use it to logroll for his friends and to pay off old scores against his enemies, as well as to clarify for himself periodically his own aesthetic prejudices. Also, the forced attendance at concerts that writing criticism entails keeps him informed of current trends in musical production. Left to himself, he has rather a tendency to avoid hearing music, to insulate himself against all currents and to fecundate in a vacuum. Now a vacuum is not a very good place to fecundate in; at least it is not a good place to cook up collaborative art. Daily intercourse with other men's music deforms any composer's work in the direction of a rather timid traditionalism. Such is the music of the school-teachers, the choir-masters, the touring virtuosos, and the conductors. But a complete ignorance of what is going on in the world of music is even more deforming. One doesn't so much need to know what the other composers are up to as one needs to know what the interpreters are up to. One needs to keep in touch with what happens when scores get made audible.

Painters can fecundate in a vacuum if they really have to; the naïve painters are numerous. Poetry too can flourish far from the madding crowd and often does, going off periodically into hermit-like retirement being quite a habit of poets. Think too of all the excellent lyrical verse that gets written year after year by private persons. Music, even naïve music, has always been written in or near the great centers of musical activity. The isolated composer, like the isolated surgeon or architect, is a rare animal.

As I said before, contributive sources of income seldom influence a composer's stylistic orientation. Only a full support can do that. Their chief influence is technical. Just as a little teaching is good for any musical executant, and a little musical execution for any composer, a little criticism is a valuable experience too for any musician. It teaches him about audiences. Nobody who has ever tried to explain in writing why some piece got a cold reception that he thought merited better, or why some musical marshmallow wowed them all, has ever failed to rise from his desk a wiser man. And the composer who has written criticism with some regularity—who has faced frequently the deplorable reality that a desired audience-effect cannot be produced by wishful thinking—inevitably, unconsciously, in spite of his most disdainful intentions, cannot help learning a good deal that is practical to know about clarity, coherence, and emphasis.

Composers' criticism is useful to the layman also. As I have said before, the function of criticism is to aid the public in digesting musical works. Not for nothing is it so often compared to bile. The first process in that digestion is the breaking-up of any musical performance into its constituent elements, design and execution. In this analytic process, the composer is of the highest utility. All musicians can judge the skill of a musical execution, because all musicians are executants. (The practice of publishing musical criticism written by musical illiterates is disappearing from even the provincial press.) But if the critic is only an executant and has never practiced musical creation, his interest is held far more by the refinements of execution than by the nature of the music itself. Inevitably he tends to glorify the executant (with whom he identifies himself) and to neglect or to take for granted the piece played. Because of the fact that performers advertise and composers don't, the criticism of composition in the musical trade-weeklies is a complimentary gesture only and is extremely limited in space. Even the daily press, for all its official good will toward novelty, cannot get around the fact that the work of prosperous persons like conductors, opera-singers, and touring virtuosos has more "news-value" than the work of composers, most of whom don't even make a living from their work. So that inevitably most musical criticism is written from the performer's point of view.

The composer-critic identifies himself imaginatively with the author of any work he hears. He knows exactly (or has a pretty good idea) when the composer and the interpreter are in the groove and when they are getting in each other's hair. He is likely to be a shade indifferent about execution, unless the latter is quite out of keeping with the style of the work executed. Nevertheless, he does know about execution, in addition to knowing about design; and he can explain to others wherein their pleasure or displeasure is due to the design and wherein to execution and where to a marriage of the two.

The criticism of poetry is written nowadays almost exclusively by poets for other poets to read. It is highly technical and bitterly controversial. The layman scarcely ever sees it. It has nothing to do with any absorptive process among the reading public, because there isn't any reading public for poetry. The criticism of painting is written by collectors, museum-directors, and dealers' hired men.

Since a painting is a piece of property and hence always belongs to somebody, any criticism written by the person it belongs to or by anybody connected with him or by anybody who has a rival picture or kind of picture to sell or who makes his living by showing pictures or by advising buyers, is about as interesting as musical criticism would be if it were written by the manager of the New York Philharmonic. Painters writing about one another, when they don't go over-fulsome, can be pretty nasty; they often lack even that commercial courtesy that dealers' representatives preserve toward one another. Prefaces to the catalogues of dealers' shows and many of their reviews are blurbs by unemployed poets; they are not even openly paid advertising. The writing of art-history (which is criticism too, of course) is more reliable. At least it is when it is written by scholars with a steady job and no dealer- or museum-connections. On the whole, there just is no criticism of contemporary painting and not very much of poetry. There is only blurb and bitterness.

Music, theater, and architecture have a copious literature of contemporary criticism, because they have, to begin with, a public, and because that public is essentially disinterested. It doesn't own works of music or plays; and works of architecture, though they are real property, are not often owned by the persons who use them. The dominating rôle in this copious literature of criticism is played by the composers, the dramatic authors, and the architects themselves. Dancing and the movies have also a good public, and lots of criticism of them gets published. Most of it, unfortunately, is either trivial or venal, because choreographers and cinema-directors, the only people who know anything about design in their respective arts, have so far mostly kept out of it.

No art in its first expansive period needs criticism anyway. There isn't time to bother with anything but creation and distribution. With further expansion of the movie-trades momentarily arrested by international trade-wars, by financial crises, and by the menace of television, a certain amount of soul-searching does go on in the movie-world; and a few historical books have been written. It is quite certain that if the movies continue to function as an entertainment-form we shall see an increasing amount of critical writing about them from persons experienced in their making. [Ditto for television.]

g. The Appreciation-racket

Every composer is approached from time to time by representatives of the Appreciation-racket and offered money to lecture or to write books about the so-called Appreciation of Music. Unless he is already tied up with the pedagogical world, he usually refuses. If he makes his living as a teacher, refusal is difficult. I've seen many a private teacher forced out of business for refusing to "co-operate" with the publishers of Appreciation-books. Refusal of public-school credits for private music-study is the usual method of foreclosure. The composer who teaches in any educational institution except a straight conservatory is usually obliged to "co-operate." The racket muscles in on him. His name will be useful; his professional prestige will give a coloration of respectability to the shady business. He is offered a raise and some security in his job. He usually accepts.

Every branch of knowledge furnishes periodically to the layman digests of useful information about that branch of knowledge and elementary hand-books of its technique. Simplified explanations of the copyright laws, of general medicine for use in the home, of the mathematics of relativity, of how to build a canoe, a radio-set, or a glider, of home dressmaking, of gardenlore, of how to acquaint yourself with classical archaeology in ten volumes, and of how to see Paris in ten days—this literature is in every way legitimate. Some of the most advanced practitioners in every branch of knowledge have at one time or another paused to write down in non-technical language what was going on in those branches. The artistic professions have a large literature of this sort, the present book being an example. Biographies of celebrated musicians, histories of the symphony orchestra with descriptions of the commoner instruments, synopses of opera plots, memoirs of singers and their managers, even of musical hostesses, all go to swell the general knowledge about music and how it lives. Works of a scholarly or pedagogical nature, like treatises on harmony, on acoustics, on instrumentation, or bibliographies of historical documents, need no justification at all. They are instruments for the direct transmission of professional knowledge.

What needs some explaining is the Appreciation-literature, which transmits no firm knowledge and describes no real practice. The thing nearest like it is the physical culture advertisement that proposes to augment the muscular and virile forces of any customer who will buy the book and do what it says for five minutes a day. Obviously, five minutes a day of gymnastics, any kind of gymnastics, with or without a book, will inside a week produce a temporary enlargement of the muscles exercised. Equally, the deliberate listening to music, any kind of music, five minutes a day for a week will sharpen momentarily the musical listening-ability. If the Appreciation-racket were no more than a pretext for habituating listeners to musical sounds, it would be a legitimate advertising device, destined, with luck, to swell the number of possible concert-customers.

What distinguishes it from the physical culture schemes is the large number of reputable musicians, philanthropic foundations, and institutions of learning connected with it and the large amounts of finance-capital behind it. So much money and so much respectability behind a business that hasn't very much intrinsically to recommend it is, to say the least, suspect.

When I say the books of Music-Appreciation transmit no firm knowledge and describe no real practice, you will either believe me or you won't. I have no intention of exposing in detail here the operating methods of that sinister conspiracy or of attacking by name the distinguished musicians who have signed its instruments of propaganda. If you are a musician, all I need say is, just take a look at the books. If you are not, avoid them as you would the appearance of evil.

It is as difficult for the layman to avoid contact with Music-Appreciation as it is for the musician. Children in elementary schools get it handed out to them along with their sight-singing. So far as it is just a substitution of European folklore for American folklore and made-up exercises, not much real harm is done. At least, not as long as the center of attention remains instruction in sight-singing rather than the tastefulness of the pieces sung. It is in the secondary schools, with the introduction into education of mere listening, that is to say, of a passive musical experience, to replace performance, which is an active experience, that Appreciation begins to rear its ugly head. In secondary schools, especially in those where instruction is accomplished according to the pedagogic devices known as Progressive Education, passivity seems to be the chief result sought. A proper, that is to say, an enthusiastic, receptivity to canned musical performance is highly prized by "progressive" educators.

In colleges the Appreciation of Music is a snap course, and as such it fills a need for many a busy (or lazy) student. As anything else it is hard to defend. For professional music-students it is confusing, because the explanations are esthetic rather than technical; and esthetics are a dangerous waste of time for young practical musicians. What they need is musical analysis and lots of execution according to the best living traditions of execution. For non-professional students also it is a waste of time that might be spent on musical practice. The layman's courses for adults in ordinary civil life are an abbreviated version of the collegiate Appreciation-courses. They offer nothing more (technically) than could be learned in one music lesson from any good private teacher. The rest is a lot of useless and highly inaccurate talk about fugues and sonata-form, sales-talk for canned music really.

The basic sales-trick in all these manifestations is the use of the religious technique. Music is neither taught nor defined. It is preached. A certain limited repertory of pieces, ninety per cent of them a hundred years old, is assumed to contain most that the world has to offer of musical beauty and authority. I shall explain in a moment how this repertory is chosen by persons unknown, some of them having no musical authority whatsoever. It is further assumed (on Platonic authority) that continued auditive subjection to this repertory harmonizes the mind and sweetens the character, and that the conscious paying of attention during the auditive process intensifies the favorable reaction. Every one of these assumptions is false, or at least highly disputable, including the Platonic one. The religious technique consists in a refusal to allow any questioning of any of them. Every psychological device is used to make the customer feel that musical non-consumption is sinful. As penance for his sins he must:

A. Buy a book.
B. Buy a gramophone.
C. Buy records for it.

D. Buy a radio.

E. Subscribe to the local orchestra, if there is one.

As you can see, not one of these actions is a musical action. They are at best therapeutic actions destined to correct the customer's musical defects without putting him through the labors of musical exercise. As you can see also, they entail spending a good deal more money than a moderate amount of musical exercise would entail. Persons whose viscera are not audito-sensitive need very little musical exercise anyway. To make them feel inferior for not needing it and then to supply them with musical massage as a substitute for what they don't need is, although a common enough commercial practice, professionally unethical.

If you will look at almost any of the Appreciation-books you will notice:

A. That the music discussed is nearly all symphonic. Chamber-music (except string-quartets) and the opera are equally neglected.

B. That the examples quoted are virtually the same in all the books.

C. That they are quoted from a small number of musical authors.

D. That 90% of them were written between 1775 and 1875 and are called Symphony Number Something-or-Other.

All this means that by tacit agreement Music is defined as the instrumental music of the Romantic era, predominantly symphonic and predominantly introspective. At least that that repertory contains a larger amount of the "best" music than any other. This last assumption would be hard to defend on any grounds other than the popularity of the symphony orchestras (plus their gramophone recordings and radio transmissions) performing this repertory.

A strange thing this symphonic repertory. From Tokyo to Lisbon, from Tel-Aviv to Seattle, ninety per cent of it is the same fifty pieces. The other ten is usually devoted to good-will performances of works by local celebrities. All the rest is standardized. So are the conductors, the players, the soloists. All the units of the system are interchangeable. The number of first-class symphony orchestras in the world is well over a thousand. Europe, exclusive of the Soviet Union, counts more than two hundred. Japan alone is supposed to have forty. They all receive state, municipal, or private subsidy; and the top fifty have gramophone-and-radio-contracts. All musical posts connected with them are highly honorific. Salaries, especially for conductors and management, are the largest paid anywhere today in music. The symphony orchestras are the king-pin of the international music-industry. Their limited repertory is a part of their standardization. The Appreciation-racket is a cog in their publicity machine.

It is not my intention here to go into the virtues and defects of the system beyond pointing out that the standardization of repertory, however advantageous commercially, is not a result of mere supply and demand. It has been reached by collusion between conductors and managers and is maintained mostly by the managers, as everybody knows who has ever had anything to do with the inside of orchestral concerts. To take that practical little schematization of Romanticism for the "best" in music is as naïve as taking chain-store groceries for what a gourmet's merchant should provide. For a composer to lend the prestige of his name and knowledge to any business so unethical as that is to accept the decisions of his professional inferiors on a matter gravely regarding his profession. I do not know whether it would be possible to publish a book or offer a course of instruction in music-appreciation that would question the main assumptions of the present highly organized racket and attempt to build up a listener's esthetic on other assumptions. I doubt if it would, and the experience of various well-intentioned persons in this regard tends to support my doubts. Their attempts to disseminate musical knowledge among musically illiterate adults seem to have led them eventually to substitute for instruction in listening some exercise in musical execution, such as choral singing or the practice of some simple instrument like the recorder. It would seem that such execution, which, however elementary, is a positive musical act, gives not only its own pleasure of personal achievement but also not inconsiderable insight into the substance of all music.

Do not confuse the Appreciation-racket with the practice of musical analysis or with the exposition of musical history. These are legitimate matters for both students and teachers to be occupied with. I am talking about a real racket that any American can recognize when I describe it. It is a fake-ecstatic, holier-than-thou thing. Every school and college, even the most aristocratically anti-musical, is flooded with it. Book-counters overflow with it. Mealy-mouthed men on the air serve it in little chunks between the numbers of every symphony-orchestra concert broadcast. It is dispensed in high academic places by embittered ex-composers who don't believe a word of it. It is uncritical, in its acceptance of imposed repertory as a criterion of musical excellence. It is formalist, in its insistence on preaching principles of sonata-form that every musician knows to be either nonexistent or extremely inaccurate. It is obscurantist, because it pretends that a small section of music is either all of music or at least the heart of it, which is not true. It is dogmatic, because it pontificates about musical "taste." Whose taste? All I see is a repertory chosen for standardization purposes by conductors (who are musicians of the second category) and managers (who are not even musicians), and expounded by unsuccessful pianists, disappointed composers, and all the well-meaning but irresponsible little school-teachers who never had enough musical ability to learn to play any instrument correctly.

The musical ignorance of the army of teachers that is employed to disseminate Appreciation should be enough to warn any musician off it. Most composers are wary at first. Then it becomes tempting, because the money looks easy; and they think they at least will not be disseminating ignorance. Also in academic posts there is considerable straight pressure brought to bear. Nine times out of ten the young composer who is trying to make a modest living out of teaching harmony or piano-playing is ordered to get up a course in Appreciation (the tonier institutions are now calling it Listening) whether he wants to or not. He can make his own decision, of course; but I am telling him right now what will happen if he gets caught in those toils. He will cease to compose.

It always happens that way. No professional man can give himself to an activity so uncritical, so obscurantist, so dogmatic, so essentially venal, unless he does it to conceal his fundamental sterility, or unless he does it with his tongue in his cheek. In the latter case he gets out of it pretty quick. In the former case he gets out of composition instead. He gets out with some regret, because his professional status is lowered. But there is nothing to be done about that. Appreciation-teaching is not even a Special Skill of any kind. It is on the level of Minimum Musicality, as everybody in music knows.

So your composer who sticks at it becomes an ex-composer and an embittered man. Always beware of ex-composers. Their one aim in life is to discourage the writing of music.

[These paragraphs on Music Appreciation have been preserved in the present edition because I enjoy their fine fury. Also because they brandish for the first time two fighting terms that have since been widely used in musical polemics. These are Appreciation-racket and the Fifty Pieces. Both are still capable of inflicting insult because both still bear a high percentage of truth. Within two years, indeed, after this book's appearance, documented studies of both subjects had become available—of music as it was being explained to laymen over the radio by the late Walter Damrosch, and of the standard orchestral repertory as programed by sixteen subscription societies since 1812. The Appreciation studies appeared in a quarterly published by the Institute of Social Research, *Studies in Philosophy and Social Science*, later in book form. The orchestral repertory was analyzed in a 1941 pamphlet from the University of Indiana by Dr. John H. Mueller and his wife Kate Hevner, these studies being later amplified and published in book form by Dr. Mueller.

Both books are now standard texts in musical sociology. And they are far more devastating than my remarks. The researches that went into these studies, though in progress when I wrote this book, had not yet appeared in print. Nor was I aware of them. But the disquiet that musicians felt about Appreciation and about the standardized repertory had already so far penetrated the universities that sociologists had picked these subjects out as matters meriting investigation.

As of 1960, the radio offers little of either Music Appreciation or orchestral repertory. The explaining of music to laymen in our colleges is pretty firmly in the hands of musical technicians. (Even musicologists are not generally allowed to teach the course.) And orchestral performances are disseminated for the most

part (in America) by public concerts and by recordings. The recording companies still restrict their orchestral output to fairly familiar stuff, indeed very much
so right now, the vogue for stereophonic or binaural reproduction having given
them another excuse for recording the standard works all over again. They have
usually found some such technological pretext about every ten years since recording began, and they will go on doing so, I am sure, until philanthropic (or government) subsidy shall have taken the responsibility for recording symphonic,
chamber, and operatic music out of commercial hands, as it did long ago their
performance.]

4. The Just Rewards of His Labor

This brings me to the last kind of composers' income, namely, receipts from his
own musical works as published, performed, or recorded. It is sad that these
should come last. If they were not so rare they would naturally have come first.
Well, the facts are the facts. Performing-rights fees and royalties on copies sold
are about the last thing any composer need ever expect to live on. His children
sometimes come in for a bit of gravy. (The heirs of Ethelbert Nevin are doing
quite well, thank you.)

I had better explain here something about royalties and performing-rights
fees. Printed music brings to its composer (theoretically) a fee of ten per cent of
the marked retail price for every copy sold. I say theoretically, because many
European publishers don't pay anything to the author. They think they are doing
enough for him when they publish his work at all. If he pays the expenses of publication, he is usually allowed his ten per cent. Gramophone recordings also
bring to the composer a royalty of so much per record sold. This fee is generally
paid. The performing-rights fees of published music, like the recording fees, are
currently shared between the publisher and the composer. If a piece has words,
the author of the words gets a part of the composer's share.

There exist in all Western countries mutual protective societies of composers,
authors, and publishers, whose purpose in life is to enforce the payment of performing-rights fees by producing organizations. In Europe these societies cover all
the public usages of music, whether there is an admission-charge or not, by cine-
mas, theaters, broadcasting stations, opera houses, concert halls, churches, cafés,
night-clubs, and municipalities. Even musical mendicants are not exempt from
payment. In the United States the American Society of Composers, Authors, and
Publishers, commonly known as ASCAP, functions similarly, but really covers not
much except the usages of dance music and popular songs. [More now, especially
from radio.] Theatrical music is covered, by courtesy, through the Dramatists'
Guild of the Authors' League of America. No performing-rights fees are collected
in America at all, except by individual contract (which means there is no mini-

mum payment), from symphony orchestras, traveling concert-artists, the major opera houses, the churches, schools, colleges, and clubs. [The last four are still exempt.] In many cases of unpublished works in large form played by chamber or symphonic organizations, no fee is paid to the composer at all, not even a rental fee for the use of score and parts. This situation will not long continue, but for the present it is the case. It is the unique and sole reason for the existence in Europe of a much larger number of art-composers who live off their just share in the profits of the commercial exploitation of their work than exists in the United States. [Still true.] Such composers are almost non-existent in America. Let us call them, for the sake of brevity, successful composers (successful being understood here to mean earning a living by writing music).

Of all the composing musicians, this group presents in its music the greatest variety both of subject-matter and of stylistic orientation, the only limit to such variety being what the various musical publics at any given moment will take. Even the individual members of the group show variety in their work from piece to piece. This variety is due in part to their voluntary effort to keep their public interested and to enlarge their market. (Stylistic "evolution" is good publicity nowadays.) A good part of it is due also to the variety of usages that are coverable by commercially ordered music. Theater, concert, opera, church, and war demand a variety of solutions for individual esthetic cases according to the time, the place, the subject, the number and skill of the available executants, the social class, degree of musical cultivation, and size of the putative public. Music made for no particular circumstance or public is invariably egocentric. Music made for immediate usage, especially if that usage is proposed to the composer by somebody who has an interest in the usage, is more objective and more varied.

Successful composers are often accused of repeating themselves. In real truth they repeat themselves less often than the unsuccessful ones do. The latter keep writing the same piece over and over in the hope they can make it clearer next time, make people understand somehow. Successful men are often accused of "compromising," too, of compromising with public taste (which is assumed to be bad taste and profitable to cater to). I assure you that first-string composers have reputations to keep up, and that anyone who has a paying public (however small) is less tempted to "write down" to that public than the prize-and-commission-supported are to "write up" to musical snobs. I also assure you that public taste is not necessarily bad taste, any more than private taste is necessarily good taste, and that the quickest way for a successful composer to stop being a success is for him to vulgarize his work. Success is like travel; it broadens a man, makes him at once more objective and more passionate about the things that matter to him. There must be inconveniences about living off the just rewards of one's labor, but I don't know what they are. I have never known an artist of any kind who didn't do better work when he got properly paid for it.

The composer who lives on music-writing invariably tends toward the theater. Handel and Verdi and Gershwin are classic examples. I do not know, in the last two or three hundred years, of any composer who has lived for very long off the commercial profits of symphonic and chamber music. The song-writers don't do too badly, and certainly Richard Strauss receives, now that he is old, a respectable income from his non-operatic music. [Igor Stravinsky too, since Strauss's death.] But by and large, the theater is where the money is and where most of the composers are who have once had a taste of that money. Movies, opera, incidental music, ballet, these are the musical forms that feed their man. Composers who get fed by them have plenty of time to write a more disinterested music if they wish. Many do. All I am saying is that the commercially successful professional composer (and by commercially successful I mean he eats) is likely to be a theater man. That is his occupational deformity, if any.

To sum up and conclude:

Every composer's music reflects in its subject-matter and in its style the source of the money the composer is living on while writing that music. This applies to introspective as well as to objective music.

The quality of any piece of music is not a function of its author's income-source. One has only to remember history to know otherwise. J. S. Bach and César Franck were church organists. Handel and Verdi and Gluck and Rameau were theater men. Beethoven skimped along on patronage and publishers' fees. Wagner (after his exile) and Tchaikovsky lived on gifts. Chopin and Liszt were concert-pianists and also gave lessons. Mendelssohn was a gentleman of means. Haydn received a salary for writing music and for organizing musical entertainments at the country house of one Count Esterházy. Schumann was a musical journalist. A great many modern composers are pedagogues. One might mention Hindemith, Schoenberg, d'Indy, and practically all the Americans. Bernstein and Chavez are conductors. Satie was a post-office employee, Moussorgsky a customs official, Cui a chemist. Mozart did everything in music at one time or another except journalism. Palestrina and Debussy lived on their musical receipts till they got tired of starving and married rich widows. One could go on, but I think this should be enough to show that excellent music can be written on almost any kind of money.

Anyone who wishes to follow this matter through musical history in more detail is warned not to consider contributive income as very important. It amplifies a composer's practical experience, when it has to do with music; but it does not determine either his style or his subject-matter. Nothing does that but what he is actually living on. Nothing impresses a man very deeply except what pays him a living wage.

AGE WITHOUT HONOR (1940)

This review was Thomson's legendary opening salvo at the New York Herald Tribune—a notice as lively today as it was in 1940. Other reviews in the following pages also appeared in the Trib, as it was commonly called, where his longer, more general pieces were customarily published on Sundays. In "Masterpieces" (1944), Thomson repeated his epithet "Appreciation Racket," which, like all acute critical terms, survived its initial reference to become more generally used.

The Philharmonic-Symphony Society of New York opened its ninety-ninth season last evening in Carnegie Hall with John Barbirolli conducting. There was little that could be called festive about the occasion. The menu was routine, the playing ditto.

Beethoven's Overture to *Egmont* is a classic hors d'œuvre. Nobody's digestion was ever spoiled by it and no late comer has ever lost much by missing it. It was preceded, as is the custom nowadays, by our national anthem, gulped down standing, like a cocktail. I seem to remember that in 1917 and 1918 a sonorous arrangement of *The Star-Spangled Banner* by Walter Damrosch was current at these concerts. After so long a time I couldn't be sure whether that was the orchestration used last night. I rather think not. Last night's version seemed to have more weight than brilliance. It had the somber and spiritless sonority of the German military bands one hears in France these days. That somberness is due, I think, to an attempt to express authority through mere blowing and sawing in the middle ranges of the various instruments, rather than by the more classical method of placing every instrument in its most brilliant and grateful register in order to achieve the maximum of carrying power. I may be wrong about the reasons for it, but I think I am right about the general effect, unless my seat was in an acoustical dead spot of the hall, which I do not think it was. The anthem, to me, sounded logy and coarse; it lacked the buoyancy and the sweep that are its finest musical qualities.

Elgar's *Enigma Variations* are an academic effort not at all lacking in musical charm. I call them academic because I think the composer's interest in the musical devices he was employing was greater than his effort toward a direct and forceful expression of anything in particular. Like most English composers, Elgar orchestrates accurately and competently. Now, when a man can do anything accurately and competently he is always on the lookout for occasions to do that thing. In the Continental tradition of music-writing orchestration is always incidental to expression, to construction, to rhetoric. Many of the greatest composers—Chopin and Schumann, for instance—never bothered to become skillful at it in any major way. Others, like Beethoven and Brahms, always kept its

47

fanciness down to the strict minimum of what expression needs. I've an idea the Elgar Variations are mostly a pretext for orchestration, a pretty pretext and a graceful one, not without charm and a modicum of sincerity, but a pretext for fancywork all the same, for that massively frivolous patchwork in pastel shades of which one sees such quantities in any intellectual British suburban dwelling.

Twenty years' residence on the European continent has largely spared me Sibelius. Last night's Second Symphony was my first in quite some years. I found it vulgar, self-indulgent, and provincial beyond all description. I realize that there are sincere Sibelius-lovers in the world, though I must say I've never met one among educated professional musicians. I realize also that this work has a kind of popular power unusual in symphonic literature. Even Wagner scarcely goes over so big on the radio. That populace-pleasing power is not unlike the power of a Hollywood class-A picture. Sibelius is in no sense a naïf; he is merely provincial. Let me leave it at that for the present. Perhaps, if I have to hear much more of him, I'll sit down one day with the scores and really find out what is in them. Last night's experience of one was not much of a temptation, however, to read or sit through many more.

The concert as a whole, in fact, both as to program and as to playing, was anything but a memorable experience. The music itself was soggy, the playing dull and brutal. As a friend remarked who had never been to one of these concerts before, "I understand now why the Philharmonic is not a part of New York's intellectual life."

MASTERPIECES (1944)

The enjoyment and understanding of music are dominated in a most curious way by the prestige of the masterpiece. Neither the theater nor the cinema nor poetry nor narrative fiction pays allegiance to its ideal of excellence in the tyrannical way that music does. They recognize no unbridgeable chasm between "great work" and the rest of production. Even the world of art painting, though it is no less a victim than that of music to Appreciation rackets based on the concept of gilt-edged quality, is more penetrable to reason in this regard, since such values, or the pretenses about them advanced by investing collectors and museums, are more easily unmasked as efforts to influence market prices. But music in our time (and in our country) seems to be committed to the idea that first-class work in composition is separable from the rest of music writing by a distinction as radical as that recognized in theology between the elect and the damned. Or at the very least by as rigorous an exclusion from glory as that which formerly marked the difference between Mrs. Astor's Four Hundred and the rest of the human race.

This snobbish definition of excellence is opposed to the classical concept of a Republic of Letters. It reposes, rather, on the theocratic idea that inspiration is less a privilege of the private citizen than of the ordained prophet. Its weakness lies in the fact that music, though it serves most becomingly as religion's handmaiden, is not a religion. Music does not deal in general ideas or morality or salvation. It is an art. It expresses private sentiments through skill and sincerity, both of which last are a privilege, a duty, indeed, of the private citizen, and no monopoly of the prophetically inclined.

In the centuries when artistic skills were watched over by guilds of workmen, a masterpiece was nothing more than a graduation piece, a work that marked the student's advance from apprenticeship to master status. Later the word was used to mean any artist's most accomplished work, the high point of his production. It came thus to represent no corporate judgment but any consumer's private one. Nowadays most people understand by it a piece differing from the run of repertory by a degree of concentration in its expressivity that establishes a difference of kind. And certain composers (Beethoven was the first of them) are considered to have worked exclusively in that vein. The idea that any composer, however gifted and skillful, is merely a masterpiece factory would have been repellent to Bach or Haydn or Handel or Mozart, though Gluck was prone to advertise himself as just that. But all the successors of Beethoven who aspired to his authority— Brahms and Bruckner and Wagner and Mahler and Tchaikovsky—quite consciously imbued their music with the "masterpiece" tone.

This tone is lugubrious, portentous, world shaking; and length, as well as heavy instrumentation, is essential to it. Its reduction to absurdity is manifest today through the later symphonies of Shostakovich. Advertised frankly and cynically as owing their particular character to a political directive imposed on their author by state disciplinary action, they have been broadcast throughout the world as models of patriotic expression. And yet rarely in the history of music has any composer ever spread his substance so thin. Attention is not even required for their absorption. Only Anton Rubinstein's once popular symphony, *The Ocean*, ever went in for so much water. They may have some value as national advertising, though I am not convinced they do; but their passive acceptance by musicians and music lovers can certainly not be due to their melodic content (inoffensive as this is) or to their workmanship (roughly competent as this is too).

What imposes about them is their obvious masterpiece-style one-trackness, their implacable concentration on what they are doing. That this quality, which includes also a certain never-knowing-when-to-stop persistence, should be admired by laymen as resembling superficially the Soviet war effort is natural enough. But that what these pieces are up to in any musical sense, chiefly rehashing bits of Borodin and Mahler, is of intrinsic musical interest I have yet to hear averred by a musician. And that is the whole trouble with the masterpiece cult. It tends to substitute an impressive manner for specific expression, just as oratory does. That music should stoop to the procedures of contemporary political harangue is deplorable indeed.

There are occasions (funerals, for instance) where the tone of a discourse is more important than its content, but the concert is not one of them. The concert is a habitual thing like a meal; ceremony is only incidental to it. And restricting its menu to what observes the fictitious "masterpiece" tone is like limiting one's nourishment to the heavier party foods. If the idea can be got rid of that a proper concert should consist only of historic "masterpieces" and of contemporary works written in the "masterpiece" tone, our programs will cease to be repetitive and monotonous. Arthur Judson, the manager of the Philharmonic, remarked recently that the orchestral repertory in concert use today is smaller than it was when he went into concert management twenty-five years ago, and this in spite of the fact that orchestras and orchestral concerts are many times more numerous. I suspect that this shrinkage may be due to a popular misconception about what constitutes quality in music.

If the Appreciation Racket were worth its salt, if the persons who explain music to laymen would teach it as a language and not as a guessing game, the fallacy of the masterpiece could be exposed in short order. Unfortunately, most of them know only about twenty pieces anyway, and they are merely bluffing when they pretend that these (and certain contemporary works that sort of sound like them) make up all the music in the world worth bothering about.

CONDUCTING MODERN MUSIC (1942)

The prime consideration in interpreting new musical works is to avoid doing anything that might possibly make these appear to be emulating the music of the past. Such emulation may or may not have been a part of the composer's intention, but playing it up in presentation produces a false relation between a work and its own time that is fatal to the comprehension of the work by its own time. Dressing and directing *Hamlet* as if it were a modern play is a piquant procedure. Treating a modern play as if it were Shakespeare's *Hamlet* can only make for pretentiousness and obscurity.

There is a prestige attached to any art work that has survived the death of its author that no work by a living hand can enjoy. This fact of survival is correctly called immortality, and that immortality surrounds the surviving work with a white light. In that radiance all becomes beautiful. Obscurities disappear, too; or at least they cease to bother. When I refer, as not infrequently I do, to live music and dead music, I mean that there is the same difference between the two that there is between live persons and dead ones. The spirit and influence of the dead are often far more powerful than those of the living. But they are not the same thing, because you can only argue *about* them, never *with*. The dead have glory and a magnificent weight. The living have nothing but life.

The glorification of the dead is a perfectly good thing. Indeed, the greater civilizations have always done it more than the lesser. But a clear separation of the dead from the living is also a mark of the higher cultures. That is the fecundating drama between tradition and spontaneity that keeps peoples and empires alive. Consequently no good is accomplished by pretending, or seeming to pretend, that a work by Igor Stravinsky or Aaron Copland or myself is a museum piece, because it isn't and won't be till we're dead, if then. And framing such a work among museum pieces in such a way that it appears to be subsidiary to them invariably makes the living work seem deader than a doornail. Its lack of white-light immortality makes it appear gravely inferior to the works on the same program that have such an aura and glamour.

The moral of this explanation is that new works must be played alone, in company with other new works, or surrounded by old ones carefully chosen, if one wishes to bring out their resemblances to the traditional past as well as their essential differences from that past. A new work may not be the most important piece on the program; but unless it is the determining item in the choice of the whole program, it will always sound like second-rate music, because it is pretty certain to be placed in unfair glamour competition with the classics of repertory. Modern music indiscriminately programmed, no matter what kind of music it is, is framed to flop.

Neither can it be interpreted in the same style as older music. Insufficient rehearsal often works to a new piece's advantage. When there isn't time to do much but read the notes and observe the author's tempos, it gets a neutral reading that is at least better than a false interpretation. If the conductor has time to work it up into an imitation of all his favorite war-horses or to streamline it into a faint reminder of Beethoven and Tchaikovsky, it is very difficult for the listener to hear anything in it but a memory of these authors, or at most a feeble attempt to dethrone them by being arbitrarily different.

The best international style for playing the classics is one that reduces them to a common denominator of clarity and elegance. That was always Toscanini's forte as a conductor of standard repertory. He was never very effective as a conductor of modern music (and he avoided it whenever possible, for that reason, I imagine), because he knew no other way of conducting anything. Characteristic national differences, which are of minor importance in standard repertory but which are the very essence of modern stylistic comprehension, seem to have escaped him. And being a musician of too high temperament to be satisfied with a mere neutral reading of anything, he wisely refrained from taking on a job in which neither he nor the living composer was likely to do much shining.

The conductors who do best by the music of our century are seldom equally good at interpreting all the kinds of it. Koussevitzky does well by anything Russian and fair by the English and the Americans, provided these last are not too local in flavor. He is not bad with German music, adds to it a Slavic elegance that is sometimes advantageous. French music escapes him utterly, in spite of his many years' residence in Paris. Mitropoulos is at his best with the central-European styles. Beecham is fine for English music, for all Slavic, for some German, for anything that has lyric afflatus or rhythmic punch. The Germans are rather messy when they play German music—always were, as Richard Wagner pointed out. Some are excellent with French music, however, Furtwängler, for instance, and Stock, of Chicago. Italians do not always do their best by Italian works, especially those of strong French influence, though they do beautifully by anything Germanic, even Brahms. Only the French (and a few Germans) make sense with French music. Nobody, literally nobody, who has not passed his formative adolescent years in this country ever conducts American music with complete intelligibility.

The basis of American musical thought is a special approach to rhythm. Underneath everything is a continuity of short quantities all equal in length and in percussive articulation. These are not always articulated, but they must always be understood. If for any expressive reason one alters the flow of them temporarily, they must start up again exactly as before, once the expressive alteration is terminated. In order to make the whole thing clear, all instruments, string and wind, must play with a clean, slightly percussive attack. This attack must never be sacrificed for the sake of a beautiful tone or even for pitch accuracy, because it is more important than either. Besides, once a steady rhythm is established, the music plays itself; pitch and sonorities adjust themselves automatically; as in a good jazz band the whole takes on an air of completeness.

French music is the nearest thing in Europe to our music, because French rhythm, like ours, is less accentual than quantitative. Keeping downbeats out of a Debussy rendition, for instance, is virtually impossible to anybody but a Frenchman. Steady quantities, a little longer than ours and requiring no percussive definition at all, are its rhythmic foundation. Definition is achieved by a leisurely breathing between phrases and an almost imperceptible waiting before attacking, with no added force, what in any other music would be played as a downbeat. As with American music, a proper rhythm is cardinal and must be achieved before the pitch and the tone-production can be polished up.

Modern German music is not very interesting rhythmically. It needs no exact quantities, only a thwacking downbeat. Even that can be advanced or held back, as is the Viennese custom, to express sentiment. What is most important is to get the harmony right, for pitch is all-important to the German mind. Get the harmony right and don't go *too* sentimental. Nothing else counts, provided care for the harmony includes a clear plotting out of the key-relations in the whole piece. This means being sure there is always plenty of bass at the piece's joints.

Russian music is an alternation of very free rhythms with rigid and insistent ones. The latter are easy to render. But few conductors ever take enough liberties with the sentimental passages. English formulas are always closely related to the Russian (*vide* the English novel and the English Church). In music, both peoples conceive of rhythm as either nonexistent or quite inflexible. Both observe beat-rhythms, too, not quantities. And both alternate speech inflections with foot-work, as in a song-and-dance. The chief difference between them is that the Russian mind dramatizes itself with a grandiloquent simplicity, whereas the English tradition values a more intimate and personal kind of forthrightness in the expression of tender thought. The grander passages of both repertories may be rendered with the utmost of pomp and of panache.

Matters like these seem to me more important to restate than international aesthetic principles. All conductors know nowadays what the Neo-Classic style is all about. Also the Neo-Romantic style and the twelve-tone syntax. And certainly the survivals of late Romanticism are not difficult to decipher. But these are the stylistic elements that underlie all modern music; they have been written about *ad infinitum* and *ad nauseam.* What I am pointing out is that underneath these international tendencies and observances there are ethnic differences that must be taken account of. Also to remind my readers that these ethnic differences preclude the possibility that conductors of foreign upbringing now resident among us will play a leading role in our present musical expansion. They render great service by their constant acts of goodwill toward homemade music. But they have only the vaguest idea of what it's all about. And so has that part of our musical public that hears it only through their well-intentioned but unconvincing renditions.

THE INTELLECTUAL AUDIENCE (1950)

Anyone who attends musical and other artistic events eclectically must notice that certain of these bring out an audience thickly sprinkled with what are called "intellectuals" and the others do not. It is managements and box offices that call these people intellectuals; persons belonging to that group rarely use the term. They are a numerous body in New York, however, and can be counted on to patronize certain entertainments. Their word-of-mouth communication has an influence, moreover, on public opinion. Their favor does not necessarily provoke mass patronage, but it does bring to the box office a considerable number of their own kind, and it does give to any show or artist receiving it some free advertising. The intellectual audience in any large city is fairly numerous, well organized, and vocal.

This group, that grants or withholds its favor without respect to paid advertising and that launches its ukases with no apparent motivation, consists of people from many social conditions. Its binding force is the book. It is a reading audience. Its members may have a musical ear or an eye for visual art, and they may have neither. What they all have is some acquaintance with ideas. The intellectual world does not judge a work of art from the talent and skill embodied in it; only professionals judge that way. It seeks in art a clear connection with contemporary aesthetic and philosophic trends, as these are known through books and magazines. The intellectual audience is not a professional body; it is not a professors' conspiracy, either, nor a publishers' conspiracy. Neither is it quite a readers' anarchy. Though it has no visible organization, it forms its own opinions and awards its own prizes in the form of free advertising. It is a very difficult group to maneuver or to push around.

In New York it is a white-collar audience containing stenographers, saleswomen, union employees of all kinds, many persons from the comfortable city middle-aged middle class, and others from the suburban young parents. There are snappy dressers, too, men and women of thirty who follow the mode, and artists' wives from downtown who wear peasant blouses and do their own hair. Some are lawyers, doctors, novelists, painters, musicians, professors. Even the carriage trade is represented, and all the age levels above twenty-five. A great variety of costume is always present, of faces and figures with character in them. Many persons of known professional distinction give it seasoning and tone.

The presence of such an audience at a musical event is no result of paid advertising or of standard publicity. Its representation is small at the Metropolitan Opera, the Philharmonic, and the concerts of the N.B.C. Symphony Orchestra, though it will go to all these places for special works. Dimitri Mitropoulos, for example, drew a brilliant audience for his recent performance at the Philharmonic of Strauss's *Elektra*. The smaller symphonic ensembles, the City Center opera, the New Friends of Music, and the League of Composers bring out lots of intellectuals. So do certain ballet performances and the spectacles of Martha Graham, though not, on the whole, for musical reasons. The International Society for Contemporary Music, the Composers' Forum, concerts and opera productions at the Juilliard School and at Columbia University, and certain recitalists are definitely favored. Wanda Landowska, harpsichord players in general, Jennie Tourel, Maggie Teyte, Martial Singher, Gold and Fizdale, sometimes Josef Szigeti are all notable for the interest they offer to persons of high mental attainments.

The conductors chiefly favored by this group are Reiner, Monteux, and Ansermet. The intellectuals often come in a body to hear them. They come individually from time to time to hear Toscanini, Koussevitzky, Bernstein. They have shown no consistent interest in Rodzinski, Mitropoulos, Munch, Ormandy, or in recent years Stokowski. Beecham's audience appeal, for all his high cultural equipment, remains strictly musical, though his recordings are collected by many persons from other professions.

Flagstad, too, is a purely musical phenomenon; and so is Horowitz. The latter, indeed, no longer pleases wholly even the musical world, if I read his public right. One sees fewer and fewer known musicians at his recitals, more and more a public clearly not familiar with standard piano repertory. The music world attends *en masse* Landowska, Schnabel, and Curzon. The last two, however, have never made full contact with the world called intellectual, the world of verbalized ideas and general aesthetic awareness.

Management's aim is to mobilize the ticket-buying and propaganda power of this world without alienating the mass public. The latter is respectful of intellectual opinion, which it learns about through the magazines of women's wear, but resistant to the physical presence of the intellectual audience. The varieties of fancy dress and interesting faces, the pride of opinion expressed in overheard conversations, the clannish behavior of these strange and often monstrous personalities are profoundly shocking to simpler people. Their behavior expresses both a freedom of thought and a degree of ostentation that are not available to the standardized consumer. Much as he would like to enjoy everything that is of good report, he is really most comfortable among his own kind listening to Marian Anderson. This is why the Philharmonic and the Metropolitan managements make little or no play for the intellectual trade and discourage efforts in that direction from the musical wing. They have a mass public of sorts already, do not need intellectual promotion. They seem to fear, moreover, that the intellectual influence, bearing always toward the left in program-making, may keep away more paying customers than it brings in.

Beneath all of management's dealings with the intellectual group lie two assumptions. One is that intellectuals like novelty and modernity. The other is that the mass public dislikes both. I think the first is true. I doubt the second. I am more inclined to believe, from long acquaintance with all sorts of musical publics, that it is management which dislikes novelty and everything else that interferes with standardization. I suspect that management's design is toward conditioning the mass public to believe that it dislikes novelty. Some success has already been achieved in this direction. If intellectual opinion has any carrying power beyond the centers of its origins, there is a job to be done, a war to be fought across the nation. The intellectuals' own survival, even, may depend on winning it. For unless these bright ones carry some weight in the forming of everybody's opinions and tastes, they are a useless body and can be by-passed by any power-group that wants to use art for its own ends.

Conservative Institution (1947)

The symphony orchestra, among all our musical institutions, is the most firmly established, the most widely respected and, musically speaking, the most efficient. It is not, however, either the oldest or the most beloved. The opera and the singing society, I should think, have better right to the latter titles. Nevertheless, the orchestra is what all music, its prestige, its exploitation, and its teaching, turns round. It is the central luminary of our contemporary musical system.

Someone, I cannot remember who, suggested several years ago that the strength of the institution comes from the fact that the concert orchestra is a representation in art, a symbol, of democratic assembly. Certainly it is so conceivable. And certainly its rise is contemporaneous historically with the rise of parliamentary government. The fact that its most glorious period, as regards composition, the working years in Vienna of Haydn, Mozart, and Beethoven, was a time when, in that place, there was no parliamentary government at all, does not disprove the identification. It merely suggests that the parliamentary ideal, as represented then by England, was strong enough to influence democratic-minded men everywhere and that its picturing through music, an art difficult to censor, is more than probable in a country which would not have tolerated at the time any such representation through the less hermetic techniques of painting and literature.

In any case, these men in Austria, not the composers of liberal England or of revolutionary France, transformed the court symphony into the popular symphony. Never again, after they had lived, was the symphony an elegant or decorative form. It was larger, louder, more insistent, more humane, broader of scope, and definitely monumental. Its performance ceased to be a private entertainment and became a public rite. Also, there has remained with the symphony ever since an inalienable trend toward, in the broad sense, political content.

Professional symphony orchestras today remain associated with a political unit, the city. They are a privilege and symbol of civic pride. States and central governments rarely support them. Even municipalities do not like contributing taxpayers' money to them, though in a few American cities—Baltimore, Indianapolis, and San Francisco—there is a budgetary provision for such aid. Normally they are a civic proposition, and their deficits are met by public-spirited citizens. Rarely are great orchestras associated with our religious or scholastic foundations (as our finest choruses are more often than not) or directly with the world of big business and finance and fashion (as our best opera companies have always been). They are wedded to our great cities. They are monuments to civic pride and symbols not only of musical achievement but of their communities' whole cultural life.

There are really two kinds of orchestras, the monumental and the directly functional. The latter kind exists in large numbers connected with educational institutions and with the amateur musical life of neighborhoods and of semirural communities. In 1937 there were about 30,000 of these in the United States alone. Their chief purpose is the musical training or musical enjoyment of the players, though they also provide in increasing numbers nowadays professional players to what I call the monumental orchestras. The latter are strictly professional and perform only for the edification of the listener.

The functional orchestras, being educational in purpose, play a larger repertory than the others do. And their style of execution is less standardized. The monumental orchestras, being more ceremonial by nature, are highly standardized in both repertory and execution, internationally standardized, in fact. The players, the conductors, the pieces played (save for a very small number that represents local taste only) can be removed from one orchestra and inserted in another anywhere in the world. Even language is no barrier to rehearsal efficiency. Indeed, it is exactly their international standardization that enables our orchestras to represent localities, to symbolize to the whole world the cultural level—by internationally recognized standards—of the particular city that supports any one of them.

The civically supported symphony orchestra is the most conservative institution in the Western world. Churches, even banks, are more open to experiment. The universities are daring by comparison. This does not mean that new music does not get played by the orchestras. The rendering of contemporary works along with familiar classics is one of their firmest traditions. No orchestra can live that plays only the music of dead composers. As a matter of fact, no orchestra ever essays so radical a policy. The public objects to modern music, naturally, because modern music, however great intrinsic musical interest it may present, simply can never compete as edification with the hallowed past. But the same public that objects to hearing modern music objects far more vigorously to being deprived of the privilege. Just as the musical execution of our symphony orchestras is the most conservative and correct that money can buy, so also is the repertory they play, a certain appearance of musical progressiveness being required by tradition itself.

The encouragement of musical advance, however, is not the chief purpose of symphony orchestras. The first-line trenches of that lie elsewhere. They lie in many places, but always the rapidest progress of musical invention takes place where the attention of so large and so pious a public is not present to discourage the inventor. Small groups of musicians working under private or university patronage can produce more novelty in a year than will be heard at the subscription concerts in twenty. Invention takes place sometimes, even under the very eye of a large public, provided that public is looking at something else.

If theatrical entertainment is there to give novelty a *raison d'être*, as at the ballet or at the opera, or if the occasion is not too respectable socially, as in jazz dives, then the circumstances for musical invention are at their most favorable. The symphony orchestra favors musical advance officially, but it dare not offer much of it at a time. It must advance slowly, because it deals with a large public, which necessarily is slow of comprehension, and because the basis of its whole operation is the conserving of tradition anyway. Stability rather than variety is what the faithful chiefly demand of it.

Our symphony orchestras, historically viewed, are solider than our banks. They are always getting born; they rarely die. Constantly threatened with financial disaster (a talking point during campaigns to raise money or in union negotiations), they almost never cease operations. Nor will they, so long as civic pride exists and so long as democratic government through parliamentary procedure shall seem to us a beautiful ideal worthy of representation in art.

ENGLISH AT THE MET (1947)

There is no doubt that the performance of opera in English to an English-speaking audience brings enormous benefits in the way of general understanding. There is also no question but that such performance presents unusual difficulties to an organization like the Metropolitan Opera Company, which was long ago set up for another purpose. Ideally, and naïvely, viewed, this troupe has usually been considered a polygot repertory theater, prepared to offer a proper performance of almost any known opera in its original tongue. Actually it has rarely been convincing in any languages but the Italian and the German. It still has enough good Italian singers to cast and render Italian opera correctly and enough German-speaking Central Europeans (mostly of Swedish or Hungarian birth) to give a reasonably satisfying performance of Wagner. French opera rarely sounds like French opera at the Met; and English, though the mother tongue of many of the artists, more often than not leaves much to be desired in the way of clarity.

Russian opera, when performed there, is offered in translations more or less fortuitously chosen. Mussorgsky's *Boris Godunov* is currently given in Italian, that being the native language of Ezio Pinza, who sings the title role. Rimsky-Korsakov's *Golden Cockerel*, formerly given in French, has been heard of late years in a language that might be described as Basic Bromide English. Similarly, the Czechish *Bartered Bride*, by Smetana, has been moved from the German in which it used to be given over to our own vernacular, and none too effectively, I may add.

The Metropolitan is lucky to have a chorus capable of singing German, Italian, French, and English and enough soloists to cast any opera with moderate effectiveness in those languages. To offer the Slavic ones as well, though not at all out of the question in New York City, would require firing most of the present Italo-German chorus and hiring a Russo-Polish one with Western language accomplishments. Even the giving of *Boris* in Italian is condonable on the ground that it leaves the excellent Mr. Pinza in the cast, though why this artist should not, in his more than twenty years' American residence, have learned, even accidentally, to speak and sing our language passes my comprehension. One would have thought that simple curiosity might have led him somewhere in that direction.[1]

The same slow progress that has got all the Slavic operas but *Boris* into English at the Metropolitan has begun now to work on the production in translation, one every two or so years, of operas from the more familiar European repertory, chiefly, so far, from the German. Mozart's *Magic Flute* and *Abduction from the Seraglio* and Humperdinck's *Hansel and Gretel* are now given in an English that, if not exactly of the highest literary distinction, is perfectly clear and for the most part inoffensive. Little by little, if present trends continue, the Met will go on augmenting its in-English list, though the Italian wing of the company, as Italian wings have always done everywhere, will no doubt oppose progress in this direction by every means in its power. Since one of these means is the refusal to co-operate, to sing in English on any stage, the in-English productions will, of course, be deprived of all the best acting talent in the company, which is, to a man, Italian.

Articulating the English language clearly in a house of that size, though this has not always in the past been accomplished impeccably, is not an insoluble problem. The present production of Mozart's *Seraglio* is highly presentable in that regard, and that of Bernard Rogers's *The Warrior* is well nigh perfect. Opera in English for an English-speaking audience requires a good initial fitting of words to music by the composer, if the opera is composed in English; a good literary and prosodic translation, if it is a foreign work; and a clear projection of the verbal text by all the singers on the stage, including the chorus. Without these elements the show is bound to be second-class and to disappoint any audience that expects a first-class entertainment for its seven dollars. But both are in the long run, with patience on everybody's part, obtainable, as current productions prove.

What is going to give trouble from now on is acting. Acting in English to music has no local tradition; and one must be formed, in however elementary a fashion, right away. So far the Metropolitan management has tried to side-step the problem by giving in English only comedies and fairy-tale fantasies. The acting in Humperdinck's *Hansel and Gretel* will do. That in Mozart's *Seraglio* will not. I do not believe, moreover, that a proper technique of rendering grown-up comedy is available among the Met's English-singing artists. Neither do I believe that bad acting is more nearly acceptable in the comic style than in the tragic. On the contrary, an amateur *Hamlet or Macbeth* is far easier to listen to than an amateur *Twelfth Night* or *Tempest*. Anybody can act *Il Trovatore*, and the popular Puccini operas—*La Tosca*, *La Bohème* and *Madama Butterfly*—are foolproof in any language. Tears need no timing, only insistence. Farce and fantasy are a monopoly of the great stage technicians.

Here, I think, is the reason why Mozart's *Seraglio*, for all its sound musical execution, has not yet caught public favor at the Metropolitan. It has a silly plot that does not lend itself to easy rendering. *Figaro*, on the other hand, which makes sense as a play, is rarely ineffective in any language, played by no matter whom. Even Debussy's *Pelléas et Mélisande*, for all its intimate French tone and its throughly French vocal line, can be convincing in English, as the Philadelphia Opera Company demonstrated several years back. But silly plots and silly jokes are all the sillier when one can understand them. Those are the operatic elements that profit best from being left in a foreign tongue.

To the Metropolitan management, therefore, the writer suggests that the next time an opera is to be translated and refurbished, one with a serious story be chosen. If our English-speaking singing actors and actresses are going to learn to act, which they must do eventually, they must be given, for their early efforts in that enterprise, something that is capable of being acted. *Seraglio*, *The Magic Flute*, and *The Golden Cockerel* are hard jobs for the most expert and imaginative comedians. For average singing actors they are hopelessly difficult. We must give our American singers every facility. Give them young love, irate parenthood, sexy seduction, the royal mien, maternal sentiments, jealousies, noble friendships, priesthoods, vendettas, tears, and tuberculosis. And if the Met must do farce comedy, let some insistence be made that Baccaloni learn to sing English. Or, failing that, how would it do if a stand-by sang the bass solos while somebody like Bobby Clark did some real clowning?

Notes
1. Pinza sings English in concert.

BIGGER THAN BASEBALL (1953)

Among all of America's leisure activities, the most widely indulged, believe it or not, is the art of music. I am not talking about radio music, the universal background of home life, or the various forms of transmitted music that are the steady accompaniment to public eating and drinking, to bus-riding, automobile trips, and shopping. "Canned" music has become an auditory decor so constantly present in American life that virtually nobody can escape from it.

But music in this sense cannot be called a leisure activity any more than sleeping in a bed or wearing shoes can. An activity is something one is active about. Well, the latest bulletin of the National Music Council, a very serious documentary publication, reports over the signature of Mrs. Helen M. Thompson, executive secretary of the American Symphony Orchestra League, that thirty million people in this country are "actively interested in concert music." This does not mean jazz or popular ditties, or hillbilly dance-bands, or shows and films employing music, or hymn singing, or wedding marches. It means the classical music of the last three centuries, including the one we live in. And thirty million people are one-fifth of our population.

The statement is even more difficult to believe when one realizes that only half that number, fifteen million, watched major league baseball games last year, that only thirteen million ordinarily engage in hunting, and that a mere five million, according to the same report, play golf. Considering classical music as a spectator sport, its total cost in a recent year, says Mrs. Thompson, was $45,000,000, compared to the following gross revenues of organized sports:

Baseball $40,000,000
Professional football..............9,000,000
Horse and dog tracks.........38,000,000

In addition to the $45,000,000 paid at the gate for public performances of classical music, which represents 30,000,000 separate paid admissions, last year's sales of classical recordings totaled $60,000,000. This amounts to 24 per cent of all record sales. And among the ten best sellers were two full-length classical symphonies.

Let me give you some more details about our professional music life. America has eighty opera companies operating in nineteen states. We have 150 music periodicals, 750 music critics, 1,196 writers on musical subjects. We have 938 symphony orchestras, all or in part professionally staffed. One of our large booking organizations reports that last year three times as many concerts were given in the United States as in all the rest of the world put together. Music in general—its teaching, performance, manufacture of equipment, and distribution—has for some years now ranked sixth among America's industries in volume of business, being somewhat smaller than food or motor cars but a much bigger affair than steel.

As for music on the non-professional level, let us begin by noting the existence, again according to the National Music Council, of 20,000,000 music students. More than one-tenth of our population is taking lessons of some kind toward the acquisition of musical skill. Seventy-five lay organizations comprising over 600,000 members aid in disseminating international standards of work-

manship. Fifteen thousand school orchestras actually perform symphonic repertory. For adults who enjoy playing string quartets and the like there is a society of
more than 3,000 members called Amateur Chamber Music Players. They have a
national directory, too, where they are graded A, B, C, D for skill, and they can
phone one another anywhere, just like Alcoholics Anonymous. As for choruses,
choirs, glee clubs, and singing societies, they number surely upward of a million.
There are very few citizens among those able to carry a tune at all whose lives
have not at one time been permanently enriched by participation in this most
rewarding of all forms of musical exercise.

Now with a large part of our nation involved in some way with music,
nobody has to worry right now about the state of the art. It is in every way a
going concern. But it might help to understand how deeply music is honey-
combed into American life if I sketch, even superficially, music's organization.
For with the possible exception of medicine, music is the most highly organized
activity in the Western world. Religion has its sects, literature its language barri-
ers. Sports have different rules in different countries. Love and war, as we know,
have no rules at all. But the symphony orchestra is a machine so standardized
that any conductor, any player, any piece in its repertory can be replaced
overnight by a conductor, player, or composition from any other orchestra in the
world of similar skill-category. And the skill-categories are only about three. All
this without language difficulties. The instruments used, the manner of sounding them, and the compositions performed do not differ in any notable way
from Tel-Aviv to Valparaiso.

And since the symphony orchestra is the kingpin of our whole musical system, the conservatories of music from Tel-Aviv to Valparaiso and from Cape
Town to Murmansk, by way of Seattle and Tokyo, are devoted to the production
of players, conductors, and composers who will be ready at a moment's notice to
step into any symphonic operation. Also, since a standardized art needs a standardized public, our schools, colleges, and universities have set themselves the
task of teaching to future orchestral subscribers an accepted history of music
(with orchestral composition at the top), a standard method of musical analysis
(for the understanding of orchestral music), and a standard hierarchy of values
for the admiration of orchestral works.

Contributory to this effort of our educational system is a network of music
clubs, laymen's auxiliary aid societies, technical guilds, and trade groups.
National associations of music teachers, of instrument manufacturers, of piano
tuners, of flute players, societies for the pooling of copyrights and the collection
of royalties, groups opposed to the performance of contemporary music, others
who agitate for it, a managers' association, a union of soloists (in addition to the
great Musicians' Union itself), a half dozen sororities devoted to general do-
gooding, musical therapists, music publishers, collectors of recorded music,

youth organizations of music lovers world-wide in membership, statisticians devoted to the collecting and pooling of information about how symphony orchestras are financed—everybody, literally everybody connected with the music world belongs to something, has a part in its complex organization.

This organization has no hierarchy or center. It is not a professional clan, a business monopoly, or an exercise in amateur philanthropy, though it is something of all these. It is basically a vast network of spontaneous co-operation that happens to work efficiently because the modern world loves music and because musicians themselves are, among all workers in the intellectual branches, the most given to effective organization. Their talent for this is probably associated with their private feeling of consecration. In this they are like the clergy, which is also good at organizing everybody. In any case, the music world is a maze of powerlines in which the professional, the amateur, the educator, the student, the man of business, and the woman of society are equally involved.

Some years ago the late Louis Kirstein, at that time president of Filene's department store in Boston, received a visit from some trustees of the Boston Symphony Orchestra. The orchestra needed $75,000 quickly; could Mr. Kirstein help? Mr. Kirstein, aware of the suburban business which the concerts brought to his store every Friday afternoon, though he himself rarely attended, recognized his responsibility, gave $25,000 and telephoned two other retail merchants, who gave the same. The orchestra's emergency was closed.

Another case of business tie-up came to attention recently in the decision of the General Electric Company to build a subsidiary plant in Louisville.

The cultural advantages of that city, of which the symphony orchestra is one, had determined its being chosen. Culture works as follows in the decentralization of industry. You cannot establish a branch factory without moving executives and technicians. And your executives and technicians cannot move their families without their wives' consent. And their wives will not consent unless the city proposed can offer educational advantages in the form of (and prized in this order) good schools, a near-by college, a symphony orchestra, a public library, and an art museum.

Mayor Charles Farnsley of Louisville demonstrated some years ago in a doctoral thesis that municipal prosperity follows from city to city a curve parallel to the availability in these cities of (in this order) music, theater, and art. In those cities department store business is good, restaurant business is good, hotel business is good; and there is a traffic problem, infallible index of prosperity.

It has long been known from history that culture follows commerce. Today it is clear also that commerce follows culture. And it is also clear to any one who deals with the world of classical, or "serious," music that music is purely a cultural and educational manifestation and forms no part of the entertainment trades, of show business. On the contrary, it is esteemed beneficial like religion;

and people give money to it. Musical exercise is well known to be good for the body, the feelings, and the mind. A further presumption that it can also lift up the soul, though rarely stated, is ever present in the American view of life.

To occupy the young, to ennoble adulthood, to train the hand, elevate the mind, lift up the spirits, and at the same time make business boom—all these are what America expects out of music and, surprisingly enough, gets. No country before us, not Germany nor Austria nor Italy nor the England of Tudor times, ever quite so gleefully turned itself over to the tonal art. What will come of it all there is no way of knowing. But for this century at least, music is our hobby and our habit; and the chiefest, after breadwinning, among all our avowable preoccupations.

THE BURNING QUESTION (1966)

By the time Thomson turned seventy, late in 1966, he was less an intruder than an Elder American Sage, in the following two pieces talking in general about American opera and musicology.

The opera gets reformed about every fifty or seventy-five years, and it's badly in need of reform right now. This matter of art forms needing renewal is especially true of the theatrical forms. The ballet gets reformed every seventy-five years, too, and the reform is always the same: a reintroduction of touching subject matter. Ballet tends to grow cold and lack expression when it's in a routine state, just being distributed but not renewing itself. Then a little revolution inside the ballet world takes place in one of the capitals somewhere, like the Diaghilev revolution—or before that, about 1841—when the ballet suddenly became extremely vigorous and interesting. The reform in Diaghilev's time was due to the combination of an imaginative impresario with a new step-up in the dancing techniques, and it brought vigor again to the ballet.

But the ballet is running down now. It's all distribution, rather than original creation. And the opera is all distribution, too. There are opera companies everywhere, but the repertory is relatively static, and even the new operas are so often written deliberately in the vein of the old ones that they are rarely successful.

When I was a very young man, and earlier, there was vigor in the opera; and there were good contemporary operas performed. From 1890 on, for instance, you had the last works of Verdi, the realistic works of Mascagni and Leoncavallo, then the particular gifts and brilliance of Puccini. On the intellectual side, you had the operas of Strauss from around 1900 in Germany and Austria. And there were still Massenet operas, so that things were coming along all the time, and it was very interesting to see them. I remember an early performance of *La*

Fanciulla del West around 1911. Here was a powerful opera writer, much more powerful than anybody now, and the way he was writing operas was fresher than anything is now. Also around that time I saw *Pelleas et Mélisande*, which was still fairly recent, and a great many other French operas with Mary Garden, such as *Louise*, all of which were new and sounded like the twentieth century, not the nineteenth. But not many of the operas now sound the way those operas sounded then.

During the period of the First World War and the avant-garde time of the '20s opera didn't make a fresh start, because the musical theater was taken over by ballet. Diaghilev came to Paris in 1909 and remained functioning, there and on tour, until he died in '29, using the most advanced painters for his sets: Picasso, Braque, Derain and Matisse. The finest composers, too—at least in the West, the school of Paris, everybody but the Austrians—were writing for the ballet: Stravinsky, Prokofiev, Milhaud, Sauguet, Auric, Falla, Rieti. That was a form of musical theater far more vigorous than anything that was going on in opera. The opera had made its own refreshment, from the '90s up until World War I. About the only thing of any vigor that appeared after that was Alban Berg's *Wozzeck*, which came out in Berlin in 1925. It made an enormous impression and was produced all over Europe. During the composer's lifetime it was so much produced in Germany, for instance, that he lived for that lifetime on his box-office receipts. *Wozzeck* was not unsuccessful, however recondite the music might have seemed. Indeed, anybody who does well in opera makes money. The prosperous composers throughout history have always been the theatrical ones, like Handel, Verdi, Donizetti, Puccini, Strauss. Even today, Benjamin Britten does very well, and so does Hans Werner Henze—probably even better than Menotti.

When the great symphonic boom occurred in the '30s, it found the American composer with plenty of playable scores in his desk. But the opera boom, which came up in the late '30s and then resumed with enormous force after World War II, found the American totally unprepared to write operas. He had never been taught to write vocal music; he had never worked very much on the stage. To this day, American composers tend to be a little inept when the curtain is up.

But opera is just as critically ill in Italy, France, Germany and Russia, where the tradition is valid, as it is in England and America, where the tradition was either never established or has long since been broken. Opera inevitably ran downhill after its last energetic period, which ran roughly from 1890 to 1914. It is in need of rejuvenation now. Foundations pour money into it, but the musical and dramatic interest in their operas is low. A new venue has to be established, and I think the only one possible is the poetic theater. I don't think the realistic theater, or even the theater of the absurd, is likely to produce a very vigorous opera movement. But the poetic theater, yes; there you've got something to sing, something to get your teeth into. Movies and television supply all the melodrama you want, and you don't have to vulgarize your stage with that. The opera stage must have something that is not available elsewhere: imagination, poetry, *language*. What's not worth saying is certainly not worth singing, and it would be silly to waste a year or two of one's life setting it to music.

The burning question in opera today is making it a part of the intellectual and artistic world, instead of routine entertainment or a vehicle for vocalism. That has always been the classical reform of the opera, and it has to be every time: getting poetry and imagination back into it, and removing the routine elements that tend to weigh new works down into an ineffective imitation of the past. Opera is not going to get anywhere any more with the straight-forward realistic or naturalistic prose theater; that we've had. The nineteenth century got its own plays beautifully into nineteenth-century music, but they will not go effectively into twentieth-century music, and nobody today can write anything else. Nineteenth-century opera ran through Puccini. It is now, in spite of my dear friend Gian Carlo Menotti, dead as a doornail. Nobody is really writing it in a way that works.

So you have to have twentieth-century librettos—real ones that feel like twentieth-century librettos and not like nineteenth-century ones. I feel very deeply about this matter, very urgently. We're past the middle of our own century, and it's been very brilliant in music. There is twentieth-century music, and anybody knows it, and anybody can even recognize it, whether it's the farthest out or not; no twentieth-century music sounds like nineteenth-century music. On the other hand, practically all the twentieth-century plays read and act like nineteenth-century ones, because Bernard Shaw lived too long. Sardou is not played today, but Arthur Miller is—and they're the same. The plays of Genet and Edward Albee, on the other hand, *are* twentieth-century plays. There has recently been quite a reasonable success for three plays on historical subjects by Robert Lowell. That kind of contemporaneousness in the hands of a poet can give you something, if the poet has not lost the stage sense that poets used to have but don't seem to have much any more.

The trouble with contemporary poets, you see, is that they can't keep themselves out of the play. They are so used to personal lyrical expansion that it's very difficult for them to remain within the dramatic convention that it is the other people who talk. There are ways of getting around that. Sometimes you can cut out those passages or introduce other people to say them, like asides. There are many dramatic availabilities, provided you've got something worth arranging your stage for.

There have been adventures in the direction that I said would be the only possible solid one. Britten has written *Peter Grimes*, after a story by Crabbe; *The Turn of the Screw*, after a story by Henry James, with a very pretty libretto by Myfanwy Piper; and *A Midsummer Night's Dream*, using the actual words of

Shakespeare, though not all of them. Henze's *Elegy for Young Lovers*, his most successful work so far, has a full poetic text by W. H. Auden. And the best opera I've seen in the last ten years is Hugo Weisgall's *Six Characters in Search of an Author*, based on Pirandello. That's a serious subject, treated by a serious composer. The whole thing appeals to the higher faculties and is interesting. I myself wrote two operas on poetic texts by Gertrude Stein. I love working for the stage, and opera is the most complete form of the musical stage. But I am very fussy about librettos. I don't start with the subject. I start with the person—the literary person, the poet with whom I'm going to work. Then we must find a subject that is agreeable to us both, capable of sustaining him and me through the labors of composition. As of last fall, I have a poet, a theme and a completed libretto for a new opera, and I am working on it.

As for style, it's been a sore point in opera forever. The older members of the public always find the newer music non-melodic, while the young people don't find it that way at all. You have *cantilena* styles that move by neighboring notes and others that jump around. How far one goes toward tone-speech depends on the nature of the words and the theatrical idea in which they are involved. Also, how loud the music needs to be; you can't use tone-speech triple *forte*. If you're going to have the full orchestra going, the voices have to sing full volume, and there's no way of doing that except to put them all in the high register on open vowels. There are plenty of musical styles around, and opera can put any of them on the stage, from the tweet-tweet electronic happening through the twelve-tone down to the old do-mi-sol triad. The more variety the better! The public is willing, the singers are good—but the theatrical conceptions available are very much in retard of the musical conceptions available.

It's true that the most lastingly popular operas have been the ones that presented the public with easily remembered melodies. On the other hand, what do you remember of *Pelléas*? It doesn't make as much money as *La Bohème*, but it's still around. It's not just memorable melody that ear-minded people like. Every now and then there are memorable melodies in Wagner, but they don't come one right after another. What does go on for several hours is the harmonic bath, which is very agreeable on the back of the neck. That, and the fact that Wagner really holds the stage. What is the problem of getting something on the stage? It is to animate a dramatic action, or the concept of a dramatic action. And Wagner does animate it. His music doesn't start and stop; it goes on. It may go on like a slow stream, but it's there, and not only the music but the play moves from beginning to end.

There's some confusion about what the opera audience is, because the larger establishments in the United States and Europe are all repertory theaters, producing a given work a few times each year. Since they nearly all play in quite large houses, and since the basis of their repertory is still nineteenth-century or early twentieth, involving a sizable orchestra, the standard repertory acts as a constraining element on musical and theatrical novelty. Because your regular singers—not the guests who come in and sing three weeks and go away, but the people who are there all season—are all hired for their ability to be the bedrock of the standard repertory, not for their adaptability to do out-of-line roles.

Since I have always written operas fairly far out of line with the standard repertory, I do much better to cast them myself and perform them in middle-sized Broadway theaters or even in college workshops, because they would get awfully rough treatment under the repertory system; they would be turned into something that somehow or other fits in with *Don Pasquale* and *Götterdämmerung.* So the repertory system tends to act as an extremely conservative, almost reactionary element in the choice of new repertory—or in the composing of new repertory. The repertory setup, however advantageous for singers, public and management, is not the most advantageous for experimental opera; and experimental opera is very much needed right now. Some of that goes on in the college workshop—more than anywhere else, at least.

I don't think the critical press has much influence. The only people seriously influenced by it are the foundations, because they have to have a favorable press to show their trustees, and to show the federal tax people to keep their exemption. I worked on the critical press for fourteen years, and in front of the public as a composer for something like forty, and I assure you that the musical press has almost never, in my experience of it, had very great influence on the survival of a work. I was talking to Aaron Copland last year about this. When we were young, we were close friends and used to give concerts together, and our works would appear on the same programs at the modern-music-giving societies along with other contemporaries, such as Roy Harris and Roger Sessions. The critics would say we were ignorant, uneducated, impudent and without ability. Regularly they would say all those things about all of us. And then, maybe fifteen or twenty years later, they would admit to a quality here and there, and now that we're old they treat us with great respect and say we are the authors of such-and-such classical works, and so forth. But those works have become classical, if they have, entirely without the benediction of the press.

Among music reviewers, anybody who keeps a decent job for ten years is in some way on the inside of music. A workman of some competence in the field is likely to be more interesting when discussing that field than a non-worker. That's the trouble with film criticism today: there are far too few reviewing films who have ever had any contact with the making of them. They are obliged to review from a naive audience point of view, rather than that of the skilled or consecrated workman. I don't say that in order to write a good bridge column you have to be a tournament champion, but you sure have got to understand the game. Otherwise the bridge people won't read your column.

I don't feel the spectator has any basis for judging, except that which is individual, intuitive and capricious. What, then, is a critic's column? It's a shopping service. And a shopping service should go a little deeper than superficial observation. For women's wear it's advantageous to know what are the durable qualities of certain things, rather than whether it's the latest funny style. Where can it be worn? How does it get that way? All sorts of things like that are interesting.

When I was in the newspaper business I used to tell the boys who came to work for me, "Keep your mind on the object, not on yourself. Tell us what took place and what it was like. If you're worried about the expression of your own opinion, just stop worrying, because it will come through automatically in your choice of words. But don't get self-centered about this. You have a public. Your public is your readers. You have to inform and, if possible, enlighten them. If there is going to be any defending, don't defend the public against the artist, defend the artist against the possible ignorance of the public."

ON WRITING OPERAS AND STAGING THEM (1982)

Let me begin by talking about feeling at home in theaters, having stage-sense. In France they call it "*le sens du théâtre.*" In any language it means an awareness of the fact that in show business—any kind of it—there is a show and there is an audience. It takes two to play theater.

It actually takes three to play bullfight. The oldest boy plays matador; he shakes his little jacket at the next oldest, who holds up two fingers above his forehead, like horns, then darts at the jacket as it is waved over him. This symbolizes the show as performed by man and bull. But there has to be a third child, the youngest, who simply stands there and when the pass is made says, "*Olé!*" So we are back to our two basic elements, the show and its audience.

Historically speaking, not all the great poets, nor musicians either, have been gifted for the stage. Shakespeare, Ben Jonson, Marlowe, Ford, and Dryden all were. Milton was not. Nor were the great Romantics—Byron, Shelley, Keats, and Coleridge. Any more than were the novelists and storytellers, from Sterne through Dickens and on to Henry James, Proust, and Joyce.

George Frideric Handel was thoroughly a stage man. Johann Sebastian Bach was not, though his *Saint Matthew Passion*, with its moving recitatives for Jesus, its terrifying crowd scenes, and its audience-participation hymns, approaches the dramatic oratorio. Mozart had an enormous stage gift; Haydn a very small one in spite of his 15 operas; Beethoven almost none, though he aspired to it. But Weber was wise in the theater, and Wagner virtually infallible.

What is this mysterious talent that seems to have skipped half the population? It shows up in children as impersonation, or as simply showing off, in the manipulating of family and friends through charm, later as an exploitation of adolescent sex-appeal. Wherever the stage-sense is true, it is accompanied by an instinct for timing. In playing comedy, as in telling a joke, timing is almost the whole trick. Tragedy, sob-stories, and soap opera require a less wary trajectory. Just keep them going, tears will eventually flow.

Composers of our own century have often worked well for the stage. Richard Strauss wrote upwards of ten successful operas; Debussy with *Pelléas et Mélisande* only one, though there are also a fine pair of ballets, *Khamma* and *Jeux*, as well as two dramatic oratorios, *The Prodigal Son* and *The Martyrdom of St. Sebastian*. Stravinsky's *The Fire Bird, Petrouchka*, and *The Rite of Spring*, to mention only his early ballets, are tops in their field, while *Les Noces* (in Russian), *Perséphone* (in French), and *Oedipus Rex* (in Latin) are impressive ballet-cantatas. There are also two far-from-negligible Stravinsky operas, relatively early *The Nightingale* (in Russian) and quite late *The Rake's Progress* (in English). Alban Berg's *Wozzeck* and his uncompleted *Lulu* are operatic adaptations of German literary classics. Ravel, in France, wrote two successful operas, *L'Heure Espagnole (On Spanish Time)*, and *L'Enfant et les sortilèges (The Spellbound Child)*, as well as one world-famous ballet score, *Daphnis et Chloë*. The French composers of our time have in fact, like their predecessors, virtually all composed for both the singing and the dancing stage. Hence the abundant theatrical production of Milhaud, Honegger, Sauguet, and Poulenc. While in England Benjamin Britten, and in Russia Shostakovich, Prokofiev, and others have produced both operas and ballets with stage-quality.

If modern poets—Rimbaud, Valéry, Yeats, Rilke, Pound, and the surrealists—have written more often for silent readers than for actors, T.S. Eliot did write four thoroughly practical plays and Gertrude Stein, in addition to quite a lot of texts that she called plays (and which have indeed been played), was the author, along with the ballet-with-words *A Birthday Bouquet*, of three genuinely effective opera librettos—*Four Saints in Three Acts, The Mother of Us All*, and *Doctor Faustus Lights the Lights*.

In Germany, Russia, Norway, France, Italy, Spain, and England, play-writing is still high literature, with Chekhov and Ibsen and Shaw and Pirandello ranking among the classics. American authors have on the whole worked less well for the stage than at storytelling, reporting, history, and polemics. Or to compare them with novelists alone, no American playwright, not Tennessee Williams nor Thornton Wilder nor Edward Albee nor even Eugene O'Neill, has produced anything comparable in power to Melville's *Moby Dick* or to the novels of Hawthorne, Henry James, Theodore Dreiser, John Dos Passos, and William Faulkner. It is *not* that Americans lack stage sense. Our light musicals are today's world model, and we have produced both fiction films and documentaries of the highest prestige. Also our designs for dancing are quite original and often first-class. It is only on the speaking stage that show business has in America tended to be low business.

A good deal of this has been pointed out before; much of it is covered in a lecture I sometimes give called *America's Unrequited Love for Opera*. Just now I am taking the love for granted, though you may not esteem it unrequited. And since so many of our composers are now writing operas, or planning to do so, I am going to take the liberty of suggesting certain things about the nature of opera which may be helpful.

Opera, and let us understand this right off, is not light entertainment. It is drama at its most serious and most complete. It is also the most complex operation in music and the most complex in stage-production.

Its complexity, moreover, involving the collaboration of poetry, visual design, and often dancing too—along with music both vocal and instrumental— creates necessities that are different from those of the concert hall. An opera is not a concert in costume. Neither is it just a play with music laid on. It is a dramatic action viewed through poetry and music, animated and controlled by its music, which is continuous. It owes to poetry much of its grandeur, to music all of its pacing. But since opera involves both intoned speech and mimed action, its pacing must allow for both verbal clarity and convincing impersonation. The Anstendig Institute, musico-acoustical investigators in San Francisco, makes the definitive statement about music's role in general:

> Music is the highest, most powerful, most overriding, of all the arts. In the presence of music, all the other arts take on the character of the music, not vice versa, and it is capable of, and can produce in us, the finest, most delicate, of possible human reactions.

Now the opera is no such ancient form as verse tragedy, miracle-plays, or even the sentimental comedy with songs. It has in fact a history of only four centuries. Born around 1580 as Italian-language tragedy to be sung throughout (which is its profound originality and from birth its unshakable integrity), opera moved into French during the late seventeenth century, into German during the very late eighteenth and early nineteenth, and into Russian just before the middle of the nineteenth. It has never created a repertory in Spanish, Portuguese, Greek, Dutch, Polish, or the Scandinavian languages, though it has enjoyed a certain popularity, through translation, in English and in Flemish. The twentieth century has witnessed sustained efforts, not yet wholly successful, toward making opera seem to grow naturally in the English and American languages. Whether these experiments can be stabilized remains uncertain, but the problems they raise are being labored at on both sides of the Atlantic.

For a successful outcome, certain preliminaries are essential. The composing fraternity must first master the musical prosody of its language. This is in general better handled in the United Kingdom than in the United States. Over there the history of it all goes quite far back, to Henry VIII at least, and is preserved in libraries, remembered in the schools. Here the matter is neglected in schools and largely ignored in the homes where so many of our finest musical creators have grown up without ever hearing English spoken idiomatically.

For experimental opera productions, there needs to be available also a galaxy of young voices naturally well-placed and with access to lessons. This situation is better on our side, Britain's colloquial speech, save for the Welsh and the Irish, being notably lacking in the nasal content necessary for differentiating vowels and for enabling them to cut through an orchestra. Canadian speech and South African are similarly soft, but the Australian is very good for singing. That continent has long produced great voices; it may one day write operas for them.

In the matter of production Britain and the U.S. are both active, though they approach their opportunities differently. England lends its best facilities (Covent Garden, Sadlers Wells, and the big festivals) to its best composers. The works of Benjamin Britten, William Walton, Michael Tippett, and Peter Maxwell Davies have been effectively launched from these. Thea Musgrave, being a woman and Scottish, seems to get better treatment in America.

The opera houses of New York, Chicago, and San Francisco, on the other hand, though they have mounted works by famous composers like Victor Herbert, Reginald de Koven, Deems Taylor, and Samuel Barber, seem not yet to have set a trend or created a school. Our most lively new operas have, with few exceptions, come out of the Opera Workshops in our colleges and universities. Among the exceptions are George Gershwin's *Porgy and Bess* and Marc Blitzstein's *Regina*, both of which originated in commercial theaters, and my own *Four Saints in Three Acts*, which began its playing life in an art museum, the Wadsworth Atheneum of Hartford, Connecticut. The University of Indiana, where John Eaton's *The Cry of Clytemnestra* was first heard, has the finest facilities of any college for producing operas, also a remarkable voice faculty and nine theaters on campus. Columbia University's now defunct Opera Workshop is deeply regretted. It is there that Menotti's *The Medium* and my own *The Mother of Us All* were born. Unhappily, Columbia no longer has a home for it. It once had, in the small Brander Mathews Theatre borrowed from the Drama Department, an ideal casting situation whereby professionals from the New York pool, all unpaid, could give tone to students playing small roles and understudying large ones. Singing on a stage with even one artist of experience is like playing in an orchestra at the same desk with a professional. That sort of apprenticeship, though hard to come by, is unutterably valuable. And so, of course, is hearing one's own composition conducted, staged, and sung by people who know what *cannot* be done in opera.

One of these things, believe me, is to "act," to simulate emotion by any means whatsoever except through the singing voice. Impersonation yes. That is created by costume and aided by a minimum of controlled movement (call it choreography if you like). But the emotions of high tragedy, insofar as these make up the substance of opera, are projected by the singing voice alone, not by any contributing circumstance. The success of opera recordings, which bear no visual aids to comprehension, has long been witness to that fact. Comic moments, let us admit, do permit a modicum of acting.

Regarding the advantages of British versus American production of operas in English, let us not underestimate the power of Great Britain's promotion machinery, which operates through its embassies and consulates. Henry Barraud, formerly music director of the French Radio and Television, told me not long after World War II that foreign pressures toward performance did not tend to come, as was commonly supposed, from the Soviet Union. "I don't hear twice a year from the Russians," he said, "but not a week goes by without my receiving a demand from the British Culture Office to perform some work by Benjamin Britten."

American artists' careers, on the contrary, practically all suffer from official neglect. The chief American composer to profit abroad from the State Department's blessing was George Gershwin, whose opera *Porgy and Bess* toured internationally, with partial government support, for two years. An opera of mine, *Four Saints in Three Acts*, got from the State Department a small contribution toward its Paris trip of 1952, and Douglas Moore's *The Ballad of Baby Doe*, similarly blessed, went later to Berlin and Yugoslavia. Otherwise, official encouragement for trips abroad has been generous to performing groups without specifying at all that U.S. music be played. And lecture tours have been awarded occasionally to concert composers. Unfortunately the countries where performance might help a composer professionally are likely to be omitted from the State Department's plan. England, France, Germany, Italy, and Scandinavia are not judged to be "sensitive areas" meriting the support that has regularly promoted good will toward our country in Turkey, Burma, India, South America, and black Africa.

In any case, operas are being written all over the U.S. and the U.K. and many are produced, listened to, and nationally reviewed. Americans do tend, however, to go off half-cocked. They are without any serious mastery whatsoever of the words-and-music techniques (and I mean orchestral accompaniment as well as word setting). The British are limited in their productions by a lack of critical support from the universities and also by their music publishers, who, like most other British businesses, are monopoly-oriented. Literary publishers there, responsible to an older and grander history, still enjoy a somewhat competitive set-up. English composers, however, unless they are pushed by the establishment, very frequently get squeezed out of distribution. The late Stanley Bate, a fecund and charming composer rarely heard of today, is a case in point. Lord Berners is another.

Both countries have libretto trouble. The British tend to emulate their own literary classics—Sir Arthur Sullivan in *Ivanhoe*, Vaughan Williams in a version of Shakespeare's *Merry Wives of Windsor* called *Sir John in Love* and of *Riders to the Sea* by John Millington Synge. Benjamin Britten, by using minor poets, was more successful. It is to foreign-language opera, not English, that Shakespeare and Sir Walter Scott have made their most valid contributions through (in Italian) *The Bride of Lammermoor, Hamlet, Falstaff, Macbeth,* and *Othello*; (in French) *Hamlet* and *Romeo and Juliet.*

English masterpiece poetry in the original can throw almost any composer. The British suffer too from the lack of a solid history in composing for the stage, their musical strength lying mainly in the comic vein and the liturgical. Nor is there a history of serious libretto writing; both Nahum Tate's *Dido and Aeneas* and Dryden's multi-media *King Arthur,* though among the best, do skirt danger-ously the tempting shallows of light verse. In general the British composer has neither found good serious librettos nor, with the exception of Britten's *Peter Grimes* (based on a poem of George Crabbe), shown marked ability for handling a dramatic theme.

The current American trend is to use for librettos cut-down versions of suc-cessful plays. The playwriting techniques of Eugène Scribe and Victorien Sardou applied to stories by Dumas *jeune,* Victor Hugo, and similar sources have pro-duced in Europe such unshakable repertory works as *La Traviata, Rigoletto,* and *La Tosca.* These same techniques applied to materials non-dramatic in origin have caused the creation of *Faust, Carmen,* and *Louise* (all faultless librettos). By pursuing this course of facile story-interest and by including lots of historical subject-matter, libretto writing achieved in nineteenth-century France, Italy, and Germany an acceptable standard which replaced for a post-Revolutionary public the earlier models of Metastasio and da Ponte. Actually, libretto writing on the continent has by now well over three centuries of history as a literary form that can be entrusted by those administering public funds to poets, or even prose writers, with a tolerance for music and some sense of the stage.

The American libretto, whether poetic or in prose, has suffered from the banality of American playwriting. Even music cannot bring to life its common-place emotional occasions nor sustain its garrulous dialogue. I realize that dia-logue is in general the American playwright's first gift, but even this at its com-pact best cannot hold up a tragedy of which the emotional content provokes no terror.

Invigorating the opera repertory by modernizing radically its musical tex-tures and by introducing up-to-date story-themes are classical ways of keeping contemporary opera a part of the intellectual life. Any holding back in such mat-ters by poets and composers is bound to discourage the endowed production agencies, which prefer a bold approach. Commercial producers—in films, T.V., or theater—are more timid. They like the excitements of novel sex, psychology, politics, manners, and religion, fearing box-office failure, however, for modern music styles.

But opera is rarely commercial; it is almost entirely endowed. Virtually none of it is self-supporting, not even the works of Wagner and Puccini. The whole operatic establishment, whether its funds be of high capitalist origin, as with us, or Marxist-Leninist bureaucratic, as in Russia, is endowed, subsidized, tax-exempt. And its operators are subject to criticism for the way they spend public monies both by the press and by the head people of our universities, conservatories, and libraries, all of whom are also spending public monies. The result, for all the squabbling that goes on about "advanced" versus "conservative" repertory, is a higher degree of both freedom and responsibility in operatic production than is dreamed of in commercial show-biz.

There is actually lots of courage around, as well as money, for opera production. So much indeed that I wonder whether the timidities of opera composition in America and Britain may not be due less to under-developed musical skills than to hesitancies about subject matter. Certainly there is a dearth of strong librettos in the English-speaking countries.

Now let me go back to the beginnings of opera in the years just preceding 1600. We can do this because the basic format has changed very little since. The variations of this can be infinite, and the story-line is always a bit colored by local needs whenever the format moves into a new language. But that format must be preserved, or opera will fail to take root. In my view of it, the basic recipe reads somewhat as follows.

What is an opera?

It is a dramatic action involving impersonation, words, and music. Without impersonation it is a cantata. Without music, but with impersonation, it is a play. Without words, but with impersonation and music, it is a dance spectacle, a ballet. With only impersonation it is a pantomime. Any of these can be comical, serious, or mixed.

A comic opera mainly impersonates without dignity, makes fun of us all, alternates jokes with musical numbers, lays charm on with a trowel.

A serious opera tells a mythological story which leads, unless interrupted by some superhuman agent, to a tragic outcome. The mixed, or tragi-comedy, is always, like Mozart's *Don Giovanni*, more tragic than comic.

Now what is a dramatic action?

It is what happens inevitably to persons opposed to one another by character, circumstance, or desire. The energy leading to this outcome is latent in their differences of character and in the unalterable nature of desires and circumstances.

It is not a drama unless events are described or mimed by one or more actors impersonating the characters involved.

It is not an opera unless both words and action are expressed through music and carried forward by it.

It is not a satisfactory opera unless the words, the action, and the circumstances are made more vivid through music than they could ever be without. Because words sung carry farther than words spoken (or even shouted); because instrumental music can intensify suspense or calm, explosions of energy or its complete arrest; and because landscapes, weather, history and its monuments, all sorts of contributory detail can be evoked by musical device.

This is not to say that musical tragedy is any grander than poetic tragedy. The fact is simply that after opera came into existence in any language, poetic tragedy became a thing of the past, however glorious, with opera taking over the chief contemporary effort toward complete theater.

Moreover, your spectacle will not be an opera at all, will not hold the stage, unless the story of it, the dramatic action, moves forward. Otherwise you may be left with a static spectacle on your hands—something like an oratorio in costume, Stations of the Cross, or a song cycle.

Music, please remember, is the great animator. Without it dancing goes dead and so do liturgies. Only spoken plays can survive without it. Even films and T.V. spectacles tend to freeze up, just as dancing does, without some musical help. Music is warming, emotional, acoustically surrounding, a bath. The visual always keeps a certain distance, hence is cooler than the musical experience. (Lincoln Kirstein says, "The life of a ballet is the life of its musical score," meaning that when the dancers are no longer moved (literally) by the music, the work drops out of repertory.)

Let's look at this musical element, the slippery substance that can so firmly change the specific gravity of anything. Seriously employed, it is a "noble" material, and for any serious subject needs to be carefully composed and carefully executed. The slapdash may go down in nightclubs or drinking joints. Similarly for casually selected materials and for their arrangement in some accidentally determined order. Such elements are too frail to sustain a serious mythological subject or to prepare us for a tragic ending.

While we are discussing mythology, let us stipulate that history, fairy-tales, lives of the saints, anything anybody can almost believe can be subsumed under that head. From *Samson and Delilah* through *Cinderella, Tannhäuser,* and *Boris Godunov* to *Madama Butterfly, Joan of Arc,* and *Billy the Kid,* all are believable stories about believable people. And music makes these people seem bigger, blows them up to mythological size. It even overblows them toward collapse in the case of Cinderella (who is hence better for dancing than for song). Also for the super-monumental and political (say George Washington, Napoleon, Abraham Lincoln). Singing could only diminish them.

But let us say you have a sizable heroine or hero in mind. How do you go about generating a libretto? My own way is to address myself to a poet. This is dangerous because English-language poets have over the last century and a half been most of them quite clumsy at handling a dramatic action. They can't avoid talking in their own person, seem unable to write dialogue objectively. But I think there is no way around that obstacle. The poets must simply re-educate themselves if they are even a little bit stage-struck.

How can they do this? I do not know. But I am sure that the poets who have no innate stage-instinct (that well-known *sens du théâtre*) cannot be taught it, though a latent stage-sense can perhaps be brought to life. The matter is a difficult one. If the composer himself has a feeling for the stage, that fact solves only half the problem. But it may help him in choosing a poet. If he does not have it he should leave opera alone, and if he cannot pick a poet who also has a little of it, the collaboration is not likely to produce a viable stage work. There is no final test of that, of course, short of full-scale production. The history of every opera establishment is strewn with costly failures.

It is just possible that further research into the history of libretto-writing may reveal standards by which the English-language libretto can be adjudged a legitimate poetic form. If so, then the poets may come to face it without thinking of themselves as possibly betraying their art. Actually poets are less fearful of music (they all love being sung) than of the stage itself.

Opera, to be worth looking up to, has to be poetic theater. And librettos, I think, are best when custom-built. Readymades, even in the form of a well-structured prose play cut down to libretto size, are rarely satisfactory in English. They are not even literature, chopped up like that, pinched here and let out there to accommodate musico-emotional timings, which are quite different from the verbo-emotional.

By musical versus verbal timings I do not mean that communicating emotion to an audience by words alone takes any more time, or less, than by music or by words and music. On the contrary, a strong emotion can be extended in any medium to last, say, twenty minutes, if variety of texture is available. But twenty minutes of speech will pour out more words than twenty minutes of music can handle. A love scene from *Romeo and Juliet* set to music as recitative would be jabber; and if set uncut as cantilena, with all the vocal extensions needed to make singing eloquent, could seem interminable. Too many words can get in music's way. So also, I may add, can too many notes obscure the words.

A libretto needs to be, in general, much shorter than a play. Otherwise it may lack flexibility for being fitted into musical forms and continuities. It also needs poetic language. Not pompous language, nor florid nor overloaded with imagery. But nobly plain, if possible compact, and somehow appropriate to myth-size characters.

An opera libretto must be animated by music, and the emotional progress of the drama must conform to musico-emotional timings, not speech-play timings. To sustain and extend to its acceptable limit any musico-emotional situation, the use of structural devices specific to music is the available method, the only method. This is what is meant by the earliest Italian name for opera, *dramma per musica,* as well as by Richard Wagner's demand that his own theater works be referred to as *Musikdrama.*

For the best musical result, poetic textures and all characterizations need to be a little plainer than for spoken tragedy, and an excess of verbal imagery is to be avoided.

In my opinion, plots, intrigues, and planned suspense, however exciting they may be on the comic or the melodramatic stage, tend to make a tragic outcome seem not inevitable. Operas based on legend, myth, fairytale, biography, or national history tend therefore to be both poetically and musically richer than those corseted by a tight play-structure.

Complex musico-dramatic structures dealing with humor and sentiment or with satire are a not uncommon variant of "serious" opera. Mozart's *The Marriage of Figaro* and its theatrical companion-piece Rossini's *The Barber of Seville,* Wagner's *Die Meistersinger von Nürnberg,* Strauss's *Der Rosenkavalier,* Verdi's *Falstaff,* and Puccini's *Gianni Schichi* are notorious cases in which the domination of a whole work by its musical continuity has turned comedy into a serious enterprise. Actually these works, which survive almost exclusively in the larger houses, are far more monumental than funny.

The comic speaking-stage shows no history of growth, development, or decline since the earliest antiquity, in the West since Greece and Rome. The tragic stage in poetry, on the other hand, has a history. It matures in any language once, then dies, leaving behind monuments of literature that live forever.

The tragic opera, a late invention, has not yet died out in any language. It has left us moreover three legacies previously unknown—the proscenium stage, the pit orchestra (a curtain of instrumental sound through which all other is filtered), and the monumental singing voice.

The comic musical stage, liturgical ceremonies, and song recitals do not, in general, require great vocal range or power. An eleventh, say C to F, is the usual spread, with loudness when needed laid on by brass instruments and choral masses.

The tragic musical stage, the opera, or *dramma per musica,* had perfected by the middle 1630s a training for loudness and flexibility in all the vocal ranges (as well as a name for it, *bel canto*) that has survived to this day as the training system for operatic voices, those with a minimum range of two octaves at all levels of loudness. Operas are still written to be sung by such voices, and pit orchestras in our opera houses are also of monumental proportions, rarely fewer than fifty players.

Such is the equipment available today in the professional houses, the conservatories, and the colleges. It also includes usually some kind of built or painted scenery, artificial lighting, appropriate costuming, and a modicum of controlled stage-action.

I say a modicum because with any musical production being completely rehearsed and always conducted, and with today's other popular serious stage medium, the dance, equally controlled and regulated, it is not wise to allow singers to improvise their "acting." Still less is it wise to allow stage directors the kind of freedom toward distortions and even contradictions of the stated dramatic action that have lately been current in many houses.

On the other hand, singers are not dancers or acrobats. Excessive pantomime is not suitable either to vocalists or to their bodies, which need to save breath for singing. The best solution of the "acting" problem is to use choreographers with a sense of music and some taste, for moving the singers around (with grace if possible, and minimally) so that at major musical moments they can stand still in a good acoustical spot and proceed to act with the voice, which is after all what the art of singing is.

Enabling singers to make words clear and meaningful is part of the composer's art. Another is to reveal character and feelings by musical device. This may be operated within the vocal line, as with Mozart and the Italians, or by orchestral means, as with Wagner and many French composers.[1] In any case, specific expressivity is more easily achieved through line, vocal or instrumental, than through harmony, the latter being highly valuable for structure, for holding our attention on the expressive line. Orchestration too may be useful in pointing things up. Extreme variety in the orchestra, however, though delicious in concert music, can seem finicky in opera, as it so often does with Berlioz and Rimsky-Korsakov. Wagner, Debussy, Mozart, Verdi, even Stravinsky, have offered more dependable support to the expressive element by keeping orchestral color steady and clearly related at all times to the voice. Never forget that no matter how interesting orchestral sound may seem to be, singing is what opera is about. And this is as true of Wagner's stage works as of Bellini's. Actually Wagner's music-dramas are today opera's chief vehicles for vocalism. In every house they receive the most careful musical treatment and offer us the grandest voices.

So let us restate the situation in reverse order.

Opera is singing. This singing is both monumental and flexible—loud, soft, high, low, fast, slow.

Opera exposes through impersonation and poetic dialogue a serious dramatic action. This is a serious action because it faces at all times the possibility of a tragic outcome. And it is moved forward toward whatever outcome may be its destiny by instrumental music and by singing. A dramatic action is opera's thread and purpose. Poetry is its explanatory method. Singing is its *sine qua non*.

As regards the words-and-music factor, that is a constant in any mature language, established early on by musicians, and is not likely to alter much after that. So that the vocal line of Italian music, or French or English or German or Russian, tends to remain closely tied to the classical pronunciation of these languages.

Other musical textures, however, such as harmonic and contrapuntal styles, rhythmic devices and orchestral coloration, insofar as these are expressed instrumentally, vary with history and fashion. From Monteverdi to Nono, from Rameau to Poulenc, from Purcell to Britten, from Schütz to Schönberg, and Glinka to Stravinsky, the voice parts of operas and oratorios in any language are almost interchangeable, though their instrumental accompaniments can vary from Baroque, Rococco, and Romantic to polytonal, non-tonal, even twelve-tone serial. Excellent opera music has indeed been composed in all these styles.

A similar history seems to obtain for librettos. Opera stories certainly have varied far less in the last four centuries than has poetic diction. Dryden, Molière, Metastasio, Racine, Goethe, Maeterlinck, von Hofmannsthal, Claudel, T. S. Eliot, W. H. Auden, and Gertrude Stein have all, in consequence, served effectively the lyric stage.

My recipe for the structure of serious opera, as stated above, is the classical one and not likely to be radically altered. In the domain of stylistic orientation, however, poetic as well as musical, anything goes, provided the voice parts are correctly prosodized, and can be heard to dominate clearly all other kinds of sound.

Now let us suppose you have an opera, well enough written for the words and for the voices that are to sing them, embodying a story-line, or myth, that the authors consider worthy and touching, the whole supported throughout by appropriate instrumental music. Let us suppose also that you have an offer of production under reputable circumstances. How do you go about protecting your conception?

If you cannot procure for the occasion a producing director whom you trust to understand your dramatic concept, you are out of luck. Stage directors, designers, costumers, and choreographers, all working along different stylistic lines (and with no deep knowledge of the script, plus none at all of the music), will turn your work into a vaudeville show. Musical direction and casting are less of a hazard, since the conductor will surely have read the score. And there are lots of good conductors around. But the miming and movements, as improvised by the stage director, and the clumsy efforts of singers to act while singing will be very hard to correct unless your producer is friendly.

Singers, let me say it firmly, must not be allowed to stagger, lurch, weave about, or make faces. Musical expression comes from singing the words and the music, not from mugging. Nor from doing anything else, in fact, while singing. The movements required should be done at other times, between phrases, practically never on the phrase, except in comedy.

Neither should singing be done in profile. Maximum beauty of sound and maximum verbal clarity come from facing the audience. With a quarter-turn, half the sound and sense is lost. With a half-turn, you lose three-fourths of the words. Singing at full turn, back to the audience, can be used occasionally for dramatic effect, but only on clear vowels sung ff. No consonants will carry. Conversations in opera can be carried on very effectively with all faces turned out, hands and arms being used to identify the person addressed. To look at people when they sing, that offers them attention. Let them also look at you when you sing. But everybody, while singing, must look straight out at all times, even in love duets. There is no other way to achieve musical balance or verbal clarity.

The acoustical necessities of opera, different from those of the spoken stage, require therefore, instead of the improvised bits of "business" that so often light up a spoken speech, a form of regulated movement not far from what the dance world calls choreography. In opera the music is completely planned; in ballet so is the dancing. In serious opera all stage movements should be directed. When this is done, the singing improves, character clears up, and emotion communicates.

The planning of such movement, with all attention to acoustical needs and full visibility between singers and conductor, can be done quite early in the rehearsal time. A *Sitzprobe*, though valuable for musical cues and choral balances, need not involve intense expression. (Some singers will always be "saving their voices" anyway.) It is in the later rehearsals and the early run-throughs, after movements and positions have been set, that individual expression and an interplay of feeling can be encouraged. These will for the most part come about automatically, once they have been facilitated by appropriate gestures and positions. In my recommendations for operatic staging, expressive intensity is never demanded until the moves and positions are right. Then it comes without asking and can be further refined in coaching sessions with the *répètiteur*.

Moves and positions are a matter of stylistic authenticity, hence of choreographic skill. Every opera needs a stage director aware of acoustical needs and of singers' limitations, but for the best results musically he needs also a co-director skilled in dance expression and in regional ways. English characters, for example, do not move like Italians. Neither do French or Germans.

Regarding the cuts that many conductors like to make, all I suggest is that they be tried out in rehearsal. Then, if both the composer and the librettist are consenting (but only then) leave them in during the early performances. After all, nothing, during the first years of an opera's life, is to be thought of as permanent. This remark applies strongly to interventions of the stage-director. With the conductor matters are different; by the fifth performance all tempos and volume levels should be firm, the pacings too, even the overall timing of the show. And his markings can then pretty safely be considered as part of the score.

As a last word, since I am writing for a literary publication, let me preach a little to the poets. It is a good two hundred years now since a sense of the stage was required of you. Some, nevertheless, have still a certain yearning for the boards, and all of you, I think, love to hear your lovely verses set and sung. The opera libretto may be a secondary form, but it is a worthy one, honored by many of poetry's best names, just as incidental music to poetic plays has been composed by practically all of music's great ones. And don't be afraid of asking help from someone instinctively wise in stage matters. Auden, by himself theatrically weak, with the help of Chester Kallman made his work stick on the stage, even the singing stage, the most demanding of them all.

And don't get mixed up with composers who have no respect for poetry, who think they can pick up a plot anywhere and then treat their librettist like a hired man. The subject of a serious opera has to be something that touches both you and the composer deeply enough to inspire both of you through the labors of composition. Opera writing, in my view, is a two-man job. It takes a poet and a composer, working at the same theme, to pull it off. It also helps if they can bear each other's company for the length of time they may be working together. But if they share a liking for the opera's theme, that should be fairly easy. That and keeping other poets' and other composers' noses out of the enterprise.[2]

Notes

1. An example of characterization by vocal line is the coloratura of the flighty young page Oscar in Verdi's *Un Ballo in Maschera*. On the other hand, it is orchestral chord sequences that identify with such massive weight Wotan in Wagner's *Ring*, and with an elusive evasiveness Debussy's Mélisande.
2. Two books can be warmly suggested for perusal: *Words for Music* by V.C. Clinton-Baddeley, Cambridge University Press, 1941, and *The Tenth Muse*, a historical study of the opera libretto, by Patrick J. Smith, New York, Knopf, 1970.

MUSIC DOES NOT FLOW (1981)

Comparing history to a stream, no doubt an urgent idea when new, seems nowadays less vigorous, especially regarding the arts. So also does belief in their continuing progress, as if any series of related events involved necessarily a destination.

Myself, I prefer to think of the arts as a museum or as a wine cellar. These comparisons would leave room for paying honor to great soils, great years, great workmen, also for preserving ancient methods. Museums and libraries are mainly devoted anyway to conserving works and ways that it is no longer practical to imitate.

Gertrude Stein used to say that nothing changes from generation to generation except what people are looking at. Actually, what people have thought they were looking at, arranged in chronological order, makes up whatever consistent fairy tale that history can be imagined to illustrate. And though repeating patterns do seem to recur in any such narrative, organic development is notoriously difficult to identify. In the arts, certainly, the creating, elaborating, and transmitting of techniques are basic procedures, but among these there are few long-term growths. They are more like inventions—say the fish net, the wheelbarrow, or pie crust—which once they have come miraculously into being stay on. And as for the game of "influences," which reviewers, and sometimes even historians, like to play, it is in my view about as profitable a study as who caught cold from whom when they were all sitting in the same draft.

Nevertheless, since what people are looking at changes constantly, everything can seem to be changing. Also, the things that don't change, like wheelbarrows and fish nets and pie crust, are always there. Playing games and eating and childbirth and death, for example, change almost not at all; they merely get arranged into stories about people doing them, into literature. And in this literature people move around and talk; sometimes they even sing. This makes for plays and films and operas. And in all these kinds of entertainment the element that affects people most intensely, that makes chills to run up and down the spine, the digestive apparatus to work faster, and the breath to hold or catch, is music. This element has no precise meaning and no dictionary. But it does provoke intensities; and it provokes these so rapidly and so powerfully that all the other elements—the verbal ones and the visual ones for sure—more often than not call on music's transports for reinforcing their own cooler communications. Music's lack of specific meaning, moreover, allows it to be attached to other continuities without contradicting them. The way that singing can give acoustical reinforcement to speech—can shape it, help it to run along and to carry—this is music's gift to liturgical observances, to prayers, hymns, and magical incantations, as well as to mating ceremonials like social dancing.

The composition of music not intended for provoking movement or for singing, and involving no spectacle other than that of men at work, is a quite recent invention, dating as a public show from, at the earliest, about 1600. But its elaboration during the last four centuries has made of music in Europe and in the West generally an art independent of liturgical circumstances, of dancing, of poetry, even of the singing voice.

Now how can an activity without meaning hold the attention of people who are not doing anything but just sitting there? Well, it would seem that over recent centuries there has developed for instrumental music, if not a vocabulary of meanings, a way of suggesting things that is capable, shall we say, of halfway evoking them and thus of attaching its own intensities to quite a variety of thoughts.

These evocations are of three kinds. There is that of the human voice singing metrical verse or intoning unmetered prose. Everything verbal, from lullabies to oratory to rigmaroles, is receptive to this kind of treatment. Instrumental music of this kind is in Europe called strophic.

A second kind, though perhaps it should have come first—it is so ancient and so easy to do—is known as choric; and it can remind us, through a one–two, one–two beat, of marching, or through more fanciful countings-out, of dancing, either ritual and religious, or social.

There can also be attractions for the mind through the following of some tonal texture, as in Sebastian Bach's fugal patterns. I do not know a Greek-origin word for this kind of music; but when it is enlivened by unexpected waits and irregular stresses, this exploiting of the surprise factor, as both Bach and Beethoven practiced it so masterfully or as we encounter it nowadays in a jam session, could be called, I suppose, spastic.

In any case, it is one of the things that instrumental music does, music that is made only for being listened to. And the assemblage of all these kinds of musical gesture—the poetico-oratorical, the movement-provoking, the intellectually complex and surprising—into a composition involving many kinds of variety is the very special achievement of our Viennese masters—Mozart, Haydn, Beethoven, and Schubert. And what do all their grand sonatas and symphonies communicate? Anxiety-and-relief patterns, I should say, experiences cerebral from their ability to hold attention, but surely emotive and visceral in their immediate effect.

The continuity devices that purely instrumental music has employed toward these ends are the only discoveries I know of in music's history that even remotely resemble new species. And they were certainly not arrived at by organic evolution. Even today they are so far from having a clear morphology that there is no textbook anywhere for teaching them, no *Formenlehre*, old or new.

Now let us look a little into the permanent materials of music, which are tones, intervals, and their ordering in time. By time I mean measured time. The recitation of prose and poetry also exists in time, but that time is not a chain of fixed durations. Movies also are a time art; and their small bits joined together into a continuity, though this final cutting can be measured, every second of it, these bits really make up only a psychological pattern not meant to be perceived independently.

Music's time patterns, on the other hand, are there to be noticed. Their rhythmic and metrical structure controls the tonal one so powerfully that it actually gives to music most of whatever clear meaning it may seem to have. Rhythm is therefore both a stable and a stabilizing element and can be viewed as a constant, something of which neither the nature nor the function changes, though its designs may be infinitely various. And these designs, for all their constantly recurring elaborations in different times and places, are limited by the inability of the human mind to perceive as a unit any count larger than two, three, or just possibly a fast five. Rhythm, therefore, is hopelessly tied up to footwork and to language, to meaning, to expression. It can copy, but it cannot grow or evolve.

Speeds and loudnesses, moreover, being subject to choice by performers, are no firm part of any pattern.

The so-called "harmonic series"—all the intervals that can be generated from one fundamental bass tone—are another constant in musical organization. The pitch of the fundamental on which a composition is based can vary from piece to piece, or even from one performance to another. But the relation of that fundamental to its overtones remains the same whatever its exact pitch may be. These intervals are fixed by nature, and our awareness of them is very ancient.

Actually the Greeks knew much of what we know regarding the first dozen or more of these, the Hindus and the ancient Chinese possibly more than the Greeks. Their number, though theoretically infinite, is for practical performance limited to about half a hundred, or fewer. Mixing them gives great variety to sound color. Transposing them into a single octave for use as modes or scales is a convenience. Falsifying them to facilitate pattern-making has long been common practice, the European "tempered scale" of twelve equidistant semitones being already more than two centuries old. A somewhat less acceptable tuning practice is to mix the overtones of slightly different fundamentals. This produces an acoustical interference known as vibrato. Mixing those from distant fundamentals is likely to cause more complex interferences and to erase clear pitch. We call these mixtures noise.

Sound patterns made from scale tones, commonly called "music," have long been thought to be good for the spirits and to give pleasure. Noise has no such reputation; indeed it is known to produce exasperation and bad temper. And though it is easy to compose noises into a pattern, it has been a fancy of only recent times to call such arrangements music. Modern art-workers, I must say, do like joining contradictions into a single concept. Nevertheless, the contradictory terms embodied in the idea of noise-music are not by any means terms of equal semantic weight. In fact the sounds of noise, being governed by no single harmonic series, are only weakly interrelated and thus cannot lend themselves nearly so well to acoustical structuring as the sounds of music do. Entertaining they can be, as we know from our percussion orchestras. And at places in Africa, notably Nigeria and the Cameroon, persons at some distance are said to communicate words without the help of any pronouncing voice. All this is both lively and useful. It makes a valued addition, in fact, to our repertory of ear experiences, and is capable, by isolating the rhythmic element, of encouraging rhythm's growth in complexity. There is nothing wrong with it so long as it is not offered as a substitute for music's ancient and visceral tone ecstasies.

Moreover, the harmonic series and its intervals are not only a delight, they are another of music's constant elements. They exist in nature, and though refinements in their perception may (just may) show a history of progress, the way these are perceived is built into the human body. I am not a specialist in this matter, but I can tell you a few things I have read. One is about an experiment carried out some years ago in Switzerland that tends to demonstrate that musical intervals are received by the brain not as a mixture of tones but as a resultant of their overlay.

The experiment goes as follows. You channel into one ear a pure pitch electronically produced and low enough in volume so that there will be no convection by the skull. Into the other ear you feed a similar sound pitched higher by the interval of a fifth. According to the account published in *Gravesaner Blätter*, July 1955, the brain does not hear these two pitches as an interval but only as a noise. On the other hand, if you feed both tones into one ear, either ear, the brain will instantly recognize the fifth.[1]

More extended speculation about music's relation to acoustical perception is to be found at the beginning of a very long book by a famous Swiss conductor, the late Ernest Ansermet. This is entitled *Les Fondements de la musique dans la conscience humaine* (or "The Basis of Music in Human Consciousness"). Its reasonings are derived from further evidence regarding the human ear's attachment to the harmonic series, even perhaps of its evolution therefrom. This evidence, according to Ansermet, is that the semicircular canals of the middle ear have a shape, definable by natural logarithms, which compels the air within them to vibrate in response to the harmonic series, also governed by natural logarithms.

Our learned conductor argues further that twelve-tone-row music, which uses only twelve intervals, all tempered and all uncorrectable on keyboard instruments, is a road leading to no musically pleasurable destination. Arnold Schönberg, its inventor, has been said to boast that this method of composition would assure for at least two more centuries the predominance of German music. Myself, I find that in the music of the chief twelve-tone masters—Schönberg, Berg, and Webern—though it bears many marks of individual genius, the actual sound of its built-in off-pitchness tends to be sensuously not very satisfying. Also, I see no reason why music today should seek to perpetuate a German domination. Neither can I do more about the new researches on musical hearing than to hope they are right. And I cherish this hope because I like music to be in tune and to sound well. I also think that the intervals when sounded in tune have a great variety of expressive power, whereas twelve-tone-row music has always tended rather toward monotony of expression.

What I do hope for sincerely is proof that not only do intervals exist as an experience built into the brain but that chords as well may turn out to have a real existence. From my own experience I would willingly award this to six of them, which any musical child can recognize. They include the major and minor triads, the diminished seventh, the dominant seventh, the augmented triad, and any three or four notes out of a whole-tone scale. All mixtures outside of these I tend to identify as either real chords with added notes, as tone clusters, or as agglomerates. Real chords sounded simultaneously can, of course, create a polychordal complex, and the acoustic principles that govern the use of these in composition, as well as the psychological ones involved in their perception, merit investigation by composers as well as by psychologists. Polyharmony is after all a natural extension of the contrapuntal principle.

Moreover, in spite of Arnold Schönberg's practice of treating all the intervals as having equal rights, whether they are scored in stack-up to look like chords or laid out in a row like melodies, we all know, I think, that they differ in strength, by which I mean their power to build a loudness. Also, they may well differ in expressive intensity, in their relation to our built-in awareness of them, and thus to some kind of pleasure-pain gamut. In Berlin at the Institute for Comparative Musical Research there is an instrument that produces electronically (that is to say, in a pure state) the first fifty or more of them; and among these there is a major seventh so sharp, as related to our experience of this interval in its more common varieties, so sharp that I found hearing it actually painful. The belief of Alain Danièlou, the institute's former director, is that the whole interval gamut is allied to our repertory of feelings. And though it is far from certain that any such relation is codifiable verbally, we may well be able to experience fifty shades of emotion.

Certainly we have no such number of names for identifying them. And they unquestionably vary in their *affect* through associations, proximities, colorations, stresses, and durations—their rhetoric, in short. Actually I see no reason to deny that the constants of music, which begin with rhythm and meter and go on to cover all the possible combinations of tones within any harmonic series, are not only structural elements for aiding memory but expressive vocabularies as well. Not dictionaries of emotion, not at all, but repertories of device for provoking feelings without defining them.

Now the defining of our sentiments has long been a preoccupation of religions and of governments. And the most powerful of these tie-ups has always been music's marriage to poetry. Music has no connection at all with touch, taste, or smell; and Muzak piped into art galleries has never taken on. Films and dancing do require music, but they don't want it overcomplex. Actually Igor Stravinsky's most elaborate ballet scores—*Petrouchka*, say, and *The Rite of Spring*, even *The Firebird*—have tended to shed their choreographies and to survive purely as concert pieces.

More durable matings have long taken place between music and words, and the music in any such union is likely to prove stronger than the words. How often has a fine melody worn out its verse and taken on another! Or crossed a frontier and changed its language! Tunes move as easily from the secular to the sacred as from the Ganges to the Mississippi. And all that is part of the way things change in what people are looking at.

What does not change, or hardly at all, is the way words and music fit when they do fit. That too seems to be a constant. Instrumental styles vary with fashion, but the singing of prose and poetry changes little throughout the life of a language. During the Middle Ages, so long as Latin was for Western Christians the language of worship, the musical settings of liturgical texts, being monolinear, could be melodically quite elaborate. For much of this time, of course, Latin was a dying language, immobilized by its plethora of long vowels and by the progressive erosion of its quantities. Nor was understanding it essential. No wonder Church music tended toward the flowery and the complex.

With the Protestant reform, a German syllabification came into use. With the English prayerbook of Edward VI, 1549, pattern was discovered, for that is basically the character of Anglican chant, as it is a propensity of spoken English. In Italy and France, where Church Latin still survived, the seventeenth-century invention of musical tragedy in the vernacular, or opera, forced the local languages to find each its own musical characteristics.

My point is that when any language becomes a mature language, with a dictionary and a grammar, almost immediately the musical wing establishes a prosodic declamation for singing it. And this prosody remains. Instrumental style in music shifts constantly, vocal style very little. Here is therefore another constant element. Just think of Italian opera from Claudio Monteverdi to Luigi Nono. The handling of words in recitative, aria, or arioso has hardly changed at all, even when the vocal treatment was at its most florid. The stories of Italian opera have changed a little, and the music illustrating them quite a lot. But the words-into-music factor has hardly moved at all. The same is true in French opera from Lully and Rameau to Debussy and Poulenc. And if *Pelléas* contains little in the form of aria or set-piece, its vocal line is nonetheless French recitative that Rameau himself might have written.

The German cantatas of Schutz and the oratorios of Sebastian Bach are vocally of the same family. And the songs of Franz Schubert were so clearly the model for all who came after, including Hugo Wolf and Mahler, even for Arnold Schönberg, that Richard Wagner himself, the master of them all for theatrical German, could so nearly copy Schubert's practice while enlarging it for the stage that one might almost call the singing parts of any Wagner opera just lieder louder.

A special treatment of the vocal line needs to be mentioned here, which is that of Arnold Schönberg's *Pierrot Lunaire* and which he called *Sprech-stimme*. This is a stretching out of normal German speech cadences to their farthest limits, with no precise pitch controls observed save by five accompanying instrumentalists. It is not quite melodrama (or speech-to-music); rather is it a sort of yelping-to-music all the more effective for its exaggerated naturalism. And the vocalist's role in these twenty-one tiny pieces is actually easier to perform than would be any on-pitch musical line jumping about like that. Moreover, since the German language often does jump about and feels right doing so, the voice part of *Pierrot* is not unrelated to the recitatives of Jesus in Bach's *St. Matthew Passion* or to the upward full-octave swoops of Brunhidlde's battle cry in Wagner's *Die Walkure*.

As for Igor Stravinsky's cantata in French, *Perséphone*, and his English opera *The Rake's Progress*, though they contain what seem to be faults of prosody, they do come over as language quite clearly. And their resemblance to classical French or English declamation is much closer than any parallel that might be drawn between their instrumental textures and those of historic composers English or French. English musical declamation from Tallis through Purcell, Handel, Sullivan, and Britten is virtually unchanging, especially if you recognize Anglican chant as one of its sources. And the extremely high ranges in certain songs of William Flanagan, or of the Italian Silvano Bussotti, are merely flights of musical fancy. They do not alter very much the vowels or at all the stresses of spoken language.

In enumerating the musical elements that are not subject to change, no matter how much the ways of using them may vary, I must not omit to point out that the invention, elaboration, and eventual abandonment of technical devices do tend to follow a repeating pattern. That pattern is especially clear with regard to the historic periods of music's successive expansions. I speak of the West, of course, of Europe, of the music we know as ours. In Asia, Africa, and Indonesia, music may not behave the same way. From this distance the musics of India and of China-Korea-Japan seem relatively permanent, at any rate subject to changes in method that come about far more slowly than with us.

Our musical energy-booms, if I may call them that, have averaged over the last twelve hundred years an active life of about three centuries each. I refer to the monolinear music of early medieval times, which after its codification in the time of Pope Gregory VII created a large and fully written-down repertory, came to the end of its creative strength in the twelfth century. At that time a contrapuntal music very different in methods and procedures, as well as in expressive content, had been invented. Originally called *organum novum* (or a new tool), this music was no longer monolinear but composed as two and three tunes made for being heard together in pitch relations governed by intervals of the harmonic series. These were primarily fifths, fourths, and octaves, with secondary permissions accorded to major seconds and minor sevenths; also, to allow for fluidity of movement, to passing thirds and sixths.[2] Superposing on all such elaborations metrical observance no less elaborate came to produce in the fourteenth century liturgical music of a high complexity.

Whether the sound of it was ever as complex to the ear as it appears in score would depend on the technical sophistication of those who heard it. In any case, toward the beginning of the fifteenth century these particular complexities were quite rapidly abandoned. Their replacement for the Renaissance centuries, roughly the fifteenth and sixteenth, was a polyphony far easier to follow, being dominated by the more sentimentally appealing thirds and sixths and even by common chords. But eventually that music too went the way of all repertories.

For it is not humanity's habit with music to incorporate its predecessors' high skills into those used by succeeding generations. It is rather that these skills, along with the kind of expressivity that they deal in, tend to be abandoned whenever a new kind of expression, embodied in a new technique, comes into favor. And if the high practices are not altogether lost, that fact is due to their preservation in manuscript and occasionally, in some privileged liturgical corner, of a permitted archaic practice. Such survivals also tend to disappear eventually, so that even the notation of yesteryear's music now needs scholarship for its deciphering.

In cases where older music survives along with the new, the older tends to assume an antiquarian rigidity. Establishments may go on performing earlier music, but nobody writes new music in the old way. These simultaneous existances are visible today in Japan and Korea, where an ancient court music is still preserved and taught, still played as a homage to history, while the new musics—Eastern, Western, and pop—carry on virtually the whole of music's creative life.

It is visible too in Roman Catholic churches, where every modernism, after repeated papal denunciation, finally gets admitted to the service. A researched version of Early Medieval repertory was decreed in 1906 to be the authorized music for Catholic worship. And twentieth-century styles of composition have still more recently been blessed in an encyclical of 1946. But the ancient Gregorian plainchant, however devoutly performed, is not a method by which anybody today is likely to compose. And to make survivals further precarious, the ecumenical rules, ordering services to be held no longer in Latin but in any convenient vernacular, will inevitably put our still-enjoyed modernisms, along with the revived plainchant and restorations of Late Medieval *organum* and Renaissance polyphony, all of them right back into the library.

Today's music may also be approaching the end of a major expansion. Everything we can still feel as ours dates from, at the earliest, around 1600. From then, or a bit earlier, come the Anglican chant, the Lutheran hymns, the opera, the ballet, the oratorio. Also the fully developed keyboard instruments such as the pipe organ and the harpsichord with their terraced dynamics, all those blessed violins which made possible the orchestra, and the pianoforte with its facile crescendo.

In the late eighteenth century the stiff continuity-texture of canon and fugue came to be somewhat abandoned in favor of the freer, almost organic expansions of symphonic and chamber music. We call the noblest of these layouts—as used by Haydn, Mozart, Beethoven, and Schubert—sonata-form, though that term was unknown to any of these masters. The historian Paul Henry Lang once told me that he had found the word only as far back as 1838, when Schubert, the youngest of them all, had been dead for ten years.

It is these masters, rather than Bach and Handel, who occupy the central position in today's repertory. And it is the codification of their practices in harmony, free structure, freely differentiated counterpoint and rhythm, and eventually, by Berlioz, in orchestral scoring, that define current music. So also, of course, do the operatic procedures of Mozart, of the Italian and French theater composers, and of Richard Wagner.

Also, with the impoverishment of noble patrons through the French Revolution, and with the building of public halls for the orchestra's growing possibilities of loudness, a paying public had come into existence. And along with this came publishers, managers, copyright laws, and a vast reorganization of pedagogy. All these still exist. They are today's musical establishment, enlarged of course by the recording industry, which preserves (though for how long we do not yet know) performances of the central repertory and also of music's outlying regions. These last include every kind of music available in every part of the world. And music of all kinds is also distributed by radio and by recordings to every part of the world, indeed to every hut and palace in it.

All this has created not only a codification of the Baroque and Romantic repertories but also a sales empire so large and so powerful that its eventual collapse, if earlier empires are a model, can be easily envisaged. The date of such a collapse is not available to me, nor do I see it as imminent. Empires take a long time to fall. I must say that many composers in our time have seemed to be working toward a speed-up of such destruction. And along with these intellectual efforts there has taken place through radio and the jukebox such a massive distribution of music's mere presence that inattention has long been quasi-universal. And inattention, as we know, can kill anything.

Now the ideas that evolution is a constant and that perpetual enrichment of the musical art is inevitable are ideas I have been endeavoring to disprove here, or at least to discourage. And the thought that music, for all the present hypertrophy of its distribution, may be in one of its historic declines regarding creative energy is one that has been pressing itself upon me for some time. Nor do I perceive any prospect of a major renewal.

The practical methods of Baroque and Romantic music, their exploitation, expansion, and codification, as well as their embodiment in a repertory of concert and theater pieces that both professionals and straight music lovers can accept, all that seems to have come to term about 1914. The constants of music have not altered, but their utilization within the assumptions of our recent centuries would seem to have reached some kind of a terminus. Their high point of interior organization and of expressive intensity had already come with the work of the Viennese symphonic masters roughly between 1775 and 1825. Some amplification of volume, extension of length, and intensification of sensuous appeal have taken place since, but these achievements too had all been pretty well finished off, I think, by World War I.

One may point out also that the United States came to participate in this European history at only about that time, too late to have taken a major part in music's major branchings out or in any decline of its flowering. Our musical needs therefore and our contributions, if any, are likely to lie outside of Europe's narrative. Our folklore and our jazz, now studied in many European academies, are phenomenal creations. Indeed, they may lead us elsewhere than toward joining Europe. If jazz could replace classical counterpoint, it might justify our abandoning the classical line. I find such an eventuality quite improbable. But I have observed that the commercial establishment, by fighting jazz relentlessly, has strengthened it. Also, that in its fight for life, black music, jazz, has developed a remarkable ability to reject impurities. Actually it is a persecuted chamber music with nearly three-fourths of a century's history of survival.

Among our century's incompleted efforts, music for electronic tape has not lived up to what many thought was its early promise. Neither has noise-composition. As for the arithmetical overlays that some had put faith in for renewing music, the twelve-tone-row method has now, in spite of a vigorous burst after World War II, virtually faded away. The aleatoric, or accidental, ways of composing have probably, except for John Cage, now approaching seventy, lost much of their attraction for the young. Stochastics, or the calculation of probabilities, has one brilliant adherent, Yannis Xenakis. And the electronic big machines, though valuable for calculation, have actually invented nothing. Processed sound effects are what their taped products most strongly resemble.

The philosophers of modernism show, along with some hope toward music's renewal, a notable willingness to abandon most of its past except for teaching purposes. But there is also among educated people (today a mass public in itself) a distaste for being manipulated by managers and marketeers. The composer Milton Babbitt has even proposed that musicians go underground. To a laboratory, I presume, in which tape composers would work alone or in small groups.

This idea is a tempting one for circumventing the addicts who make up most of music's public, including the opera fans, the electronics wing, the rock-music youth, and the more intellectually oriented but no less maneuverable school-and-college trade, the complexity-lovers. Obviously the only way to escape from them would be to turn toward something fresh. But there is very little available in music today, or in any contradictory non-music, nothing existing anywhere to my knowledge that was not in existence thirty years ago.

The question often asked, "Where is music going?" is to my mind unanswerable because I cannot see it going anywhere. Nor is anyone standing on its bank. Music, to my view, is not a stream in which a composer drops his line and with luck pulls up a fine fish. Nor is it a mysterious wave-force traveling from past to future which may, also with luck, carry us to higher ground. It is not like that at all. It is merely everything that has been done or ever can be done with music's permanent materials. These are rhythm, pitch, and singing. The first, being mainly imitation, is highly communicative. The second, let us call it harmony, is calculative in the handling, intensely passional in the result. The third, the words-and-music operation, appeals to everybody and is the avenue, almost the only avenue, to lasting fame. But it is also a discipline, never forget, and a game, like chess or contract bridge, to be played for high stakes against religions, governments, and music's whole secular establishment. That play, which will decide your life or death as an artist, cannot be avoided.

The purpose of this essay is to warn young composers away from a relaxed attitude toward their art. Look out, I say, lest its permanent pitfalls trip you. Music itself is not in motion. But you are. So do be watchful. Please. Unless, of course, you are a "natural" and can write music without remembering its past. But that involves the discipline of spontaneity, the toughest of all disciplines. Just try it sometime.

Notes

1. An attempt to reproduce this experiment made several years ago in Princeton, New Jersey, gave indecisive results. The operating engineers from RCA found it successful, but the musicians present all maintained that they could identify as separate tones the pitches independently produced.
2. This may sound strange because it is contrary to later practice. It is true nevertheless for the thirteenth and fourteenth centuries.

THE NEW GROVE...(1981)

When a wide-coverage report is issued by a business or a government, the issuing agency can be held responsible for every statement in it. When a work of scholarship is issued by a publishing house, only the author is responsible for his remarks, unless libel, obscenity, or blasphemy is involved. When the work has been written by many different people, however carefully selected by committees and controlled by an editor, nobody can reproach directly either the publisher or his editor, let alone the writers, with individual misstatements, outlandish opinions, or careless language. A reasonable proportion of such accidents is to be expected; what portion is tolerable depends on the price of the work. In *The New Grove Dictionary of Music and Musicians,* there are surprisingly few stumbling blocks and many occasions for gratitude, so huge is its gamut of information, so peaceable its continuing attitudes, so generally easy to read its English writing.

All the same, one looks for an editorial attitude regarding, say, contemporary composers. Everybody, or nearly everybody is there. Serious efforts have been made to describe their work and to identify it. Also, in considering it, in estimating what one might call its specific gravity, care seems to have been used toward distinguishing small achievers from real minor masters, and both of these from careers which, no matter how limited their world public may be (as with Arnold Schoenberg, for instance), are unquestionably Big Time. Not that any of these terms is applied. But I do note the prevalence of judicious attitudes and a civil tongue, to such a generalized extent indeed that some briefing from the editor must be assumed. Either this, or simply that a choice of writers predominantly from among those professionally occupied with writing about music rather than with performing it or composing it (predominantly British too, I may add) has assured throughout the work a tone of informed common sense that is both easy-going and easy to follow.

This kind of bland civility makes the dictionary a delight to cruise in. And an infinitude of unexpected refreshment tables makes it actually more fun for chance encounters than any other work of its kind I know, even the jolly and somewhat irresponsibly French *Encyclopédie Fasquelle*.

Its novel approaches to musical lexicography comprise—in addition to usual subjects like harmony, modes, scales, notations, and the like and of course composers, theorists, and performers—a truly vast array of locales and geographic situations. Music is covered by cities (including Canada's Halifax), states (including the Vatican), countries (including all the United Nations), regions (Anatolia, East Asia, Micronesia), and all the continents with their subdivisions.

It is these extra parts of the world that provide such rich reading in ethnomusicology. And with this come lots of photographs of inhabitants playing instruments. Indeed the volumes reflect abundantly our century's musicological adventures, and its lively illustration department has made of it a picture book showing sculpture, painting, pottery and portraits, architecture, landscape, and show business from innumerable times and places.

Going back to composers, the living and the near living, there does seem to have been editorial control over the length of the entries that discuss them. To each a given number of words was assigned, this to be accompanied by lists of compositions, of books and articles *by* the subject, and of references *about* him. The writers of the articles have in most cases made out these lists. Whether *their* length was assigned I do not know, but that of the prose treatment was. And this measurement in advance, though needed for controlling the dictionary's volume, does constitute an editorial comment, one sometimes quite surprising, in fact.

For the following list of examples, I have measured entries by the number of pages covered, including photographs, music quotations, catalogues, and bibliographies. They are selected cases, but typical I hope of main threads in the tissue of Western music.

From Germany and Austria, Richard Wagner has 41 pages, his father-in-law Franz Liszt (actually not German save for his music) has 45, Brahms comes next with 34, then Hugo Wolf with 28, and Mahler with 26½. Close to that stand Arnold Schoenberg (24), Richard Strauss (22), and Bruckner (19). Hindemith comes next with 15, then Alban Berg (13), Anton Webern (11½), Stockhausen (8), Henze (7), Max Reger (6). Distinctly minor, according to editorial apportionment, are Hanns Eisler (just under 5), Busoni (3½), Boris Blacher (3), and Mauricio Kagel (3). Not German at all but cousins to the German line are Bartók with 28 pages, Janáček with 15½ , and Grieg with 13.

Among the Russian masters, Glinka has 13 pages; then there are Moussorgsky (13), Rimsky-Korsakov (14), Balakirev (9), Borodin (8), and Prokofiev (15). Topping all these are Tchaikovsky's 27 and Igor Stravinsky's 25 (these last two topping also, but just, Richard Strauss and Schoenberg). Szymanowski, a Pole and closer musically to France, gets 5.

In Italy Verdi takes the sweepstakes with 30 pages, Puccini placing far behind with only 10. Among the stragglers one finds Gian-Francesco Malipiero (6½), Luigi Dallapiccola (5), Luciano Berio (5), Luigi Nono (4), Alfredo Casella (3), Sylvano Bussotti (3), and Ottorino Respighi (less than 2).

In the French group, Berlioz rides strong with 30 pages, Debussy following with 22. Bizet gets 14, Fauré 12. Ravel also 12, Gounod 11. Boulez 8, and César Franck 7. Darius Milhaud and Olivier Messiaen also chalk 7 each. Among slow runners we find Erik Satie (5), Vincent d'Indy (4½), Charles Koechlin and Emmanuel Chabrier (4 each). The nineteenth-century pianist-composer Valentin Alkan comes in next with 3½, Gilbert Amy also with 3½, and Arthur Honegger a bit short of 3. André Jolivet scores just over 2 pages, Georges Auric, Henry Barraud, and Henri Sauguet slightly under that. Lili Boulanger and her sister Nadia are each awarded half a page.

Benjamin Britten leads the British line-up with 15½ pages. Ralph Vaughan Williams rates 12, Michael Tippett 11, Sir Arthur Sullivan 9, and Frederick Delius 6. Sloping down from there, William Walton and Peter Maxwell Davies measure 4½, Lennox Berkeley 3½. At 2½ and 2 we find Arthur Bliss, Frank Bridge, Elizabeth Lutyens, Thea Musgrave, Peter Warlock, and Sir Hubert Parry. Lutyens and Musgrave, unless I have read hastily, are the only female composers from anywhere to receive two pages of attention. Even the French-American Betsy Jolas, though warmly praised, is confined to a bit over one column.

American composers receive in general brief treatment, except for Charles Ives's 14½ pages, of which 8½ are lists, and Kurt Weill's 10½. Aaron Copland's entry runs to 6 pages, John Cage's to 5½, Edgard Varèse's and Elliott Carter's to 5 each. Four-page entries honor Louis Moreau Gottschalk, Edward MacDowell, Henry Cowell, and Roger Sessions. Three-page treatments go to Gian-Carlo Menotti and Virgil Thomson.

Most of the following have received just two pages, a few 2½: Louis Armstrong, Milton Babbitt, Samuel Barber, Marc Blitzstein, Duke Ellington,

George Gershwin, Charles T. Griffes, Roy Harris, Lowell Mason, Walter Piston, Wallingford Riegger, William Schuman, Harry Somers (Canadian), and Carl Ruggles.

Those limited to one page or a bit over include Arthur Berger, Leonard Bernstein, William Billings, Henry Brant (born Canadian), Earle Brown, Henry F. Gilbert, Lou Harrison, Andrew Imbrie, Leon Kirchner, Otto Luening, Daniel Gregory Mason, Nicolas Nabokov, Dika Newlin, Ned Rorem, Gunther Schuller, Carlos Surinach, Randall Thompson, Vladimir Ussachevsky, Hugo Weisgall, Cole Porter, Quincy Porter, and John Philip Sousa.

Of those receiving less than one page one notes Ernst Bacon, Theodore Chanler, Ruth Crawford, Edward Burlingame Hill, Howard Hanson, Frank Loesser, Dane Rudhyar, and David Tudor. From the other Americas Heitor Villa-Lobos rates 3½, Carlos Chavez and Alberto Ginastera each a little over 3.

Please note that these ratings represent in no direct way popularity, fame, genius, or distinction. They are an editor's judgment, after consultations, of course, of each composer's probable Importance in a historical panorama that might be visible on a clear day from England. And any composer, at no matter what length, can receive high praise or summary judgment.

Let me cite a few examples. Charles Hamm writes, "John Cage [5½] has had a greater impact on world-wide music than any other American composer of the twentieth century." Bayan Northcott says that Elliott Carter (also 5½) "at his best sustains an energy of invention that is unrivalled in contemporary composition." He also shows "a grasp of dynamic structure comparable, among twentieth century composers, only with Berg." Aaron Copland's (6) constant use of material from folk sources is admired by William A. Austin as "the individual quality he [has] given so many borrowed melodies." This individual quality in his own music is further diagnosed as what "listeners all over the world continue[d] to respond to . . . and to recognize."

In the entry on Benjamin Britten I have not been able to isolate any statement quite so comprehensive as these, but I did notice that the genuinely informative essay about him, if not entirely drenched in honey, is certainly spread with the very best butter. More abrasive is the brief article on Byron the poet. Here his lordship is jostled by the word "outsider"—upper-class epithet for the socially unacceptable—and his love-life with Augusta, the half-sister by whom he had a child, is dismissed as an "affair."

Two cases of an apologetic use of "perhaps" occur in otherwise straightforward sentences. One of these picks out Hugo Weisgall as "perhaps America's most important composer of operas" (Bruce Saylor). The other remarks of Arnold Schöenberg that "perhaps no other composer of the time has so much to offer" (O. W. Neighbour).

For a real "rave," as such writing is known journalistically, I offer the following on Karlheinz Stockhausen by G. W. Hopkins:

He has gathered in a great synthesis all the means available to the composer of the twentieth century, not excluding his heritage from the past, and he has drawn from serial thought the techniques—indeed, the new language—which can present them in a fashion at once ordered and elemental. It is this elementality which explains the 'drama' of Stockhausen's music, and in the breadth of the synthesis it achieves lies all the justification for its grandeur.

So you see, this dictionary has every kind of writing in it. There are pictures too and lots of them. It approaches the multiple aspects of music from many angles and makes a good show out of the whole. If a few slip-ups occur, I must say I ran across only a very few, and no real howlers. Among the slips let me note (without reproach, only surprise) the absence from individual consideration of two poets whom many composers have set—the English mystic William Blake and the French visionary Max Jacob, as well as the German playwright Georg Büchner, source for *Dantons Tod* by Gottfried von Einem and Alban Berg's *Wozzeck*. Also, for whatever the fact may mean, the Eastman School of Music at Rochester, New York, which Americans hold in high esteem, is summed up in one line and a half.

Actually the coverage of anything, twentieth-century music for instance, is so dispersed that reading it up means jumping about in all twenty volumes. For American music alone there is excellent information under United States Music, also under thirty or more U.S. cities, under Orchestra, Orchestration, Oratorio, Opera, Symphony, Film Music, Theatre Music, Folk Music, Dance, Jazz, Rock, Chamber Music, Stage Design and stage designers, Librettos and librettists, as well as under names of individual composers.

In many cases it is the larger subjects that have been the most wisely written about, since these have been mostly assigned to highly knowledgeable writers, or even to groups of them. Single composers tend to get more casual treatment on account of the limited space allowed them, and certainly in some cases from the acceptance of such assignments by writers of lesser preparation.

Famous modern composers, on the other hand, are more likely to be covered by specialists capable of treating them in depth—Stravinsky by Eric Walter White, Debussy by Edward Lockspeiser, and Ives by John Kirkpatrick. Schoenberg and Boulez have, I think, been treated with less authority. The account of "serious," or classical composition, in the article on United States Music, benefits from the knowing hand of Gilbert Chase, as do many references to Latin America and Spain from that of Robert Stevenson. A very brief piece called Libretti (1½ pages only) is signed by two specialists of that subject, Edward Dent and Patrick J. Smith. And there is a remarkably fine essay on music Criticism from the historian Winton Dean.

One is happy with *The New Grove* for much good reading. Americans may feel impatience with it for certain strangenesses in the proportions, as if its values were not quite either those of an enlightened Europe nor yet of informed

America. All the same no German, French, or other encyclopedia of its kind has so far granted to America anything like the amount of space that *Grove* has. This generosity was inevitable, I suppose, since there were bound to be hopes over there for selling sets here. Nevertheless, there it is.

After all, what comparable compendia have American scholars or their publishers ever produced? We have not rivaled so far the *Encyclopedia Britannica*, nor so far Oxford's *New English Dictionary*. Till we do even half as well regarding music, let us all be grateful to *Grove*.

PRECURSORS

Like any good critic/composer, Thomson publicly sorted what was best in his pre-decessors—not only W. A. Mozart and Richard Wagner but, closer in time, Igor Stravinsky—in reviews for Modern Music, *prior to 1940;* The New York Herald Tribune, *between 1940 and 1954; and* The New York Review of Books, *after 1966.*

Persons of humanitarian, libertarian, and politically liberal orientation have for a century used Beethoven as their musical standard-bearer. I employ the word *use* deliberately. Because it is hard to find much in Beethoven's life or music—beyond the legend of his having torn up the dedication of his "Heroic" Symphony to Napoleon when that defender of the French Revolution allowed himself to be crowned Emperor—to justify the adoration in which he has always been held by political liberals.

Wagner, yes. Wagner was full of political theory; and he got himself exiled from Germany (losing also his conducting post at the Dresden Opera) for participating in the unsuccessful revolutionary uprising of 1848 beside his friend, the philosopher of anarchy, Mikhail Bakunin. If he had not gone pseudo-Christian and jingo at the end of his life, he would probably be venerated by members of the Third and Fourth Internationals in the same way that Beethoven is worshipped (rather than really listened to) by adherents of the Second.

Mozart, both his life and his works inform us, was more continuously occupied than either of these other composers with what we nowadays call "leftism" (not to be confused with "left wing," [a] Communist Party euphemism meaning the Communist Party).

Mozart was not, like Wagner, a political revolutionary. Nor was he, like Beethoven, an old fraud who just talked about human rights and dignity but who was really an irascible, intolerant, and scheming careerist, who allowed himself the liberty, when he felt like it, of being unjust toward the poor, lickspittle toward the rich, dishonest in business, unjust and unforgiving toward the members of his own family.

As a touring child prodigy Mozart was pampered by royalty, though he worked hard all the time. But after the age of twelve he was mostly pushed around by the great, beginning with Hieronymus Colloredo, Archbishop of Salzburg, going on through Grimm and Madame d'Epinay in Paris, and ending with the Emperor Francis I of Austria. He took it like a little man, too. Few musical lives bear witness to a more complete integrity of character in sickness and in health, in riches and in poverty, such little riches as he knew.

Mozart was not embittered by illness and adversity; he was tempered by them. Furthermore, he was acquainted with French libertarian ideas, having been fully exposed to these in Paris, where he spent his twenty-third year. But he was never at any time a revolter. He was an absorber and a builder. He never tried to throw out of the window his Catholic faith or his allegiance to his Emperor, in spite of much unpleasant treatment from both Church and State. He merely added to them his belief in human rights and the practice of Masonic fellowship as he had learned these in Paris and in Vienna.

The three great theater-pieces of his maturity, *Die Zauberflöte, Le Nozze di Figaro*, and *Don Giovanni*, are all of them celebrations of this faith and fellowship, of what we should call liberalism or "leftism" and what the eighteenth century called Enlightenment.

Die Zauberflöte, in spite of its obscure libretto, is the easiest of these to grasp. Mozart, like practically all other self-respecting men in those days, like the French King and his own Emperor Josef II and like our own George Washington and Benjamin Franklin, was a Freemason. Freemasonry was not the anti-Catholic secret society it became in nineteenth-century America, and it was far from being the conspiracy of job-holding that it developed into under France's Third Republic. It was more like Rotary. Something between that, perhaps, and organized Marxism. It softened the manners and broadened the viewpoint of all classes in society. Even in Austria, the most retarded country in Europe politically, its fellowship was practiced, at least after Maria Theresa's death, without interference or suppression.

On account of changes that were operated upon the libretto of *Die Zauberflöte* during its composition and mounting, the fairy-story allegory it tells has always been considered obscure. Obscure it is in its details, if you like, in its mixing up of Zoroaster with Egypt and Japan. But surely its main moral is clear, that married happiness and dignity are to be won only by renouncing pride and snobbery and by conducting oneself as an ethical being. And certainly its textual references to liberty, equality, and fraternity are unmistakable.

If this were Mozart's only work with ideas of the kind in it, we could discount its humanitarian content as we discount the stilted verses of *Idomeneo*. But it is not. *Figaro*, to Beaumarchais's satirical play, was revolutionary in its egalitarianism; and *Don Giovanni* is the most humane and tolerant piece about sacred and profane love that anybody has ever written.

In Lorenzo da Ponte, who made the libretti for *Figaro* and *Don Giovanni*, Mozart had a collaborator ideal to his taste. They worked together so closely that the libretti seem almost to have been made to fit the music, the music to come spontaneously out of the libretti. With a da Ponte text he was able to do completely what he was able later to do only partially with Schikaneder's fairy tale *Die Zauberflöte*—namely, to transform the whole thing into an expression of his own ideas.

The reason why the "meaning" of the two more naturalistic works is less easy to grasp than that of the fairy tale is that the humanitarianism of the fairy tale is its only easily comprehensible element. In the others practically everything is stated directly *but* the composer's attitude toward his characters.

Beaumarchais's *The Marriage of Figaro* is straight social satire, a poking fun at the nobility for not being noble enough. It is closer to pamphlet journalism than it is to humane letters. It is what we might call a snappy and sophisticated little number. Mozart and da Ponte changed all the accents, made everybody human, gave to all the characters, to masters and servants alike, the human dignity of their faults and of their virtues. They produced out of a piece of propaganda that was scarcely literature one of the most touching pictures of eighteenth-century life that exists.

Don Giovanni is a tragicomedy about sacred and profane love. Its dramatic tone is of the most daring. It begins with a dirty comic song, goes on to a murder, a series of seductions, a sort of detective-story pursuit of the murderer in which one of the previously seduced ladies plays always a high comedy role; a party, a ballet, a supper scene with music on the stage, a supernatural punishment of the villain, and a good-humored finale in which everybody reappears but the villain.

The villain is charming; the ladies are charming; everybody in the play is charming. Everybody has passion and character; everybody acts according to his passion and his character. Nobody is seriously blamed (except by the other characters) for being what he is or for acting the way he acts. The play implies a complete fatalism about love and about revenge. Don Giovanni gets away with everything, Donna Elvira with nothing. Donna Anna never succeeds in avenging her father's unjust murder. Punishment of this is left to supernatural agencies. Love is not punished at all. Its sacred (or at least its honorable) manifestations and its profane (or libertine) practice are shown as equally successful and satisfactory. The only unsatisfied person in the play is Donna Elvira, who is not at all displeased with herself for having sinned. She is merely chagrined at having been abandoned.

Mozart is kind to these people and pokes fun at every one of them. The balance between sympathy and observation is so neat as to be almost miraculous. *Don Giovanni* is one of the funniest shows in the world and one of the most terrifying. It is all about love, and it kids love to a fare-ye-well. It is the world's greatest opera and the world's greatest parody of opera. It is a moral entertainment so movingly human that the morality gets lost before the play is scarcely started.

Why do I call it leftist? I don't. I say the nearest thing we know to eighteenth-century Enlightenment is called today liberalism or leftism. But there is not a liberal or leftist alive who could have conceived, much less written, that opera. It is the work of a Christian man who knew all about the new doctrinaire ideas and respected them, who practiced many of the new precepts proudly, and who belonged to a humanitarian secret society; but who had also suffered as few men suffer in this world. He saw life clearly, profoundly, amusingly, and partook of it kindly. He expressed no bitterness, offered no panacea to its ills. His life was the most unspeakable slavery; he wrote as a free man. He was not a liberal; he was liberated. And his acquaintance, through doctrine and practice, with all the most advanced ideas of his day in politics, in ethics, in music, was not for nothing in the achievement of that liberation.

THE OFFICIAL STRAVINSKY (1936)

Igor Sravinsky's *Chroniques de ma Vie* (Volume II, Paris, Denoël et Steel, 1935) is brief and smug. Smug is perhaps too strong a word to describe the neat aplomb of it, but there is something in the work somewhere, or in the author's attitude toward it, that gives one the feeling that Mr. Stravinsky has just swallowed the canary and doesn't mind our knowing it.

It is all surprisingly like his post-war music. I say surprisingly, because although composers have often written voluminously and well, almost none has ever carried quite the same conviction on foolscap as on music-paper. Stravinsky does. He writes French with the same tension, the same lack of ease with which he writes music. It is a tight little package, like the *Sonate pour Piano*. It is as neatly filled up, too. It may be stiff and *guindé,* but it is not empty.

It seems strange he should continually pose himself such limited problems, that he should never for once really want to do something large and easy. But restriction is apparently of his nature. It certainly is in his later music, much as I admire many of the works. They have tension and quality but no *envergure,* no flight. He seems for some years to have been quite content to say small things in a neat way and to depend on instrumental incisiveness to turn his little statements into concert- or theatre-pieces. He is objective and impersonal like the notices in railway carriages, and not without the same authority.

Objectivity is fine. But how can a man of his vigor be so dry? Reticence about one's family life and feeling is only genteel. But when he stops his narrative to write a formal cadenza in honor of Diaghilev, why do I feel at the end of it that his affection for his life-long friend and patron has been exactly measured out to cover the qualities he discerned in him, just that much and no more. Completeness there is, but never any abundance. There is no evidence of his ever having had a musical idea he didn't develop into a piece. An exact adjustment between inspiration and labor seems to be back of all this ant-like neatness.

He apportions out paragraphs of praise to musicians past and present very much like a college president conferring honorary degrees. Glinka, Tchaikovsky and Beethoven, Weber, Gounod. Satie and Chabrier receive certificates of merit for having existed and for having been of some service to the art of Mr. Stravinsky. Debussy, Ravel, and Prokofieff come in for honorable mention. The megalomania of orchestral conductors is reproved, but most of the orchestral celebrities get nevertheless a button for having performed some work of the author in a satisfactory manner.

Scattered throughout the book at appropriate intervals are clearly-stated maxims about music. There is nothing in these to quarrel with. They are the truisms of the modern world. They could be framed and exposed (they *should* be indeed) in every conservatory and college. None of these principles are, so far as

I know, original with Stravinsky. None of them are at all shocking any more either, though they might be inspiring to the young.

And yet the book is interesting. Because a good workman writing about his trade is always interesting. Also because it convinces one by making it evident all over again through a different medium that the stiff little man we have had to deal with these last fifteen or so years is exactly what he seems to be, a stiff little man, and that we shall probably have to deal with him as that for the next fifteen or so years if we care to deal with him at all.

Acquaintance with Wagner (1943)

About once a year your reviewer ventures to dip an ear again into the Wagnerian stream. He thinks he ought to find out whether anything about it has changed since the last time or if anything has possibly changed in him that might provoke a reversal of judgment about it all and a return of the passionate absorption with which he used to plunge himself into that vast current of sound. This season's expedition took him to hear *Die Walküre* last Tuesday at the Metropolitan Opera House. So far as he could tell, nothing has altered since last he heard the work.

The tunes are the same tunes as before, some excellent and some not so excellent. The symphonic development of the leitmotives continues to vary in interest according to the musical value of the leitmotives themselves. Those that contain chromatic progressions, arpeggios, or skips of a major sixth still become monotonous on repetition, while those based on narrower skips and diatonic movement continue to support expansion without strain. Wagner never learned the elementary rules of thumb that aided Bach and Handel and Haydn and Mozart and even Schubert to estimate the strength of melodic materials. His rhythmic patterns are frequently monotonous, too; and he has a weakness for step-wise modulating sequences.

The instrumentation remains rich in sound and highly personal. And if it often creates its theatrical excitement by the use of mere hubbub, that excitement is still a dependable effect and the instrumental dispositions involved are acoustically sound. It has long seemed to me that Wagner's original contributions to musical art are chiefly of an orchestral nature. Indeed, orchestration is the one element of musical composition in which Wagner had sound training, exception being made for the rules of German declamation, which he derived for himself by studying the works of Mozart and Weber and Meyerbeer. His music-writing is more varied in quality than is that of any other composer of equal celebrity, even Berlioz; but no matter what the quality, it always sounds well. It is always instrumentally interesting and infallibly sumptuous.

Sometimes the musical quality runs high, too. There are unforgettable moments of invention in any of Wagner's operas, though the percentage of memorable pages out of his whole production will probably be inferior to that in Verdi and certainly far less than what one can find in Mozart. And their excellence is not due wholly to orchestral orotundity; he often wrote charmingly for the voice, as well. He wrote rather more effectively, however, it seems to me, for the higher voices than for the lower. His tenor and soprano roles are more pleasing and more expressive than his alto, baritone, or bass writing. His Ortruds and his Frickas are always a slight bore; and King Marke, Wotan, Hunding, Fafner, even for habitual Wagnerians, are proverbially great big ones. He had little feeling for the heavier vocal timbres, and there is no real liberty in his handling of them.

Well, all that is all that. Wagner was a gifted and original composer, though an unusually uneven one. And his lack of early musical instruction is probably the cause of his major faults, though I doubt if ignorance can be held responsible for any of his virtues. He was not, as a matter of fact, an ignorant man; he was merely an autodidact, lacking, like most autodidacts, more in aesthetic judgment than in culture. He read voluminously and understood what he read; he reflected in a penetrating way about aesthetic matters, and he mastered easily any musical technique he felt he needed. His troublesomeness on the musical scene has always been due less to the force of his musical genius (which was recognized from the beginning) than to the fact that neither instinct nor training had prepared him to criticize his own work with the objectivity that the quality of genius in it demanded. As a result, every score is a sea beach full of jewelry and jetsam. Fishing around for priceless bits is a rewarding occupation for young musicians, just as bathing in the sound of it is always agreeable to any musical ear. But musicians are likely to find nowadays that the treasure has been pretty well combed and that continued examination of the remnants yields little they hadn't known was there before.

What continues to fascinate me is not Wagner's music but Wagner the man. A scoundrel and a charmer he must have been such as one rarely meets. Perfidious in friendship, ungrateful in love, irresponsible in politics, utterly without principle in his professional life, and in business a pure confidence-man, he represents completely the nineteenth-century ideal of toughness. He was everything the bourgeois feared, hoped for, and longed to worship in the artist. The brilliancy of his mind, the modernity of his culture, the ruthlessness of his ambition, and the shining armor of his conceit, even the senile erotomania of his later years, all went into a legend that satisfied the longings of many a solid citizen, as they had long before made him an attractive figure to aristocrats and intellectuals.

To know him was considered a privilege by the greatest figures of Europe, though many of these found the privilege costly. His conversation was stimulating on every subject; his wit was incisive and cruel; his polemical writing was expansive, unprincipled, and aimed usually below the belt. He was the most inspiring orchestral conductor and the most penetrating music critic of his century. His intellectual courage and the plain guts with which he stood off professional rivalries, social intrigues, political persecution, and financial disaster are none the less breathtaking for the fact that his very character invited outrageous fortune.

All this remains; it is available in many books. The music remains, too; and it is available at virtually every opera house in the world. It would not bring out the crowds or incite conductors and vocalists to the serious efforts it does if it did not have, in spite of its obvious inequalities, strength beneath its fustian skill. To deny that strength were folly. To submit to it is unquestionably a pleasure. But what your reviewer would like most of all is to have known the superb and fantastic Wagner himself.

FAIRY TALE ABOUT MUSIC (1945)

Richard Wagner's *Die Meistersinger von Nürnberg*, which was given again at the Metropolitan Opera House last night after an interval of five years, is the most enchanting of all the fairy-tale operas. It is about a never-never land where shoemakers give vocal lessons, where presidents of musical societies offer their daughters as prizes in musical contests, and where music critics believe in rules of composition and where they get mobbed for preferring young girls to young composers.

It is enchanting musically because there is no enchantment, literally speaking, in it. It is unique among Wagner's theatrical works in that none of the characters gets mixed up with magic or takes drugs. And nobody gets redeemed according to the usual Wagnerian pattern, which a German critic once described as "around the mountain and through the woman." There is no metaphysics at all. The hero merely gives a successful début recital and marries the girl of his heart.

And Wagner without his erotico-metaphysical paraphernalia is a better composer than with it. He pays more attention to holding interest by musical means, wastes less time predicting doom, describing weather, soul states, and ecstatic experiences. He writes better voice leading and orchestrates more transparently, too. *Die Meistersinger* is virtually without the hubbub string-writing that dilutes all his other operas, and the music's pacing is reasonable in terms of the play. The whole score is reasonable. It is also rich and witty and romantic, full of interest and of humanity.

French Music Here [Erik Satie] (1941)

Darius Milhaud has communicated to me the catalogue of an exhibit held recently at Mills College, Oakland, California, of Erik Satie's manuscripts. These manuscripts, the property of Milhaud, were brought by him last summer from France at some inconvenience, since the traveling facilities available at that time did not always include transportation of unlimited personal impedimenta. That Monsieur Milhaud should have made room for these at the cost of leaving behind manuscripts and orchestral material of his own for which he might have need during his stay here is evidence of the esteem in which he holds the unpublished works of the late Sage of Arceuil.

The collection, as one can see from the above brief digest, is an extensive one. Its importance depends on what one thinks of Erik Satie as a musical figure. This writer is in agreement with Darius Milhaud and with some of the other contemporary French composers in placing Satie's work among the major musical values of our century. He has even gone so far in print, nearly twenty years ago, as to parallel the three German B's—Bach, Beethoven, and Brahms—with the three S's of modern music—in descending order of significance, Satie, Schönberg, and Stravinsky.

French and other Parisian music of the 1930s has been but little performed in America. (That is an old quarrel of mine with the League of Composers.) Such of it as has been performed here is usually considered to be mildly pleasant but on the whole not very impressive. This estimate is justified only on the part of persons initiated to its aesthetic. And its aesthetic, as was that of Debussy, is derived directly from the words and from the works of Satie, whose firmest conviction was that the only healthy thing music can do in our century is to stop trying to be impressive.

The Satie musical aesthetic is the only twentieth-century musical aesthetic in the Western world. Schönberg and his school are Romantics; and their twelve-tone syntax, however intriguing one may find it intellectually, is the purest Romantic chromaticism. Hindemith, however gifted, is a neo-classicist, like Brahms, with ears glued firmly to the past. The same is true of the later Stravinsky and of his satellites. Even *Petrushka* and *The Rite of Spring* are the Wagnerian theater symphony and the nineteenth-century cult of nationalistic folklore applied to ballet.

Of all the influential composers of our time, and influence even his detractors cannot deny him, Satie is the only one whose works can be enjoyed and appreciated without any knowledge of the history of music. These lack the prestige of traditional modernism, as they lack the prestige of the Romantic tradition itself, a tradition of constant Revolution. They are as simple, as straightforward, as devastating as the remarks of a child.

To the uninitiated they sound trifling. To those who love them they are fresh and beautiful and firmly right. And that freshness and rightness have long dominated the musical thought of France. Any attempt to penetrate that musical thought without first penetrating that of Erik Satie is fruitless. Even Debussy is growing less and less comprehensible these days to those who never knew Satie.

When Satie used to be performed here occasionally, the works were found difficult to understand. French music in all centuries has been rather special, not quite like anything else. In our century it has become esoteric to a degree not currently admitted even in France. It has eschewed the impressive, the heroic, the oratorical, everything that is aimed at moving mass audiences. Like modern French poetry and painting, it has directed its communication to the individual.

It has valued, in consequence, quietude, precision, acuteness of auditory observation, gentleness, sincerity and directness of statement. Persons who admire these qualities in private life are not infrequently embarrassed when they encounter them in public places. It is this embarrassment that gives to all French music, and to the work of Satie and his neophytes in particular, an air of superficiality, as if it were salon music written for the drawing rooms of some snobbish set.

To suppose this true is to be ignorant of the poverty and the high devotion to art that marked the life of Erik Satie to its very end in a public hospital. And to ignore all art that is not heroic or at least intensely emotional is to commit the greatest of snobberies. For, by a reversal of values that constitutes one of the most surprising phenomena of a century that has so far been occupied almost exclusively with reversing values, the only thing really hermetic and difficult to understand about the music of Erik Satie is the fact that there is nothing hermetic about it at all.

It wears no priestly robes; it mumbles no incantations; it is not painted up by Max Factor to terrify elderly ladies or to give little girls a thrill. Neither is it designed to impress orchestral conductors or to get anybody a job teaching school. It has literally no devious motivation. It is as simple as a friendly conversation and in its better moments exactly as poetic and as profound.

These thoughts occurred to me the other evening at a League of Composers concert of recent works by Milhaud. Not a piece on the program had a climax or a loud ending. Nothing was pretentious or apocalyptical or messianic or overdramatized. The composer's effort at all times was to be clear and true. And when I saw the catalogue of the Satie manuscripts and learned how Milhaud had brought them to America at the cost of not bringing all his own, when I remembered also the brilliant and theatrically effective works of Milhaud's youth, *Le Bœuf sur le toit* and *Le Train bleu* and *La Création du monde*, I realized that after Satie's death he had been led, how unconsciously I cannot say, to assume the mantle of Satie's leadership and to eschew all musical vanity. That, at any rate, is my explanation of how one of the most facile and turbulent talents of our time has become one of the most completely calm of modern masters; and how, by adding thus depth and penetration and simple humanity to his gamut, he has become the first composer of his country and a leader in that musical tradition which of all living musical traditions is the least moribund.

[Edward] MacDowell's Music (1944)

Revisiting the music of Edward MacDowell, through copies found in a borrowed house, was one of the pleasures of your reviewer's late summer vacation. What the larger works would sound like nowadays—the two Suites for Orchestra, the two piano concertos, and the four piano sonatas—he does not know, because he has not for many years handled their scores; and they have almost disappeared from our metropolitan programs. But the shorter piano works—the *Woodland Sketches*, the *New England Sketches*, and the *Sea Pieces*—have kept an extraordinary freshness through the years. Rereading them brought the reflection that although no living American would have written them in just that way (the Wagnerian harmonic texture having passed out of vogue), no living American quite *could* have written them, either.

Let us take them for what they are, not for what they are not. They are landscapes mostly, landscapes with and without figures, literary or historical evocations, *morceaux de genre*. The test of such pieces is their power of evocation. Couperin, Mendelssohn, Schumann, and Debussy are the great masters of genre painting in music, Grieg, Smetana, and possibly Albéniz or Villa-Lobos its lesser luminaries. MacDowell might well rank with these last if he had had access to a body of folklore comparable in extent to theirs, an access that Americans do have, in fact, now. He divined the problems of style that face American composers, but he was not able to solve them singlehanded. So he borrowed more from German sources than he would have liked, I think, and more than anybody has to do today.

Nevertheless, the scenes he describes are vivid. His rhythmic contours evoke the stated subject quickly, accurately. No other American composer has painted a wild rose or an iceberg, a water lily or a deserted farmhouse so neatly. The rendering is concise, the outline definite. No piece is a rewriting of any other. Each is itself, economical, elegant, clearly projected. The impersonality of the procedure is proof of the author's sincerity; its evocative power is proof of his high skill as a craftsman. MacDowell did not leave his mark on music as a stylist; he left us merely a repertory of unforgettable pieces, all different from one another and all charming. And he left to American composers an example of clear thought and objective workmanship that has been an inspiration to us all.

There is a movement on foot toward influencing the American Academy of Arts and Sciences to place his bust in the Hall of Fame at New York University.

Stephen Foster is the only writer of music there honored at present. MacDowell could not be in better company, because his music, like that of Foster, is part of every American's culture who has any musical culture. Everybody has played it, loved it, remembered it. Just as no student who ever attended MacDowell's classes at Columbia University ever forgot the master's penetrating observations about music, no musician or no music lover has ever forgotten the delicate firmness of MacDowell's melody, the exactitude with which his rhythm (and his piano figuration, too) depicts the picturesque. To have become, whether by sheer genius for music making, as in Foster's case, or, as in MacDowell's, by the professional exercise of a fully trained gift and by an integrity of attitude unequaled in our musical history, part and parcel of every musical American's musical thought is, in any meaning of the term, it seems to me, immortality.

[CARL] RUGGLES (1971)

This appreciation of the idiosyncratic American composer Carl Ruggles first appeared in American Music Since 1910. *That book concludes with a page or two apiece of notes on other native composers, including himself (e.g., the "(Auto)biography" reprinted at the beginning of this book).*

There is nothing notably genteel about Carl Ruggles. He is a bohemian rather, who up to the age of forty earned a living out of music, then found a patron on whose kindness he has lived for over fifty years, supporting also till her death a wife passionately loved and bringing up one son. He has also been for many years a landscape painter. Music he has followed from his youth without qualms about failure, poverty, disapproval, or what-will-people-say. Wiry, salty, disrespectful, and splendidly profane, he recalls the old hero of comic strips Popeye the Sailor, never doubtful of his relation to sea or soil.

A revealing story about him is the familiar one told by Henry Cowell twenty years ago. Having gone to see him in Vermont, Cowell arrived at the former schoolhouse that was Ruggles's studio and found him at the piano, playing the same chordal agglomerate over and over, as if to pound the very life out of it. After a time Cowell shouted, "What on earth are you doing to that chord? You've been playing it for at least an hour." Ruggles shouted back, "I'm giving it the test of time."

As of today, all of Ruggles's music has withstood that test, as has the man. His oldest surviving piece—a song to piano accompaniment composed in 1919— is more than fifty years old; his latest, from 1945, is twenty-five; and he himself, as I write, is ninety-four. His works have traveled in America and in Europe; and though they have not experienced the abrasions of popularity, they have been tested microscopically by the toughest analysts without any examiner finding anywhere a flaw. Excepting perhaps himself, since he has rescored some works several times before settling on their final sound and shape.

Born in 1876 of whaling folk on Cape Cod, he learned to play the violin in Boston and had lessons in the composer's craft at Harvard. Then he got experience of the orchestra in the good way, by conducting one for eleven years. That was in Minnesota. During all this learning time he wrote no music that he cared later to preserve.

There was some work done on an opera, its subject Gerhard Hauptmann's play *The Sunken Bell*; but this was never finished, Ruggles having gained through the effort a conviction that he had no talent for the stage. His earliest work that he has allowed to survive is the song called *Toys*, composed in 1919 when he was forty-three. Over the next twenty years he produced virtually all his surviving repertory, each piece intensely compact, impeccably inspired, exactly perfect, and exactly like all the others in its method of workmanship.

This method, of which the closest model is the music that Arnold Schönberg composed before World War I, can be classified among musical textures as non-differentiated secundal counterpoint. By non-differentiated I mean that the voices making up this counterpoint all resemble one another in both character and general shape; they are all saying the same thing and saying it in much the same way. This manner of writing music, whether practiced by Bach or by Palestrina or by Anton Webern, for all of whom it was their usual method, produces a homogeneity highly self-contained, and more picturesque than dramatic.

By secundal counterpoint I mean that the intervals present at the nodal points of the music (say roughly at the downbeats) are predominantly seconds and sevenths. This interval content distinguishes it from the music dominated by fourths and fifths (composed chiefly between the years 1200 and 1500; we call this music quintal) and from the music colored by thirds and sixths (the tertial) that followed the quintal for four centuries. Secundal writing, compared with quintal, which is rocklike, and with tertial, which is bland, produces through continuous dissonance a grainy texture that in most of Ruggles's music is homogenized, or made to blend, by the use of closely similar timbres, such as an all-string or all-brass instrumentation. And as happens in most of Bach, the music comes out polyphonic as to line but homophonic as to sound.

In spite, however, of all its homogeneity (exterior mark of its introspective nature) music like this is never quite without objective depiction. For observing this in Ruggles, the early song *Toys* is most revealing. The words, written by Ruggles himself, are:

Come here, little son, and I will play with you.
See, I have brought you lovely toys.

Painted ships,
And trains of choo-choo cars, and a wondrous balloon,
that floats, and floats, and floats, way up to the stars.

Let us omit reference, save in passing, to the fact that the father seems to have let go of the balloon before his son could lay hands on it. Also, since stars are mentioned, that the play hour seems to be taking place out of doors on a moonless night, a most unlikely circumstance. But these are literary quibbles.

Musically the piece, for all its steadily dissonant sound-texture, is illustrative throughout.

It begins with a gesture-like call in the piano accompaniment, stated both before and after the summons, "Come here, little son, and I will play with you."

The phrase "painted ships" is accompanied by a rocking motion that leads to a splash.

The "choo-choo" mention is followed by rhythmic sounds, low in the register and accelerating, that clearly picture a steam-driven locomotive.

And the "balloon that floats" not only does so in the piano part, which arpeggiates upward, but also in the vocal line, which leaps and leaps till on the word "stars" it reaches high B-natural and stays there.

Similarly, the piece for strings called *Lilacs*, though I doubt whether any description quite so specific is intended, is all of short rounded lines at the top and of long gangling tentacular rootlike curves in the bass.

And *Portals*, another string piece, has high-jutting points to it that might be either Gothic arches or simply man's aspiration. The quiet moment at the end of an otherwise energetic work could represent man's humility on entering the high portals; but if the earlier part is not the noble gates themselves but merely the soul of man climbing toward them, then the ending must represent him arrived and sitting down to rest. The motto on the score tells us nothing so specific; it merely asks, "What are those of the known but to ascend and enter the unknown?"

Angels, for seven muted trumpets and trombones, is quietly ecstatic from beginning to end, and the angels are not individualized. They are clearly a group, a choir perhaps. I do not even know whether they are singing; they may be merely standing close together and giving off light, as in the engravings of William Blake. Whatever is happening, they are doing it or being it together, for the instruments all pause together, breathe together, start up again together, as in a hymn. Whether this close order depicts a harmony of angels or merely one man singing about them in seven real parts is not important; it could be both. But in any case, the music's sentence structure, always clear in Ruggles, is nowhere more marked than in his work, where ecstasy is communicated through a series of statements about it, each with a beginning, a middle, and a tapered ending, and all separated from one another like formal periods.

The Sun Treader and *Organum,* both scored for large orchestra rather than for a blended small ensemble, achieve homogenization of sound through the constant doubling of strings by wind instruments. And this device, so dangerous in general to the achievement of variety, is here not monotonous, but eloquent rather, as if one speaker were carrying us along on winged oratory. The Ruggles counterpoint is there too, constantly chromatic, flowing, airily spaced but also compact and dissonant, and speaking, for all its rhythmic diversity, as with a single voice. This may be the voice of the sun treader, or it may be a picture of his actions; it matters little. What matters is that the piece goes on. It lasts eighteen minutes (long for Ruggles) without any let-up of intensity. *Organum* is longish too, but less choreographic, more songful. Both are full of their message, which is apocalyptic, and yet systematically, intensely self-contained.

The way that Ruggles has of making his music always come out in nonsymmetrical prose sentences—a planned spontaneity, one might call it—is not really in opposition to his preoccupation with ecstasy. For that ecstasy in the expression, that unrelenting luminosity of interval and sound, is needful for producing the quality that was his overall intent and which he calls "the sublime." Now what does he mean, what does anybody mean, by "the sublime"? I should say that this word, when applied to a work of art, can only mean that the work expresses and hence tends to provoke a state of ecstasy so free from both skin sensuality and cerebral excitement, also so uniformly sustained, that the ecstasy can be thought of as sublimated into the kind of experience known as "mystical." Ruggles, in fact, once said as much, that "in all works there should be the quality we call mysticism. All the great composers have it."

The titles of his works and their explanatory mottos mostly tend to evoke, if not a mystical experience, at least the familiar cast and décor of religious visions—*Men and Mountains, Men and Angels, The Sun Treader, Vox Clamans in Deserto, Organum,* or, quite vaguely for once, just *Evocations.* These subjects, save for the presence of angels and for a voice from the wilderness, are not nearly so close to Christian mysticism as they are to pantheism, to a spiritual identification with nature such as can be called forth in almost any New Englander by the presence of lilacs, or of mountains measurable by the size of man.

But it is not the subjects of his ecstasy that create sublimity. Many a witness has gone dizzy looking at beauty. With Ruggles it is with the need for sublimity that dizziness ends and hard work begins. For there is no sublimity without perfection; and for Ruggles there is no perfection until every singing, soaring line, every subtle rhythm and prose period, every interval and every chord has received from his own laborious hands the test of time. There must be no gigantic proportions, no ornamental figurations, no garrulous runnings-on, no dramatization, no jokes, no undue sweetness, no invoking of music's history, no folksy charm, no edifying sentiments, no erotic frictions, no cerebral cadenzas, no brilliance, no show-off, and no modesty. There is nothing in his music but flexible melodies all perfectly placed so as to sound harmonious together, and along with these a consistently dissonant interval-texture, and a subtly irregular rhythm that avoids lilt.

The auditory beauty of Ruggles's music is unique. It actually sounds better than the early Schönberg pieces, *Verklärte Nacht* and *Erwartung*, that are perhaps its model, almost I should say its only model. It sounds better because it is more carefully made. Its layout is more airy; no pitch gets in any other's way; the rhythm is more alive; it never treads water, only sun. It is by very hard work and all alone that this perfection has been attained. And it is through perfection, moreover, the intensely functioning refinement of every musical grain and chunk, every element of shape and planning, that a high energy potential has been both produced and held in check, like a dynamo with its complex insulation. And it is this powerful energy, straining to leap a blue-white arc toward any listener, that constitutes, I think, what Ruggles means by sublimity. It is no wonder that out of a ninety-year lifetime there remain fewer than a dozen pieces. Intensities like that cannot be improvised.

Wilfrid Mellers, comparing Ruggles to Arnold Schönberg, has written in his book of praise to America, *Music in a New Found Land*, that "both were amateur painters who, in their visual work, sought the expressionistic moment of vision. Both, in their music still more than in their painting, found that the disintegrated fragments of the psyche could be reintegrated only by a mystical act. Schönberg, as a Viennese Jew, had an ancient religion and the spirit of Beethoven to help him; Ruggles had only the American wilderness and the austerities of Puritan New England. For this reason he sought freedom—from tonal bondage, from the harmonic straightjacket, from conventionalized repetitions, from anything that sullied the immediacy and purity of existence—even more remorselessly than Schönberg."

Ruggles's dilemma, of course, has been the perpetual dilemma of American composers. On one side lie genius and inspiration, on the other an almost complete lack of usable history. We have access to the European masters, to Bach and Mozart and Beethoven and Debussy, but only through their music; we cannot remember them nor reconstruct what they were thinking about; and what we *can* remember, through our documents and our forebears, is so different from anything Europe knows or ever knew that both to the European listener and to the American, naïf or learned, every inspiration is a scandal. A Frenchman or an Austrian of gifts can be fitted early into his country's immortality machine—nurtured, warmed for ripening, brought to market. An American of talent is from the beginning discouraged (or overencouraged), bullied by family life and by schoolteachers, overworked, undertrained, sterilized by isolation or, worse, taken over by publicity, by the celebrity machine.

American composers have tried several solutions. One has been to fake a history; that is to say, to adopt some accepted European method of working and to hide behind it so effectively that the ignorant are impressed and the intellectuals immobilized. Horatio Parker, Edward MacDowell, and Walter Piston did this. And their inspiration, discolored by its own shield, lost personality and some of its meaning; but these men did write music of distinction that has not died.

Another way of facing the awful truth is to face it squarely—to discard the concept of distinction, to use any and all materials that come to hand and to use them in any context whatsoever. Walt Whitman did this in poetry, Charles Ives in music, also Henry Cowell in his early years. And though they mostly could not make their art support them, they produced in quantity and their inspirations were not deformed. By sacrificing the ideals of perfection and distinction, as well as all hope of professional encouragement—Ives actually for twenty years hiding away (and wisely, I think) from the danger of professional persecution—they achieved in their work an enormous authenticity.

Ruggles faced the dilemma in still another way, which was to slowly construct for himself a method for testing the strengths of musical materials and a system of building with them so complex, so at every point aware of tensile strengths and weaknesses, that by this seemingly neutral application of psychological and acoustic laws, works were constructed that are not only highly personal in content but that seem capable of resisting wear and time. Poe is a somewhat parallel case in letters. In music Elliott Carter is surely one. And in all three cases—Ruggles, Carter, and Poe—not only has authentic inspiration survived, but beauty and distinction have not been sacrificed. Such artists may wear their integrity like a chip on the shoulder, but it is real. Ambition, "that last infirmity," though it may torment their sleep, has been kept from their work. With Ruggles and Carter the output has been small; but no compromise has taken place, nor has any hindrance occurred to the artist's full ripening.

Good music, reputable and palatable, has been composed in all three of the circumstances I describe—by copying Europe, by working without rule, or by constructing a method—and I fancy that all three ways for getting around the American dilemma will continue to be used. For there is still no "spirit of Beethoven" here, either walking beside you down the street as he does in Vienna, or buried nearby in any of our graveyards. It will be some time before one of our young musicians, feeling the call to speak to man of God, to God of man, or of man to men, will find his feelings channeled by understanding or his consecration accepted. Everything is set here to educate him, to brainwash him, and to reward him with success; nothing is prepared to help him become a great man, to carry out his inspiration, or to fulfill his blessedness.

For inspiration, as we can learn from all great work, comes only out of self-containment. And style, that touchstone of authenticity, comes only from authentic inspiration. What is style? Carrying power, I say; nothing more. At least, carrying power is style's direct result. From carrying power come distinction and fame, recognition while one is still alive. And from them all—from inspiration, style, and distinction, provided the inspiration be authentic, the carrying power through style very strong, and the distinction of personality visible to all—from all these comes immortality.

Now both Ives and Ruggles have through their music achieved a modicum of that. To Ives has come also, of late, popularity. The music of Ruggles, far more recondite, is also more intensely conceived and more splendidly perfected. Ives belongs (though he is grander, of course) with the homely tinkerers like the eighteenth-century tanner William Billings, and also with the roughneck poets of his own time Carl Sandburg and Vachel Lindsay. But for all of Ives's rude monumentality and his fine careless raptures—welcome indeed in a country vowed to a freedom that its artists have rarely practiced—he falls short, I think, of Whitman's total commitment, as he does also of Emerson's high ethical integrity. Ruggles, judged by any of these criteria, comes out first class. Europe, where he has been played more than here, has never caviled at such an estimate; nor has his music, under use or after analysis, revealed any major flaw. Standing up as it does to contemporary tests, including public indifference, how can one doubt that it will also stand the test of time?

REACTIONARY CRITIC (1951)

Eduard Hanslick, a Bohemian born in 1825 in Prague, came to Vienna in 1846 as a law student. He had already received a musical education, had met Schumann and Wagner, corresponded with Berlioz, and written music criticism. While preparing his doctorate in law, which he took in 1849, he continued to write music criticism, for most of which he was not paid. His first Viennese contribution was an analysis of Wagner's *Tannheuser*, published by the *Wiener Musikzeitung* in eleven installments. Hanslick was at this time a deep admirer of Wagner's genius and music. Till his death he continued to admire the genius; but from *Lohengrin* on, which he reviewed from the Vienna production of 1858, he did not approve the music.

Meanwhile, by easy stages, he had given up law (or rather the civil service career for which it had prepared him) and become a salaried reviewer of music in the daily press. From 1855 to 1864 he wrote for *Die Presse* and from 1864 to his retirement in 1895 for *Die Neue Freie Presse*. From 1861 he was Extraordinary Professor of the History and Aesthetics of Music at the University of Vienna. In the middle 1850s he had written a book on *Beauty in Music*. Thereafter, at the university and in print, he posed as world-expert and final authority on the subject. A classical education and a facile pen enabled him to defend his assumed position with ingenuity and wit. His determination to uphold the cause of classicism in music involved him in systematic denial of the artistic validity of Liszt, Berlioz, Wagner, Bruckner, Hugo Wolf, Verdi, and Richard Strauss. He barely tolerated Tchaikovsky and Dvořák, ignored wholly the rising movement in Russia and France. Henselt, Lachner, and Johann Strauss he always mentioned benevolently. The dead—Schumann, Schubert, Mendelssohn, Weber, Beethoven, Mozart, Handel, Bach—he treated with respect. The only living composer of class that he deigned to defend was Brahms. His banner Hanslick carried aloft as the banner of counter-revolution till his own death in 1904.

Except for his early brochure on *Beauty in Music* Hanslick's work has not till now been available in English. Henry Pleasants III, formerly music critic of the *Philadelphia Evening Bulletin*, has recently edited and translated admirably a selection of Hanslick's reviews, complete with notes and biographical preface, under the title of *Vienna's Golden Years of Music: 1850–1900* (Simon and Schuster, New York, 1950). One is grateful for even this brief acquaintance with the man Wagner pilloried as Beckmesser in *Die Meistersinger*. One is pleased to learn that he was not, as Wagner gave him to us, a bad composer, a lecher, and a boor, but a skilled belles-lettrist and a master reporter. One is charmed, too, by his literary culture, his musical penetration, and smooth easy man-of-the-world ways. Reading him lightly, one might almost take him for the perfect music critic, if perfection is conceivable in so invidious a genre.

But no, three times no! Once because there was no real warmth in the man. Twice because the truth was not in him. And thrice because he never stuck his neck out.

To those who may think a twenty-five-year war with Richard Wagner enough bravery to ask of any man, I recall that Wagner did not live in Vienna and that Hanslick's readers, who did, were middle-aged, well-to-do, bourgeois. He wrote for a conservative paper. His readers asked no better than to see a man of novel genius reduced to the level of an incompetent entertainer. Critics writing all over Europe on conservative papers—Chorley in London, Fétis in Paris, not to speak of the German reviewers—had given Wagner the same treatment; and in 1856 *The New York Times* had denied to *Lohengrin* "a dozen bars that could be called real melody." Anybody knows it is easier to defend the public against novelty in art than it is to defend an original artist against the public's comfortable conservatism.

Actually there is not a point in Hanslick's attacks on Wagner that had not been made before. Berlioz, Meyerbeer, Rossini, and the young Bizet had long since put their finger on the inequalities in his talent. These were common knowledge in music circles. Time had not altered, moreover, their reality. Wagner's contemporaries, including Hanslick, denied him no excellence for which he is still cherished. Nor were even his closest friends, save a few, unaware of his imperfections. Even Hanslick's main theme about how for all its beauties this music is not "the music of the future," not a beginning but a glorious and dangerous dead end, that too was a familiar idea. That is what the famous Wagner "case" has always been about, and Hanslick did not invent it. As a matter of fact, his reviews spent far more space unmasking Wagner's literary weaknesses, which he was capable of doing quite well, than analyzing the musical structure which he could not always follow, even with a score. He knew that Wagner could orchestrate, paint tremendous musical landscape scenes, and prosodize in German; but he had not the musical technique to understand Wagner's complex chromatic harmony and asymmetrical rhythm. So he complained about the "lack of melody," made fun of the librettos, and refuted the advertising. Compared with Nietzsche on Wagner, he was thoroughly superficial.

To protect himself against the possible charge of not patronizing home industry, Hanslick had sagaciously picked on Brahms as his "side" in the Brahms–Wagner war. He was sold this position by a surgeon named Billroth, who was a close friend of Brahms, and who, according to Dr. Max Graf, Hanslick's successor on the *Neue Freie Presse*, furnished the critic with analyses of Brahms's works. Hanslick cared little for Brahms; what he really liked was waltzes, light airs, and Offenbach. But Brahms was useful to him, and he to Brahms. The pair of them, if stories of the time and Bruckner's letters are to be believed, carried on a relentless intrigue, aided by two other critics who were also friends of Brahms, to prevent Bruckner's rise in popularity from endangering the carefully constructed celebrity of the older man. Brahms's ironic gesture of gratitude was the dedication to Hanslick of his *Love Waltzes*. To Billroth, who understood depth and complexity, he dedicated two of his grander quartets.

Hanslick could describe a performer to perfection—Liszt, von Bülow, Clara Schumann, Lilli Lehmann, Adelina Patti. He tells you what they looked like, the kind of sounds they made, the nature of their technique, and the character of their temperaments. His musical analysis of any composition was elementary and timid, reads like a quoted program note. Also he was a dirty fighter. He was a dirty fighter because his extraordinary intellectual and literary powers were used solely to convince people that he alone was right and all the living composers, except for a few minor melodists and for Brahms, were wrong. A mere reviewer, a belles-lettrist, a reporter, and a professor of Music Appreciation (the first, I believe), he pitted himself in his own column against the creative forces of the age. Anywhere but in his own column, or surrounded by its glamour in a Viennese salon, he was just another irate customer complaining about modern music. In his column, and in private intrigues, he was formidable.

Having gone through my two provable indictments in reverse order, I am now back to the first, which is a matter of feeling. For me there is no warmth in the man, no juice, no passion for music. Sensuality, grace, some sparkle, a gift for ridicule, and a colossal vanity shine through his selected reviews. So does the insincerity of his pretended love for Brahms's music. He states it over and over, but he cannot make it glow. What comes through everything is an ever-so-careful conformism to the bourgeois tastes of his time, which, I am very sorry to say, are still the tastes of bourgeois Vienna at home and abroad. But he did not invent even these. He invented nothing but the style and attitude of the modern newspaper review. That, with all its false profundity and absurd pretensions to "sound" judgment, he will probably have to defend at everybody's Last Judgment. He was second-rate clean through, and he had no heart. Max Graf thinks highly of Hanslick's literary gift. "His essays and articles," says Dr. Graf in his excellent book, *Critic and Composer*, "have been published in twelve volumes, in which his intelligence, charm, clarity, and wit are preserved, like drugs and poisons in cut-glass vessels on the shelves of a pharmacy." "Venom from contented rattlesnakes" was the late Percy Hammond's term for similar critical contributions.

III

CONTEMPORARIES—PERFORMERS

As a contributor to Modern Music, *Thomson wrote primarily about composers; but as a reviewer for a daily newspaper, he had to evaluate performers, some of whom were prima donnas accustomed to fawning notices. Safely ensconced in his position at the* Trib, *Thomson did not hesitate in being severe—indeed, very severe—even about Arturo Toscanini, who had the status of a deity in New York in the 1940s. Thomson's reviews also had an abundance of bon mots that his readers could declaim aloud over breakfast, say, as in this about Dimitri Mitropoulos: "For the most part he did everything to the orchestra but conduct it. He whipped it up as if it were a cake, kneaded it like bread, shuffled and riffled an imaginary deck of cards, wound up a clock, shook a recalcitrant umbrella, rubbed something on a washboard, and wrung it out." Here, as elsewhere, Thomson repeatedly pits European artists against American experience, for instance noticing that, even though the pianist Artur Rubinstein was born in Poland, his two-hand technique resembles that of "a good swing band."*

It is not easy to define what we mean by great music, but it is very easy to agree that the nineteenth century produced lots of it. It is also easy for musicians to agree that Frédéric Chopin was one of the great composers of that century, quite possibly the very greatest of them all. Last night a whole fistful of Chopin's greatest works were played in Carnegie Hall by one of our greatest living pianists, Artur Rubinstein.

Mr. Rubinstein is a delight to watch as well as to hear. Though he is as fastidious as one could wish in his musical execution, his platform manner is straightforward, well bred, businesslike. His delicacy is delicate, his forte powerful, his melodic tone rich and deep. He can play loud and soft and fast and slow without interrupting the music's rhythmic progress. He is a master of his instrument and of the music he plays, and he finds no reason for attracting undue attention to anything else. He is authoritative, direct, and courteous, like the captain of a transatlantic liner.

His pianism is of the close-to-the-key school. Hence the good marksmanship. Hence, also, its lack of any bright, pearly brilliance. His arms and torso are of stocky build. Hence the power of his climaxes, the evenness of his pianissimo. He is Polish by birth, if I mistake not. Hence his complete at-homeness in Chopin's music, like a host in his father's house.

He is most at home in straightforward pieces, like the études, and in long, massive works like the sonatas, the ballades, the scherzos, works that call to action his mastery of dramatic line, of architectural sweep. He plays the tricky mazurkas and nocturnes with less ease. They don't give him enough room to move around in, and so he rather streamlines them than builds them.

His rubato is of the Paderewski tradition. I do not know how that tradition got started, but I do not think it comes from Chopin. It sounds Viennese to me.

Chopin's prescription for rubato-playing, which is almost word for word Mozart's prescription for playing an accompanied melody, is that the right hand should take liberties with the time values, while the left hand remains rhythmically unaltered. This is exactly the effect you get when a good blues singer is accompanied by a good swing band. It is known to the modern world as *le style hot*. The Paderewski tradition of Chopin-playing is more like the Viennese waltz style, in which the liberties in the melody line are followed exactly in the accompaniment, the two elements keeping always together and performing at the same time a flexible distortion of strict rhythm that manages by its very flexibility to keep the procedure from seeming arbitrary or the continuity from collapsing. Mr. Rubinstein is skillful with this kind of rubato. He keeps the music surging. But I don't believe for a moment it resembles anything Frédéric Chopin ever did or had in mind.

On more than this count does Rubinstein make one think of Paderewski. Among his encores (he played the C-sharp minor Waltz and the Étude for the Little Finger also) he did such a rendition of the A-flat Grande Polonaise as it has not been my pleasure to hear in many a day. Such speed, such power, such fury, such truly magnificent transcending both of the pianoforte's limitations and of his own customary accuracy were the very substance of Paderewski's greatness. They were Mr. Rubinstein's last night, a final jewel in his already laureate crown.

PIPE-ORGAN OBSESSION [LEOPOLD STOKOWSKI] (1940)

It becomes increasingly clear to this listener that Leopold Stokowski's concept of orchestral music is derived from organ-playing. He cares nothing for the spontaneous collaboration that is the joy of ensemble players, the kind of perfect concord that swingsters call being "in the groove" and that French instrumentalists refer to as "the little blue flame." He treats his men as if they were 110 stops of a concert organ, each complete with swell-box, all voiced for solo use and mutually adjusted for producing balanced chords of any timbre at any degree of loudness or softness.

His latest seating arrangement is an adaptation to orchestral uses of pipe-organ antiphony. He long ago did away with the classical symphonic antiphony of first violins on one side against seconds on the other, through both of which pierce succeeding layers of supporting woodwind, brass, and percussion. He has his musicians arranged now with all the strings massed at back center as if these were a single homogeneous body of foundation tone, like Great Organ diapasons, with woodwinds out in front, like a Choir Organ or *positif*, and with the brasses at the right and left downstage corners, like the heavy solo reeds of a French organ, the horns playing antiphonally on one side against the trumpets and trombones on the other.

This massive acoustico-architectural layout established, he proceeds to play on the whole thing with his bare fingers as if it were a solo instrument. Nothing is left to the musicians' personal taste or feeling. He even went so far last night as to mold William Kincaid's flute passages by hand, an insulting procedure toward an artist of Mr. Kincaid's stature, but a necessary procedure for producing the kind of one-man musical performance that Mr. Stokowski has in mind.

He carries his pipe-organ obsession to the extent of imitating organ rhythm, even. Now the organ, a mechanical wind instrument, knows no lilt or swing. It executes an even scale and an evenly progressive crescendo or diminuendo. It can play *sforzando* and *fortepiano*, but its accent knows no beat. Its rhythm is entirely quantitative, a question of long and short note-values, never of beat-stresses varied within the measure.

To have made Brahms's *Haydn Variations*, with their Viennese lilt and only occasional passage of non-accentual music that sets off by contrast their otherwise steadily swinging rhythm, into something that sounded like nothing so much as a skillful organ transcription of these same *Variations* is a triumph of will power as well as of conductorial skill. The thoroughness and clarity of the technical procedures by which this deformation was operated make any questioning of its aesthetic value seem like quibbling, since, as always with Stokowski, the means employed, no matter what aesthetic end is achieved by them, are a contribution to orchestral technique.

It is just as well that he chose for his technical exhibition last night music that could take it. Beethoven's *Leonora* No. 3, Brahms's *Haydn Variations*, and Siegfried's *Death Music* from *Die Götterdämmerung* are all foolproof and virtuoso-proof. No matter how you play them, they sound.

Shostakovich's *Sixth Symphony*, like all the later works of that gifted and facile composer, is pretty hard to conceal, too. It is clear, obvious, effective, old-fashioned. It is not, perhaps, as successfully pulled off as his First and Fifth. Its allegiance seems to be divided between a romanticized, and hence attenuated, neo-classicism and a full-blooded Muscovite orientalism à la Borodin. Each movement begins with a gesture of goodwill toward the lately reputable International Style and goes off as quickly as possible into the atmospheric market-place-and-landscape painting that Russians have always loved. It is a pleasant piece and not without a certain concentration. If it were signed by an American composer, say Harl McDonald or Walter Piston, it would be classifiable as good salable academicism.

MASTER OF DISTORTION AND EXAGGERATION [VLADIMIR HOROWITZ] (1942)

If one had never heard before the works Vladimir Horowitz played last night in Carnegie Hall, or known others by the same authors, one might easily have been convinced that Sebastian Bach was a musician of the Leopold Stokowski type, that Brahms was a sort of flippant Gershwin who had worked in a high-class night club, and that Chopin was a gypsy violinist. One might very well conclude also that Liszt's greatest musical pleasure was to write vehicles for just such pianists as Vladimir Horowitz. The last supposition would be correct. Liszt was that kind of pianist himself, and he turned out concert paraphrases of anything and everything from the *Faust* waltz to Palestrina motets. Whether he was quite the master of musical distortion that Horowitz is, history does not record; but I think there is little doubt possible that a kindship of spirit exists between the two pianists. One has only to hear Horowitz play Liszt's music to recognize that.

Do not think, please, that my use of the word *distortion* implies that Mr. Horowitz's interpretations are wholly false and reprehensible. Sometimes they are and sometimes they are not. His Bach is no worse and no better than Stokowski's, on which I take it to be modeled. His Brahms may be less light-minded on other occasions than it was last night. His Chopin varied a good deal during the evening. The B-flat minor Sonata was violent, coarsely conceived, melo-dramatic. He made its *Funeral March* sound like a Russian boat song by accenting all the off-beats of the bass, and he turned its serene middle section into the most affected of nocturnes. His Études, however, were recognizable and, of course, quite brilliant, as they should be; and the A-flat Waltz (an encore) was as normal as his Liszt.

Supernormal would be a better word for the way he renders the works of the great Hungarian Romantic. He seems to have a perfectly clear understanding of what they are about and a thorough respect for them. He exaggerates when exaggeration is of the essence, but he never tampers with their linear continuity. He makes all the right effects, and he makes them in the right places. The only distortion is one of aggrandizement. He plays the Liszt pieces faster and louder and more accurately than anybody else ever plays them. Sometimes he plays the music of other composers that way too, and the effect is more tremendous than pleasant. In Liszt it is both tremendous and pleasant, because Liszt's music was written for that kind of playing and because Mr. Horowitz really loves and understands that kind of music. It is the only kind that he approaches without fidgeting, and last night it was the only kind the audience didn't cough through.

If I speak chiefly of interpretation, it is not that I am wanting in admiration of Mr. Horowitz's justly acclaimed technical powers. But these powers are exploited by a violent and powerful personality that is, after all, a part of his virtuoso equipment. Paderewski had and Artur Rubinstein has a strength of crescendo comparable. E. Robert Schmitz has an equal cleanness of articulation and a more even trill. Josef Lhévinne's octaves and general marksmanship are at least as good. And almost any of the more poetic virtuosos, Rudolf Serkin or Robert Casadesus, for example, has a lovelier tone. But none of these pianists is so free from respect for the composer's intentions, as these are currently understood. Horowitz pays no attention to such academic considerations. He is out to wow the public, and wow it he does. He makes a false accent or phrasing anywhere he thinks it will attract attention, and every brilliant or rapid passage is executed with a huge crescendo or with a die-away effect. It is all rather fun and interesting to students of what I like to call the wowing technique. It is a great deal more than that, however, when he gets into his own arrangement of Liszt's arrangement for one piano of Saint-Saëns' arrangement for two pianos of the latter's orchestral version of his own song called *Danse Macabre*. His rendition of that number is in every way the berries.

SILK-UNDERWEAR MUSIC [JASCHA HEIFETZ] (1940)

Robert Russell Bennett's *Hexapoda*, musical sketches of the jitterbug world, are pretty music. Also they are evocative of swing music without being themselves swing music or any imitation of swing music. They manage with skill and integrity to use swing formulas as a décor for the musical depiction of those nerve reflexes and soul states that swing-lovers commonly manifest when exposed to swing music. They are, in addition, expertly written for the violin. They come off, as the phrase has it, like a million dollars.

Jascha Heifetz's whole recital rather reminded one of large sums of money like that. If ever I heard luxury expressed in music it was there. His famous silken tone, his equally famous double-stops, his well-known way of hitting the true pitch squarely in the middle, his justly remunerated mastery of the musical marshmallow, were like so many cushions of damask and down to the musical ear.

He is like Sarah Bernhardt, with her famous "small voice of purest gold" and her mastery of the wow-technique. First-class plays got in her way; she seldom appeared in one after thirty. Heifetz is at his best in short encore pieces (the Bennetts are beautifully that) and in lengthy chestnuts like Spohr's *Gesangscene*, where every device of recitative style, of melodic phrase turning, and of brilliant passage work is laid out, like the best evening clothes and the best jewelry, for Monsieur to put his elegant person into. No destination, no musical or emotional significance, is implied.

The Richard Strauss *Sonata*, a work of the author's early manhood, lacks none of that composer's characteristic style. The themes could only be his (albeit one was practically straight out of *Carmen*), bombastic, second-rate (I except the one that starts the last movement, which is bombastic and first-rate), inflated, expressing nothing but the composer's fantastic facility, his jubilant gusto at writing music. Mr. Heifetz's execution of this was almost embarrassingly refined.

Of his Mozart, the less said the better. It is of the school that makes a diminuendo on every feminine phrase-ending, that never plays any phrase through with the same weight, that thinks Mozart's whole aim was to charm, that tries so hard to make out of the greatest musician the world has ever known (those are

Joseph Haydn's words) something between a sentimental Pierrot and a Dresden china clock that his music ends by sounding affected, frivolous, and picayune. If that is Mozart, I'll buy a hat and eat it.

I realize that my liking or not liking what Mr. Heifetz plays and how he plays it is a matter of no import to the stellar spaces in which he moves. But it happens that I did go to the concert last night and that I did observe pretty carefully his virtuosity. It was admirable and occasionally very, very beautiful. The fellow can fiddle. But he sacrifices everything to polish. He does it knowingly. He is justly admired and handsomely paid for it. To ask anything else of him is like asking tenderness of the ocelot.

Four-starred super-luxury hotels are a legitimate commerce. The fact remains, however, that there is about their machine-tooled finish and empty elegance something more than just a trifle vulgar.

THE TOSCANINI CASE (1942)

Arturo Toscanini's musical personality is a unique one in the modern world. One has to go back to Mendelssohn to find its parallel. A reactionary in spirit, he has none the less revolutionized orchestral conducting by his radical simplification of its procedures. Almost wholly devoted to the playing of familiar classics, he has at the same time transformed these into an auditory image of twentieth-century America with such unconscious completeness that musicians and laymen all over the world have acclaimed his achievement without, I think, very much bothering to analyze it. They were satisfied that it should be, for the most part, musically acceptable and at all times exciting.

Excitement is of the essence in Toscanini's concept of musical performance. But his is not the kind of excitement that has been the specialty of the more emotional conductors of the last fifty years. Theirs was a personal projection, a transformation through each conductor's own mind of what the conductor considered to be the composer's meaning. At its best this supposed a marriage of historical and literary with musical culture. It was derived from the conducting style of Richard Wagner; and its chief transmitters to us have been the line that is von Bülow, Nikisch, and Beecham. For musicians of this tradition every piece is a different piece, every author and epoch another case for stylistic differentiation and for special understanding. When they miss, they miss; but when they pull it off, they evoke for us a series of new worlds, each of these verifiable by our whole knowledge of the past, as well as by our instinctive sense of musical meaning. Theirs is the humane cultural tradition. And if their interpretations have sometimes been accompanied by no small amount of personal idiosyncrasy and a febrile display of nerves, that, too, is a traditional concomitant of the sort of trancelike intensity that is necessary for the projection of any concept that is a product equally of learning and of inspiration.

Toscanini's conducting style, like that of Mendelssohn (if Wagner is to be believed about the latter), is very little dependent on literary culture and historical knowledge. It is disembodied music and disembodied theater. It opens few vistas to the understanding of men and epochs; it produces a temporary, but intense, condition of purely auditory excitement. The Maestro is a man of music, nothing else. Being also a man of (in his formative years) predominantly theatrical experience, he reads all music in terms of its possible audience effect. The absence of poetical allusions and of historical references in his interpretations is significant, I think, of a certain disdain for the general culture of his individual listeners. In any case, whatever he may have inherited of nineteenth-century respect for individualistic culture was sacrificed many years ago to an emphasizing of those musical aspects that have a direct effect on everybody. It is extraordinary how little musicians discuss among themselves Toscanini's rightness or wrongness about matters of speed and rhythm and the tonal amenities. Like any other musician, he is frequently apt about these and as frequently in error. What seems to be more important than all that is his unvarying ability to put over a piece. Like Mendelssohn, he quite shamelessly whips up the tempo and sacrifices clarity and ignores a basic rhythm, just making the music, like his baton, go round and round, if he finds his audience's attention tending to waver. No piece has to mean anything specific; every piece has to provoke from its hearers a spontaneous vote of acceptance. This is what I call the "wow technique."

Now, what are we accepting when we applaud a Toscanini rendition? Not personal poetry, certainly; nor any historical evocation; nor a literal reading of a classic score. I think it is his power of abstraction we are acclaiming, the abstraction of a piece's essential outline. If he has reduced conducting motions to their basic outline, too, that is not mere elegance on his part, nor ostentation either; it is a systematic throwing away of all refinements that might interfere with his schematic rendition. His whole accent is on the structure of a piece. Its thematic materials are the building blocks with which that structure is erected. Expression and ornamentation are details to be kept in place. Unity, coherence, and emphasis are the qualities that must be brought out.

Both theatrical experience and poor eyesight are probably responsible for the Toscanini style. When one cannot depend on reading a score in public, one must memorize everything. And when one memorizes everything, one acquires a great awareness of music's run-through. One runs it through in the mind constantly; and one finds in that way a streamlined rendering that is wholly independent of detail and even of specific significance, a disembodied version that is all shape and no texture. Later, in rehearsal, one returns to the texture; and one takes care that it serve always as neutral surfacing for the shape. For shape is what any piece is always about that one has memorized through the eye and the inner ear.

Playing a piece for shape and run-through gives (if the piece has shape at all) the most exciting effect that can ever be produced. It is the same procedure as that of directing a melodrama on the stage, character and dialogue being kept at all times subsidiary to the effects of pure theater, to the building up in the audience of a state of intense anxiety that is relieved only at the end of the last act.

The radical simplification of interpretative problems that all this entails has changed orchestral conducting from a matter of culture and of its personal projection into something more like engineering. Young conductors don't bother much any more to feel music or to make their musicians feel it. They analyze it, concentrate in rehearsal on the essentials of its rhetoric, and let the expressive details fall where they may, counting on each man's skill and everybody's instinctive musicianship to take care of these eventually. Poetry and nobility of expression are left for the last, to be put in as with an eyedropper or laid on like icing, if there is time. All this is good, because it makes music less esoteric. It is crude because it makes understanding an incidental matter; but it is a useful procedure and one wholly characteristic of our land and century. About its auditory result I am less enthusiastic than many. I find Toscanini's work, for the most part, spiritually unenlightening, except when he plays Italian music. But that is only a personal experience; many musicians find otherwise. And those of us who like more differentiation, more poetry, and more thought in our music, who find his much advertised fidelity to the notes of musical scores to be grossly exaggerated, his equally advertised "perfection" to be more so, and both of these aims, even when achieved, to be of secondary importance, even we must admit, nevertheless, the reality of Toscanini's musicianship and achievements. For good or for ill, and most probably for good, orchestral conducting will never be the same again.

I say most probably for good, because it is noticeable already that lesser conductors analyze music better than they used to and that this simple extraction of a work's formal essence tends to facilitate rather than to obfuscate differentiations of style and expression in the conducting of men whose musical experience is more limited but whose general culture is more ample than Toscanini's. Many of his contemporaries and most of his famous predecessors have had more interesting minds. Almost none has been so gifted a natural musician and so strictly professional a showman. He has simplified the technique of the art by eliminating all the hangovers of Late Romantic emotionalism and by standardizing a basic technique of musical rendition that is applicable to any piece in the world, whether one understands its spirit or not. This may be treason to culture, or it may be merely a radical purging of culture's own fifth column. I fancy it includes a bit of both. In any case, I believe that the introduction of a new cultural understanding into orchestral rendition, as one observes this in the work of Alexander Smallens, for instance, and in that of most of the other good American conductors, is as directly traceable to Toscanini's having previously eliminated practically all cultural understanding from it as the means of their doing so have been facilitated by his radical simplifications of conducting procedure.

Toscanini's influence lies, so far, chiefly in America. Europe follows Furtwängler and Beecham and great French conductors like Monteux and Münch. It has no need of exchanging their interpretations or their working methods for anything so oversimplified as Toscanini's. The Romantic tradition has already transformed itself there into a modern tradition that is as rich and as complex and as generally satisfactory to the mind as the tradition of Wagner and Nikisch was. That tradition is too complex for us. We admire the work of the great European conductors, but we do not quite understand how it is done. A century of importing them has not revealed their secrets to our local boys. We watched Toscanini work for ten years at the Philharmonic; and now there are 30,000 symphony orchestras in the United States, practically all of them led by the local boys. He is the founding father of American conducting. Whether we like or not the way he interprets music (and I don't much, though many do), his place in our musical history is certainly an important one.

In any European sense, he is not a complete musician, as the late Karl Muck was, and perhaps not even a great technician, as Reiner is, for example. He is too completely self-taught to be wholly responsible to any Great Tradition. But he is a thoroughgoing professional, although self-taught; and he has shown our musicians how to be thoroughgoing professionals too, although self-taught. The value of this contribution to our musical life cannot be overestimated. Any influence Toscanini might possibly have on European musical life would be anti-cultural. His ruthless clearing away here, however, of Romantic weeds and unsuccessful implantations has made a space where conductors are already being grown locally. And a steady supply of good American conductors to the local market is the thing above all else needful right now to the public understanding and the autochthonous development of American musical composition.

VIOLENCE AND CHARM [RUDOLF FIRKUSNY] (1944)

Rudolf Firkusny, who played a recital of piano music in Carnegie Hall last night, is a dynamic temperament with lots of punch in his fingers. He plays very loud and very fast most of the time. He plays most of the written notes, too, and often adds extra ones by accident. I once heard him play a concerto with orchestra most prettily. But concerto playing doesn't show up faults of musicianship as a recital does. Last night's concert revealed a pianist with far from negligible (though not complete, by any means) keyboard mastery and a musical temperament of such banal violence as it has not often been my lot to encounter among reputable performers.

Excepting for two of the Chopin *Études*, which were sensibly and agreeably read, everything—literally everything—was so deformed by speed and pounding that it was difficult to tell one piece from another. Under such circumstances it was not possible for one to have any clear impression of Martinů's *Fantasy and Rondo* beyond recognition of the fact that it is a work of serious intentions and some length. What a listener not familiar with Beethoven's *Waldstein* sonata might have made of the piece is difficult to imagine. It was recognizable to your reviewer only by the notes of it, its expressive content, as rendered, being chiefly reminiscent of the movie pianism of his youth.

The first movement might have been entitled "A Day at the Races," with steeplechase hazards being got over at full speed and ponies constantly coming lickety-split down the homestretch. The rondo was like the accompaniment to a class-B Western. A young miss of pastoral upbringing had apparently been seized by a band of outlaws on horseback, taken to a lonely spot, and left there. She was very sad about this, and then the outlaws took her to an even lonelier place and tied her hands behind her. A gallant young cowboy, however, came to her rescue and galloped her away. On the ride home the two had a tender moment in which she thanked him for his trouble. And when they got back to town there was general dancing.

If you think I am making fun of either Beethoven or Mr. Firkusny, just try playing the *Waldstein* Sonata at 120 half-notes to the minute. You will see that the effect is somewhat as I have described it, especially if you play all the passages marked f as if they were marked $ffff$. The result is both piquant and trite. If you play a whole program through in this way you will discover that only so tough a work as this particular sonata is capable, under the speed-up and the pounding process, of sounding as if it had a subject at all. Music fast and furious is not always fun. If Mr. Firkusny were less charming as a platform personality, it is doubtful whether his kind of music making would be as appealing to music lovers as it clearly was, I must admit, to last night's audience.

THE KOUSSEVITZKY CASE (1947)

Serge (or Sergei) Koussevitzky, conductor of the Boston Symphony Orchestra since 1924, is an aristocrat among American conductors and in Boston music circles something of an autocrat. Born seventy-two years ago in Russia and reared there in poverty (his family, though Orthodox Jews, never lived in a ghetto), he has attained wealth, world-wide fame and the highest distinction in his profession. As a virtuoso on the double-bass viol and as a conductor his ranking, by any standards, has been for many years among that of the very greatest in our time. As a composer he has contributed to the reputable literature of his instrument. As a publisher and a patron of contemporary music he has probably made a more lasting contribution to the art than any other single person living, excepting five or six composers. His place in its history is already assured and glorious.

Just to make assurance doubly sure, the Boston immortality machine has started issuing this winter what looks like a series of books bearing the papal imprimatur of the good doctor (LL.D., *honoris causa*, Harvard, 1929, and elsewhere). M. A. DeWolfe Howe, official biographer to the Bostonian great, has furnished *The Tale of Tanglewood, Scene of the Berkshire Music Festivals* (Vanguard Press, New York, 1946), prefaced by Mr. Koussevitzky himself. And Hugo Leichtentritt, a musicologist of repute and a former Lecturer of Harvard University, has fathered *Serge Koussevitzky, the Boston Symphony Orchestra and the New American Music* (Harvard University Press, 1946).

And now to supplement these two books, which are clearly official and more than a little superficial, arrives a full-length biography of the maestro which is neither. It is entitled simply *Koussevitzky*, by Moses Smith (Allen, Towne, and Heath, 1947). Announced for sale on February 15, its distribution has been held up for the time being by an injunction that prohibits its publication, sale, and distribution till Justice Shientag of the New York Supreme Court shall have determined whether the book's circulation will do its subject "irreparable harm." If the present writer, who has read an advance copy received before the injunction was issued, is in any way typical of the American reading public, it certainly, in his opinion, will not. The only possible harm he can envisage to so impregnable a reputation as that of Serge Koussevitzky is that already done by his own efforts to suppress the book.

Moses Smith, a trained newspaper man, for many years music critic of the *Boston Evening Transcript*, as well as a friend of Mr. Koussevitzky, has produced a far more thorough study, a better work of scholarship than either Mr. Howe or Mr. Leichtentritt, scholars both by trade. There seems little in the book of factual statement that is subject to question. Whether Mr. Koussevitzky, in view of his great devotion to the memory of his second wife, Natalie, is made unhappy by mention of his first marriage, hitherto not publicized in America, is scarcely germane. Neither is his possible sensitivity to reports of his quarrels with musicians and with blood relatives. These are, as a matter of fact, common knowledge; and they legitimately form part of the whole story of his musical life, just as his first marriage does of any complete biography.

Judgments and opinions, expressed over any writer's signature, are, of course, personal. The conductor's legal complaint objected to Mr. Smith's statement that Koussevitzky had succeeded as a conductor in spite of imperfect early training in musical theory and score reading. This also, if I may make so bold, has long been common knowledge among musicians. Nor is the estimable doctor unique among the conducting great for being in a certain sense self-taught. Leopold Stokowski, Sir Thomas Beecham, and Charles Munch, great interpreters all of them, did not come to conducting through early mastery of the conservatory routines. They bought, muscled, or impressed their way in and then settled down to learn their job. They succeeded gloriously, as Koussevitzky has done. All honor to them. They have all, Koussevitzky included, contributed more of value to the technique of their art than most of the first-prize-in-harmony boys ever have.

But great pedagogues, and the good doctor is one, do hate hearing that their own education has not been conventional, though it rarely was. And all great artists loathe criticism. They do; they really do. What they want, what they need, what they live on, as Gertrude Stein so rightly said, is praise. They can never get enough of it. And sometimes, when they have come to be really powerful in the world, they take the attitude that anything else is libel. Dr. Koussevitzky's complaint, as I remember, did not use the word "libel." It spoke of possibly "irreparable injury." Well, criticism is often injurious; there is no question about that. Many a recitalist, receiving unfavorable reviews, finds it more difficult to secure further engagements than if the reports had been less critical. Minor careers have been ruined overnight that way. Major careers are rarely harmed by criticism, because major artists can take it. They don't like to; but they have to; so they do. All the same, it is the big boys, the great big boys that nothing could harm, that squawk the loudest. I know, because I have been in the business for several years now.

Mr. Smith's book makes Koussevitzsky out to be a very great man indeed, but it also makes him human. Gone is the legend of his infallibility. Renewed is one's faith in his sincerity, his consecration, his relentless will to make the world permanently better than he found it. Nobody, I am sure, can read the book through without admiring him more. And the faith of the pious need not be shaken by reading that he has not always been toward his fellow man just and slow to anger. Civilization would be just a racket if we had to learn all we know about the lives of great men from their paid agents.

Mr. Koussevitzky is not the only first-class conductor in the world, though he is one of the best. Nor is he the only first-class conductor the Boston Symphony Orchestra has enjoyed. Nor does he any longer play the double bass in public, though when he did he was, by common consent, world champion. His unique position in a world full of excellent conductors, many of them devoted to contemporary music, is that he has played more of it, launched more of it, published more of it, and paid for more of it than anybody else living. That is the clear message of Mr. Smith's biography. Everything else, a petulant gesture here and there, a musical or family quarrel, a pretentious remark, a vainglorious interview, the present court action—all these things serve the picture; they bring him more vividly to life. How can anyone mind knowing them? Only he himself, apparently, hasting fearfully toward Parnassus, though his throne there has long been reserved for him, and involved, no doubt, in a publicity apotheosis that has already begun, would see any value in posing before an already worshiping universe without the customary habiliment of one human weakness. His lawsuit, of course, adds to the tableau that he has essayed so carefully to compose just that.

IN SPITE OF CONDUCTING [DIMITRI MITROPOULOS] (1953)

William Lincer, playing viola solo last night in the Philharmonic's opening concert of the season at Carnegie Hall, was a delight for his dark tone and the grace of his phraseology. If he did not project dramatically the solo part of Berlioz's *Harold in Italy* as one sometimes hears it done and did not attempt to make a concerto out of a work that is nothing of the kind, that reluctance was welcome, too. It enabled one to hear the piece as what it is, an orchestral landscape "featuring," as show business would put it, the viola.

Dimitri Mitropoulos, conducting, was less discreet. He did not cover the viola with noise when it was playing. But he crowded it, when it was not, with sudden loudnesses and brassy balances. Indeed, our Philharmonic's celebrated conductor overplayed his brasses most of the evening. And in the *Symphonie Konzertante* of Karl Stamitz, which "featured" seven other of the orchestra's first-desk musicians, he pushed his soloists for time as well as for volume.

The conductor's personal excitement, bordering on hysteria, was least under control in the Schumann Third, or *Rhenish* Symphony. Here the rhythm was often unclear, the counterpoints lost, the shape of the lovely work distorted by a nervous passion. If its reading nowhere lacked eloquence, it was everywhere lacking in elegance, in sweetness, in proportion, and in that spontaneity that is the heaven-sent grace, the unique gift of Robert Schumann.

Actually, when the conductor, in moments of calm, conducted straightforwardly and with a minimum of motion, his orchestra followed with a maximum of beauty and with the authority of style that is our Philharmonic's way. But for the most part he did everything to the orchestra but conduct it. He whipped it up as if it were a cake, kneaded it like bread, shuffled and riffled an imaginary deck of cards, wound up a clock, shook a recalcitrant umbrella, rubbed something on a washboard and wrung it out. Really, there were very few moments when a film taken of the conductor alone, without sound, would have given any clue to the fact that he was directing a musical composition.

JAZZ (1924)

To a 1977 magazine reprint of his pioneering writings on American vernacular music Thomson penned his own new headnote: "As a composer with professional interests to protect, Thomson regarded popular musicians as performers who had esthetic value intrinsically but no importance to compositional arts."

Jazz, in brief, is a compound of (a) the fox-trot rhythm, a four-four measure (*alla breve*) with a double accent, and (b) a syncopated melody over this rhythm. Neither alone will make jazz. The monotonous fox-trot rhythm, by itself, will either put you to sleep or drive you mad. And a highly syncopated line like the second subject of the Franck *Symphony in D minor* or the principal theme of Beethoven's third *Leonora* overture is merely syncopation until you add to it the heavy bump-bump of the fox-trot beat. The combination is jazz. Try it on your piano. Apply the recipe to any tune you know. In case you are not satisfied with the result, play the right hand a little before the left.

The fox-trot, which appeared about 1914, is the culmination of a tendency in American dancing that has been active ever since ragtime was invented in the early years of the century. The Viennese waltz and its brother, the two-step, died about 1912. For two years following, fancy steps like the tango, the maxixe, and the hesitation, with their infinite and amazing variations, made anarchy in the ballroom. This was resolved by a return to the utmost simplicity, and the common language of legs became a sort of straight-away walk. Any man could teach his partner in ten steps his peculiar form of it, whether he called it the Castle walk, the lame duck, or what not.

Soon after this primitive step became established ballroom dancing began to show the disturbance that shook all of polite society when the lid of segregation was taken off of vice and the bordello erupted into the drawing-room. Ragging, a style of dancing with slight footwork, but with much shoulder-throwing, came home from the bawdy house bearing the mark of the earlier hoochie-coochie, a monotonous beat without accentuation. It infected the walk-steps, had a convulsion called the turkey-trot, which proved too difficult to keep up, and finally, calling itself both the one-step and the fox-trot, became national and endemic. The former name, which merely indicated a tempo, is no longer used. The tempo of the latter has been expanded to include it.

At present the fox-trot is our only common dance rhythm. Its speed varies from 66 to 108 half-notes to the minute. It will bear any amount of muscular embroidery, from the shimmy to the halt, because its rhythm is in the simplest possible terms. The Viennese waltz is practically extinct in America. What is now called a waltz is simply a three-four fox-trot, as the two-step was a four-four waltz. The rhythm of the Viennese waltz is ♩ ♩ or ♩. ♪ ♩ and that of the hesitation ♩ ♩ 𝄽 or ♩ ♩. ♪ . There is one accent to a measure, as indicated. The two-step also had one accent, ♩. ♪ ♩ ♩ or ♩. ♪ ♩ . But the fox-trot has two, ♩ 𝄽 ♩ 𝄽 , and the jazz waltz has three, ♪𝄽 ♪𝄽 ♪𝄽 . The waltz, however, is not at home in jazz. After a century of Europeans, from Schubert to Ravel, had played with it, there was small possibility for further rhythmic variation. It is not comfortable now, for the true waltz-step is almost impossible to do unless the music has a flowing rhythm to tempt a flowing motion of the body.

We learned syncopation from three different teachers—the Indians, the Negroes, and our neighbors in Mexico. [This is quite wrong; a Scottish source is more likely. V.T.] It had become firmly established before the Civil War. It is the characteristic twist of nearly every familiar old tune. The dance craze of the last twenty-five years has simply exaggerated it. Because the way to make a strong pulse on 3 is by tying it to 2, thus, ♩ ♩‿♩ ♩ . A silent accent is the strongest of all accents. It forces the body to replace it with a motion. But a syncopated tune is not jazz unless it is supported by a monotonous, accentless rhythm underneath. Alone it may only confuse the listener. But with the rhythm definitely expressed, syncopation intensifies the anticipated beat into an imperative bodily motion. The shorter the anticipation the stronger the effect. The systematic striking of melodic notes an instant before the beat is the most powerful device of motor music yet discovered. But a fluent melody with a syncopated accompaniment is an inversion of the fundamental jazz process, and its effect is sedative.

If certain formulas of beat produce motion, probably certain motions have suggested these formulas. But I have no stake in the hen-and-egg controversy. I wish merely to show that the peculiar character of jazz is a rhythm, and that that rhythm is one which provokes jerky motions of the body. Instead of the following "normal" rhythms, ♩ ♩ ♩ ♫ and ♩ ♫ ♩ ♫ and ♩ ♩ ♫♫ , we have ♫ ♩ ♩ ♩ and ♬♩ ♩ and ♪ ♪ ♬♩ and ♪ ♬♩ —in brief, all the divisions which the masters of music-not-meant-for-dancing have used sparingly or with special antidotes, for the very reason that they make the body move instead of keeping it quiet so that the music can go forward.

Instrumentation is not an essential element in jazz, as anyone knows who has heard a good performer play it on the piano. It is possible to practically any group of instruments, because, above the rhythmic accompaniment, which also sets the harmony, it is contrapuntal rather than homophonic and does not require balanced timbres. Certain instruments and effects, however, are characteristic, especially the use of the saxophone, which, in pairs or in quartets, makes a rich and penetrating diapason, and the monotonous banjo accompaniment, giving out the ground-rhythm—a rhythm so sonorous that it would be unendurable were not its hypnotic effect turned into motor stimuli by cross-accents.

Another characteristic of jazz is its constant use of glissando. This has long been common on the trombone. It is also possible on the clarinet and the saxophone for about a major third. A descending succession of little glissandi makes the "laughing saxophone." The Frisco whistle plays a continuous glissando; and the glissando on a plucked string, introduced from Hawaii, has been applied to almost every stringed instrument except the banjo. It is difficult there because of the frets and because the banjo, having no sound-box, gives a tone which, though powerful, is of short duration.

With the growth of the contrapuntal style, necessary to disparate combinations, the varieties of wind tone have been considerably extended. Passionate or startling expression has been found in all sorts of vibrati and flutter-tonguing and in the covered tones of the muted trumpet and trombone, the muted clarinet, and the trombone played through a megaphone. Most of these devices, of course, are not new. Rimsky-Korsakov knew all the tricks on the trumpet that you now hear in the dance hall, and more. Berlioz employed the muted clarinet. Richard Strauss and Vincent d'Indy wrote years ago for quartets of saxophones. Stravinsky has even written glissandi for the horn! But the megaphone trick, which takes the blare out of the trombone and makes it sound like a euphonium, is probably new. Certainly the use of a free-hanging mute is new, though when it takes the form of a tin can or a silk hat it is no great addition to orchestral elegance.

In the current jazz one hears piano figures that are ingenious, counter-melodies that are far from timid, and experiments in instrumental balance that are of interest to any composer. The harmony itself is at times varied and delicate. The blues formula—subdominant modulation with alternations of tonic major and minor—is simple and effective. The chromatic (or diatonic) succession of dominant ninths so dear to Franck and Chabrier has become popular, and the mediant or sub-mediant tonality for modulation offers a pleasing relief from the more obvious dominant. The Neapolitan sixth is quite common and even the "barbershop" chord—the augmented six-five-three, or German sixth—is sometimes used in a manner that is not at all crude.

These characteristics of jazz are partially supported by serious music and partially contributory to it. Classical composers snap up quickly any novelty that the makers of jazz invent. Union musicians often play one night at the movies, and the next night with the local symphony orchestra. They bring a few tricks to the latter, and they take home many more. Orchestral and harmonic styles in jazz are still experimental and shifting. But the essence of the thing remains free melody with a fox-trot rhythm underneath. That rhythm shakes, but it won't flow. There is no climax. It never gets anywhere emotionally. In the symphony, it would either lose its character or wreck the structure. In that respect it is analogous to the hoochie-coochie beat.

SWING MUSIC (1936)

Swing music is for the layman just a new name for what another generation called jazz. It serves not infrequently, even among its intellectual amateurs, to distinguish jazz of some artistic value from the commercial product. Among professionals, however, it means a certain kind of rhythm. In defining the nature of that rhythm I am going to write a brief history of popular dance steps and their music from the beginning of jazz, around 1912, to the present day.

Primitive, or pre-swing, jazz is definable as an ostinato of equally accented percussive quarter-note chords (these take care of rhythm and harmony) supporting a syncopated melodic line.

I am defining here dance-jazz as it was to be heard almost anywhere between 1912 and 1932. The introduction into popular dance music of the jazz formula, or unvarying accent, was a basic simplification that made possible an added complexity in the ornamental and expressive structure.[1]

Elsewhere in print are lists of musical means and devices commonly employed in jazz performance. All I care to recall here is that an ostinato of percussive quarter-note chords was their basic support both rhythmically and harmonically.

Swing music is based on a different kind of ostinato. Its rhythm (to use the language of versification) is a rhythm of quantities, not a rhythm of stresses.

Let us examine dance rhythms a little and see how they got that way.

Pre-jazz Ragtime Two-step.

Jazz Fox-trot. Basic simplification.

Tango. Enter the Latin influence.

Parisian Tango. Takes on jazz accent.

Charleston. Jazz takes a tango accent.

Rumba. Spanish America goes Negroid.

Beguine. Spain is buried in the jungle.

Lindy Hop. Swing approaches.

Continental. Swing is here.

Spain is back on the dance floor and Africa at her drums, while the richest fancies of melody and harmony frolic in uncontrolled improvisation through the agency of our old friend the two-step.

Let us examine this tabulation more closely. All these dances are of New World origin. The tango is a modern name for an Argentine version of the nineteenth-century habañera (from Havana). The two-step is a 4/4 (*alla breve*) version of the Boston, as distinguished from the Viennese, or whirling waltz. Hesitations, maxixes, barn dances, turkey trots, lame ducks, the superb and buoyant Castle walk, were all New World steps. The fusion of the Hispanic, Anglo-Celtic, and Negroid elements of all these into a single formula was a twenty-years' dance war. It was fought out in Paris mostly, where the Hispanic and the Anglo-Celtic elements could meet on neutral ground. Each side, as we shall see, had its Negro troops.

By 1918 Anglo-America had stripped herself down to the fox-trot and the one-step, Latin-America to the tango. In the mid-twenties the battle was still a stalemate. Since French tax laws obliged all nightclubs to have both kinds of orchestras, American trumpet players were fraternizing at the bar with Argentine accordion players. The two sides didn't mix musical efforts much, but the tango unconsciously equalized its accents.

The folks back home were getting bored with all this undramatic trench war. The United States went wild first, and when the dust died down, it was evident that their new wildness, the Charleston, had somewhere or other acquired a suspiciously Hispanic accent. (It had long been the custom of W. C. Handy and the Mississippi Valley school to use a tango-bass in the middle section of a Blues number.)

Then Latin America got jittery too. She went Negroid in the form of rumbas and beguines. The original habañera downbeat reappeared along with floor-length dresses and the Boston waltz. The United States countered with the even fancier Lindy hop and a return to the prewar two-step (off the beat).

With swing music approaching, Latin America held out for a strong downbeat, Anglo-America for a strong offbeat. Latin America offered a percussive shimmer on its other beats, Anglo-America a rest. Swing rhythm was the solution. The shimmer was kept, but on the offbeats only, and accents were sacrificed by both sides. The percussive shimmer would stop where a beat was expected to occur, only the beat didn't occur. The treaty was signed in the form of an international ballroom accomplishment named appropriately for the chief battleground and popularized from Hollywood, the Continental.

All the characters of our little history are now happily united. The 4/4 Boston waltz, or two-step, is the new basis of operations. Body positions and some footwork are added from the Lindy hop and the tango (all passion restrained, however).

The percussive basis of the new music is now the West Indian shimmer. Downbeats are expressed only by a cessation of that shimmer. Here, therefore, is the special characteristic of swing music. It is founded on a purely quantitative (rather than an accentual) rhythm.[2]

Melody, harmony, and all thumpy percussion are henceforth liberated from formal rhythmic observances. The melodic instruments are not obliged even to syncopate, either by delay or by anticipation. They are free to improvise (it is more often the harmony that remains fixed than the tune) in that sort of spontaneous lyrical effusion mixed with vocal imitation and instrumental virtuosities that the French call so charmingly "le style hot."[3]

They are not really free not to play "hot"; that is to vary and to contradict at every possible point the underlying measure, because quantitative rhythm is a very powerful thing, as impressive and as boring over any length of time as organ music. Its emotional impassivity incites to emotional wildness, to irregular pattern, to strange timbres, to mysterious outbursts and inexplicable tensions.

It also liberates for free expressive use all the short or thumpy sounds of the percussion section. And few things in music are as expressive as a thump. One cymbal or snare drum being sufficient to keep up the swing, regularly placed *sfz* stresses become in themselves a form of hot solo exactly as they do in the *Sacre du Printemps*.

Liberating the percussive banjo, guitar, and piano also liberates the harmony section from rhythmic control. Hence we have all the emotional elements of the orchestra disengaged from point-counterpoint and released for free polyphony. Steady support underneath by a nonemotional quantitative rhythm both stimulates and accentuates the superposed emotional expression. The result at its best is sumptuous.

I shall not here go into detailed recounting of the higher points of contemporary swing art. They are discussed vigorously in Monsieur Hugues Panassié's fine volume, *Le Jazz Hot*.[4] You will find there a wealth of fact about "le style Chicago" and "le style New Orléans." About the instrumental innovations of Bix Beiderbecke and Muggsy Spanier (good jazz and swing music have never been Negro monopolies). Of what distinguishes "le style hot" from "le style straight." Of the art of five-part improvisation. Of the diverse merits of the divers famed "solistes hot." Of the difference between real and merely commercial jazz. You will be inducted into an orderly study of the historical and stylistic development of the whole business from Handy to Ellington, with special attention to the Chicago school, where the categorical German and the spontaneous Negro musicalities united to produce in Louis Armstrong (originally from New Orleans) a master of musical art comparable only (and this is my comparison, not M. Panassié's) to the great castrati of the eighteenth century. His style of improvisation would seem to have combined the highest reaches of instrumental virtuosity with the most tensely disciplined melodic structure and the most spontaneous emotional expression, all of which in one man you must admit to be pretty rare. You will also learn something (though not really enough) of the fascinating lingo the swing people use. You will weep tears over the author's efforts to define the word in French, its musical significance being hardly covered by *balancement* and matters being in no way helped by the already accepted French usage of *swing* as a term in pugilism. You will find all this and many more matters of both historical and esthetic importance discussed in *Le Jazz Hot*, the whole topped off by photographs of great men, indexes, and a bibliography of records.

I cannot compete with M. Panassié in either learning or enthusiasm. I can only come back to what I started out to do, which is to state in these pages (being asked) a definition of swing music (the estheticians of swing having neglected that point) which I believe to be correct. That definition, to sum up, is this. Swing music is a form of two-step in which the rhythm is expressed quantitatively by instruments of no fixed intonation, the melodic, harmonic, and purely accentual elements being freed thereby to improvise in polyphonic style.

POSTSCRIPT: I haven't stated, I find, just why swing music swings and beat music doesn't. Remember the Viennese waltz? Well, the whole story is there. It isn't the strong downbeat that makes a dancer swing. A strong downbeat only makes him whirl. A strong offbeat makes him jerk. A percussive roll or trill is what makes him swing. Give him the roll and no beat and he can neither whirl nor jerk. He can only swing and that lightly, because there is no place for the swing to take him. He can also sit still and listen.

Notes

1. Stravinsky's *Sacre du Printemps*, written in 1912, exploits an identical procedure. (It opens, by the way, with a "hot" solo for bassoon beginning on high C.) The *Danse des Adolescents* begins with equally accented percussive chords to which are added irregularly placed *sfz* stresses and, later, hot solos in nonvertical counterpoint. The contrast between control and spontaneity is the most striking thing of its kind in classical music.

   I mention the parallel to show that the dissociation of rhythm from beat took place in different kinds of music and on two continents at the same time. It was nobody's invention.
2. Quantitative rhythm is not new in musical art. The merry-go-round, the hurdy-gurdy, and the pipe organ have no accents at all, only quantitative rhythm.
3. The technic of this improvisation was developed from the free two-measure "breaks" of the early Blues.
4. Hugues Panassié, *Le Jazz Hot*, Paris, 1934. (*Hot Jazz: The Guide to Swing Music*, 1936 American edition reprinted by Negro Universities Press.)

SACRED SWING [GOSPEL MUSIC] (1941)

Last Sunday I went to Newark to attend the evening services of a Negro congregation known as The Church of God in Christ, where Brother Utah Smith, a traveling evangelist of that denomination, was closing his engagement. Brother Smith is a stocky gentleman in the mid-forties, neither old nor young, whose musical accomplishments had been signaled to me by swing experts. He is known in religious circles as The One-Man Band, was so introduced, in fact, by the local pastor. His whole musical equipment is an electric guitar, his only vestment an ordinary sack suit of dark blue, with a pair of white wings made of feathered paper attached to his shoulders like a knap-sack by crossed bands of white tape.

His religious message is delivered more by music and dancing than by preaching. Only after the preliminary prayers, solos and congregational hymns are over does he take charge of the meeting. Then an open space is cleared between the chancel rail and the first congregational seats. These last are allowed to be wholly occupied, no mourners' bench being reserved at all, since the nature of the service is one rather of general rejoicing than of personal penitence. The Brother makes a few remarks to the congregation and then, without any formal address or other preface, goes straight into his number, if I may so refer without irreverence to his music-making.

He plays the guitar with a high pick-up that fills the auditorium with a rich and booming sonority. He does not sing. He only plays and, like all swingsters, pats his foot. His musical fancy is of the highest order. I have rarely heard such intricate and interesting swing. From time to time he shouts: "I've got wings! Dust my feet!" Persons in the congregation reply with: "Dust my feet!" with "Praise the Lord!" and similar ceremonial phrases, as is customary among many colored religious groups. Practically everybody claps his hands in time to the music, claps on the off-beat, as is also customary in swing circles.

The music goes on for quite a long time, the Brother swinging chorus after chorus with ever increasing fantasy and insistence. Various persons of the congregation who feel so inclined first edge timidly toward the edge of the open space and then one by one start dancing. Each dances alone, some with raised and some with lowered head, all with eyes closed. Some jerk a little; others do rapid and complex footwork. The floor sways with their impact as if about to collapse. When the music stops, the dancers come out of their trancelike absorption and regain their seats as calmly as persons leaving any ballroom floor.

At no time during my stay did I observe any licentious behavior or other evidence that the ceremony was not a bona fide religious manifestation. Brother Smith himself, though full of humor and jollity, and not without a certain naïve showmanship, impressed me as sincere. And if I was not conscious during my one brief visit to his services of any extraordinary or commanding inspiration in them, neither was I aware of anything that might make me think them phony.

In any case, his musical gift is real and his musical imagination abundant. I am, consequently, taking occasion this Easter Sunday to make reference to what struck me as an interesting musical manifestation and to point an example from contemporary life of the truism that in those societies or groups where religion is most vigorous there is no difference whatever between the sacred and the secular musical styles, the consideration of what is sacred and what is profane in music applying only to the moral prestige in society of the ceremonies that it accompanies. As a swing artist Brother Utah Smith is worthy to rank among the best. As a stimulator of choric transports he incites the faithful to movements and behavior not very different from those of any true jitterbug. Myself, I found it distinctly pleasant to hear good swing and to observe its effects in surroundings imbued with the white magic of Protestant Christianity, rather than among alcoholic stupidities and even more somber diabolisms of the nightclub world.

"La Môme" Piaf (1947)

The presence among us of Edith ("la Môme") Piaf, currently singing at the Playhouse, is a reminder, and a very pleasant one, that the French *chanson* is an art form as traditional as the concert song. It has a glorious history and a repertory. Its dead authors and composers have streets named after them. Its living ones, just like the writers of operas, symphonies, and oratorios, enjoy a prestige that is not expressed in their income level. Its interpreters are artists in the highest sense of the term, easily distinguishable in this regard from the stars of commercialized entertainment.

If the official art music of our time expresses largely the life and ideals of the bourgeoisie and penetrates to the basic strata of society *from above*, the *chanson* is almost wholly occupied with depicting contemporary life from the view-point of the underprivileged and comes to us *from below*. The habitats of the official style are dressy places with a sanctimonious air about them. The *chanson* lives in neighborhood "music halls," as the French call them, or what we refer to, using a French term, as "vaudeville" houses. The *chanson* has nothing to do with farm life, either. Farm workers, unless they are itinerants who spend their winters in town, sing, when they sing at all, an older repertory, that which we denominate folklore. The *chanson* is a musical art form of the urban proletariat.

Its social origins and preoccupations are expressed not only in the words of the songs but also, in performance, by a vocal style opposed in method to that of the vocal studios. The latter consider high notes their greatest glory and make every effort, in training the voice, to spread the quality of these downward through the middle and chest ranges. The *chansonniers* use principally chest resonances, carrying these as high in the vocal range as possible and avoiding pure head tone as rigorously as singers of the official school avoid an unmixed chest tone. Head tone is used, if at all, for comic or character effects, to represent the voices of children, of the not very bright, and of the socially hoity-toity.

Miss Piaf represents the art of the *chansonnière* at its most classical. The vocalism is styled and powerful; her diction is clarity itself; her phrasing and gestures are of the simplest. Save for a slight tendency to overuse the full arm swing with index finger pointed, she has literally no personal mannerisms. She stands in the middle of a bare stage in the classic black dress of medium length, her hair dyed red and tousled, as is equally classical (Yvette Guilbert, Polaire, and Damia all wore it so), her feet planted about six inches apart; and she never moves, except for the arms. Even with these her gestures are sparing, and she uses them as much for abstractly rhetorical as for directly expressive purposes.

There is apparently not a nerve in her body. Neither is there any pretense of relaxation. She is not tense but intense, in no way spontaneous, just thoroughly concentrated and impersonal. Her power of dramatic projection is tremendous. She is a great technician because her methods are of the simplest. She is a great artist because she gives you a clear vision of the scene or subject she is depicting with a minimum injection of personality. Such a concentration at once of professional authority and of personal modesty is no end impressive.

If Miss Piaf had not impressed me so deeply with the authenticity of her repertory and her convictions about its rendering, I should have used my column today for praising Les Compagnons de la Chanson, a male chorus of nine singers who precede her on the program. They sing folksongs to the accompaniment of athletic pantomime with a perfection of drill, vocal and muscular, that is both side-splitting and utterly charming. If anybody wants to find a political reference in their song about a bear that terrified the village but became, when legally elected, as good a mayor as his predecessor, I pressume such an interpretation could be discovered without too much effort, since otherwise the number has little point. Their imitation of an American radio quartet accompanied by a swing band, however, needs no further point than its excellent satire. Their work in every number is funny and unusually imaginative. "La Môme," or "Pal" Piaf, to translate her cognomen, may be strong meat, artistically speaking, for American theater audiences, but Les Compagnons are more the sort of act we can take without any effort at all.

CONTEMPORARIES—COMPOSERS

Whereas some professional artists refuse to talk publicly about their contemporaries, Thomson in his prime was not so self-consciously insecure. He wrote often and well about people roughly his age, some of whom he knew well, socially as well as professionally.

Gershwin, Cole Porter, and [Jerome] Kern are America's Big Three in the light musical theater. Their qualities are evident and untroubling. Mr Gershwin has, however, for some time been leading a double musical life. This is the story of his adventures among the highbrows.

His efforts in the symphonic field cover a period of about twelve years and include, so far as I am acquainted with them:

A Rhapsody in Blue, for piano and orchestra
Harlem Night, a ballet
Two concertos for piano and orchestra
An American in Paris, symphonic poem

to which has now been added an opera on a tragicomic subject, *Porgy and Bess*.

The *Rhapsody in Blue*, written about 1923 or 1924, was the first of these and is the most successful from every point of view. It is the most successful orchestral piece ever launched by any American composer. It is by now standard orchestral repertory all over the world, just like Rimsky-Korsakov's *Scheherazade* and Ravel's *Bolero*.

I am not acquainted with *Harlem Night* or the second *Piano Concerto*. I am not even certain that a second one exists, although I have been told so. I can only speak, therefore, of the *Concerto in F* and of *An American in Paris*. Both of these show a rather lesser mastery of their materials than the *Rhapsody* does. They have not, however, altered Mr. Gershwin's prestige. He has remained through everything America's official White Hope, and he has continued to be admired in music circles both for his real talent and for his obviously well-meant efforts at mastery of the larger forms. Talent, in fact, is rather easier to admire when the intentions of a composer are more noble than his execution is competent.

Just why the execution is not so competent as in the *Rhapsody* is not clear to me. I used to think that perhaps he was cultivating a certain amateurishness because he had been promised that if he was a good little boy and didn't upset any apple carts he might maybe when he grew up be president of American music, just like Daniel Gregory Mason or somebody. Either that, or else that the air of timid and respectable charm which those pieces play up was simply a blind to cover a period of apprenticeship and that one day he would burst out with some more pieces like the *Rhapsody in Blue*, grander. It seemed that such a gift as his, with ten years of symphonic experience, couldn't but turn out eventually something pretty powerful.

It has now turned out *Porgy and Bess*. When a man of Gershwin's gift, experience, and earning capacity devotes in his middle or late thirties three years of his expensive time to the composition of a continuous theatrical work on a serious subject, there is no reason to suppose that it represents anything but his mature musical thought and his musical powers at near their peak. The music, however, is not very different from his previous output of serious intent, except insofar as staging helps cover up the lack of musical construction. Hence it is no longer possible to take very seriously any alibi for his earlier works.

The *Rhapsody in Blue* remains a quite satisfactory piece. Rhapsodies, however, are not very difficult to write, if one can think up enough tunes. The efforts at a more sustained symphonic development, which the later pieces represent, appear now to be just as tenuous as they have always sounded. One can see through *Porgy* that Gershwin has not and never did have the power of sustained musical development. His invention is abundant, his melodic quality high, although it is inextricably involved with an oversophisticated commercial background.

That background is commonly known as Tin Pan Alley. By oversophisticated I mean that the harmonic and orchestral ingenuity of Tin Pan Alley, its knowledge of the arts of presentation, is developed out of all proportion to what is justified by the expressive possibilities of its musical material. That material is straight from the melting pot. At best it is a piquant but highly unsavory stirring-up-together of Israel, Africa, and the Gaelic Isles. In Gershwin's music the predominance of charm in presentation over expressive substance makes the result always a sort of *vers de société*, or *musique de salon*; and his lack of understanding of all the major problems of form, of continuity, and of straightforward musical expression, is not surprising in view of the impurity of his musical sources and his frank acceptance of them.

Such frankness is admirable. At twenty-five it was also charming. *Gaminerie* of any kind at thirty-five is more difficult to like. So that quite often *Porgy and Bess*, instead of being pretty, is a little hoydenish, like a sort of *musique de la pas très bonne société*. Leaving aside the slips, even, and counting him at his best, that best which is equally well exemplified by *Lady, Be Good* or *I've Got Rhythm* or the opening of the *Rhapsody in Blue*, he is still not a very serious composer.

I do not wish to indicate that it is in any way reprehensible of him not to be a serious composer. I only want to define something that we have all been wondering about for some years. It was certain that he was a gifted composer, a charming composer, an exciting and sympathetic composer. His gift and his charm are greater than the gifts or the charms of almost any of the other American composers. And a great gift or great charm is an exciting thing. And a gifted and charming composer who sets himself seriously to learn his business is a sympathetic one. I think, however, it is clear by now that Gershwin hasn't learned his business. At least he hasn't learned the business of being a serious composer, which one has long gathered to be the business he wanted to learn.

Porgy is nonetheless an interesting example of what can be done by talent in spite of a bad setup. With a libretto that should never have been accepted on a subject that should never have been chosen, a man who should never have attempted it has written a work that has considerable power.

The more conventionally educated composers have been writing operas and getting them produced at the Metropolitan for twenty or thirty years. Some of them, Deems Taylor in particular, know quite well how to write in the larger formats. Year after year they write them, perfectly real operas on perfectly good subjects. And yet nothing ever happens in them. No significant musical misdemeanor ever seems to have been perpetrated. Gershwin does not even know what an opera is; and yet *Porgy and Bess* is an opera, and it has power and vigor. Hence it is a more important event in America's artistic life than anything American the Met has ever done.

But before I finally get around to saying all the nice things I have to say about it, let me be a little more specific about its faults and get all the resentments off my chest. Because I do resent Gershwin's shortcomings. I don't mind his being a light composer, and I don't mind his trying to be a serious one. But I do mind his falling between two stools. I mind any major fault he commits, because he is to me an exciting and sympathetic composer.

First of all, the opera is vitiated from the beginning by a confusion as to how much fake it is desirable or even possible to get away with in a work of that weight. The play, for instance, and the libretto derived from it, are certainly not without a good part of hokum. That can be excused if necessary. *La Traviata* and *Tosca* are not free of hokum either. Hokum is just theatrical technic got a little out of hand, tear-jerking for its own sake, an error of proportion rather than a lack of sentiment. The artificiality of its folklore is graver. I must hasten to add that Mr. Gershwin is here a greater sinner than Mr. Heyward, because his work was executed later. Folklore subjects recounted by an outsider are only valid as long as the folk in question is unable to speak for itself, which is certainly not true of the American Negro in 1935.

Let me be clear about folk opera. *Lucia di Lammermoor* and *Madama Butterfly* are not Scottish or Japanese folk operas; they are simply Italian operas on exotic subjects. *Carmen* comes nearer because of its systematic use of Spanish popular musical styles. It is nonetheless a fake. Smetana's *Bartered Bride* is a folk opera and it is not a fake, because it is Bohemian music written by a Bohemian. It is not so fine a theater work as *Carmen*, but it is better folklore. Hall Johnson's music for *Green Pastures* and the last act of his *Run, Little Chillun* are real folklore and also folk opera of quite high quality. *Porgy and Bess*, on the other hand, has about the same relation to Negro life as it is really lived and sung as have *Swanee River* and *Mighty Lak' a Rose*.

The most authentic thing about it all is George Gershwin's sincere desire to write an opera, a real opera that somebody might remember. I rather fancy he has succeeded in that, which is pretty incredible of him too, seeing how little he knew of how to go about it. His efforts at recitativo are as ineffective as anything I have heard since Antheil's *Helen Retires*, where a not dissimilar effect was got by first translating the play into German, then composing music for the German text, and finally translating this back into English. The numbers which have rhymed or jingled lyrics are slick enough in the Gershwin Broadway manner. But his prose declamation is full of exaggerated leaps and unimportant accents. It is vocally uneasy and dramatically cumbersome. Whenever he has to get on with the play he uses spoken dialogue. It would have been better if he had stuck to that all the time.

As for the development, or musical build-up, there simply isn't any. When he gets hold of a good number he plugs it. The rest of the time he just makes up what music he needs as he goes along. Nothing of much interest, little exercises in the jazzo-modernistic style, quite pleasant for the most part but leading nowhere. The scoring is heavy, overrich, and ineffective. Throughout the opera there is, however, a constant stream of lyrical invention and a wealth of harmonic ingenuity.

There is little drama in the orchestra and little expression in the melodies, prettily Negroid though they be. The real drama of the piece is the spectacle of Gershwin wrestling with his medium, and the exciting thing is that after all those years the writing of music is still not a routine thing to him. Such freshness is the hallmark of *les grandes natures*. Every measure of music has to be wrought as a separate thing. The stream of music must be channelized, molded, twisted, formed, ornamented, all while it is pouring out molten hot from that volcano of musical activity, Mr. Gershwin's brain. Never is the flow inadequate. Never does his vigilance fail to leave its print on the shape of every detail. *Porgy* is falsely conceived and rather clumsily executed, but it is an important work because it is abundantly conceived and executed entirely by hand.

There are many things about it that are not to my personal taste. I don't like fake folklore, nor fidgety accompaniments, nor bittersweet harmony, nor six-part choruses, nor gefiltefish orchestration. I do, however, like being able to listen to a work for three hours and being fascinated at every moment. I also like its lack of respectability, the way it can be popular and vulgar and go its way as a professional piece without bothering about the taste-boys. I like to think of Gershwin as having presented his astonished public with a real live baby, all warm and dripping and friendly.

In a way, he has justified himself as a White Hope. He has written a work that can be performed quite a number of times, that can be listened to with pleasure by quite different kinds of people, and that can be remembered by many. If its eminence, as Shaw once said of John Stuart Mill, is due largely to the flatness of the surrounding country, that eminence is nonetheless real.

[CHARLIE] CHAPLIN SCORES (1940)

Before saying what I have on my mind about Mr. Chaplin as a musical engineer, I should like, with all apologies to persons more skilled than I in judging films as literary and pictorial art, to register one vote of approval for *The Great Dictator*. It seemed to my lay eye and taste as nearly perfect a creation as I have ever witnessed in that medium, up to the point, six minutes from the end, where Mr. Chaplin steps out of character, comes right down to the foot-lights, so to speak, and makes a recruiting speech for the British army. I think that if the film were cut short at that point, the rest would turn out to be a sort of truncated masterpiece like the Venus de Milo.

As we know, Mr. Chaplin, though no musician, plans his own musical scores, working through a trained composer of course. In this case, the musical direction is credited to Meredith Willson. It is to be presumed that the opening fanfares and such occasional bits as occur throughout the film that are not recognizably quotations are of his composition. They are not very good; they are musically uninteresting.

What is good and extremely interesting is Mr. Chaplin's way of using music in films. This concept has been clear since his first sound film, *City Lights*. His way of integrating music with animated photography is to admit auditive elements to the rank of co-star with the poetic and visual elements in the final unified effect.

He does not try to use music as mere accompaniment, as neutral background. He knows that a well-cut film can get along without that. Nor does he try to drag in tonal appeal by making one of his characters a music student who can go into a song if necessary. Unless he can coordinate music with the action in such a way that the two play a duet, each commenting upon and heightening the other, he leaves it out altogether. For the same reason, he has hitherto omitted the speaking voice from his own characterizations, because there was no need of it. It would have introduced a jarring naturalistic element into his far from naturalistic acting-style.

The Mayor's wordless speech, sounded on a trombone, in *City Lights*, is one of Chaplin's procedures. The dictator's speeches in semi-nonsense German are the same trick done with his own voice. His bubble dance (to the *Lohengrin Prelude*) and the shaving scene (to a Brahms *Hungarian Dance*) are a different form of musical integration. The first procedure is a substitution of stylized sound for naturalistic speech. (Note then when he is acting naturalistically he speaks naturalistically.) The second procedure is not a substitution; it is an adding of stylized sound to stylized movement without speech, to pantomime. He has here introduced the straight music-hall turn he was brought up to, as artificial a thing as the classical ballet, into movies, the most naturalistic form of theatre that has ever existed. The result is artistically successful.

Mr. Chaplin has not made a complete musical film. He has made a silent film with interpolated musical numbers. But he has obviously reflected about the auditive problem, and so far as he uses music at all, his use of it is unfailingly advantageous. He uses all the auditive effects correctly. He employs very little naturalistic noise, for instance. He takes as his basic esthetic principle the fact that movies are pantomime. Anything expressible by pantomime is not expressed otherwise. He introduces speech, music and sound-effects only when they are needed to do something pantomime can't do. There is a little bombing in the war scenes, a strict minimum. When he belches after having swallowed three coins, he lets the coins jingle. But nowhere does he overlay the film with speech that says nothing, with music that just accompanies, with noises that merely express hubbub.

This is the proper way to integrate auditive elements into any visual spectacle, not to use them at all unless you can use them to heighten the visual effect directly. The Hollywood idea of using background music for its emotional value without anybody ever noticing it is there is nonsense. Because music has to be either neutral or expressive. If it is neutral it has no expressive value. If it is expressive (in the same way and at the same time as the incidents of the photographic narrative; that is to say, accurately expressive), then it is not neutral. It is very noticeable indeed and must be well written and correctly integrated with the action.

Nobody knows how to write neutral music nowadays anyway, as I have explained elsewhere. Bromides are all that ever result from that effort. And bromides solve no esthetic difficulty. They merely obfuscate expression.

There are others in the world beside Chaplin who have sound instincts about musical usage with films. The wailing Russian locomotive at the end of *The Road to Life* was a case of what music and sound-effects can do together. René Clair too has often used music and sound to advantage as a substitute for complete visual depiction. Chaplin has not included in *The Great Dictator* every device known to film art of incorporated auditive effect. That was not his aim. But in no other film that I have seen are speech and music and sound incorporated into a photographed pantomimic narrative with such unvarying and deadly accuracy, nor omitted from the spectacle so rigorously when no way seems to present itself for using them to advantage.

STAR DUST AND SPUN STEEL [ANTON WEBERN] (1950)

Anton Webern's *Symphony for Chamber Orchestra*, the novelty of last night's Philharmonic concert in Carnegie Hall, was "advanced" music when first played here twenty years ago; and it still is. For all the worldwide spread of the twelve-tone technique that has taken place since then, it would be hard to find today five living adepts of it whose writing is so firm and so sophisticated as Webern's was. The audience effect of this work attested also to its vitality. Not only were repeated bows taken by Dimitri Mitropoulos, there was actually booing in the hall, a phenomenon almost unknown at the Philharmonic.

The piece itself offends, as it delights, by its delicacy, transparency, and concentration. The first movement, for all its canonic rigor, is something of an ultimate in pulverization—star dust at the service of sentiment. Each instrument plays just one note, at most two; then another carries on the theme. The theme itself is a row of tones isolated from one another by scale skips. The texture is thin, too. One note at a time, just occasionally two or three, is the rule of its instrumental utterance. And yet the piece has a melodic and an expressive consistency. It is clearly about something and under no temptation to fidget. Its form, I may add, is roughly that of a binary, or Scarlatti-type sonata; and its rhythmic pulse, save for a few retards in the second movement, is steady.

This movement (there are only two) is a set of variations on the work's whole twelve-tone row, first stated completely at this point. Rhythm is broken up into asymmetrical fragments. The melodic pulverization is less fine, however, than that of the first movement. Occasionally an instrument will articulate as many as eight or ten notes at a stretch. Some of these are even repeated notes. Metrical fragmention has taken the place of melodic. The sonorous texture becomes even thinner at the end than anything one has heard previously. A tiny sprinkle of sounds; two widely spaced ones on the harp; and vaporization is complete.

There is every reason to believe the Philharmonic's reading of this tiny but ever so tough work to have been correct. Musicians following the score could question only the size, here and there, of some minute crescendo. The rendering was clear, clean, tonally agreeable, and expressive. Expressive of exactly what, would be difficult to say, as it is of any work. Nevertheless, consistency and self-containment, ever the signs of expressive concentration, were present to the ear, just as they are to the eye reading the score. Once again there was cause to be grateful to Mr. Mitropoulos for his assiduity toward neglected distinction and for his enormous loyalty to the text of a work rare, complex, and in every way difficult.

MOST MELODIOUS TEARS [KURT WEILL] (1933)

Kurt Weill is a new model of German composer. There is no flavor of scholasticism or officialdom about him. His training, or at least his early experience, is that of a writer of sad popular songs, mostly about whores and gangsters, the kind of thing that the French call *chansons réalistes*. The *Dreigroschenoper* is full of these, the most current one in Paris nightclub repertory being *La Fianeée du Pirale*.

The elaboration of such matter into dramatic pieces of some pretension has been aided by two perfect collaborators, a poet named Bert Brecht, his librettist, and his wife Lotte Lenya, a singer, or rather a diseuse of most extraordinary personality. The formula for these works is always the same. There is a story about simple, very simple people. There are songs for the chief actors, choral passages of dramatic or moral comment and a few instrumental passages. There are also costumes and a kind of elementary mise-en-scène. They are little morality-plays.

The accompaniments are meant to imitate a not-too-competent jazz-band. They are well-scored. The songs have a perfection of prosody that is unequaled by any European composer. Without degenerating into mere sprechstimme, keeping at all times the formal contour of a popular song, there is a union of words and tune that, once made, is indissoluble. No one who has heard *Mahagonny* can recall either element of *O Moon of Alabama* without recalling something of the other. The choral parts are less striking in that work, but the children's chorus *Er hat Ja Gesagt* from *Der Jasager* is memorable. Madame Lenya has a tiny voice, seemingly untrained, with no resonance, no placing, and no power. She sings or rather croons, with an impeccable diction that reaches to the farthest corner of any hall and with an intensity of dramatization and a sincerity of will that are very moving. She is, moreover, beautiful in a new way, a way that nobody has vulgarized so far, and her simple costumes are admirable. It will not be long, I imagine, before some moviegang gets hold of her and stuffs her down our throats like Garbo.

The program of the Sérénade concert in London, while neglecting to print the names of the interpreters, went to the trouble of explaining to the supposedly ignorant English that the music of Kurt Weill had "something of Mozart and the better moments of Cole Porter." This means nothing of course. It is just a citing of impressive names to warn the listener that he is about to be impressed by Exhibit A. He usually is and sometimes gets mad. The music has a heaviness that is not far from real power and a melodic line that, seemingly cheap and tawdry, doesn't let itself be easily forgotten. Most of all, in the subject matter of the poetry, in the lay of the tunes, in the monotony of the accompaniments, is an authentic flavor of the ghetto which is recognizable by anybody as a thing depicted and which is completely touching to anyone who has ever had any real contact with the ghetto.

Kurt Weill has done for Berlin what Charpentier did for Paris. He has dramatized its midinettes and their family life. He has thrown a certain aspect of it sharply against the sky. He has touched hearts. He has almost created style. One can be indifferent to the subject-matter. One cannot say that the work is non-existent or entirely low. Its authenticity, plus the fact that it is all very easy to understand, is why it is so eagerly received by the Paris fashionables ever alert for a new kind of gutter.

There is no use pretending that it is profoundly new or in any way recondite. Weill's work is far more commonplace than Satie's, but his esthetic is the esthetic of *Mercure*. Such a homage, and from Germany of all places, is of course irresistible to the French.

The stories of his little cantatas are very moral. The *Yes-Sayer* is a little boy whose mother is about to die for lack of certain medicines. When the doctor asks for volunteers to cross a dangerous mountain pass in the snow and get the medicine, the little boy says yes; and later when he gets sick and risks causing the loss of the entire expedition by having to be carried, he again does his duty by jumping over a cliff.

Les Sept Péchés Capitaux (in English, *Anna-Anna*) is about a young girl who leaves home to make money for her aging parents. She has two spirits in her, one lazy and easy-going, the other devoted to the job she has to do, which is building a little house in Louisiana by the Mississippi fluss for said parents. Naturally, the more dutiful spirit manages to egg her on through everything and get money sent home periodically as she commits with profit most of the allegedly deadly sins. Gluttony only is denied her, as I remember, because it spoils her figure; and true-lust is discouraged because an *amant de coeur* costs money. The little house in one front corner of the stage gets bigger with each check, and the male quartet that represents the family ceases eventually to complain about her laziness and appears finally before the completed cottage dressed as Southern mammies to welcome home the tired but noble prostitute. This was presented at the Ballets 1933, Lotte Lenya singing the part of the family spirit in Anna and Tilly Losch dancing the adventures of the real one. The spectacle is heavy and monotonous. The relentless length to which that poor girl is dragged through sin after sin is, well the best one can say is that it is very German. The piece has some style, just the same. The accompaniment is not uninteresting, in spite of its weight. The purely instrumental portions, as is often true of a composer with a good gift for vocal writing, are less interesting.

Mahagonny is pathos about the street-life of pre-Hitler Berlin, the Berlin of night-clubs, of low bars, of universal destitution, of universal prostitution. Fragile and underfed youth with no mother to guide it imagines, from having heard it sung about, that somewhere in Alabama is a *pays de cockaigne* called *Mahagonny* where everything is jake, so to speak. They all go looking for it. The little girl describes her life and how she learned very early to ask gentlemen, "Wünschen Sie mich mit Wäsche oder ohne Wäsche?" But even in Alabama they find no promised land. There is a very pretty song in English to these words:

"O moon of Alabama
I now must say goodby,

There is no dear old mama
And I know the reason why."

It is all very unsuitable to the taste of these urchins. "Here is no whiskey-bar, goddam. Here is no telephone." "I must get whiskey, must get whiskey or I die," sings Lenya.

This is tender and touching and fortunately Lotte Lenya did her own miming at the Sérénade, so that we were spared the contortions of Tilly Losch, who beside Lenya's sweet voice and fragile beauty is everything one can imagine of competent vulgarity. *Mahagonny* is fresher than *Anna-Anna*. The music more inspired or at least more trouvé, the whole less made-to-order.

A great deal of the press was taken in by the apparent cynicism of Anna and mistook the poem for a sort of communism-to-amuse-the-rich. This is quite wrong. It is a story of filial devotion like *Der Jasager*. The music has all the weight and authority of a sermon. There is nowhere any flippancy or trifling. It is just plain sad all the way through. So is *Mahagonny*.

Weill is not a Great Composer any more than Charpentier is. He has a warm heart and a first-class prosodic gift. The rest is moving enough, perhaps too moving. It smells of Hollywood. It is hokum like *Louise*, sincere hokum. If it really touches you, you go all to pieces inside. If not, it is still something anyway, though not so much.

The line between hokum and real stuff is far from sharp. Many a serious career has been made in the no man's land that lies between the two, provided there was talent and a sincere passion about something or other, like Byron with his loves or Toulouse-Lautrec and his night-life. Let him who has never wept at the movies throw the first stone at Weill's tearful but elegant ditties about the Berlin ghetto.

OLIVIER MESSIAEN (1945)

"Atomic bomb of contemporary music" is the current epithet for Olivier Messiaen. Whether France's thirty-seven-year-old boy wonder is capable of quite so vast a work of destruction as that unhappy engine I could not say. But certainly he has made a big noise in the world. And the particular kind of noise that his music makes does, I must say, makes that of his chief contemporaries sound a bit old-fashioned.

What strikes one right off on hearing almost any of his pieces is the power these have of commanding attention. They do not sound familiar; their textures—rhythmic, harmonic, and instrumental—are fresh and strong. And though a certain melodic banality may put one off no less than the pretentious mysticism of his titles may offend, it is not possible to come in contact with any of his major productions without being aware that one is in the presence of a major musical talent. Liking it or not is of no matter; Messiaen's music has a vibrancy that anybody can be aware of, that the French music world is completely aware of, that has been accepted in France, indeed, for the postwar period as one of the facts of life.

Messiaen's pieces are mostly quite long; and their textures, rhythmic and harmonic, are complex. In spite of their length and their complexity, their sounds are perfectly clear. They are nowhere muddy in color but always sonorous. Their shining brightness takes one back to Berlioz. So also does their subject matter. "Dance of Fury for the Seven Trumpets," "The Rainbow of Innocence," "Angel with Perfumes," "The Crystal Liturgy," "Subtlety of the Body in Glory," "Strength and Agility of the Body in Glory," "God with Us," and "Vocal Exercise for the Angel Who Announces the End of Time" are some of the simpler subtitles. And the renderings of these are no less picturesque than Berlioz's description of doomsday (in the Dies Iræ of his *Requiem Mass*) for chorus and full orchestra plus twenty-eight trumpets and trombones and fourteen kettledrums.

Messiaen is a full-fledged romantic. Form is nothing to him, content everything. And the kind of content that he likes is the convulsive, the ecstatic, the cataclysmic, the terrifying, the unreal. That the imagery of this should be derived almost exclusively from religion is not surprising in a church organist and the son of a mystical poetess, Cécile Sauvage. What is a little surprising in so scholarly a modernist (he is organist at the cultivated parish of La Trinité and a professor of harmony at the Paris Conservatory) is the literalness of his religious imagination. But there is no possibility of suspecting insincerity. His pictorial concept of religion, though a rare one among educated men, is too intense to be anything but real. Messiaen is simply a theologian with a taste for the theatrical. And he dramatizes theological events with all the *sang-froid* of a man who is completely at home in the backstage of religious establishments.

The elaborateness of Messiaen's procedures is exposed in detail in a two-volume treatise by him called *The Technique of My Musical Language*, (*Technique de mon language musical*; Alphonse Leduc, Paris, 1944). The rhythmic devices employed, many of them derived from Hindu practice, are most sophisticated. The harmonic language is massively dissonant but not especially novel. It resembles rather the piling of Ossa on Pelion that formerly characterized the work of Florent Schmitt. There are layer cakes of rhythms and of harmonies but there is little linear counterpoint. The instrumentation is admirably designed to contrast these simultaneities and to pick them out. Derived from organ registration, it exploits the higher brilliancies (as of mixture stops) to great advantage. The weaker elements of Messiaen's style are his continuity, which, like that of many

159

another organist-composer, is improvisational rather than structural, and his melodic material, which is low in expressivity. The themes are lacking in the tensile strength necessary to sustain long developments because of his predilection for weak intervals, especially the major sixth and the augmented fourth, and for contradictory chromatics.

Among the works which one hopes will soon be heard in New York are *Forgotten Offerings* (*Les Offrandes oubliées*) for orchestra, by which Messiaen became known way back in 1935 as a major talent, and *The Nativity of Our Lord*, nine meditations for organ, published in 1936. These pieces have charm and youth in them and a striking virtuosity of texture. Among the more recent works of some length are *Seven Visions of the Amen*, for two pianos; *Twenty Admirations of the Infant Jesus* (unless I mistranslate *Vingt Regards sur l'enfant Jésus*), for solo piano; *Three Short Liturgies of the Divine Presence* (they last a good half-hour, all the same), for women's voices and orchestra; and a *Quartet for the End of Time*, which was composed during his German captivity.

The most satisfactory of these works to me is the two-piano work. The most impressive to the general public, however, is the orchestral one, which was first presented last April at a concert of *La Pléiade* in the Salle du Conservatoire. I have heard a recording of these liturgies, made from a subsequent broadcast under the direction of Roger Désormière; and though certainly they have a spasmodic flow (and no little monotony) they do make a wonderful noise.

The instrumentation, though top-heavy, is utterly glittering. It consists of vibraphone, celesta, maracas, gong, tamtam, nine sopranos singing in unison, piano, *les ondes Martenot* (a form of theremin), and strings. The three sections are entitled: "Antiphon of Interior Conversation (God present in us . . .)," "Sequence of The Word, Divine Canticle (God present in Himself . . .)," and "Psalm of the Ubiquity of Love (God present in all things . . .)." The text employed by the singers is of Messiaen's composition, as were also program notes printed on the occasion of the first performance. Of the "Antiphon" he writes:

> Dedicated to God present within us through Grace and the Holy Communion. After a most tender beginning ('My Jesus, My Silence, Abide with Me'), accompanied by the songs of distant birds (on the piano), there follows a contrapuntal middle section of great polyrhythmic and polymodal refinement. ('The Yes which sings like an echo of light.' 'Red and lavender melody in praise of The Father.' 'Your hand is out of the picture by one kiss.' 'Divine landscape, reverse your image in water.')

All these are clearly a believing organist's ideas. César Franck and Anton Bruckner, though neither had Messiaen's humor, worked from just such preoccupations. I once described this religio-musical style as the determination to produce somewhere in every piece an apotheosis destined at once to open up the heavens and to bring down the house. Certainly the latter action is easier to accomplish in modern life than the first. And certainly Messiaen has accomplished it several times in the *Liturgies*. The success of his accomplishment is due to a natural instinct for making music plus the simplicity and sincerity of his feelings. These are expressed, moreover, through a musical technique of great complexity and considerable originality. The faults of his taste are obvious; and the traps of mystical program music, though less so, are well known to musicians, possibly even to himself. Nevertheless the man is a great composer. One has only to hear his music beside that of any of the standard eclectic modernists to know that. Because his really vibrates and theirs doesn't.

MUSIC NOW (1961)

This essay began as a speech delivered at the American Academy of Arts and Letters, a self-perpetuating club located in upper-upper Manhattan. When Thomson addressed equally prominent colleagues in literature and visual art, rather than writing for a disinterested audience or an authoritarian editor, he produced some of his strongest late-career critical writing: not only the following essay and the memoir about music reviewing reprinted in the autobiographical section of this book, but his short appreciations of Leonid and Eugene Berman, Edgard Varèse, and the third of his four essays on Aaron Copland. Curiously, none of these AAAL texts have been reprinted before.

A report on the state of music today will have to begin with some recall of its state in other modern times.

Back in 1914, on the verge of World War I, musical modernism was already mature and successful. The works of Debussy, Ravel, Schoenberg, and Stravinsky had thrown sharp profiles against the sky; and these were clearly not nineteenth-century profiles. Nor was the sky a nineteenth-century sky. The Wagnerian storms were over and the rainbows of Valhalla washed white. It was clear and ready for anything, with just enough windiness around to carry forward the fires of revolution.

For the advanced composers of the time did appear in those days, both to the radical-minded younger musicians and to the conservative older ones, as leading a revolution. And the revolution they were leading, as most revolutions do, had provoked a war. If today the war about modern music is no longer a cause, that is because, like all wars between generations, it has been won through the mere survival of the younger side. We all take the twentieth century for natural, simply because most of the people now active either as creators or as consumers were born and brought up in it.

After World War I it had already come about that the musical climate was one of successful, or achieved, revolution. The bases of a new musical expression and of a slightly fresh way of dealing with musical sound, had all been laid down by our great leaders. The next generation were merely sons of the revolution. And though innovation was still being admired, as a matter of modernistic principle, the main musical activity between the two World Wars was what Gertrude Stein, in her 1926 Oxford lecture, called "equilibration and distribution." Distribution we shall be speaking more about later, because after World War II it becomes really massive.

Contemporary music between the two World Wars did not, however, in spite of its faithfulness to a revolutionary past, obey any unified command. Modernism in one form or another was the order of the day; but its practice was sectarian and the members of different schools did not fraternize easily. Igor Stravinsky and Arnold Schoenberg, for instance, though both resident in Los Angeles during the late 1930s, never met, even in battle, and never felt the need, for all the world-wide leadership they both exercised, of anything resembling a summit conference. The Russian impresario Diaghilev and the Austrian Reinhardt did, it now appears, have a cartel agreement by which Reinhardt's productions were not shown in western Europe and the Russian Ballet refrained from invading the central regions.

On the verge of World War II, in 1939, let us say, there were about five separate kinds of contemporary music available, all of them reputable, all skillfully practiced, and most of them with a history of at least two decades of public acceptance. Composers representing the five kinds could be viewed as occupying a fanshaped enclosure rather like the French Chamber of Deputies, where those who favor change sit on the left and the defenders of privilege on the right.

On music's right, twenty years ago, sat the survivors of Late Romanticism. These included Richard Strauss, Sergei Rachmaninoff, and Ernst von Dohnányi, all still writing music, and Jan Sibelius, still an impressive figure, though he had ceased to compose about 1926.

Next to them on the left, though still to right of center, sat the eclectical modernists, composers like Hans Pfitzner in Germany and certain young Americans of the time whose work was animated by some delight in dissonance and some brash sound, but of which the nineteenth-century allegiance was betrayed by its basic structure, all built of sequences and working toward climaxes.

The central section, and by far the largest, was occupied by composers whom one may call either neoclassical writers or Impressionists, since they worked both veins. This large and powerful group still exists; and it still operates, as it did then, under the intellectual hegemony of Igor Stravinsky, Darius Milhaud, and Paul Hindemith. They occupied, and still occupy, virtually all the seats of power; and they distribute the patronage. For several decades now they have headed just about every conservatory in the world, every college music department, every musical magazine of distinction. They have conducted the symphony orchestras, run the publishing houses, written the musical criticism, distributed the prizes, the travelling fellowships, the commissions and the cash awards. In Europe they administer the radio too. In America they advise the foundations.

The reason why our century's neoclassic composers are the same men as the musical landscapists is that they do not essay to emulate history, like Brahms (who was called a neoclassic in his time), but rather to evoke it, as if history itself were a series of picturesque landscapes, like Scotland or Ceylon. Their relation to music's past, even among our most academical types, is a product of modern historical awareness and the modern style-sense. They adapt to present-day service details from older times very much as our parents turned square pianos into writing desks or—as I once saw back in the 1920s—used a mediaeval chalice for an ash tray.

A smallish branch of the neoclassical and Impressionist group is sometimes called, or used to be, neo-Romantic, though the term is embarrassing because of its earlier association with such heirs of real Romanticism as Sibelius and Rachmaninoff. I mention this group because I am one of its founding fathers, along with Henri Sauguet. We seem to have started it in Paris about 1926. The idea for it, like many of our ideas, probably came out of Erik Satie. Our parallel workers in painting (and our close companions) were Pavel Tchelitcheff, Christian Bérard, Eugene and Leonid Berman. What we had in common was a respect for the integrity of our own and of one another's personal sentiments.

Now most of the century's earlier artists—Debussy and Ravel, for instance—had viewed with disfavor the use of poetry, music, or painting to express personal sentiments. Even today Picasso, Stravinsky, Hindemith, and T. S. Eliot are not likely to allow themselves any such indulgence. Nevertheless, a century before, personal sentiments had furnished some of poetry's and of music's best material—as in Schubert and Schumann and Chopin, for instance, or in Blake and Byron. It was our scandal, in an objective time, to have reopened the old Romantic vein and to have restored, in so far as our work was successful at all, private feelings to their former place among the legitimate themes of art.

This curious move on our part, which many observers mistook for reactionary, actually brought us over to the very left-most position possible within the middle party of contemporary music. That was a position contiguous through its choice of subject-matter to that of the chromatic and atonal world, which occupied the terrain just to the left of our central grouping.

The chief subject-matter of these last composers had long been abnormal psychology and their method of treatment something one might call emotional micro-analysis. Schoenberg's cantata *Pierrot Lunaire* and Alban Berg's opera *Wozzeck* are characteristic and fine examples of chromatico-atonal music from our century's first quarter. The one contact between their studied luridness and our spontaneous lyricism was the fact that both described interior rather than exterior realities. Our methods of composition and our climate of feeling were as different as Paris can be from Vienna. Nevertheless, we did together open up the hard flank of Impressionist and neoclassical objectivity and thus rendered possible, I think, the transfusions and the graftings that have made blood-brothers today out of all composers.

My fifth and farthest-left grouping of pre-War days we might call the rhythmic research fellows. Henry Cowell and Edgard Varèse were its leaders. The movement was small but outspoken. Nowadays this group is quite large and includes within its wide arms not only the percussion writers and the specialists of pure noise-composition but the tape-tamperers too, those who construct music directly on magnetic ribbon without the intervention of hand-played instruments. Also, their use of arithmetical structures, which are about the only structures available to nontonal music, has been picked up by the chromatic composers, especially by those accustomed to employing tone-rows in fixed numerical series.

Today the fences between our five stylistic groupings are all broken down, and desegregation is general. The Late Romantics have all died. The eclectical Romantics, with no conservative support left them, have moved into the neoclassical and neo-Romantic neighborhoods. And these neighborhoods are in constant flirtation with both the chromatic composers of the former middle-left and with the arithmetical constructors from music's engineering or factory suburbs. The result is a melting pot, where everybody practices at least a little bit all the techniques and where everybody's music begins to sound more and more alike.

Such a consolidation seems on the whole desirable both for music and for its business. For its business it provides a standard product to meet the demands of massive international distribution. With thousands of symphony orchestras in the world, millions of radio listeners, millions of gramophone recordings sold, and every government exporting music to every other as a form of political propaganda, some standardization both of the product and of the consumer has been inevitable. From an artistic point of view the standardization has some virtue too. It may well be that our century's styles and devices are coming to be amalgamated into a classical style, or universal idiom, that will serve the masters of our century's last decades for the creation of master works.

Such a consummation, I hope, is not far off; but I do not think it is complete just yet. Most of the music written since World War II has been, on the whole, over-chromatic tonally and over-elaborate rhythmically. As a result, it has tended toward obscurity, toward poverty of expression rather than toward wealth and variety. In a time of fears and conformities, of cold wars and urgent concealments, the composers of Europe and America who consider themselves leaders seem to have ambushed themselves against all possible interrogation, and behind a thick wall of complexity to be hopefully hiding their hearts from the common view.

We all speak a common idiom nowadays, but one not perfected yet for full communication. It may be that the stabilization of our vocabulary will come through opera. Certainly the Western composers are making a massive assault on this ever-so-resistant fortress. The fortress is resistant because nineteenth-century opera, which is still our basic repertory, had got its stories and its music so admirably fitted together that they cannot now be torn apart. A nineteenth-century type of play just will not work with twentieth-century music, and a really twentieth-century play, if there is such a thing, seems to need less musical complexity than any opera house is accustomed to furnish to its patrons; or at least it requires a different kind of sensitivity from that for which the standard repertory-house routines have been designed.

In general, most modern operas have too many notes in them; their music tends to crush both words and meaning. Nevertheless, the opera is the place where modern music will have to be made to work. Complexities and other games played for their own sake can be entertaining in the concert hall, even quite impressive. But in the theatre everything must serve. Today our century's own proud and raucous musical idiom may be preparing itself to serve, and thus to conquer, the opera. But I do not know a composer living, not an old one or a young one, who has yet made more than just a tiny dent on the masonry of that moated monument.

Our composers are a united front for action, and the distribution of their works is global business. But I wish they were better prepared for global distribution. Maybe in ten years they will be speaking more clearly, saying more things. Just now I cannot help feeling that they are being at once garrulous and secretive. Also that there is far too much music in the world.

I do not feel this because I get tired of musical sound itself. Musical sounds are always a pleasure. It is unmusical sounds masquerading as musical ones that wear you down, and the commercializing of musical distribution has given us a great many of these as a cross to bear. It has also given such currency to our classics that even these the mind grows weary of. Because though musical sound is ever a delight, musical meaning, like any other meaning, grows stale from being repeated. Perhaps that is why so many of our contemporary composers feel safer hiding it.

After all, most of the arts today, save possibly history and reporting, reflect a manneristic epoch. Music is merely the latest to assume the mask. When one remembers the high and hilarious hermetisms that both poetry and painting have enjoyed in our century, one need not be surprised that music, in its own slow time and for its own quite private reasons, should at last have got into the game.

EDGARD VARÈSE, 1883-1965 (1966)

Edgard Varèse was born in 1883, not in 1885, as had been believed till the time of his death. He was part Franco-Italian and part Burgundian, part engineer and part musician (a pupil of the École Polytechnique as well as of both the Schola Cantorum and the Paris Conservatoire), a conductor both of modern orchestral repertory and of Renaissance choral music, a friend of Debussy and of Busoni, and a composer the most modern of them all. A broadly-based European (ten years resident in Italy, fifteen in France, seven in Berlin, those last brilliant years before World War I), he took to America so completely in his thirty-third year that all his preserved music is American work.

Debussy's assumption that chords do not move, Busoni's advice that there was more future outside of classical harmony than within the thorough-bass convention, and America's freedom of artistic expansion (unique in 1916) made him the leader of our musical advance—and indeed of the world advance—a position which he held unchallenged during the time of his major production as a composer, or about fifteen years. During five of his last twelve years, beginning at seventy, he composed again, this time with electronic materials. And again he was the farthest out among the far-outs, partly because he had a first-class ear for sound and partly because he had long since by-passed, way back in his Berlin days, the attempt to make non-tonal music out of only tonal instruments and materials, an effort that later came to represent for him a doctrinaire, or establishment-type, modernism.

Varèse's own music, for all its awareness of acoustical theory and of sound-source technology, remains highly resistant to analysis. This fact represents no small achievement, as indeed it does also in the case of Europe's older masters from Mozart through Debussy. For the explainable loses interest. And Varèse's music, over a nigh on to fifty-year period, has not lost its interest. It is still exciting, sometimes shocking, often vastly beautiful as sound, and always the work of genius—in other words, of imagination and brains. Aspects of it are surely arcane, the result of unstated but systematic calculations; others are just as certainly irrational, spontaneous, and inspired; and the whole of it has long seemed to me, by exactly these qualities plus that of never showing fatigue, great music.

Melody, harmony, and form, in the classical sense, it seems to have shaken off completely in spite of its author's classical education. From *Amériques* of 1919 to the *Poème électronique* of 1957 he worked with timbre alone, with kinds of sound, chunks of it, organized these into a polyphony comparable perhaps to the intersecting polyhedrons that are the shapes of modern architecture. Nevertheless, these pieces are not static like a building, nor even like the music of Debussy; they move forward, aerodynamic, airborne. What moves them forward? Rhythms, I think, rhythms counterpointed to create tension and release energy. There are also in the timbre contrasts and loudness patterns designs for producing anxiety and relief, just as there are in tonal music. And these designs create psychological form, though the music is not overtly planned for drama.

It seems to hang together not from themes and their restatements but from tiny cells or motives which agglomerate like crystals. As Varèse himself described this phenomenon, "In spite of their limited variety of internal structure, the external forms of crystals are almost limitless." To have produced with so cool a concept of artistic creation music of such warm sonorous interest and such urgent continuity makes of Varèse, and I think there is no way round this, the most original composer of the last half century and one of the most powerfully communicative.

HENRY COWELL: BY WEIGHT AND BY VOLUME (N.D.)

Henry Cowell's music covers a wider range in both expression and technique than that of any other living composer. His experiments begun three decades ago in rhythm, in harmony, and in instrumental sonorities were considered then by many to be wild. Today they are the Bible of the young and still, to the conservatives, "advanced." His vast repertory, on the other hand, of choral music for school use and of band music is a model of technical and of expressive accessibility. Between these extremes lie eleven symphonies and many other works at once humane of content and original in style. No other composer of our time has produced a body of works so radical and so normal, so penetrating and so comprehensive. Add to this massive production his long and influential career as a pedagogue, and Henry Cowell's achievement in music becomes impressive indeed. There is no other quite like it. To be both fecund and right is given to few.

AARON COPLAND

None of his colleagues preoccupied Thomson as much as Copland (1900–1990), his near-contemporary, with whom he had an intense relationship involving both admiration and envy, love and hate, respect and skepticism, that lasted their entire adult lives. (I remember seeing sparks flying between them as one gave the other an award at the annual ceremony of the American Academy of Arts and Letters sometime in the 1960s.) These four essays explicitly about Copland, published over nearly four decades, here collected together for the first time, document Thomson's changing opinions and sympathies.

I (1932)

Aaron Copland's music is American in rhythm, Jewish in melody, eclectic in all the rest.

The subject matter is limited but deeply felt. Its emotional origin is seldom gay, rarely amorous, almost invariably religious. Occasionally excitation of a purely nervous and cerebral kind is the origin of a scherzo. This tendency gave him a year or two of jazz-experiment. That has been his one wild oat. It was not a fertile one.

He liked the stridency of high saxophones, and his nerves were pleasantly violated by displaced accents. But he never understood that sensuality of sentiment which is the force of American popular music nor accepted the simple heartbeat that is the pulse of its rhythm, though it is the pulse of his own rhythm whenever his music is at ease.

His religious feeling is serious and sustained. He is a prophet calling out her sins to Israel. He is filled with the fear of God. His music is an evocation of the fury of God. His God is the god of battle, the Lord of Hosts, the jealous, the angry, the avenging god who rides upon the storm. Far from Copland's thoughts are the Lord as shepherd in green pastures, the Lord as patriarch, the God of Jacob, the bridegroom of the Shulamite, the lover, the father, the guide-philosopher-and-friend. The gentler movements of his music are more like an oriental contemplation of infinity than like any tender depiction of the gentler aspects of Jehovah.

Hence the absence of intimacy. And the tension. Because his music has tension. His brass plays high. His rhythm is strained. There is also weight; five trumpets and eight horns are his common orchestral practice. They give the tension and weight of battle. The screaming of piccolos and pianos evokes the glitter of armaments and swords. His instrumentation is designed to impress, to overpower, to terrify, not to sing. All this I write is overstated. But I put it down because it seems to me to provide as good an evocative scheme as any for fitting together various observations about the way his music is made.

I note the following:

His melodic material is of a markedly Hebrew cast. Its tendency to return on itself is penitential. It is predominantly minor. Its chromaticism is ornamental and expressive rather than modulatory. When he sings, it is as wailing before the Wall. More commonly his material is used as a framework for a purely coloristic compilation.

By coloristic I mean it is made out of harmonic and instrumental rather than melodic devices. This compilation is picturesque and cumulative. It tends to augment its excitement, to add to weight and tension. His dominant idea of form is crescendo. This is Russian, because it is a crescendo of excitement. Of development in the classic German sense, the free development of Haydn and Beethoven, there is none.

His conception of harmony is not form but texture. Hence the absence of marked tonal modulation. His conception of instrumentation is not variety but mass. He has no polyphonic conception at all, because he is alone in his music. His commonest contrapuntal device is a form of canon, usually at the octave or unison, everybody doing the same thing at a different moment. This is counter-point but not polyphony. He is not walking with God or talking with men or seducing housemaids or tickling duchesses. He is crying aloud to Israel. And very much as if no one could hear him.

The *Piano Variations* have not even this canonic counterpoint. They are a monody, one line repeated, not developed, lengthened out from time to time by oriental flourishes, accented and made sharp, orchestrated, as it were, by slightly dissonant octaves, by grace-notes and arpeggios.

I find the music of them very beautiful, only I wish he wouldn't play it so loud. One hears it better unforced. I miss in his playing of it the singing of a certain still, small voice that seems to me to be clearly implied on the written page.

I also note this:

There is a certain resemblance of procedure between Copland, Antheil, Varèse, Chávez. This in spite of antipodal differences in their personalities and sentiments. Their common homage to Stravinsky honors the White Russian master more than it profits them. It creates a false community and obliterates distinctions. It also smothers quality.

The quality that distinguishes American writing from all other is a very particular and special approach to rhythm. It is in these composers when they forget Stravinsky; it is in all American music whatever its school or origins. It is a quiet, vibratory shimmer, a play of light and movement over a well-felt but not expressed basic pulsation, as regular and as varied as a heartbeat, and as unconscious. It is lively but at ease, quiet, assured, lascivious.

Stravinsky knocked us all over when we first heard him, because he had invented a new rhythmic notation, and we all thought we could use it. We cannot. It is the notation of the jerks that muscles give to escape the grip of taut nerves. It has nothing to do with blood flow. It is spectacularly effective when used to express the movements it was invented to express. It is the contrary when imposed upon our radically different ones. How infinitely superior in simple effectiveness are our popular composers over our tonier ones. They have no technical drama of composition. They are at ease in their notation.

Our highbrow music, on the other hand, is notoriously ineffective. It is the bane of audiences at home and abroad, in spite of the very best will on everybody's part.

I deny that it is really as dull as it sounds. I think our gift, our especial gift, is the particular rhythmic feeling I have described. That is enough to make an epoch. It takes very little. The rest is framing. Our weakness is timidity, hence snobbishness and eclecticism.

Today we ape Stravinsky. Yesterday it was Debussy. Before, it was Wagner. Copland's best recommendation is that he is less eclectic than his confreres. I reproach him with eclecticism all the same.

There is real music in his pieces, true invention, and a high nobility of feeling. He is not banal. He has truth, force, and elegance. He has not quite style. There remain too many irrelevant memories of Nadia Boulanger's lessons, of the scores of Stravinsky and Mahler and perhaps Richard Strauss.

I wish they were plain thefts. Theft is refreshing and legitimate. Copland is like certain American poets (very distinguished ones; supply your own examples), who cannot quite forget their collegiate loyalty to Keats and Browning and who are more occupied with the continuation of some foreign tradition than with style, which is personal integrity.

This may explain a little why Aaron Copland is at the same time an inspired composer and only a comparatively effective one. Comparatively, because most American music is less effective in performance than his. In fact, his music is often so near to a real knockout that I am sometimes left wondering whether it is a case of a knockout not quite achieved or of an unwise application of the knockout technic to a case where persuasion were more to the point.

In any case, there is a problem of rhetoric for the American composer. The problem of adjusted emphasis, the appropriate stating and effective underlining of personal invention. This means selection and variety. Forcing every idea into the key of the grandiose and the sublime is obviously false and in the long run monotonous.

I fancy there is more of use to us in the example of Verdi than in that of Wagner, Puccini even than Hindemith, certainly Bizet than Debussy, Schubert than Brahms. Simple clarity is what we need, and we will get it only by a radical simplification of our methods of composition. If Copland's simplifications are perhaps not radical enough for my taste, they are important simplifications all the same.

Because he is good, terribly good. A European composer of his intrinsic quality would have today worldwide celebrity and influence. It is a source of continual annoyance to me that his usefulness and his beauty are not fully achieved because he has not yet done the merciless weeding out of his garden that any European composer would have done after his first orchestral hearing.

The music is all right, but the man is not clearly enough visible through it. An American certainly, a Hebrew certainly. But his more precise and personal outline is still blurred by the shadows of those who formed his youth.

II (1949)

Aaron Copland's musical accompaniments to a film called *The Red Pony* (by Milestone, out of Steinbeck) are the most elegant, in my opinion, yet composed and executed under "industry conditions," as Hollywood nowadays calls itself. Other films shown this winter have had ambitious scoring or talented sonorous detail, but those this writer has seen have not offered any consistently distinguished music. Mr. Copland himself, Hollywood's most accomplished composer, has not in his earlier films—*Of Mice and Men, The North Star*, and *Our Town*—produced for cinematic drama a musical background so neatly cut and fitted.

It is the perfection of the musical tailoring in this picture that has made clear to me in a way I had not understood before just where the artistic error lies in the industry's whole manner of treating musical backgrounds. Hollywood has often engaged high-class composers, but Hollywood has also been notoriously unable to use these in any high-class way. European films have made better use of the big musical talents than we have. Honegger, Auric, Milhaud, and Sauguet in France, William Walton in England, Kurt Weill in Germany, Prokofiev and Shostakovich in Soviet Russia have all made film music that was more than a worthy contribution to film drama. Here privately produced or government-produced documentaries have occasionally made film and music history, but our industry-produced fiction films have not included in their whole lifetime five musico-dramatic productions worthy to rank beside the fifty or more European films that as musico-dramatic compositions merit the name "work of art."

It is not talent or skill that is lacking here. It is not intelligence, either, or general enlightenment on the part of directors and producers. The trouble goes deep and has, I think, to do with our distribution rather than with our production system. But first let me talk a bit about *The Red Pony*.

The film itself, as a visual narrative, is far from perfect. It is diffuse; it tries to tell more stories than it can integrate with the main one or bring to a conclusion. Also, it has too many stars in it. It is about a boy and a pony, both admirably played. What the child star and the animal need is acting support, not glamour support. What they get, however, is not acting support at all but the glamour competition of Robert Mitchum and Myrna Loy. As a result, the composer has been obliged to hold the show together with music. There are some sixty minutes of this; and Mr. Copland has made it all interesting, various, expressive. If he has not made it all equally pointed, that is not his fault. He has met beautifully and effectively all the possible kinds of musical demand but one. That one is the weak spot in all American fiction films. It is a result of our particular treatment of the female star.

Wherever Copland has provided landscape music, action music, or a general atmosphere of drama he has worked impeccably. Here his music sets a scene, illustrates action, advances the story. Wherever he has essayed to interpret the personal and private feelings of Miss Loy, he has obscured the décor, stopped the action, killed the story, exactly as Miss Loy herself has done at those moments. His music at such times goes static and introspective, becomes, for dramatic purposes, futile. In a landscape picture, which this is, interpreting emotion directly in the music destroys the pastoral unity of tone. Miss Loy's sadness about her marital maladjustment might have been touching against a kind of music that suggested the soil, the land, the farm, the country life—all those attachments which, not shared by her husband, are the causes of her sadness. But the sadness itself, when blown up to concert size and deprived of specific musical allusion, loses point. The composer here may have helped to build up the glamour of the actress; but he has, by doing so, allowed the author's narrative to collapse.

American films have occasionally omitted all such fake *Tristan und Isolde* music, using simply dialogue or sound effects to support the stars' close-ups. It is much easier, moreover, to handle musically a male star in emotional crisis than a female one, since our mythology allows character and even picturesqueness to the hero. Our heroines, on the other hand, are supposed to be nymphs—all grooming, all loveliness, all abstract desirability, though capable of an intense despair when crossed in love. It is not easy to make a successful picture about one of these goddesses unless the contributing elements—music, costumes, furniture, housing, male adoration, effects of weather, and triumphs of technology—are made to contribute to the myth. Our industry, our whole design, manufacture, and distribution of fiction films, is the commerce of this goddess's image. She is what Hollywood makes and sells. It is easy for a classically trained composer, one for whom art means reality, to enhance the reality of scenic backgrounds, to animate passages of action, to emphasize dramatic values, to give shape and pacing to any narrative's progress. But it is quite impossible for him to be a salesman of soul states in which he does not believe.

No composer working in Hollywood, not even the great Copland himself, has ever made me believe that he believed in the reality of our female stars' emotions. That is the spot where American films go phony, where they fail of truth to life. In so far as this spot is a box-office necessity (and with million-dollar budgets it may well be a necessity), it is impossible for the film industry to make a musico-dramatic work of art. The film, as Europe has proved, is an art form capable of using to advantage the collaboration of the best composers. The film as produced by the American industry has never been able to show any composer at his best. *The Red Pony*, in spite of its mediocrity as a film drama, comes nearer to doing this than other American fiction films I have seen. It is the nearness of its miss, indeed, that has made me realize where the fault in our Hollywood musical credo lies. It lies in the simple truth that it is not possible to write real music about an unreal emotion. An actress can communicate an unreal emotion, because tears, any tears, are contagious. But no composer can transform a feeling into beauty unless he knows in his heart that that feeling is the inevitable response of a sane human being to unalterable events.

III (1957)

It is granted to few in this life to be both a great artist and a great man. That is why Aaron Copland makes us all so happy. It has been my delight for thirty-five years to be his friend and his colleague. And so the warmth I feel toward him and the admiration in which I hold his work have been tested by a long experience. So have the warmth and the admiration many other musicians cherish for him. Consequently, I speak for us all, for the whole world of music everywhere (and Aaron Copland *is* known everywhere), when I bear witness to the fact that both the man and his music are infinitely, wonderfully rewarding.

In the thirty-five years I have known his work (and I think I know every piece of it) I have never known one piece which did not embody a real and truly held personal sentiment and which was not couched in a musical language at once straightforward, original, and strong. The sincerity of his thought and the drive behind his highly individual spare workmanship reveal an artist whose integrity has no place in it for self-indulgence or for devious ways. His orchestral works, his chamber music, his film scores and his ballets have raised for us all standards of power, of honesty and of general excellence that are hard to meet because they are world standards. They are the standards of the great workmen of all times and places. No wonder we are all grateful, the plain public as well as the professionals.

As for the musical colleagues, young and old, Copland has befriended them all. For thirty-five years he has given concerts of their music, expounded it in books and lectures, organized publishing enterprises to make it available, produced it in Canada, the United States, Mexico, South America and Europe. He has founded a society that collects and distributes to them money in payment for performance rights. He has counseled the young, brought them up to maturity as artists, got them jobs, commissions, and private subsidies, made enemies in their defense and taken the rap when their work has disappointed the backers. There is scarcely a composer in the hemisphere (and there are few even in Europe) who is not under gratitude to Copland for valuable and specific services of a professional character.

Clearly all this, the music as well as the career, the authenticity of his art as well as the moral elevation of his professional conduct, deserves a medal. And what a pleasure it is to see him receive it as he has received so many honors already, with that characteristic unconscious grace of a modest but perfectly real prince! Allow me therefore, as I bestow upon him in the name of the American Academy of Arts and Letters The Gold Medal for Music presented once every five years by the National Institute of Arts and Letters, to speak not only for the Institute membership but for the whole world of music as well, when I say to Aaron Copland the composer, the man, the whole heavenly artist that he is, "We thank you for everything."

IV (1971)

Julia Smith's book on Aaron Copland refers to him on its first page as "this simple and great man in our midst." And indeed from his youth Copland has so appeared. Having known him as friend and colleague for nigh on to fifty years, I too can attest that his demeanor is sober, cheerful, considerate, his approach direct and at the same time tactful. I have never seen him lose his temper or explode. His physical appearance has not radically changed since 1921; nor have the loose-hung suits and unpressed neckties, the abstemious habits and seemly ways which by their very simplicity add up to a princely grace.

Considering the irritability of most musicians, Copland's diplomat-façade might well be thought to conceal a host of plots and poutings, were it not so obviously his nature to be good-humored and an ancient principle with him not to quarrel. When he came home from Paris at twenty-four, his study time with Nadia Boulanger completed, and began to be a successful young composer, it is said that he determined then to make no unnecessary enemies. It is as if he could see already coming into existence an organized body of modernistic American composers with himself at the head of it, taking over the art and leading it by easy stages to higher ground, with himself still at the head of it, long its unquestioned leader, later its president emeritus.

This consecrated professionalism was Copland's first gift to American music; it had not been there before. Varèse and Ruggles, though consecrated artists, showed only a selective solidarity with their colleagues. Ives had been a drop-out from professionalism altogether. And the earlier professionals, the lot of them, had all been individual operators. Copland was the very first, I think, to view his contemporaries as a sort of peace corps whose assignment in history was to pacify the warring tribes and to create in this still primitive wilderness an up-to-date American music.

His first move in that direction in 1924 was to take over de facto the direction of the League of Composers. This gave him a New York power enclave; and his classes at the New School for Social Research, held from 1927 to 1937, were soon to give him a forum. He also wrote in magazines, listing about every three years the available modernistic young and offering them his blessing. Also from the beginning, he had established a Boston beachhead, where the new conductor Serge Koussevitzky, taking over from Walter Damrosch Copland's Symphony for Organ and Orchestra, 1925, thereafter performed a new work by him every year till well into the 1930s.

Copland had in New York from 1928 to 1931, in addition to his access to the League of Composers, his own contemporary series, shared with Roger Sessions and called the Copland-Sessions Concerts. At these he played both American and European new works, attracted attention, distributed patronage, informed the public. His collaboration with Sessions, the first in a series of similar teamings-up, marks a second stage of his organizational work. Having by that time solidified his own position, he could enlarge his American music project by calling on, one after another, personalities comparable to his own for weight and influence.

After the Sessions concerts ended in 1931, Copland shared briefly with Roy Harris, just returned then from his studies with Boulanger, an influence centered chiefly in Boston, where Koussevitzky was launching Harris with the same steadfast persistence he had used for Copland. A close association with Walter Piston began in 1935, when Copland took over for a year the latter's composition class at Harvard. In 1937 with Marc Blitzstein, Lehman Engel, and myself, the four of us founded the Arrow Music Press, a cooperative publishing facility, and with several dozen others the American Composers' Alliance, a society for licensing the performance of "serious" music, a need at that time not being met by existing societies.

During the mid-1930s there were five composers—Copland, Sessions, Harris, Piston, and myself—whom Copland viewed as the strongest of his generation both as creators and as allies for combat. And all were to serve under his leadership as a sort of commando unit for penetrating one after another the reactionary strongholds. Their public acknowledgment as co-leaders of American music took place in 1935 at the New School through five concerts, one devoted to each composer's work, all presented as Copland's choice for contemporary excellence in America.

Two foreign composers—Carlos Chavez, during the 1930s conductor of the Orquesta Sinfónica de México and an official of the Fine Arts Ministry, and Benjamin Britten, England's most accomplished composer since Elgar—were to benefit from Copland's friendship, as he from theirs. But his American general staff did not participate in these alliances. Nor have they shared in Copland's influence over our two remarkable composer–conductors Leonard Bernstein and Lukas Foss—though as recognized composers they have all been played by these leaders. In general Copland's foreign affairs and post-war domestic alliances, as well as his worldwide conducting tour of the 1960s, seem more specifically aimed at broadening the distribution of his own music than at sharing the wealth. And this no doubt because his commando comrades had all become successful independently, while the post-war young, having placed their hopes in a newer kind of music (Elliott Carter, Boulez, Cage, the complexity gambit, and the serial-to-noise-to-electronics gambit), have not been able to muster up the personal loyalties needed for calling on his organizational experience.

I have dwelt on Copland as a colleague, a career man, and a mobilizer, because I consider his contribution in those domains to be no less remarkable than that of his music. This music has been analyzed in books by Julia Smith and by Arthur Berger. All its major items are in print and most are recorded. It comprises piano music, chamber works, orchestral works, and ballets, all of high personal flavor and expert workmanship. Less striking, I think, are the vocal works—consisting of two operas, several sets of songs, an oratorio, and a handful of short choral pieces. Among these the choral works are possibly the happiest, because of their animated rhythmic vein. And five Hollywood films made under first-class directors (three, I think, were by Lewis Milestone) on first-class themes (two from John Steinbeck, one from Thornton Wilder, one from Lillian Hellman, one from Henry James) are imaginative and distinguished in their use of music.

Julia Smith has discerned three stylistic periods in Copland's work. His first period, from age twenty-four (in 1924) to age twenty-nine, includes but one non-programmatic, non-local-color work, the Symphony for Organ and Orchestra, composed for Nadia Boulanger to play in America. I found this work at that time deeply moving, even to tears, for its way of saying things profoundly of our generation. The rest of that production time—*Music for the Theatre*, the *Concerto for Piano and Orchestra*, the necrophiliac ballet *Grogh*, the *Symphonic Ode*, the trio *Vitebsk* (study on a Jewish theme), and divers smaller pieces—is largely preoccupied with evocation, as in *Grogh* and *Vitebsk*, or with superficial Americana, characterized by the rhythmic displacements that many in those days took for "jazz" but that were actually, as in George Gershwin's vastly successful *Rhapsody in Blue*, less a derivate from communal improvising, which real jazz is, than from commercial popular music. No wonder the effort to compose concert jazz came to be abandoned, by Copland and by others.

Its last appearance in Copland's work is in the otherwise nobly rhetorical *Symphonic Ode* of 1929, which led directly into the *Piano Variations*, high point of his second period, which in turn initiated a series of non-programmatic works that was to continue for the rest of his productive life. *The Vitebsk* trio, in spite of its allusions to Jewish cantilation, can on account of its tight musical structure be listed, I think, among Copland's abstract works. And so can the orchestral *Statements* of 1933–34, so firmly structured are these mood pictures. Of more strictly musical stock are the *Short Symphony* of 1932–33, later transcribed as a

Sextet for Piano, Clarinet, and Strings, the *Piano Sonata* (1941), the *Sonata for Violin and Piano* (1943), the *Piano Quartet* (1950), the *Piano Fantasy*, and the *Nonet for Strings* (these last from the 1960s). One could include perhaps the *Third Symphony* (1946) on grounds of solid form, but I tend to consider it, on account of its incorporation of a resplendent *Fanfare for the Common Man* (from 1942), one of Copland's patriotic works, along with *A Canticle of Freedom* and the popular *A Lincoln Portrait*.

The initiation of a third period, or kind of writing, followed that of the second by less than five years; and it too has continued throughout his life. This embodied his wish to enjoy large audiences not specifically musical, and for that purpose it was necessary to speak simply. Its major triumphs are three ballets— *Billy the Kid* (1938), *Rodeo* (1942), and *Appalachian Spring* (1944)—all of them solid repertory pieces impeccable in their uses of Americana and vigorous for dancing.

Actually the dance has always been for Copland a major inspiration, largely as an excitement of conflicting rhythms, contrasted with slow incantations virtually motionless. As early as 1925 the unproduced ballet *Grogh* had been transformed into the prize-winning *Dance Symphony*. And his jazz experiments of the later 1920s were closer to dancing than to blues. In 1934 he composed for Ruth Page and the Chicago Grand Opera Company a ballet, or dance drama, entitled *Hear Ye! Hear Ye!*, satirizing a murder trial and based largely on night-club music styles. It was not a success, and with it Copland said good-by to corrupt musical sources, as well as to all attempts at being funny.

Actually his return to ballet and his entry into other forms of show business had been somewhat prepared that same year by the production on Broadway of my opera *Four Saints in Three Acts*. Its willful harmonic simplicities and elaborately-fitted-to-the-text vocal line had excited him; and he had exclaimed then, "I didn't know one could write an opera." He was to write one himself with Edwin Denby three years later, *The Second Hurricane*, designed for high-school use. But my opera had set off trains of powder in both our lives. In 1936 it led me into composing a symphonic background for *The Plough that Broke the Plains*, a documentary film by Pare Lorentz, in which I employed cowboy songs, war ditties, and other folk-style tunes. Again the effect on Copland was electric; as a self-conscious modernist, he had not thought that one could do that either. Shortly after this, Lincoln Kirstein proposed to commission from Copland a work for his Ballet Caravan (the parent troupe of today's New York City Ballet), an offer which Copland declined, no doubt still unsure of himself after the failure of *Hear Ye! Hear Ye!*. I, on the other hand, with a brasher bravery, did accept such a commission and produced in 1937 *Filling Station*, another work based on Americana.

At this point Copland reversed his renunciation and returned to his earliest love, the dance, this time by my way of cowboy songs, producing in 1938 for

Ballet Caravan *Billy the Kid*, a masterpiece of a dance score and a masterpiece of novel choreographic genre, the ballet "Western." Copland's *Rodeo*, of 1942, made for Agnes de Mille and the Ballet Russe de Monte Carlo, is another "Western." And *Appalachian Spring* (for Martha Graham, 1944) is a pastoral about nineteenth-century Shakers. All make much of Americana, the hymn lore of the latter piece having as its direct source my uses of old Southern material of that same kind in *The River*, of 1937, another documentary film by Pare Lorentz.

If I seem to make needless point of my influence on Copland, it is less from vanity than for explaining his spectacular invasion, at thirty-eight, of ballet and films, and less successfully of the opera. His love for the dance was no doubt inborn, and an acquaintance with the theatre had been developed through long friendship with the stage director Harold Clurman. But his previous ballet experiments had come to naught, and his essays in writing incidental music for plays had not led him toward many discoveries. He yearned, however, for a large public; the social-service ideals of the 1930s and the musical successes of Dmitri Shostakovich having created in him a strong desire to break away from the over-intellectualized and constricting modernism of his Paris training. To do this without loss of intellectual status was of course the problem. Stravinsky's neo-classical turn toward conservatism, initiated in 1918, had offered guidance to the postwar School of Paris and to all those still-young Americans, by the 1930s quite numerous and influential, who through Nadia Boulanger had come under its power.

But they had all preserved a correct façade of dissonance; and this surfacing, applied to every species of contemporary music, was making for monotony and for inflexibility in theatre situations. The time was over when composers—Debussy, for instance, Alban Berg, Richard Strauss—could comb literature for themes suited to their particular powers. On the contrary, themes appropriate to a time of social protest and of trade-union triumphs seemed just then far more urgent, especially to Copland, surrounded as he was by left-wing enthusiasts. He wanted populist themes and populist materials and a music style capable of stating these vividly. My music offered one approach to simplification; and my employment of folk-style tunes was, as Copland was to write me later about *The River*, "a lesson in how to treat Americana."

A simplified harmonic palette was being experimented with everywhere, of course; and a music "of the people," clearly an ideal of the time, was one that seemed far nobler then than the country-club-oriented so-called "jazz" that many had dallied with in the 1920s. And thus it happened that my vocabulary was, in the main, the language Copland adopted and refined for his ballet *Billy the Kid* and for his first film *Of Mice and Men*. The German operas of Kurt Weill, which were known to him, performed no such service, though they were all-important to Marc Blitzstein, whose *The Cradle Will Rock* was produced in 1937.

Shostakovich's rising career and some Russian film music may have also been in Copland's mind. But his break-through into successful ballet composition, into expressive film-scoring, and into, for both, the most distinguished populist music style yet created in America did follow in every case very shortly after my experiments in those directions. We were closely associated at the time and discussed these matters at length.

Copland's high-school opera *The Second Hurricane* (to a text by Edwin Denby), produced in 1937, followed Blitzstein's lead into a city-style harmonic simplicity, rather than to my country-style one. It contains delicious verse and a dozen lovely tunes, but it has never traveled far. Nearly twenty years later he wrote another opera, *The Tender Land*, again a pastoral involving Americana-style songs and dances; but that also failed in spite of resonant choruses and vigorous dance passages. When he moved from ballet to films (*Of Mice and Men*, 1939; *Our Town*, 1940) he carried with him no such baggage of vocal ineptitude; nor was he obliged to use the dance for animation. His powers of landscape evocation in pastoral vein and his slow, static, nearly motionless suspense-like moods were useful for psychological spell-casting; and a struggle-type counterpoint, suggestive of medieval organum with rhythmic displacements—taken over from his non-programmatic works—gives dramatic intensity, as in the boy-fights-eagle passage toward the end of *The Red Pony*. For a man so theatre-conscious and so gifted both for lyrical expansion and for objective depiction to be so clearly out of his water on the lyric stage is surprising. The choral passages in his operas are the happiest, for in these he can mobilize four parts or more to produce the same polyrhythmic excitements that are the essence of his dance works, as indeed they often are of his abstract, or "absolute," music. But for vocal solos and recitatives none of that is appropriate; and his dramatic movement tends in consequence to lose impetus, to stop in its tracks. There is no grave fault in his prosodic declamation, which is on the whole clear, though here and there, as in the Emily Dickinson songs, the solo line may be a little jumpy and the vocal ranges strained. His melody in general, however, his harmony, and his musical form are those of a master. What is wrong? My answer is that just as with Stravinsky, also by nature a dance man muscle-oriented, and even with Beethoven, whose work is so powerfully rhythmicized, the vocal writing, however, interesting intrinsically, neglects to support the play's dramatic line.

A strange and urgent matter is this line. And its pacing in spoken plays is not identical with the pacing required for a musical version of the same play. Mozart, with his inborn sense of the theatre is virtually infallible on a stage; and so is Wagner, even when in *Das Rheingold* and in *Parsifal* the dramatico-musical thread may unwind so slowly that it seems almost about to break. But it never does break, and as a result each act or separate scene develops as one continuous open-ended form. Composers whose music requires rhythmic exactitudes work better with the dance or in the closed concert forms. Composers conditioned to producing mood units also tend to be ill at ease about dramatic progress and to treat the story as a series of moments for static contemplation, like Stations of the Cross. On the other hand, operas constructed as a sequence of "numbers" (Mozart to Gershwin) do not of necessity lack dramatic animation. Even the musical dramas of Monteverdi, the *opere serie* of Handel and Rameau and Gluck, can move forward as drama through their closed-form *arie* da capo and their oratorio-style choruses. I suspect it is their naturalistic recitatives that carry them from set-piece to set-piece toward a finale where a priest in full robes or some deus ex machina, in any case a bass voice singing *not* in da capo form, releases the dénouement.

The basic need of any ballet or film score is an appropriate accompaniment for the dance narrative, for the photographed landscape, or for the mimed action. Opera demands of music a more controlling rein, for its function there is not to accompany a dramatic action but to *animate* it—to pace it, drive it, wrestle with it, and in the end to dominate. For that Copland lacks the continuing dynamism. His schooling in the concert forms (in the sonata with Rubin Goldmark, in the variation with Boulanger), the rhythmic and percussive nature of his musical thought, its instrumental predominance, the intervalic viscosity of his textures—all of motionless fourths and seconds, as in medieval organum, plus tenths, so beautiful when finally heard but so slow to register—have created a musical vocabulary strong, shining, and unquestionably of our century.

My favorite among the concert works, the most highly personal, the most condensed, and the most clearly indispensable to music, it seems to me, is the *Piano Variations* of 1930. The *Short Symphony* in its sextet form and the *Nonet* also remain handsome under usage. The *Piano Quartet*, though structurally imaginative, suffers from a tone-row in which two whole-tone scales just barely skirt monotony. The *Piano Sonata*, the *Violin Sonata*, and the *Piano Fantasy* have failed on every hearing to hold my mind. And the charming *Concerto for Clarinet* (1948) with strings, harp, and piano, is essentially "light" music long ago retired to the status of an admirable ballet by Jerome Robbins, *The Pied Piper*.

Suites from the three great repertory ballets, nuggets from films and operas, one overture, divers mood-bits and occasional pieces, and the rollicking *El Salón México*, constitute a high-level contribution to light music that may well be, along with Copland's standardization of the American professional composer, also at high level, his most valued legacy. Certainly these works are among America's most beloved. Nevertheless, the non-programmatic works, though not rivals to twentieth-century European masterworks, have long served American composers as models of procedure and as storehouses of precious device, all of it ready to be picked right off the shelf.

"It's the best we've got, you know," said Leonard Bernstein. And surely this is true of Copland's music as a whole. Ruggles's is more carefully made, but there is not enough of it. Ives's, of which there is probably far too much for quality, has, along with its slapdash euphoria, a grander gusto. Varèse, an intellectually sophisticated European, achieved within a limited production the highest originality flights of any. Among Copland's own contemporaries few can approach him for both volume and diversity. Roy Harris has five early chamber works and one memorable symphony, his *Third*, but he has written little of equal value since 1940. Piston is the author of neoclassical symphonies and chamber pieces that by their fine workmanship may well arrive at repertory status when revived in a later period; for now, they seem a shade scholastic. Sessions, I should say, has for all his impressive complexity and high seriousness, not one work that is convincing throughout. And I shall probably be remembered, if at all, for my operas.

But the Copland catalog has good stuff under every heading, including that of opera. He has never turned out bad work, nor worked without an idea, an inspiration. His stance is that not only of a professional but also of an artist—responsible, prepared, giving of his best. And if that best is also the best we have, there is every reason to be thankful for its straightforward employment of high gifts. Also, of course, for what is the result of exactly that, "this simple and great man in our midst."

NOTES ON COMPOSERS (1971)

In his American Music Since 1910 *(1971), Thomson offered capsule characterizations of various composers along with their works lists at the end of the book. I have selected some of the more interesting and pithy ones for inclusion here.*

GEORGE ANTHEIL

Though Antheil's career suffered from overweening ambition, his music has many qualities of excellence. Almost any work has delicious moments along with pompous ones. As a result, his music, though not strongly current in repertory, does not die. Pieces of it are constantly being revived.

THEODORE CHANLER

Chanler's chamber music, inspired by Fauré, expresses with distinction feelings really felt. His songs, among the finest of our time in English, are impeccable for prosodic declamation and imaginative in their use of accompanimental polyharmonies.

Edward Kennedy ("Duke") Ellington

Bridging the chasm between "pop" and classical styles, though not yet fully achieved, has been consistently essayed by the "Duke." Though predominantly a big-band man, his position in blues, jazz, and swing is impregnable.

Ross Lee Finney

Finney's early chamber music, especially that involving strings, is thematically delicate and richly kaleidoscopic in harmony. His 12-tone works, both chamber and orchestral, tend toward a certain opacity of sound. All his music is brightly colored; at its best it glows like the celestial firmament, with a dispersed brilliance untouched by human feeling.

George Gershwin

Lively rhythm, graceful harmony, and a fine melodic gift. Tops for his time in show music. *Porgy and Bess*, a white man's view of life among the blacks, has circled the globe. Its powerful charm puts it not far below Bizet's *Carmen*, which is after all a Frenchman's view of Spain.

Howard Hanson

Composer of a wide variety of excellent music, including symphonies, symphonic poems, choruses, solo vocal works, and concertos. His opera *Merry Mount* was produced at the Metropolitan in 1934. Though perhaps unduly attached to sequence-structure, Hanson is a Romantic composer of warm heart. He is also an excellent administrator and a master conductor.

Roy Harris

Harris's best works have a deeply meditative quality combined with exuberance. Even without citation of folklore they breathe an American air. His music reflects high artistic aims and a sophistication of thematic, harmonic, and instrumental usage that identify it as work of distinction, with frequently great beauty in the texture.

Otto Luening

A German-schooled fine all-round musician—instrumentalist, conductor, composer, teacher, and a handy man among the Foundations. There is nothing wrong about his music either, except that it is sometimes hard to remember. Could it be that constant labors in the professional vineyard have cost him a certain intensity of concentration on the creative act?

COLIN MCPHEE

A well-schooled neoclassical composer, McPhee remained essentially that, except for the orchestral evocation of Bali called *Tabuh-Tabuhan*. This work and the treatise *Music in Bali* lift him far above all present workers in the Indonesian field.

HARRY PARTCH

A specialist in true intervals and their commas, he has built his own instruments for sounding these. His aim of producing music with true tunings is admirable. One regrets that his work sometimes lacks intellectual sophistication, though it can also be very beautiful.

ALEXANDER TCHEREPNIN

A fecund and expert composer internationally successful in classical forms and also theatrically. Initially inspired by the Russian Romantic masters, he developed in France from medieval sources an original approach to modality and rhythm, later in East Asia was influenced by classical Chinese music. His work has at all periods been filled with poetry and bravura.

Himself the son of the nineteenth-century Russian composer Nicolai Tcherepnin, two of his three sons, Serge (born 1941) and Ivan (born 1943), are Harvard-trained American composers of far-out orientation including the electronic.

RANDALL THOMPSON

Widely known for his choral works (his *Alleluia* has sold over a million copies), he is the author also of a most effective symphony, No. 2, and one of America's most indigenous-sounding string quartets.

V

CONTEMPORARIES—PUBLISHERS, ARTISTS, WRITERS, AND A MUSEUM DIRECTOR

If only for dealing seriously with the business of intelligent music reviewing, the strongest and most valuable chapter of Thomson's autobiography remembers "The Paper," which is his epithet for the New York Herald Tribune. *In stressing the importance of independence and intelligence, this memoir echoes his earlier appreciation of the other principal outlet for his best music criticism, the quarterly* Modern Music *(1924–46) edited by the legendary Minna Lederman (1896–1995). Just as nothing quite like* Modern Music *exists today, so no American newspaper (or other journalistic medium) has music reviewers as strong as those at the* Herald Tribune *between 1940 and 1954.*

The *New York Herald Tribune* was a gentleman's paper, more like a chancellery than a business. During the fourteen years I worked there I was never told to do or not to do anything. From time to time I would be asked what I thought about some proposal regarding my department; and if I did not think favorably of it, it was dropped.

The city room was an open space filled with flat-top desks, the classical stage-set of a newspaper; but what went on there bore no resemblance to the behavior of city staffs in plays and films. I never saw anyone use more than one telephone at a time, and I never heard anyone raise his voice. Exception was the plaintive call of "Copy!" from someone sending a late review down to the type-setters page by page. Self-control was the rule on that floor, just as the avoidance of any haste that might make for error was the style of the linotypers and proof-readers on the floor below.

But if the *Herald Tribune* was a decorous paper, it was also a hard-drinking one. The Artists and Writers Restaurant next door, in Fortieth Street near Seventh Avenue, a former speakeasy run by a Dutchman named Jack Bleeck, received from noon till morning a steady sampling of our staff, of writers from *The New Yorker*, who seemed in general to like drinking with us, of press agents, play producers, and after-theater parties. After the Late City Edition had been put to bed (in those days around half past midnight), our night staff and the working reviewers would gather there to wait out the next half-hour till freshly printed papers were sent down. Everyone read first his own column and after that those of the others. Then we all complimented one another, as one must before going on to discuss points of judgment or style.

The whole staff was pen-proud, had been so, it would seem, since 1912, when Ogden Reid, inheriting the New York *Tribune* from his father (Ambassador to England Whitelaw Reid), had turned it into a galaxy of stars. And until his death in 1950 it stayed luminous. After that, the care for writing faded and the drinking in Bleeck's bar lacked stamina. I do not insist that drinking and good English go together, though certainly over at the *Times*, in Forty-third Street, the staff seemed neither to roister much nor to write very impressively. In my own case, Geoffrey Parsons had no sooner opened the possibility of my writing for the *Herald Tribune* than a dinner was set up at the Players' Club, with a dozen of the paper's best-drinking old hands to test my sociability. That was in September, and I passed all right.

It was still not known, of course, how I would behave in front of a deadline. And Parsons, naturally worried on my first night, prowled about till I had finished writing, then held his breath in the composing room while I checked my proofs. He suggested in these one change, the omission of a slap at the audience ("undistinguished" had been my word). At Bleeck's, when the papers came down, my piece read clearly as a strong one, though it contained, I knew, any number of faults, including seventeen appearances of the first personal pronoun. I had entitled this review of the concert that opened the Philharmonic's ninety-ninth season *Age Without Honor*, and I had snubbed the orchestra's conductor, John Barbirolli, by publishing with it the photograph of his concert-master, Michel Piastro. It was unfavorable throughout—"hard-hitting," my admirers at the bar had called it—and it ended with a quote from my companion of the evening (actually Maurice Grosser), "I understand now why the Philharmonic is not a part of New York's intellectual life."

Hired on a Thursday afternoon, I had covered the Philharmonic that night. The next day I reviewed from its home ground the Boston Symphony's opening. The following Tuesday I attended the season's first New York concert of the Philadelphia Orchestra. For the weekend after that, in my first Sunday piece, I compared these groups. And if my first review had been brutal with overstatement, my second set a far more gracious tone ("peaches and cream," Parsons called it).

The quality of this piece was not always to be kept up. Sometimes I would write smoothly, sometimes with a nervous rhythm, darting in short sentences from thought to thought and failing to carry my readers with me. But on the whole I interested them; and almost from the beginning I did observe standards of description and analysis more penetrating and of coverage more comprehensive than those then current in the press. I was aware of this; the music world was aware of it; my colleagues on the paper were immediately aware of the fact that my work had presence. Ettie Stettheimer, neither a musician nor a journalist, compared it to "the take-off of a powerful airplane." My editors, of course, knew the dangers of so showy an ascent. Also that I was heading into a storm.

For from my first review they received, as also did I, reams of protest mail. Mine I answered, every piece of it, and with courtesy. "I thank you for the warmly indignant letter," was one of my beginnings, before going on to some point raised, such as, for instance, that of my own incompetence. Before very long the editors, aware through the secretarial grapevine of how I could win over many an angry one, would send me their own mail for answering, thus making clear no protest could be made behind my back.

But at the beginning they showed me only the favorable letters. It must have been two years before Mrs. Ogden Reid, almost more active at the paper than her husband, admitted that there had been demands for my beheading. What kept the paper firm regarding me, she said, had been the fact that those who wrote to praise me were important novelists like Glenway Wescott, enlightened museum directors like Alfred Barr, art-minded lawyers like Arnold Weissberger, and public-spirited heads of university music departments, such as Douglas Moore—in short, what she called "intellectual leaders"—whereas the protesters were practically all just quarrelsome types without responsibility ("nuts") or, worse, spokesmen for the performing institutions.

The most persistent of these last turned out to be the Metropolitan Opera Association, whose powerful hostesses, bankers, and corporation attorneys seemed to feel that their names on the board of any enterprise should render it immune to criticism. At the slightest *lèse-majesté* they would make truculent embassies to the paper demanding that somebody or other, usually I, be fired. Urged thus to remove my predecessor, Lawrence Gilman, Ogden Reid had twenty years earlier inquired, "Who's running this paper?" Similarly rebuffed regarding me, the ambassadors would remark that with the death of Mr. Gilman music criticism had lost a great prose writer.

The Philharmonic board, though no less disapproving, early gave up direct intervention in favor of a business maneuver. One of them did inquire whether I would accept board membership, but I declined. And several, I believe, "spoke" to Mrs. Reid. But the business threat was early provoked, at the end of my second week, when I diagnosed the soprano Dorothy Maynor as "immature vocally and immature emotionally." From E. E. Cummings came, "Congrats on the Maynor review. Eye 2 was there." The Columbia Concerts Corporation, however, of which the Philharmonic's manager, Arthur Judson, was president, held a board meeting over it, and not for determining Miss Maynor's fate, but mine. The decision, one heard, was to withdraw all advertising until my employment at the paper should be ended. This plan might have been troublesome to carry out, since it would have denied our services to all Columbia's artists. But at the time the threat seemed real enough to provoke intervention by another impresario.

Ira Hirschmann, a business executive married to a professional pianist, Hortense Monath, and friend of another, the ever-so-respected Artur Schnabel, had been presenting for several seasons, under the name New Friends of Music, weekly Sunday concerts of the chamber repertory. But weekdays he was advertising manager of Bloomingdale's. So when Hirschmann heard about Columbia's plan, he went to our advertising manager, Bill Robinson, and said, "Mr.

Thomson has not yet reviewed my concerts unfavorably, though he well may do so. But whatever happens, I shall match, line for line, any advertising you lose on his account." This incident I also did not know till two years later. But it helps explain the patience of my editors with a reviewer who was plainly a stormy petrel. As a storm bird, I should have preferred to sail above the clouds; but to get there I often had to fly right at them, and bump my beak against their leaden linings.

After twenty years of living inside Europe, I knew well the grandeurs and the flaws of music's past, also that with a big war silencing its present, composition's only rendezvous was with the future. America, for the duration, might keep alive the performing skills. But her strongest composers had shot their bolt in the 1930s and retired, as the phrase goes, into public life, while the younger ones who had not yet done so were getting ready either to be mobilized or to avoid that. The time was not for massive creativity, but rather for taking stock. My program therefore was to look as closely as I could at what was going on, naturally also to describe this to my readers, who constituted, from the first, the whole world of music. The method of my examination and my precepts for progress turned out to be those laid down exactly one year earlier in *The State of Music*.

These principles, as I understood them, engaged me to expose the philanthropic persons in control of our musical institutions for the amateurs they are, to reveal the manipulators of our musical distribution for the culturally retarded profit makers that indeed they are, and to support with all the power of my praise every artist, composer, group, or impresario whose relation to music was straightforward, by which I mean based only on music and the sound it makes. The businessmen and the amateurs, seeing what I was up to, became enemies right off. Those more directly involved with music took me for a friend, though Germans and the German-educated would bristle when I spoke up for French music or French artists. They would even view my taste for these as a somewhat shameful vice acquired in France.

The opposite was true, of course. I had not come to admire the musical workmanship of France from merely living there; I had lived there, at some sacrifice to my career, because I found French musical disciplines favorable to my maturing. Nor did the Germans suspect how deeply I distrusted their arrogance. For French arrogance about music is merely ignorance, like Italian arrogance, or American. But the Germanic kind, based on self-interest, makes an intolerable assumption, namely, its right to judge everything without appeal, as well as to control the traffic—as if past miracles (from Bach through Schubert) were an excuse for greed. And all those lovely refugees—so sweet, so grateful, and so willing to work—they were to be a Trojan horse! For today the Germanics are in control everywhere—in the orchestras, the universities, the critical posts, the publishing houses, wherever music makes money or is a power.

I made war on them in the colleges, in the concert halls, and in their offices. I did not hesitate to use the columns of my paper for exposing their pretensions;

and I refused to be put off by sneers from praising the artists of my choice, many of them foreign to the Italo-German axis. My editors found this method not unfair, for they too, through our European Edition, were Paris-oriented. The Germanics would never admit, however, that distributed attention was not mere Francophilia.

My literary method, then as now, was to seek out the precise adjective. Nouns are names and can be libelous; the verbs, though sometimes picturesque, are few in number and tend toward alleging motivations. It is the specific adjectives that really describe and that do so neither in sorrow nor in anger. And to describe what one has heard is the whole art of reviewing. To analyze and compare are stimulating; to admit preferences and prejudices can be helpful; to lead one's reader step by step from the familiar to the surprising is the height of polemical skill. Now certainly musical polemics were my intent, not aiding careers or teaching Appreciation. And why did a daily paper tolerate my polemics for fourteen years? Simply because they were accompanied by musical descriptions more precise than those being used just then by other reviewers. The *Herald Tribune* believed that skill in writing backed up by a talent for judgment made for interesting and trustworthy reviews, also that the recognition of these qualities by New York's journalistic and intellectual elite justified their having engaged me. Moreover, in spite of some protests and many intrigues against me, all of which followed plot-lines long familiar, I caused little trouble. If some business or political combine had caused the paper real embarrassment, either through loss of income or through massive reader protest, I should most likely not have survived, for the Ogden Reids, though enlightened, were not quixotic. As Geoffrey Parsons remarked some two years later, "It is possible to write good music criticism now, because no group is interested in stopping you." Which meant, I presume, that I was not a danger to the war effort.

The *Herald Tribune* represented in politics the liberal right, a position usually favorable to the arts. The know-nothing right and the Catholic right, as well as the Marxist left, are in all such matters, as we know, unduly rigid. And papers of the moderate left tend, in art, to be skimpy of space, the sheets of massive circulation even more so. But papers that are privately owned and individually operated make their address to the educated middle class. The *New York Times* has regularly in its critical columns followed a little belatedly the tastes of this group; the *Herald Tribune* under Ogden Reid aspired to lead them. It did not therefore, as the *Times* has so often done, shy away from novelty or from elegance. So when I took as a principle for my column that "intellectual distinction itself is news," the city desk, though not quite ready to admit so radical a concept, found my results lively, especially my wide-ranging choice of subjects and my indifference to personalities already publicized to saturation, such as Marian Anderson and Arturo Toscanini. In fact, when somewhat later John Crosby, then a staff writer, was asked to start a radio-and-television column, hopefully for syndication, the managing editor warned him against overdoing big-time coverage. "Spread yourself around like Virgil Thomson," he said. "Surprise your readers."

Except for courtesy coverage of opening nights at the Philharmonic and the Metropolitan Opera, I must say that my choice of occasions was by the conventions of the time wildly capricious. My third review was of a woman conductor, Frédérique Petrides, leading thirty players in a piece by David Diamond. In my second week, reviewing two Brazilian programs at the Museum of Modern Art, I poked fun at the public image of that institution, at folklore cults in general, at all music from Latin America, that of Villa-Lobos in particular, and found an error in the museum's translation of a title from the Portuguese. I also discovered, for myself at least, a group of young people called the Nine O'Clock Opera Company, all just out of the Juilliard School, singing in English at the Town Hall to a pianoforte accompaniment Mozart's *The Marriage of Figaro*.

My attack on Dorothy Maynor appeared on October 24, a subsequently much-quoted piece in praise of Artur Rubinstein on October 26. On the 28th I reported on a W.P.A. orchestra led by Otto Klemperer. On the 31st appeared a review of Jascha Heifetz entitled *Silk-Underwear Music*, in which I called his playing "vulgar." The imprecision of this adjective and the shocking nature of my whole attack brought protests on my head from Geoffrey Parsons as well as, through intermediaries, from Heifetz. Tasteless certainly were my adjectives weighted with scorn; but I could not then, cannot now, regret having told what I thought the truth about an artist whom I believed to be overestimated. To all such reputations, in fact, I was sales resistant, like William James, who had boasted, "I am against greatness and bigness in all their forms."

That winter, along with covering a handful of standard soloists—Josef Hofmann, Jan Smeterlin, Kirsten Flagstad, Arturo Toscanini, John Charles Thomas—and with a reasonable attention paid to the orchestras and the opera, I reviewed Maxine Sullivan (singing in a night club), Paul Bowles's music for *Twelfth Night* (on Broadway, with Helen Hayes and Maurice Evans), Walt Disney's *Fantasia*, a score of musical books and magazines, a student orchestra, two youth orchestras, an opera at the Juilliard School, a Bach oratorio in a church, a Broadway musical by Kurt Weill, Marc Blitzstein's far-to-the-left almost-opera *No for an Answer*, Stravinsky's *Violin Concerto* turned into a ballet, several other dance performances involving modern music, an economics-and-sociology report from Columbia University on the "hit" trade in popular songs, the Harvard Glee Club ("fair but no warmer"), Holy Thursday at Saint Patrick's Cathedral, a Negro preacher in New Jersey who wore frilled white paper wings over his blue serge suit and played swing music on an electric guitar (he was my Easter Sunday piece), some comical press-agentry received, a W.P.A. orchestra in Newark, three other suburban and regional orchestras, a swing concert at the Museum of Modern Art, an opera at Columbia University, a *Southern Harmony* "sing" in Benton, Kentucky, the Boston "Pops" in Boston, and the Goldman

Band in Central Park. By the following season's end I had got round to examining the High School of Music and Art and to considering the radio as a serious source. Recordings I did not touch, because another member of my staff had them in charge.

This staff consisted of myself and three assistants—Francis Perkins, who also served as music editor, Jerome D. Bohm, and Robert Lawrence. Bohm, who had conducted opera in his Berlin student days under Leo Blech, was a German-oriented voice teacher and opera coach. Lawrence, already beginning his career as a conductor, was an enthusiast for French music, especially Berlioz. Perkins, though not professionally a musician, was widely read in music's history and devoted to exactitude. Since 1922 he had kept a catalog, with dates and places, of all the orchestral and operatic works performed in New York City. This was the extension of a somewhat less careful listing begun in 1911 by Edward Krehbiel, and it was unique. He also kept well-indexed clipping books containing all the reviews and news relating to music that appeared in the paper. And he had a shelf of reference books, many of them bought by him, for checking instantly the spelling of a name, the title of a work, the facts about almost anything connected with repertory. And until the department acquired a secretary, it was Perkins who kept the catalog and scrapbooks up to date, as well as sorting out the publicity and announcements, which arrived in vast abundance at the music desk.

For doing this he often worked late into the night "mopping up," as he called it, until three or four or five, then attended early Mass, had breakfast, and went home to sleep. A vintage Bostonian and proudly a Harvard man, he allowed himself no weakness or neglect, nursemaiding and housemaiding us all, lest some misstatement or a skimpy coverage make the paper inglorious. He it was who had in the 1920s and '30s widened the coverage from just the Carnegie-and-Town-Hall beat by slipping out in the course of many an event to visit half of another, something modern usually, that was taking place over at Hunter College or downtown at the New School for Social Research. At this time still a bachelor, he was, as our secretary said, "married to the *Herald Tribune*"; and if he did not sleep on the premises (as he sometimes did at concerts), he very often spent the whole night there.

Replying to my mail, to all those "letters fan and furious" that I sometimes published along with my answers in lieu of a Sunday think-piece, had early earned me stenographic aid. So when the managing editor lent me his own secretary for use on Tuesdays, his day off, this unprecedented precedent caused Perkins too to ask for help, which was granted. And eventually, at her own request, my secretarial abettor, Julia Haines, was allowed to work wholly for the music department, a happy arrangement that long survived my tenure.

Julia was a jolly and sharp-tongued Irishwoman who from having been around some twenty years was on girl-to-girl terms with the secretaries of Ogden Reid, Helen Reid, and Geoffrey Parsons. Her discretion was complete, and so was her devotion to me. She told her colleagues all the favorable news, showing them admiring letters from prominent persons and unusually skillful replies of mine to the opposition. In return they kept her informed of good opinions received in their offices. If they let her know of any trouble about me, she did not pass that on. They could hint, however, at some complaint that Parsons or the Reids would not have wished to make directly. And she would pass back my reply, embarrassing no one.

She also, on the paper's time, typed all my private correspondence—answers to inquiries about publication, to engagements offered, even to personal letters. And thanks to her use of the secretarial back fence, my life was completely exposed. I liked it that way, and so did my employers. Thus no tension that might arise risked becoming exaggerated, a situation especially valuable with regard to Helen Reid. For though we shared mutual admiration, I almost invariably rubbed her the wrong way. My impishness and my arrogance were equally distasteful, and something in my own resistance to her dislike of being rubbed the wrong way led me over and over again to the verge of offense.

Nevertheless, in spite of our tendency to draw sparks from each other, we worked together quite without distrust. After I had once procured music for the Herald Tribune Forum, a three-day feast of famous speakers held every year in the Hotel Waldorf-Astoria ballroom, she offered to pay me for doing this every year; and when I declined payment, my salary was raised. She did not interfere in any way with my department's operations, but eventually she came to ask my advice about pressures and complaints received regarding these operations. And when the general manager of the Metropolitan Opera, Rudolf Bing, surely displeased with my reviewing of his policy statements, sought to cultivate her favor through invitations to his box, she showed him where her confidence lay by inviting me, along with my chief supporter, my discoverer indeed, Geoffrey Parsons, to lunch with him at the paper.

With Parsons there was never misunderstanding. He admired me, forgave me, adopted me into his family. Besides, he was committed to making a success of me, since my appointment had been wholly of his doing. When I misbehaved, as in the Heifetz review, he would correct me kindly, clearly, with reasons, and with always a joke at the end. When during one of my contests with the Metropolitan Opera, he found in my answer to their protest a reference to the "ladies" of the Opera Guild, he reminded me that "lady" is an insulting term because of its irony. "Always attack head-on," he said. "Never make sideswipes and never use innuendo. As long as you observe the amenities of controversey, the very first of which is straightforward language, the paper will stand behind you."

Nevertheless, he would send to my office from time to time a letter pained, impatient, and unclear. These, I came to believe, meant he had been asked by someone, probably Mrs. Reid, to "speak to Virgil." The speakings were not, of course, unjustified, merely out of proportion to the visible fault. And they were not phrased in Geoffrey's normal way, which was ever of wit and sweetness. I would acknowledge them with all delicacy of phrase, almost as if Geoffrey were some irate unknown, and then be more careful for a while. These occasions were not frequent, and no enmity seemed to build up through them. After my first two years they happened rarely, and during the last ten almost not at all. I must eventually have learned smoother ways, for in 1946, on my fiftieth birthday, Carleton Sprague Smith could say, "Six years ago Virgil was one of the most feared men in New York; today he is one of the most loved." Imagine that!

My errors, when they occurred, were of two kinds, those which shocked the prejudices of readers and those which caused inconvenience to management. In the first kind of case I was merely cautioned to watch my language, use no slang, explain everything, be persuasive. For indeed, in expository writing, failure to convince is failure *tout court*. Inconvenience to management arriving through complaint from prominent persons was not necessarily unwelcome, however. The Metropolitan Opera, the Philharmonic, the Museum of Modern Art, the radio establishments that presented Toscanini or owned Columbia Concerts, these were familiar opponents; and battling with them was tonic to us all. For that sport, methods of attack and defense were our subjects of gleeful conference, punctilio and courtesy our strategy; getting the facts right was our point of honor, exposing them to readers our way of being interesting.

The orchestras from out of town, such as Boston and Philadelphia, sent us no embassies. And the standard touring soloists one rarely heard from even indirectly. What seemed most to bother Mrs. Reid and Geoffrey was unfavorable comment on a suburban affair. My questioning the civic value to Stamford, Connecticut, of a quite poor symphony orchestra brought two strong letters from Parsons. Conflict with Manhattan millionaires, I could read between the lines, was permitted, but not with country clubs. Suburbia had long supplied the nut of our liberal Republican readership, and the paper's eventual drama of survival came to be played out against the sociological transformation of those neighborhoods. Discouraging suburbia about anything, I understood, was imprudent. For suburbs, like churches, accept only praise.

Geoffrey was right, of course; he always was. My quality as a reviewer came from my ability to identify with the makers of music; and when I spoke both as an insider to music and warmly, my writing, whether favorable or not, was communicative. But I simply could not identify with organizers and promoters, however noble their motives. Going out of one's way to cover something not usually reviewed is a lark, provided you can get a lively piece out of it. If not, wisdom would leave it to the merciful neutrality of the news columns. But when you are new to reviewing and still reacting passionately, you are not always led by wisdom. And later, when you have more control, you are not so passionate. Neither are you quite so interesting. Because the critical performance needs to be based on passion, even when journalism requires that you persuade. And in the early years of my reviewing, Geoffrey was like a guardian angel, an athletic coach, and a parent all in one, hoping, praying, and probably believing that with constant correction and copious praise I could be kept at top form.

I had entered music reviewing in a spirit of adventure; and though I never treated it as just an adventure, I did not view it as just journalism either. I thought of myself as a species of knight-errant attacking dragons single-handedly and rescuing musical virtue in distress. At the same time I ran a surprisingly efficient department, organized a Music Critics' Circle (still in existence), started a guest-column on radio music to be written by B. H. Haggin and a jazz column with Rudi Blesh as star performer. When the war removed two of my staff members, I took on Paul Bowles to substitute for one of them and later employed the composer Arthur Berger; I also caused the engagement of Edwin Denby for a year and a half as ballet reviewer; and I established a panel of music writers from outside the paper who helped us keep the coverage complete. This pool of "stringers" constituted a training corps that comprised my future music editor, Jay Harrison, and the present *New York Times* staff writers Theodore Strongin and Allen Hughes. At one time or another it included the music historian Herbert Weinstock and the composers Elliott Carter, John Cage, Lou Harrison, William Flanagan, Lester Trimble, and Peggy Glanville-Hicks.

I used no one not trained in music, for my aim was to explain the artist, not to encourage misunderstanding of his work. I discouraged emotional reactions and opinion-mongering on the grounds that they were a waste of space. "Feelings," I would say, "will come through automatically in your choice of words. Description is the valid part of reviewing; spontaneous reactions, if courteously phrased, have some validity; opinions are mostly worthless. If you feel you must express one, put it in the last line, where nothing will be lost if it gets cut for space."

My copy was never cut; neither did it ever make the front page. I wrote in pencil, proofread the manuscript before sending it down, preferring, should errors occur, that they be my own. After the first year I did not go downstairs at all, checking my Sunday proofs at home, sent by messenger. In my first weeks I had asked Francis Perkins how long it would take to get over being unduly elated or depressed at a musical event. "About six years," he had said. And he was right. After that time I could write a review, go off to bed, and wake up in the morning with no memory of where I had been or what I had written. Twice, to my knowledge, I reviewed a contemporary work without remembering I had done so two years earlier. And in both cases my descriptions were virtually identical in thought, though not in words.

I had established my routines very early. During seven months of the year I wrote a Sunday article every week and averaged two reviews. During the summer months I did no reviewing; I also skipped seven or eight Sunday articles. Since these could be sent from anywhere, I toured on musical errands of my own or stayed in some country place writing music. I also wrote music in town, published books, went in and out on lectures and conducting dates. The paper liked all this activity, because it kept my name before the public. Also because I usually came back with a piece about San Francisco or Texas or Pittsburgh (after the war, Europe and Mexico and South America, too), which was good for circulation. To the Herald Tribune Forum I added for musical relief opera singers, Southern hymn singers, Negro choirs, and Robert Shaw's Collegiate Chorale. In all these arrangements, my dealings with Helen Reid were quite without friction or misunderstanding. Indeed, unless I look at my scrapbooks I can hardly remember my last ten years at the paper, so thoroughly satisfactory were they to us all and so little demanding of my time. The dramas had all come in the first four, for those were the years when I was learning my trade while working at it. These were also, of course, the war years, naturally full of emergencies, revelations, excitements, departures, arrivals, surprises, and strange contacts.

A WAR'S END [*MODERN MUSIC*] (1947)

Modern Music, quarterly review edited by Minna Lederman and published by the League of Composers, has ceased publication after twenty-three years. Musicians and laymen who are part of the contemporary musical movement will of necessity be moved by this announcement, because *Modern Music* has been for them all a Bible and a news organ, a forum, a source of world information, and the defender of their faith. It is hard to think of it as not existing, and trying to imagine what life will be without it is a depressing enterprise.

No other magazine with which I am acquainted has taken for its exclusive subject the act of musical composition in our time or sustained with regard to that subject so comprehensive a coverage. This one reported on France and Germany and Italy and England and Russia and Mexico and the South American republics, as well as on its own United States. It covered musical modernism in concerts, in the theater, in films, radio, records, and publication. Jazz and swing procedures were analyzed and Calypso discovered in its pages. Books dealing with contemporary musical aesthetics were reviewed. The only aspects of music excluded from it were those that make up the ordinary layman's idea of music, namely, its interpretation, its exploitation as a business, and its composition before 1900.

Modern Music was a magazine about contemporary composition written chiefly by composers and addressed to them. It even went into their politics on occasion. When our entry into the recent war brought to certain composers' minds the possibility that perhaps our government might be persuaded not to draft all the younger ones, thus husbanding, after the Soviet example, a major cultural resource, Roger Sessions disposed of the proposal firmly by identifying it with the previous war's slogan "business as usual." And when, on the liberation of Europe, consciences were worried about musician collaborators, a whole symposium was published, exposing all possible ways of envisaging the problem. Darius Milhaud, as I remember, said that traitors should be shot, regardless of talent or profession. Ernst Křenek pointed out that Shostakovich, who had accepted from his own government artistic correction and directives regarding the subject matter of his music, was the prince of collaborators. While Arnold Schönberg opined that composers were all children politically and mostly fools and should be forgiven.

In the atmosphere of sharp aesthetic controversy that pervaded the magazine and with its constant confrontation of authoritative statement and analysis (for there is practically no living composer of any prestige at all whose works have not been discussed in it and who has not written for it himself), wits became more keen and critical powers came to maturity. It is not the least of many debts that America owes Minna Lederman that she discovered, formed, and trained such contributors to musical letters as Edwin Denby, Aaron Copland, Roger Sessions, Theodore Chanler, Paul Bowles, Marc Blitzstein, Samuel Barlow, Henry Cowell, Colin McPhee, Arthur Berger, and Lou Harrison. My own debt to her is enormous. Her magazine was a forum of all the most distinguished world figures of creation and of criticism; and the unknown bright young were given their right to speak up among these, trained to do so without stammering and without fear.

The magazine's "cessation of hostilities," as one of its European admirers refers to the demise, is explained by its editor as due to "rising costs of production." Considering previous difficulties surmounted, I should be inclined to derive the fact from a deeper cause. After all, the war about modern music is over. Now comes division of the spoils. Miss Lederman's magazine proved to the whole world that our century's first half is one of the great creative periods in music. No student in a library, no radio program maker, dallying with her priceless back issues, can avoid recognizing the vast fertility, the originality, ingenuity, and invention that music has manifested in our time.

EUGENE BERMAN, 1899–1972 (1974)

Eugene Berman was one of four Paris painters who came to be known quite early as "neo-Romantic." The others were Pavel Tchelitchew, Christian Bérard, and Berman's brother Leonid—three Russians and one Frenchman. All had ripened in Paris and made their first frame there, between the middle 1920s and the middle thirties. Bérard remained French and Parisian; the three Russians all became American.

The terms neo-Romantic and neo-Humanist, as used by Waldemar George to describe their work, means that these painters, while painting whatever they painted, expressed also the way they felt about it. Their subjects were generally people or places; still-life never made them vibrate. And they rendered their subjects naturalistically, at the same time infusing these with a personal sentiment. So that every landscape had a *genius loci* and every person his particular pathos.

Bérard, Tchelitchew, and Berman found in the theatre an outlet for their humane compassion and their poetic view of life. Leonid created *his* mythology by painting the shores of France, later those of a larger Europe, of America, Asia, and Africa, praising everywhere the interpenetrations of land and sea as populated by working fisherfolk. The others created for Diaghilev, for Balanchine, for the repertory theatres of France, and for the great opera houses most of the memorable settings and costumings that have come into existence since 1925. I use this date because Picasso's last theatre piece—Erik Satie's ballet *Mercure*—was of 1924. Stylistic self-assertion in stage decoration went on, of course, long after that. It still goes on. And professional painters, with their wisdom about forms and colors, remain its chief masters. But the poetic ones among them—stage-struck, stage-passionate, and involved—do bring to a poetic play, a ballet, dance-drama, or opera an intrinsic vitality quite different from that of mere easel-painting-in-the-theatre, and possibly of a higher expressive order.

Genia Berman's art was always a staging of something, a presentation with poetry built in. But behind any work that got to the monumental stage, or even to that of the fine-spun pen-and-ink drawings that he regularly exposed and sold, there lay the sacred sketch books. These were his raw materials, and few beyond his intimates ever saw them. I remember well one summer day when we walked together by the Seine in its nearby fields below high-lying Saint-Germain-en-Laye. Naturally, Genia had his sketch book along, a small bound one, not a tablet. On its pages he would pencil a tree, a bush, a view, anything that tempted his hand; and everything he drew seemed of the utmost beauty. So I said, "Genia, why don't you, instead of selling only drawings worked up as pictures, why don't you show your admirers the real thing"? "But Virgil," he said, "I could never part with those. My sketch books are my capital, my sources of saleable art. They are my living."

Since Genia's death last year in Rome, where he had resided for over twenty years, surrounded by artifacts of every place, time and land (for he collected with a comprehensive and bold taste) I have often wondered where those sketch books are, and whether his estate lawyers have any inkling of their contents, even of their existence. I do hope they have been preserved, for they are witness to an artist's authenticity. His poetic feeling for half-buried monuments and his romantic attraction toward the sumptuosities of ballet and opera have given his work identity. But its authenticity lies in the raw materials of it, which he called his capital. A rich capital too it was, because like the others of his Franco-Russian group, he was forever drawing; of that skill they all were masters. And somewhere lies buried Berman's treasure of original nuggets, of findings, priceless bits of reality stored up by a painter who cherished above all his book and pencil.

LEONID BERMAN, 1896–1976 (1978)

Leonid, when I first knew him, was already an accomplished painter. That was in Paris, 1925, and he was 29.

He had also found his subject-matter, which was the shores of oceans and the people who work there. The complex interpenetrations of water and land, the sight of ships, of the elaborate manoeuvres for fishing from beaches, of tidal fishing as a way of life, these things he loved and never ceased to love. They nourished him, and they nourished his painting; they were his almost sole theme as an artist.

This obsession was so clear and so undeniable that in all the fifty years of our friendship it never occurred to me to wonder how it had come about.

Brought up in a well-to-do banking family of St. Petersburg, educated in the best *gymnasia*, in the days of Kerensky a member of the stylish Corps of Pages, then later in Paris as a young man of artistic promise, he pursued the sea as no one I have ever known. But he pursued it only as a theme. No sailor he, nor yet a fisherman, but simply one obsessed by watching, transcribing.

He cared not where he found his models. Any sea would do—Marseille, the Norman coast, Brittany, La Rochelle, later Portugal, Indonesia, Rhode Island, the Gaspé Peninsula, Egypt's Nile, the lagoon of Venice—the waters of anywhere and the people working in them.

There was a time during the German occupation in France when he actually lived with such a land-and-water family. They were a family of well-to-do peasants owning both farms and mussel-fisheries. Leonid enjoyed that period, being a part of, at last, the thing that he always before (and always afterwards, too) merely watched, even though toward the end of that period he was commandeered by the occupying army for more than a year's day-labor on the roads, in something called the Tod Battalion.

But Leonid, though small, was strong, used to sports and physical exertions, a man of action and of muscles. He used his muscles every day, just as he painted every day. I never knew him not to paint or play physical games. And few are his paintings that do not picture water or scenes of heavy sea labor, preferably both.

How this very great gentleman, a city man, an easel painter, and a sportsman came to worship so deeply seashores and their working peoples, and this moreover without sentiment or political emotions of any sort, is a mystery I never thought about until he left us. It was all so natural, so taken for granted, so accepted by Leonid himself that one hardly realized the enormity of the phenomenon, which is that of an artist whose unique subject-matter, no less than the procedures of his art, with which it early of course became bound up, constituted for fifty years, right along with the act of painting, a true vocation. Others have used persistent or recurrent themes, but I know of none other so compulsive in his devotion.

GERTRUDE STEIN

Though Gertrude Stein was more than twenty years older than Thomson—indeed, though she was born in the same year as the composer Charles Ives—Thomson seemed to regard her as a contemporary and thus a subject to which he would often return, nearly as often as he returned to Aaron Copland, likewise saying new things about her over nearly forty years. My own critical opinion is that Thomson's very best music was inspired directly by Stein—not only the opera Four Saints in Three Acts *(1927–29) but the less-known art song for four male voices,* Capital Capitals *(1927). The essay from 1953 originally appeared as the introduction to a collection of Stein's poems published in that year.*

I (1953)

Some of the writing included in this volume [*Bee Time Vine and Other Pieces*], "The Work" for instance, is easy to understand. Other poems, such as "A Sonatina Followed by Another" and "Lifting Belly," reveal their content to persons acquainted with the regions they describe or with their author's domestic life. Still others, however, like "Bee Time Vine" and "Patriarchal Poetry," are genuinely hermetic, by which I mean that the words mean what they mean in the poem by contrast with their common sense rather than by any easily discernible parallel to it.

The first kind is as clear as Kipling. The second kind invites annotation in the way that the writings of Joyce, T. S. Eliot, Pound, and Valéry do. The third kind, which is extremely resistant to exegesis, it is legitimate to consider, I think, as abstract composition. Indeed, that is the way Gertrude Stein always referred to it—as "narration" or "description" or "paragraphs" or "sentences," never in terms of its meaning.

This does not mean that it had no meaning for her or that the reader is advised against searching for one. There is every reason to suppose that she used her subjects as a painter does his models, sometimes revealing them for recognition and at other times concealing them under such an elaboration of contrasts, puns, private associations, and rhythmic patterns that their resistance to exposure is well-nigh complete.

In my notes to the present volume I have not attempted the full explanation of any text. I have merely shared with the reader such information as I have about each one. Much of this information has been given me by Miss Alice B. Toklas, Gertrude Stein's secretary.[1] The ideas expressed about "Patriarchal Poetry," the only text included that was composed during my acquaintance with Miss Stein, are wholly mine.

I have also abstained, for the most part, from expressing opinions. The high esteem in which I have long held the writings of Gertrude Stein is a matter of public knowledge. That esteem antedates by a good many years my friendship with her. Its basis, like that of all artistic admirations, is instinctive. If it required defense, however, I might offer this: that the greatness of the great poets has never been measurable by the amount of clear thought expressed in their works. It is far more a matter of their ability to compose unforgettable lines. Judged by this standard Gertrude Stein ranks very high indeed. And clarity has nothing to do with the matter. "Rose is a rose is a rose is a rose" obviously needs no bush. Neither does the compact summation, quoted from Disraeli, "What do we live for. Climate and the affections. Jews quote that." "Toasted Susie is my ice cream," though plenty obscure, is equally memorable, explained or unexplained. The second paragraph of "Patriarchal Poetry" has also its solidity, a specific gravity rare in literature, though I have not the slightest idea what it means.

Perhaps one day I may find the meaning in it. Gertrude Stein's lines do sometimes give up their secrets over the years. In *Four Saints in Three Acts* there occurs the following dialogue:

Ste. Therese: Might with widow.
Ste. Therese: Might.

I had put this to music in 1927–28, coached and conducted it many times. In 1952 Maurice Grosser, who had known it almost as long as I, surprised me (and himself) with the discovery that it must refer (and how could one have missed it?) to the "widow's mite" and, as the spelling indicates, to any widow's might, morally speaking.

Further layers of meaning may be involved also, since I do remember that in 1927, when the *Four Saints* libretto was being written, Miss Stein was seeing a certain rich and powerful American widow. This woman wore her might as visibly as she did her widowhood. She may well have come into the composition, as did Miss Stein's cook. The latter, a woman named Hélène, had worked for Miss Stein before 1914. In the middle 1920s she returned for about a year and a half. Miss Stein's gratification at the event, mixed with anxiety lest this excellent servant leave again (for she was uncompromising as she was efficient), entered the play in a long sentence beginning "To have to have have Helen." What relation in meaning this passage bears to Spain and to the saintly life I have never known for sure, but I suspect that both women reminded Gertrude Stein of Saint Teresa. Or vice versa.

The present volume has in it landscape and love poetry and much mention of people and a great deal about the War, the first World War. It also contains every kind of writing from the plainest to the virtually impenetrable. The only kind that is not here is the kind Miss Stein never wrote, the kind that people forget. As I said before, she must be one of the great, for she sticks in the mind.

Notes
1. Phrases in quotation marks, unless cited from Gertrude Stein's own text, are quoted from this source.

II. Remembering Gertrude (1982)

I knew Gertrude Stein very well. We were close friends for twenty years, from 1926 till her death in 1946, and then I knew her companion Alice Toklas for another twenty years. I was very close to them both, almost a member of the family. But that doesn't mean I know everything about them. I'll give you a day in the life of Gertrude Stein during the years when I knew her, which began when she was fifty-two.

Like all middle-aged people she woke up. She didn't wake up too early though. She would usually get up around nine. Earlier, she used to sleep in the daytime, but I never knew her in those days. She told me that she used to work at night and sleep in the daytime, and also that she smoked cigars and drank wine. When I knew her she was not smoking or drinking. She had revised her hygiene at about the age of forty-five on account of the diagnosis of an abdominal tumor, and her doctor told her she could either keep it or have it out, but since she had had a medical education herself—now this was around 1919 or 1920—she decided not to have the operation but also to follow the medical man's advice, which was to reduce her weight.

Now she had always been self-indulgent, or enthuasiastic shall we say, about eating, and the photographs and sculpture of her as a large woman do not give you the woman that I knew, because by the time I knew her she had taken off a great deal of weight. She was very short, and so she still looked monumental, but actually she wasn't the fat girl that's in the sculptures and early photographs. She ate very little, she kept her weight down, and she exercised: she walked all the time, she liked to do that.

Well, let's say that we've got her up and out of bed by nine or so in the morning, and with a small breakfast. What do we do with her? Well, she reads her mail, she answers some of it, she writes to people asking them to come around and see her or to a party, and she meditates. Gertrude was a great meditator, and by meditating she understood, or thought she understood, what people are like. Her subject was always people, and she thought of herself as a novelist, as a writer about people, and she made portraits of people all of her life, and her main interest in them was to find out exactly how their minds worked and how their destinies and compulsions worked.

Well, having fiddled around the house for three hours or more, annoyed Alice and the cook and interrupted everybody, and read the morning paper, maybe she even worked a little but not so much in the mornings I think. Then she had a bath, put on clean clothes and had lunch, and after lunch they would go somewhere in the car, or go shopping in the neighborhood, or do errands.

The afternoon was occupied with things like that and once in a while she would take the dog for a walk. That was her only duty, if any.

Alice did the housekeeping and tended to the cooking and all that, and the secretarial work, but Gertrude didn't do anything except walk the dog and her own writing and see her friends when they came in. But she never made any engagement before four o'clock in the afternoon, because it was her general practice to write every day, and if you fill your day up with engagements obviously you are not going to get any work done, and so she kept herself absolutely free until four o'clock, because at any moment she might want to write, and at some time in the day she always did.

You see, if you work every day, and if you wait till you are ready to write, then you can work quite fast, and twenty-five to thirty minutes of concentrated work is quite a lot, and if you do that every day, in the course of a long life you build up a perfectly enormous volume of writing, which she did.

But then after four o'clock she felt that it would be all right not to think that she would be likely to work, although very often between the tea hour and the supper hour she would work a bit, if nobody was around, even sometimes after supper. She could work anytime, but she always waited until she was full of readiness, and then she'd reach for the pencil and the little notebook, and she'd start writing on whatever it was that she was having at that time as her theme, method, or subject.

In the country they would sometimes go out for lunch if they had guests, but on the whole they ate at home a nourishing lunch, but a diet lunch. Alice followed all the diets. She said she couldn't be bothered having two kinds of cooking done, so whatever Gertrude's diet was that's what she ate. There was a good lunch and a light supper, and certain close friends were frequently invited if they had dropped in before supper to stay for it, and in those cases they would often sit up talking with Gertrude until twelve or even one o'clock, because Gertrude liked to sit up and liked to talk. But Alice, who got up very early, usually went to bed about eleven o'clock.

You see, Alice had to see that everything was done right. Her principle of life was that Gertrude was not to be bothered; she was there to make Gertrude's life easy, not difficult, so she never asked Gertrude to undertake any responsibility or to do anything. But Alice herself would get up in the morning, and before the maid was up she would clean and dust the big studio drawing room, simply because there were lots of objects there, some of which were fragile, and Alice was devoted to objects in the way that Gertrude was devoted to pictures, and Alice had an enormous temper, and she didn't want to get angry at a servant if a servant should break something, and so, the breakables being all in that room, that was the room that she did. Well, before Gertrude was up Alice had cleaned up the place and was at her other work, which consisted of typing all the manuscripts, organizing the meals with the cook, writing business letters, which she signed "A. B. Toklas," and on Sunday night, when the cook was out, she cooked supper.

Very often young people ask me to tell them what life was like between the two wars in Paris. They've heard so much about it because there were famous artists around who now are in the courses they take, and they say, what was it like? I say it's not like anything you ever saw. To begin with, the costume was different. Young people did not wear today's international youth costume of sneakers, jeans, and T-shirts. The youth of the world, rich or poor, dressed like stockbrokers. The artists wore perfectly regular shoes, suits, shirts, ties and hats. Only occasionally a painter, imitating the working classes, would wear a cap instead of a hat.

In France there is this very strict difference between the workers and the bourgeois. The bourgeois all wear hats—they wouldn't be caught dead in a cap except for hunting—and the workers all wear, or in those days wore, caps, and wouldn't be caught dead in a hat, even on Sunday afternoon walking out with a wife and children.

I got interested in this matter of the costume back in the 1920s and started asking the older artists around what they used to wear, and did they dress like stockbrokers, which we did, and Picasso thought for a minute and he said, "We dressed like workmen," which painters tend to do anyway. He said, "We wore sweaters and caps, but we bought our sweaters at Williams's."

Now Williams's of course was the stylish sporting goods store where you bought really good sweaters. You can dress for one class or another. That doesn't mean you are dressing cheap just because you dress up as a workman. As a matter of fact, young people today pay fifty to sixty dollars a pair for their sneakers and have five or six pairs. It's not an economy routine at all that they are involved in.

They don't understand either, because they've never lived that way, that we had no telephones. Nobody but rich people had telephones, and you had to be pretty rich to be bothered with it. Businesses had telephones, but ladies, gentlemen, artists and writers did not have telephones. You either dropped in on your friends or you saw them at cafés, and every time you said goodbye to your friends you brought out your little notebook and wrote down an engagement to see them again and you kept the appointment. If there was any emergency about that, you sent a little pneumatic telegram, *les petits bleus* they were called, but normally you lived on your program and there was no vagueness about it. There was no saying I'll call you back. Well, all these things seem very strange to the young people. They don't know how work was done. They believe me when I say that we dressed differently and lived with a different view of our time organization. They don't really quite understand it.

But anyway all that life style which I am describing applies to Gertrude Stein's house, where you didn't call up and say, "Can I come over?" You dropped in, as callers had been doing for centuries, at a suitable calling hour, and you dropped in only if you had been given the freedom of doing so by Gertrude saying, "We are always home in the late afternoon," or something like that. That meant you could drop in.

And then sometimes she would go out in the car with Alice of an evening and drop in on old friends. And if the friends were not there then you left word with the concierge that you had been there.

About once a week she used to go to the American Library and bring home lots of books, because she liked to read. She read American history, English and American memoirs, and detective stories. She paid no attention to the magazines that carry advertising, and she was usually kept *au courant* of contemporary arts and letters by what we used to call "little magazines," which were quite good reading, and she was sometimes in them, and so were her friends.

Well, the friends varied of course from decade to decade. In my time there were certain painters who had been old friends forever, such as Picasso. I think their friendship was never really interrupted except once for about a year and a half or two years, when under the influence of his surrealist friends he started writing poetry, and they even had it published for him, and when he asked Gertrude if she had read it she said yes, and what did she think of it? She said, "What would you think if I started to paint?" Well, he didn't like that at all, and so he stayed away for a couple of years, and when he reappeared again the matter was never mentioned.

Matisse had been a close friend in the earlier days, but after Matisse moved south I don't know that she ever saw him. He rarely came to Paris. She wrote a great deal about several of his wives. There was one of them that Alice had not liked very much, and so she appears quite often in the writing.

Actually Matisse was their original connection with modern art, because Gertrude's brother Michael Stein had a wife named Sarah, and Sarah had had drawing lessons from Matisse, oh way back in the earliest years of the century, and it was through Matisse that they all became a little bit aware that something was going on in the art world besides copying the past. And they started going to galleries and to the salons. The Salon des Indépendants was where you saw the work of new, shocking and outlandish painters, and the minute Gertrude saw the work of Picasso—well, Gertrude and Leo sort of found it together, they were living together and they looked at art together, actually all three of the Steins consulted one another about art, and Gertrude and Leo bought together from communal funds. Michael tended to stock up on Matisses; he had hundreds of them at one point. Gertrude and Leo fell heavily for Picasso, and they of course knew Braque and were strong on Juan Gris because of the Cubist affair.

The Cubist affair was a part of the separation that took place between Gertrude and her brother Leo around 1910 or 1911. But it was only a part of it, I think. Leo as an aesthetic specialist had reflected opinions about painting. He was two years older than Gertrude. He had been her mentor in looking at painting, and they were very close together, affectionately and sentimentally and intellectually, but when he couldn't really take Cubism and Gertrude found it exciting, that was kind of a little splinter in the gap. I think the big gap was made by Alice. Alice didn't really want them to be as close as they had been.

Alice actually was responsible, to my belief and knowledge, for four major separations. She did them so skillfully and so carefully that Gertrude hardly knew what happened, and maybe even thought that she herself was the responsible one. But there were four friendships that Alice deliberately ended. There was that closeness with the brother Leo. After the separation they divided up the furniture and the pictures, and he moved out, and they never saw each other and never even spoke, after being as close as that for fifteen or twenty years. There was more than just a quarrel about Cubism there. The second of the separations operated by Alice I think was from Mabel Dodge, whom they had both visited in Florence, and Alice sensed something that she did not wish to continue, and which she thought dangerous for her own hegemony, as they say in the newspapers. The third one took place in my own time. That was Ernest Hemingway. Gertrude and Hemingway were too close for Alice's pleasure.

The fourth one was with regard to a French poet whom I had introduced to the family, named Georges Hugnet. Gertrude was terribly taken with him and with his work, and she actually did something that she had never done for anybody else, for any living person. She translated a long poetic work of his. Now translated means into the language of her own poetry. Actually that translation was published once on opposite pages in an American literary magazine called *Pagany*. They had quarrelled before that came out, and she tried to stop it by telegram, but the telegram was too late, and so it was published in that form. But the European publication which had been planned in the opposite page form was stopped immediately, and Gertrude printed the work, that is to say her part, of the work, under the title "Before the Flowers of Friendship Faded Friendship Faded."

It was very important to Gertrude, that friendship with Georges Hugnet, and translating French poetry of a surrealistical nature. He was a member of the surrealist group, but this was not what they would call a surrealist text, that is to say it was not dictated by dreams. It's very beautiful French poetry, and what Gertrude turned up in her translation of it was the beginning of her grandest poetic period, really, which followed it in the form of a book called *Stanzas in Meditation*.

It was through those two works that she found a way to bring alive in her own poetry the devotion that she had always felt for Shakespeare's sonnets, and it is those works, particularly the *Stanzas in Meditation*, which I think are basically the source of a good deal of American poetry, including that of John Ashbery. They are hard to analyze, but the sound is that of the sonnets and the feeling is that of the sonnets, and there is a kind of real but obscure intimacy with the subject, such as in Shakespeare's sonnets. Gertrude was very devoted to those. She said, "You know, you can say that Bacon wrote the plays if you like, but Bacon could not have written the sonnets."

I now have got Gertrude up through the evening, and have spoken a little bit about her friends and enemies. After 1925, which is about the time I knew her, there was a somewhat new group of people. The painters were not the old painters, they were the neo-Romantic painters. She never really took them on, but she was always hoping that she could identify with some movement in painting as she had with the Cubist and pre-Cubist work of Picasso. In the late 1920s she took a great passion for the painting of Sir Francis Rose. He is an English painter, still extant, of fantastic gift and facility; but no major collector, dealer, or museum has ever followed Gertrude in the devotion to his painting that she took on at that time. Alice was pretty quiet about it, because she didn't want to interfere. She never interfered unless she had to. And after Gertrude's death Alice asked him to make them a joint tombstone, which he did, out of friendship—it's in the Pére Lachaise—but I don't think she saw him very much.

There were new poets around, including Georges Hugnet whom I had introduced into the household, and an American poet, whom I also introduced, by the name of Sherry Mangan, who was useful to Gertrude by getting her work published in American magazines, particularly in *Pagany*, for which he advised about European sources. She was a friend of Hart Crane's. She had got on with Jay Laughlin, who had started life as a poet, and then turned out to be a terribly useful publisher of poetry.

Edith Sitwell was around. Gertrude used to say that in the three Sitwells there was enough talent to make one first-class English man of letters. But Edith she rather liked, and didn't want to drop her or be rude to her, so she suggested that Edith have her portrait painted by Pavel Tchelitcheff who needed the money and the job. Well, they got on like a house on fire. The first time she went to pose he told her that she looked like Queen Elizabeth. She couldn't resist that, so they became very close friends, and their correspondence is still unopened. I think it will be a few more years before the twenty-five year period runs out, and then can be opened.

She did not get on with Eliot and his henchmen or hatchet men, whoever they were. He came to call one evening, and asked her if she would write something for his magazine, and since this happened to be the 15th of November she wrote a piece in her most obscure manner called "The 15th of November" which he published, but he said to his friends at the time, "Gertrude is very good, but she is not for us." Now what such a Papal character as Eliot would have meant by "us"—whom would he have meant by "us"?—I don't know.

But there were French men of letters around also. Bernard Faÿ, whom I had introduced to her, a French historian, was very close, and they remained close even throughout the war. Actually since he held the post of Director of the Bibliothèque Nationale under the Vichy Government, he was able to protect her so that she was never bothered by the Germans, though they occupied her house in the country several times.

Thornton Wilder at some point had become a very close friend. That was earlier, because when she came to America he was a professor at the University of Chicago, and he got her to give a course of six lectures there. He was very useful as a propagandist and helped her toward publication, which was always her problem. After she died his sister and Alice kept up a constant correspondence, exchanging recipes and things like that, and being very close. Thornton would write sometimes—there is some correspondence at Yale—but he didn't come to Paris very much, because the Germans had discovered him. The Germans thought that he was practically Goethe, and his play *The Skin of Our Teeth* was in 1946 being played in seventy-two German theaters all at once. The French didn't make over him quite like that. They translated his work, but as far as they were concerned he was just another novelist, a good American novelist, they liked American novelists, but they didn't open up their hearts in the way that the Germans had, and I think he felt rather sad about that. Anyway he stopped in Germany rather than coming to Paris.

Now I have talked about everything we need to talk about, except our own work together, and I don't need to take too much time for that because the evening's getting on. I had written in 1925 and 1926—I have set to music rather—certain texts of Gertrude's which were in existence. These had been performed in Paris. She knew them and liked them. Of course poets always adore being put to music, whether they like music or not, and Gertrude had very little sense of music. She was not "musical" in the way that Alice was.

But then in the spring of 1927 I said, "Why don't you write me a libretto?" We chose a subject, and she did write a libretto, and I did put it to music, and some six or seven years later it was produced. It was called *Four Saints in Three Acts*, and it was produced first in Hartford, then in New York and in Chicago, all in the year of 1934. It attracted a great deal of attention because it was the first time, I think perhaps ever in a major theater, that black actors or singers had been cast for a subject not involving black life. Also because it was the first theatrical operatic experience of both John Houseman and Frederick Ashton, whom I had got involved in the production. It was the first time that anybody had ever seen an opera directed not by a realistic stage director, but by a choreographer.

Well, I think that's the end until we get to Columbia University, when in 1945 Douglas Moore wrote to me asking if I would accept a commission from the Alice Ditson Fund to write another opera, and I said sure. I was in San Francisco, and I wrote to Gertrude and she said sure. I happened to have picked up at that moment—it was very difficult to do—a mission from the French Government which got me on an airplane to go to Europe in 1945. I also had an idea for a subject, which was nineteenth-century American political life.

So I went to Paris, and there we were together again, and she started immediately reading books about it and writing a libretto. She finished it in the early days of 1946, and sent me a typescript in February. I saw her again that spring and summer. We spoke at length about the opera, and we made plans and projects about it, and then in July she died, and I did not start writing the music until October. I wrote it in October and November. In December I played it for friends, all except the last scene, which I had saved because I wanted to get a reaction from friends before I went on to this summing-up scene. Then in January I did, in February and March I orchestrated it, and in May we produced it at the Brander Matthews Theater. Otto Luening conducted, Dorothy Dow sang the leading role, Teresa Stich-Randall, then a student here, was in the cast. Paul Du Pont did the scenery and costumes, John Taras the choreographic direction. I was always on to that idea.

I don't know why—you see there was nearly a twenty year difference between *Four Saints* and *The Mother of Us All*—I don't know why we didn't write an opera every year. We liked working together, we understood each other, she trusted me with music and I trusted her with words. I suppose it's simply that it never occurred to either of us that both of us would not always be living.

III. WORDS AND MUSIC (1989)

When I began in the early 1920s to compose music for texts by Gertrude Stein, my main purpose was musical. Or let us say musical and linguistic. For the tonal art is forever bound up with language, even though a brief separation does sometimes take place in the higher civilizations, rather in the way that the visual arts will occasionally abandon; or pretend to abandon, illustration. The musical art, moreover, in its more ambitious efforts toward linguistic union, has regularly entwined itself with liturgical texts and dramatic continuities.

Now the liturgical connection has been operating successfully ever since medieval times and even earlier; but in Western Europe it regularly had bypassed the local dialects and the budding languages, remaining attached for administrative reasons to the formalistic, the far less vivid Latin. The first modern tongues to take on music liturgically (the first gesture after their doctrinal breakaways from Rome) were English and German, both in the sixteenth century. The Latin-based local idioms had made no great effort toward entering the Catholic liturgy until today's ecumenical trend got them involved. But toward the end of that same sixteenth century, which was producing liturgically such remarkable results for English and for German, Italian musicians in Florence had begun to perfect for secular purposes (for the stage) a blending of music with language so miraculously homogenized that a new word had to be found for it. They called it opera, or "work"; and work was actually what it did, invigorating the theater internationally in a manner most remarkable. For the English poetic theater, after the times of Elizabeth I and James I, began to lose vigor at home and never seemed able to travel much abroad. But the Italian lyric theater in less than a century had begun to implant itself in one country after another and in one language after another. It took on French with Lully in the middle seventeenth century, German in the late eighteenth with Mozart, Russian in the nineteenth, beginning in the 1840s with Glinka.[1]

Serious opera seems never to have felt quite comfortable, however, in English or in Spanish, languages of which the poetic style, highly florid, made music for the tragic theater almost unnecessary. Comedies with added song and dance numbers existed of course everywhere; but music rarely served in them for much more than sentiment, being too slow, hence too clumsy a medium for putting over either sight gags or verbal jokes, except in the patter songs that are specific to the genius of English. Nevertheless, English-language composers have never stopped making passes at the opera. It is as if we bore it, all of us, an unrequited love. My own hope toward its capture was to bypass wherever possible the congealments of Italian, French, German, and Russian acting styles, all those ways and gestures so brilliantly based on the very prosody and sound of their poetry. For an American to aspire toward avoiding these may have seemed over-ambitious. But for one living in Europe, as I did for several decades, it may have been an advantage being able finally to recognize the foreignness of all such conventions and to reject them as too hopelessly, too indissolubly Italian or French or German or Russian, or even English, should some inopportune British mannerism make them seem laughable to us.

Curiously enough, British and American ways in both speech and movement differ far less on the stage, especially when set to music, than they do in civil life. Nevertheless, there is every difference imaginable between the cadences and contradictions of Gertrude Stein, her subtle syntaxes and maybe stammerings, and those of practically any other author, American or English. More than that, the wit, her seemingly endless runnings-on, can add up to a quite impressive obscurity. And this, moreover, is made out of real English words, each of them having a weighty history, a meaning, and a place in the dictionary.

The whole setup of her writing, from the time I first encountered it back in 1919, in a book called *Tender Buttons*, was to me both exciting and disturbing. Also, as it turned out, valuable. For with meanings jumbled and syntax violated, but with the words themselves all the more shockingly present, I could put those texts to music with a minimum of temptation toward the emotional conventions, spend my whole effort on the rhythm of the language, and its specific Anglo-American sound, adding shape, where that seemed to be needed, and it usually was, from music's own devices. I had begun doing this in 1923, before I ever met Miss Stein; and I ended it all by setting our second opera, *The Mother of Us All*, in the year of her death, 1946. This was actually her last completed piece of writing and, like our earlier operatic collaboration, *Four Saints in Three Acts*, from 1927, had been handmade for me.

Four Saints is a text of great obscurity. Even so, when mated to music, it works. Our next opera, separated from the other by nineteen years and by a gradual return on her part to telling a story straight, was for the most part clear. Both *Four Saints* and *The Mother* offer protagonists not young, not old, but domineeringly female—St. Theresa of Avila and Susan B. Anthony. In both cases, too, the scene is historical; and the literary form is closer to that of an Elizabethan masque than to a continuous dramatic narrative. But there the resemblance ends. The background of the first is Catholic, Counter-Reformational, baroque, ecstatic. The other deals with nineteenth-century America—which is populist, idealist, Protestant, neighborly (in spite of the Civil War), and optimistic. The saints are dominated by inspirations from on high, by chants and miracles, by orders and commands, and by the disciplines of choral singing. The Americans of *The Mother*, group-controlled not by command but by their own spontaneity, are addicted to gospel hymns, darn-fool ditties, inspirational oratory, and parades. Nevertheless the music of the work, or so Carl Van Vechten found, is an apotheosis of the military march. I do not know that this is true. All I know is that having previously set a text of great obscurity, I took on with no less joy the setting of one so intensely full of meanings, at least for any American, that it has seldom failed at the end to draw tears. For this result, my having earlier worked on texts without much overt meaning had been of value. It had forced me to hear the sounds that the American language really makes when sung, and to eliminate all those recourses to European emotions that are automatically brought forth when European musicians get involved with dramatic poetry, with the stage. European historic models, music's old masters, let me assure you, are not easy to escape from. And if any such evasion, however minor, takes place in *The Mother*, that is due, I think, to both Miss Stein and myself having for so long, in our work, avoided customary ways and attitudes that when we got around to embracing them we could do so with a certain freshness.

Notes

1. The Florentine group (or Camerata) had begun with Greek music studies by Galileo Galilei. Giulio Caccini's *L'Euridice* dates from 1600. Monteverdi's *L'Orfeo* was produced in Mantua, 1607; but, his later works were mostly performed in Venice. The latter city is said to have supported at one time in the eighteenth century seventy-five neighborhood theaters all giving opera.

On, Donald Sutherland (1978)

Donald Sutherland's most remarkable quality, outside of his devotion in friendship, is the splendor of his mind—quick, retentive, comprehensive, and penetrating, trained in Latin and Greek, accomplished in other languages and completely read in the classics of English, French, Spanish, German, Italian. It is especially in French and Spanish, I think, that his insideness of understanding is as deep as in his native English. And this particular virtuosity, operating through a broad acquaintance with historic literary methods in all these languages, with classical poetics, and with esthetics ancient and modern, has given him a unique skill as a solver of difficult problems in Comp. Lit.

His powers of poetic analysis, exercised through a sonnet of Gerard Manley Hopkins in *On, Romanticism*; through unmasking the linguistic motivations of a very difficult author in *Gertrude Stein: a Biography of Her Work*; through his detective-like exposures of meaning in French and Spanish poetry as revealed in essays on Tristan Corbiere and on Rimbaud, on Rafael Alberti and on Octavio Paz in *Parnassus* magazine—all these searchlights are evidence of a readiness both spontaneous and accurate that suggests the trained reflexes of a great bullfighter.

Nevertheless, I have the feeling that not Spanish but French is the heart of truth for Sutherland, the next great language (always excepting his own Anglo-American) after Greek. His penchant for kidding the stiffness of Spanish vocabulary as well as the arbitrary, almost dogmatic assumptions of the Spanish regarding poetry (in spite of a long history of poetic theatre both tragic and comic and of sentiments religiophilosophical ever so tenderly expressed in epic vein as well as lyrical) all this is expressed with gentleness and with a comic nudge no less firmly loving than those of the great Spaniards themselves, but still with a kiss of wit quite French, as if Spain, oh yes, were precious and like nothing else, but France and in French were where life made sense for real.

The Blue Clown is his book embodying the fullness with which he can love Spain without accepting her.

The book on Gertrude Stein is a love letter from a young scholar thanking an older woman for being a woman and difficult, and for presenting a problem worthy of his powers.

On, Romanticism offers a three-way choice of artistic temperaments and their operating methods—classic, romantic, and baroque—a proposal so radical of a problem long unsolved by the dualistic approach that it threatens the whole layout of literary and artistic history. Actually the shock of its impact seems to have stunned the scholastic world. Everybody serious about culture and its study has read the book or heard of it. Don't be deceived about that. But practically no one has taken up its offer. The quarterly reviews have kept silent about it; the dominant scholars have not mentioned it to students, won't even talk about it when asked. I presume they are waiting to see what happens to the idea eventually in the depths of their own minds and in those of their colleagues. For now, it is still an "underground" idea. In a generation or two it will no doubt surface somewhere, probably in Comp. Lit.

Not in Comp. Lit. as nowadays laid out, a pool of late nineteenth-century poets and estheticians operating from Paris, but in some fresher view of art and culture that might straddle the visual, the verbal, and the auditory. Yes, certainly, music will have to be included, and the fine-arts mafia laid low.

This outcome none of us living will ever see. But I am convinced something of the kind will come about. And when it does, *On, Romanticism* will be, if not its Bible, the voice of a major prophet.

There remains an autobiography yet to see print. I have read it. This does not expound any further the central idea of *On, Romanticism.* A great deal of it treats of a friendship with Alice Toklas. But it does continue the voyage of a remarkable mind, first seen with all sails full in the book on Gertrude Stein. With more adventures of that mind available it will be harder to keep its high powers unrecognized, unpraised, and unstudied. Its discoveries are already, I fancy, not unfeared.

EDWIN DENBY (1984)

Edwin and I were friends for well over fifty years. I first knew him in 1929. He was working in one of the German opera houses, the Hessian State Theater in Darmstadt, which was quite famous for its modernistic productions—not merely modernistic but by young and contemporary writers who were famous, far-out ones, like Darius Milhaud and Satie and so forth. Edwin wrote me knowing that I had written an opera on a text of Gertrude Stein (*Four Saints in Three Acts*), saying that his colleagues might very well like to produce it there, and what did I think of the idea that he, being bilingual in German and English, would be responsible for the translation. He was spending the summer in Collioure in the southeastern part of France; and on my way either to or from (I forget which) the island of Majorca, I stopped for a day or so there, and we had a fine visit and made friends. I had not seen him before.

After that I sent to the opera house, or sent to him for the opera house, a copy of the libretto so that they would know how far out that was. And they still wanted to see the score, so I managed to make a copy of the score and sent it along. It produced a kind of explosion. It was refused. They'd been doing perhaps too many modern or modernistic works and not enough *Trovatores*.

Anyway, the musical wing revolted at that point in regard to my opera. And the whole troupe, a rather famous director, and decorators, and the ballet people, including Edwin, all moved up to Berlin. This included Rudolf Bing, no less.[1] A couple of years after that, the thing broke up with the German political conditions, and the main part of the troupe moved off to England to Glyndebourne.

Edwin resigned from the ballet in Berlin and came to live in New York, and shortly after, many of his nice German friends turned up. He was surrounded by very nice artistic German friends, who didn't feel that there was much for them in Germany at that particular time.

I remember his giving a party for his New York friends and his nice German friends—he was already living in the loft on Twenty-First Street—and the party was going just fine. It was a very distinguished assemblage of people, and Edwin had bought and distributed large monuments of cheese and about a dozen bottles of extremely expensive Scotch whisky. One of the German composers arrived at the top of that long staircase—and, coming in there, seeing this highly simplified décor, so to speak, but with all of his nice friends there, both German and American, couldn't quite make it all out. And he wondered if this weren't—if he'd got into some kind of slum where he didn't belong. But there were friends, and it—ah! all of a sudden he understood—it was some kind of a charade. And he said, "Ach! Ich verstehe. Künstler ohne Gelt" ("Artists with no money!"). That was the number, apparently, that he thought was being done.

In 1936 Edwin and I actually worked on a show together for the Federal Theater. He made the translation of that from the French. It was a farce by Labiche known in French as *Un Chapeau de paille d'Italie*, and which we called *Horse Eats Hat*. It was a brilliant production. Oh, very brilliant. And if the names were printed today, of course, it would make an all-star cast. Nobody in it was really particularly well known then except Orson Welles. But Orson was in the cast, and Joe Cotten and Hiram Sherman, Orson's wife, Virginia, Arlene Francis, Paula Laurence. The music was by Paul Bowles, who had never done music to a show before. There was a great deal of it, and he didn't feel quite as if he could get through making an orchestra score, so I did that more or less for him. And it was all, as I say, all very brilliant indeed, and we had lots of fun. Paul was so shocked at having to have his music orchestrated by somebody else that he hastily learned how to orchestrate and he did a great many theater productions after that, all distinguished and everything nice; and he never permitted anybody to orchestrate his music.

In '37—that was the next year—Edwin was the librettist for a high-school opera, *The Second Hurricane*, by Aaron Copland, which was produced at the Henry Street or the Grand Street Theater, again under the best of circumstances, with Lehman Engel conducting and Orson Welles directing the stage.

After that I was mostly in Europe, and I didn't see Edwin until in the early forties, when I came to New York to work on the *Herald Tribune*. And after we got into the war, our dance reviewer, Walter Terry, went to the war and the post was empty. So I suggested to the management that Edwin, who had been writing for Minna Lederman's magazine, *Modern Music*, quite fine dance articles—that he be engaged as a replacement. He was; and he was a great success. Everybody adored him. Everybody adored his writing. But in slightly less than two years, the war was over and Walter Terry came back and was legally entitled to his job, and there was no way of keeping Edwin on, much as everybody wanted to. So he worked for other papers or magazines. But his dance reviews, of course, were always collected. They became famous instantly and they still are. He's probably the most famous dance critic, or the most admired, that anybody knows about now.

But you see, all this time Edwin was writing poetry. And the ease and grace of the dance criticism sort of obscured the qualities of the poetry. Only recently, after his death, Lincoln Kirstein published a piece, sort of a tribute, in *The New York Review of Books*, in which he gave Edwin full credit for the excellence of that poetry. I'd always adored it, but it was hard for other people to take. The admirers of his poetry found it a great deal harder to swallow than the dance criticism, which went down so easy. Because the poetry was complex, compact, and gritty of texture. It didn't run on like Shelley, nothing like that. It stuck in your teeth, much more like the Shakespeare sonnets.

Still later, at Frank O'Hara's funeral, Edwin Denby referred to O'Hara as the greatest living poet. I rather like to think of Edwin in that way myself.

Note

1. In 1929 at Darmstadt's Hessisches Landes theater (actually two theaters, the larger for opera, the smaller for plays and operettas, operating for a ten-month season), Denby was working as a dancer and assistant régisseur. His colleagues included Generalintendant and stage director Carl Ebert; Ebert's assistant artistic administrator, Rudolf Bing; Generalmusikdirektor and principal conductor Karl Böhm; the conductors Max Rudolf and Carl Bamburger; stage director Carl Maria Rabenalt; and designer Wilhelm Reinking. In 1931 Bing, Ebert, and others assumed artistic management of one of Berlin's three opera companies, the Städtische Oper (City Opera) in Charlottenburg, and Denby joined as a dancer. His associates here included the conductors Fritz Stiedry and Fritz Busch, designer Caspar Neher, and composer Kurt Weill, and his wife, Lotte Lenya.

THE FRIENDS AND ENEMIES OF MODERN MUSIC [EVERETT "CHICK" AUSTIN] (1958)

The idea of a cultural institution designed to spread enlightenment along the whole cultural front is dear both to our century and to the one that preceded ours. Atheneum is a name beloved of the nineteenth century for such an enterprise. Most of the establishments bearing that name have long since turned into just libraries with a lecture hall, but the ideal has never been abandoned.

Universities have essayed to embody it too, and their efforts have led to a broadening of art experience for the young. Unfortunately the immaturity of their student public tends to stabilize many of the cultural branches as practiced there, especially the spoken stage, the dance, the opera, at an amateur level. The penetration of many such efforts into the adult life of a community has remained, in consequence, somewhat superficial.

The art museum today, at least in the United States, also strives for a full cultural expression. It does not try to replace the library and the university altogether, but it does endeavor to supplement their activities. Music and the stage, pageantry and dancing, have indeed in most of our newer museum structures a built-in home where delights for the ear are offered in happy proximity to enjoyments for the eye.

Chick Austin (and for all who knew him well the formal "A. Everett Austin, Jr." was never more than a baptismal pseudonym) was a pioneer in converting an atheneum and an art collection into a museum in the modern meaning. Toward this end he caused a theater to be built into the Avery Memorial wing of the Wadsworth Atheneum, which was erected during his tenure as its director. And in that theater he produced plays, operas, ballets, all sorts of stage spectacles, old and new.

Most of these were new, so new indeed and so distinguished that their listing contains an extraordinary number of first appearances of works and artists whose names are now classical. Eugene Berman's first theater set was made for a concert which I conducted there in 1936. Here Pavel Tchelitchew produced in 1934, also for a concert, his first stage set to be seen in America. Frederick Ashton had made his American debut as choreographer earlier that year with the opera *Four Saints in Three Acts*. That same production embodied the first stage direction of John Houseman and the unique sets and costumes of Florine Stettheimer. Unique also is the mobile set designed by Alexander Calder for the *Socrate* of Erik Satie, given in 1936. Operas by Avery Claflin, George Kleinsinger, and Ernst Krenek also came out on those boards. Eva Gauthier, Ada MacLeish, Elsie Houston, and Maxine Sullivan all sang there their most distinguished programs. And Ballet Caravan (direct progenitor of the New York City Ballet) danced there in 1937 three original American works, including a world première. Among my own works that were first performed publicly in that theater are the opera *Four Saints in Three Acts* (libretto by Gertrude Stein), the ballet *Filling Station* (choreography by Lew Christensen), and a String Quartet (No. 2).

Long before the Avery Memorial was built Chick had started bringing Hartford up to date on music through concerts held in private houses. He had organized for the purpose a subscription society, which he called "The Friends and Enemies of Modern Music." They gave, as I remember, some six concerts a year; and the works played were almost all contemporary. I remember one concert, held at Chick's own house, where five American composers—Roy Harris, Aaron Copland, George Antheil, Paul Bowles, and myself—all played works by one another.

When the Avery Memorial was opened in February 1934, the Friends and Enemies moved their concerts into that theater and enlarged their scope. It was at this time that operas and ballets came into the series. We also began (I say "we" because from 1934 through 1936 I was listed as their "musical director") to give concerts in specially designed stage sets. Tchelitchew, Berman, and Calder contributed memorable ones. Chick himself designed others. All were ingenious, imaginative, and beautifully executed.

These sets involved two lines of experiment that have not, so far, been pursued further in the theater. One is the designing of stage sets for particular concerts. The other is the use of a sculptor's awareness about space and solidity as a help to theatrical mounting.

Building sets for single concerts was current in Europe till the end of the eighteenth century, and many famous artists designed them. But our present musical tradition has tended to consider these a frivolous effort and possibly distracting to auditory concentration. Certainly their design is a special problem, to make them appropriate but not illustrative, interesting but not over-busy. And certainly they are not cheap, not in time nor thought nor money. But when they are imaginative and tasteful they can add a glory to the musical occasion and a glamour all unforeseen that are ever so appropriate to music performed in an establishment devoted mainly to the visual arts.

As for sculpture on the stage, that too is not without precedent. Serge Diaghilev, of course, used easel painters to the great advantage of his ballet spectacles. Picasso, Matisse, Braque, Gris, Derain, and many others, older and younger, brought modernist excitement to his repertory. In Russia and in Germany before World War I, a movement in art known as Constructivism had already brought to the speaking stage an exploitation of vertical space through the use of ladders, steps, and runways, that the classical ballet, which works mostly from a floor, could not much use. But this kind of construction, still in style, became very early a form of functional building, useful for adding dynamism to stage direction, if not always a visual aid toward emphasizing through beauty the poetic expression of the play itself. Diaghilev also, as late as 1927, had put on the stage for Henri Sauguet's ballet *La Chatte* constructivist statuary by Gabo and Pevsner. However, in that whole rejuvenation of staging that our century has witnessed and to which the painters, like the choreographers, have contributed so abundantly, the sculptor and the architect have not been used as they should have been.

Calder's set for Erik Satie's *Socrate*, three dialogues out of Plato set to music for voice and orchestra, is so plain to look at and yet so delicately complex in its movements (for it does move and without injury to musical effect), so intensely in accord with the meaning of the musical work and yet so rigidly aloof from any over-obvious illustrating of it, that it remains in my memory as one of our century's major achievements in stage investiture.

Its layout is like this. The orchestra is in the pit. Two singers, a man and a woman, stand very far downstage and at the two sides, dressed in evening clothes and singing from black music stands. Upstage is a sky-blue backdrop or cyclorama against which hangs high at house right (by invisible wires) an enormous disk of bright red. Downstage to house right hangs (also by invisible wires and high) a large sphere made of fine aluminum tubing to represent meridians of longitude. It is hollow and transparent, a mechanical drawing in the round. Centerstage and to the left stand two tall flats of different heights, also invisibly supported, painted white.

During the first section of the work, which recounts Alcibiades's speech in praise of Socrates from *The Banquet*, no scenery moves. During the second, the walk with Phaedrus along the river Eleusis, the sphere revolves on its invisible axis at a moderate speed, neither fast nor slow. During the third movement of the work, which recounts the death of Socrates, the sphere is still, but all the other hanging objects move. The white flats tilt to the right and very slowly lie down, first on their edge and then flat, becoming visible. Then they turn over, come up black, the color of their other side, and slowly stand erect again, this time at stage right. Meanwhile, from the beginning of this section, the red disk has been moving diagonally (and very slowly) across the blue backdrop till at the end, when the movement of the flats from left to right (and from white to black) has been completed, the disk is low and on the viewer's left. Both the composition of the stage picture and the balance of its color have been changed. So has its meaning. But the music has not been interfered with, so simple are the pictorial elements and so sedately magical their movements.

Others surely will analyse Chick's sources of intellectual orientation and enumerate his many contributions to private collecting, to museum administration, and to public enlightenment. And in those achievements he will be A. Everett Austin, Jr. For me he remains Chick and a sheer delight for wholeness as a man. He had talent, taste, energy, good looks and pride in them. Passion, too, and affection and warmth and loyalty. He liked food and clothes and driving cars and buying things and putting on a show. He was never afraid to do what he wanted to do, and what he wanted to do was to make art live and to enrich everybody's life with it. He was no snob. He was simply a man of taste with a vast love for all that has beauty and distinction and with a missionary's vocation.

The man of taste in our time is so often devitalized and a prig, and the man of talent so often an ignoramus, or else all pushing and political, that Chick, in our memories as well as in his achievements, still burns with a special flame. He not only bought works of art, exposed and conserved them, he caused them to be brought into existence, to attain the fulfillment of performance. He was nobly an amateur in everything he did, but there was nothing amateurish about anything he did. He worked hard and played hard, as indeed did everybody around him. He would not tolerate us otherwise. Wherever he passed, he changed the world. Those who did not wish their world changed did better to avoid him. Trying to fight him, as trustees sometimes did, meant certain defeat, perhaps for both sides, because Chick was a whole cultural movement in one man and, in the full sense of the word, irresistible.

He used to like to say that the main purpose of a museum was to keep its director entertained. And certainly, if it doesn't do that, God help us all. Certainly, also, one wishes there were more men like him to take both culture and fun as straightforward activities and not mutually exclusive. In my view, these are the only ones safely to be trusted with the spending of public monies and with the administering of our cultural institutions.

VI

SUCCESSORS

Whereas opportunistic artists fear discussing their successors publicly (though become eager to make decisions about them privately, as in granting prizes, say), Thomson suffered no such fears—not when he worked at The Paper or afterwards. Thanks to breadth of taste, he could praise composers who opposed each other and damn equally. The 1968 essay on Pierre Boulez is extraordinarily prescient about a composer/performer whose reputation has not worn well, at least in America. Once Thomson decided he had nothing to fear, he went to work, penning capsule sketches that are really models of their kind for both insight and style.

John Cage, whose recent compositions made up the program of a concert given yesterday afternoon at the New School for Social Research, is already famous as a specialist in the use of percussive sounds. Two years ago the Museum of Modern Art presented pieces by him for a large group of players using flowerpots, brake bands, electric buzzers, and similar objects not primarily musical but capable of producing a wide variety of interesting sounds all the same. The works offered yesterday included an even greater variety of sounds, all prepared by inserting bits of metal, wood, rubber, or leather at carefully studied points and distances between the strings of an ordinary pianoforte.

The effect in general is slightly reminiscent, on first hearing, of Indonesian gamelan orchestras, though the interior structure of Mr. Cage's music is not Oriental at all. His work attaches itself, in fact, to two different traditions of Western modernism. One is the percussive experiments begun by Marinetti's Futurist Noisemakers and continued in the music of Edgar Varèse, Henry Cowell, and George Antheil, all of which, though made in full awareness of Oriental methods, is thoroughly Western in its expression. The other is, curiously enough, the atonal music of Arnold Schönberg.

Mr. Cage has carried Schönberg's harmonic maneuvers to their logical conclusion. He has produced atonal music not by causing the twelve tones of the chromatic scale to contradict one another consistently, but by eliminating, to start with, all sounds of precise pitch. He substitutes for the chromatic scale a gamut of pings, plucks, and delicate thuds that is both varied and expressive and that is different in each piece. By thus getting rid, at the beginning, of the constricting element in atonal writing—which is the necessity of taking constant care to avoid making classical harmony with a standardized palette of instrumental sounds and pitches that exists primarily for the purpose of producing such harmony—Mr. Cage has been free to develop the rhythmic element of composition, which is the weakest element in the Schönbergian style, to a point of sophistication unmatched in the technique of any other living composer.

His continuity devices are chiefly those of the Schönberg school. There are themes and sometimes melodies, even, though these are limited, when they have real pitch, to the range of a fourth, thus avoiding the tonal effect of dominant and tonic. All these appear in augmentation, diminution, inversion, fragmentation, and the various kinds of canon. That these procedures do not take over a piece and become its subject, or game, is due to Cage's genius as a musician. He writes music for expressive purposes; and the novelty of his timbres, the logic of his discourse, are used to intensify communication, not as ends in themselves. His work represents, in consequence, not only the most advanced methods now in use anywhere but original expression of the very highest poetic quality. And this has been proved now through all the classical occasions—theater, ballet, song, orchestral composition, and chamber music.

One of the works was played yesterday by the composer, the other two by Arthur Gold and Robert Fizdale, duopianists. The perfect execution of these young men, their rhythm, lightness and absolute equality of scale, and the singing sounds they derived from their instruments, in spite of the fact that the strings were all damped in various ways, made one wish to hear them operate on music less special, as well. The concert was a delight from every point of view.

GIAN-CARLO MENOTTI

I (1947)

The ballet society produced last night at the Heckscher Theater two operas by Gian-Carlo Menotti, one of them, *The Telephone*, a world première. The other, *The Medium*, had been given for the first time last May at the Brander Mathews Theater in Columbia University by the Columbia Theater Associates. Both are first-class musico-theatrical works. The first is an opera buffa, light and full of laughter. The second is a tragedy in melodramatic vein that is the most gripping operatic narrative this reviewer has witnessed in many a year.

The Medium is about the private life of a woman who evokes by trickery, for paying customers, visions and voices of the dead. Caught up in her own psychic ambience, and aided by alcohol, she imagines she feels a hand on her throat. Terrified by the experience, she renounces her racket and exposes it to her clients. They refuse to believe that what they had wanted to believe in was false. At this point, the medium goes hysterical and murders a dumb boy who was previously part of her household and an aid in her trickery setup.

No such reduction of the plot can give an idea of how absorbing this work is. I have heard it three times and it never fails to hold me enthralled. Mr. Menotti's libretto, which he wrote himself, and his music form a unit that is deeply touching and terrifying. And if the second act is a little reminiscent as theater (though not as music) of the second act of Puccini's *La Tosca*, the piece in no way suffers by comparison with that infallible piece of stage craft. The play wrings every heart string, and so does the music. I cannot conceive the whole work otherwise than as destined for a long and successful career.

The Telephone, or *L'Amour à Trois*, is a skit about a young man whose girl friend is so busy talking to people on the telephone that the only way he can get her attention for a proposal of marriage is to go out to the corner drugstore and call her up himself. It is gay and funny and completely humane. Both operas, indeed, are infused with a straightforward humanity that is a welcome note of sincerity in contemporary operatic composition. Their librettos are skillfully made, and their music is skillfully composed. But that is not the main point. Their unusual efficacy as operas comes from their frankly Italianate treatment of ordinary human beings as thoroughly interesting.

The visual production of *The Medium* was one of unusual distinction. The casting of both operas was excellent. Particularly notable for both singing and acting were Marie Powers, who sang the title role in *The Medium* (her predecessor, Claramae Turner, was immediately engaged by the Metropolitan Opera), and Evelyn Keller, who sang the part of her daughter. Leo Coleman, who mimed the mute, was admirable also. Both operas were decorated and costumed more than prettily by Horace Armistead. Mr. Menotti, who directed them, in addition to having written both words and music, proved himself no less an expert in this domain than in the others. The musical direction of Leon Barzin was, as usual, impeccable.

Evviva Menotti!

II. PATHOS AND THE MACABRE (1950)

The Consul is all Gian-Carlo Menotti's—the play, the music, the casting, the stage direction—a one-man music drama concentrated and powerful. To report on it as merely a piece of music would give no idea of its real nature. To recount it as drama would not explain its intensity. It is a play of horror and deep pathos, but these qualities in it are as much a result of musical stylization as they are of dramatic exposition.

It is musical investiture, with all the stiffness of stage movement that this involves, that has allowed the author to point up the story with irony and with a comic relief that in any realistic presentation would have been offensive to taste. Also, the story might have come out weak, from the very concentration of its appeal to pity, in a more straightforward telling. All the theater conventions, indeed—prose speech, rhyme, instrumental music, song, recitative, and choreography—have combined to give that story breadth of appeal and emotional perspective.

The musical score is apt and ever illustrative. Also, it is valuable to the narrative through its sustained emotional plan. Harmonically it is a bit chromatic and fussy, melodically a shade undistinguished. Constant undecisive modulation and the insistent repetition of melodic fragments tantalize the listener more than they satisfy musically. Recitative passages, however, are so skillfully set as to be almost unnoticeable, to provoke no listener resistance to this most perilous of all opera conventions. And the music of orchestral commentary is everywhere inventive and a help. The two big solos, a lullaby and a denunciation scene, are valuable to the play's progress and emphasis, but musically not very memorable.

The most striking and original musico-dramatic effect in the whole spectacle is the final scene, a fifteen-minute suicide by gas. Here the orchestra and choreographer take over, though there is some singing too. A vision of death beyond the threshold, set to a waltz in coffin clothes, brings the play to a moving end by exploiting in the most daring manner Mr. Menotti's gift for combining the macabre with the pathetic. A nightmare scene in the second act and a hypnotist's trick on the customers waiting in the office of the consulate had prepared stylistically this finale. All the same, it is as surprising as it is brilliant and vigorous, the most hair-raising among the many virtuoso theatrical effects that the author's fancy has conceived.

In a cast notable for musical excellence Patricia Neway, as the wife of a Resistance hero, stands out as a singing actress of unusual power. Marie Powers, the Mother, though satisfactory, is less impressive. Gloria Lane, the consulate secretary, is thoroughly pleasing in every way. All the men are good, and so are the singers of secondary roles. Lehman Engel, at the conductor's desk, produces sound orchestral balances, impeccable pacing of the whole, and unfailing dramatic animation. *The Consul* is a music drama of great power in a production remarkably efficient. I doubt if it makes musical history, but the musical elements contribute in a major way to a spectacle that may well have its place in our century's history of the stage. Mr. Menotti, though not quite a first-class composer, is surely a bold, an original dramatic author. And music is the language that he writes his dramas in.

THE GENIUS TYPE [PIERRE BOULEZ] (1968)

That the concept represented in popular esthetics by avant-garde is applicable to music today, or in our century for that matter, would be hard to demonstrate. The idea that art has a continuous history which moves forward in both time and exploration is no less a trouble for dealing with the real artifacts, though a bit of it is required for explaining short-term developments like the classical symphony—Haydn through Schubert is only fifty years—or the growth of nontonal music from its germinal state of 1899 in Arnold Schönberg's *Verklärte Nacht* to the completed formulation of the twelve-tone method around 1923.

The trouble with *avant-garde*, originally a term in military tactics, is that it assumes the adventures of individual and small-group experimenters to be justifiable only as they may open up a terrain through which some larger army will then be able to pass. But it fails to explain who constitutes this army and what is its objective, since a military advance, however massive, is not a migration. It cannot be the world public of concert subscribers and record buyers, since many important achievements, both unique and influential, arrive at such distribution far too meagerly and too late to serve culture consumption efficiently. The music of Erik Satie and of Schönberg's group are cases in point. It is all published now and largely recorded but still not much played; the armies of musical exploitation, industrial and academic, have not carried it along with them in their world conquest.

The idea that original work of this quality nourishes the younger composer is no less hard to justify. It becomes a part of his education, naturally; but his uses of it are inevitably dilutions, since innovations in art are generally brought to full term by their inventors (and a few close comrades) long before distribution gets hold of them. Actually, distributors tend to adopt only that which seems complete, presenting it as a novelty, which it may be for them, or as "experimental," which by this time it is not, save as a sales line. Short-term developments certainly represent a true evolution. But incorporating them through the professional conservatories into the living tradition of music is a hit-or-miss affair, any occupation rights in these centers of power being reserved for successful modernists, themselves mostly diluters of their sources. American universities have a way of taking up the more successful moderns, subjecting them to institutionally certified examination, and then sinking their remains in a mud puddle ironically called "mainstream."

Europeans tend to think of history less as a river and more as a library or museum, where any citizen can seek to be culturally entertained, informed, or inspired by high example. (The designers of women's fashions are forever adapting to their use models from the libraries of historic costume; working as fast as they do, they are less bound than prouder artists to the fads of merely yesterday.) Western Europe, in fact, tends to view itself altogether as a museum and the creators of its major artifacts as a special type of workman, the "genius." This kind of artist cannot be imagined without the background of a long cultural history and a pedagogical tradition based on the achievements of that history. The German composer, the French painter, the English poet—Beethoven, Schubert, Cézanne, Degas, Shakespeare, Keats—can often create remarkably with only minimal preparation, since the tradition of sound workmanship and a full history of it have been as close to his childhood as sports and cars and soda fountains to ours. In the American language genius merely means a high I.Q.; in Europe it means that you can speak for your time in language of precision and freedom.

Now the very idea that artists of genius have existed and still appear and that their works are entitled to preservation tends to destroy confidence in progress and also in history as a stream. Nevertheless, it is not possible today for the artist in any metropolitan center to conceive his talents as functioning otherwise than in some kind of continuous career. And it is equally impossible for him to carry on such a career without a belief in some version of his art's recent history. It may even become necessary for him to retell polemically that history, in order that it may appear to others a preparation for him. The European composer's view of himself as not only an heir of music's past—a member of the family—but also an end-of-the-line genius terminating an important shortterm development has turned him into an inveterate explainer of music. No major composer of our century, I think, possibly excepting Ravel, has failed to write at least one book. The painters have written too, and brilliantly; but criticism, scholarship, and the price conspiracy have all denied them authority. The writings of Schönberg, Webern, Berg, Debussy, Satie, Stravinsky, Bartók, Milhaud, Messiaen, and Pierre Boulez are living witnesses to musical thought in our time; and they constitute, right along with historical studies, a valid part of music's verbal script.

Boulez, now forty-three, is unquestionably a genius figure and typically a French one, though the Germans captured him some fifteen years ago through a publication contract (with Universal of Vienna), later taking physical possession through a well-paid composer-in-residence post in Baden-Baden at the Southwest Radio. Meanwhile he had toured the world constantly as music director for the theatrical troupe of Madeleine Renaud and Jean-Louis Barrault. From 1954 they offered hospitality in the Théâtre Marigny, later in the Odéon-Théâtre de France, for his Concerts du Domaine Musical, the only musical series in the world, to my knowledge, which attracts a broad intellectual public of not only musicians but also painters, poets, scholars, and others professionally distinguished. Along with Boulez's own works these programs contain whatever is most far-out in Germany, France, Italy, and Belgium, and quite regularly homage-performances of works by the founding fathers of dodecaphony and occasionally of Bartók, Varèse, Stravinsky, Elliott Carter, Earle Brown, Iannis Xenakis.

Boulez himself is responsible for rehearsing these concerts and for most of the conducting. Passionate, painstaking, and aurally exact, as well as long used to exercising musical responsibility, Boulez is today a conductor of such remarkable powers that although he still works chiefly in the modern repertory, he has been led (or captured) to undertake lengthy tours in Germany, England, and the United States, as well as gramophone recordings, that have in the last decade placed him among the world's most-in-demand directors and at the same time diminished radically his output as a composer.

That output, before 1960, was in spite of its textural complexity both large and, in the view of all who follow post-World War II music, of the very first importance. Actually today's modern movement, though it contains at least a dozen composers of high quality, is dominated by the three over-forty masters who genuinely excite the young—Pierre Boulez, Karlheinz Stockhausen, and John Cage. All three, moreover, have proved effective teachers of their own composing methods. And two of them, the Frenchman and the American, have long been engaged in criticism and musical polemics. As to whether the former's conducting career will remove him from critical writing, as it seems already to have done from composing, my guess is that it will, though the Boulez tongue, sharp and fearless, will not easily be kept quiet.

More than a decade back, Boulez's writing of music already showed a tendency to taper off, though without any remarked lowering of quality. On the contrary, his last contribution, of 1960, to a long-labored work in progress for divers instrumental and vocal combinations, entitled *Pli selon pli* (a "portrait of Mallarmé" in nine movements of which the last, "Tombeau," impressed me deeply) was notable for its technical maturity, sonorous vibrancy, and full freedom of expression. Should his composition cease altogether, nobody would be more regretful than I, because I like this music, find it full of energy, fine thought, and beauty to the ear. For anybody's orchestral conducting, on the other hand, I lack the ultimate in admiration. There has been so much of it around, all absolutely first class; our century has been rich that way, richer than in first-class composition. I would trade in a Toscanini any time for a Debussy.

Is Boulez another Debussy? He seems to have all the qualities. Excepting the one that only shows up in retrospect, the power of growth. Without that, or lacking confidence in that, he may be, as I have written elsewhere, another Marcel Duchamp. This case is rare, but not unknown in France. (Rimbaud is another.) The strategy is to create before thirty through talent, brains, determination, and hard labor a handful of unforgettable works, then to retire into private or public life and wait for an immortality which, when all can see production is complete, arrives on schedule. What does not arrive is technical freedom and the expressive maturing that enables a genius type to speak at forty still boldly but now with ease, with freedom, and with whatever of sheer humane grandeur may be in him.

The heartless mature artist does of course exist, even in the upper levels. Richard Wagner, though financially a crook and sentimentally a cheat, was not one. Just possibly Mallarmé was Max Jacob said of him, "a great poet, were he not obscure and stilted" (*guindé* was the word). And Boulez, who loves the deeply calculated, expressed in a very early essay (from *Polyphonie*, 1948) his private hope for a music that would be "collective hysteria and spells, violently of the present time"; and he admits to "following the lead of Antonin Artaud" in this regard. At twenty-three (he was born in 1925) some can produce hysterical effects at will. But for professional use, dependably, a method is needed; and the methodical stimulation of collective hysterias (in class warfare, in politics, in religion) has been plenty frequent in our time. I doubt that Boulez today aspires in music just to be a Beatle. Actually Boulez today is as impressive in his musico-intellectual celebrity as the Beatles are in their more modest operation. How he got that way will no doubt be told us, in some version, by recorded music's press agents. What they will not tell us is what he thought about on the way up. And that is exactly the subject of his book from 1966 called *Relevés d'Apprenti*, translated as *Notes of an Apprenticeship*.

This is an anthology of reflections on music published between 1948 and 1962, written, as he speaks, with brio and with a vast repertory of allusions. In French it is not easy to make out, because the vocabulary is overreplete with technical terms from mathematics (which Boulez seems fairly familiar with), from philosophy (less confidently used), from musical analysis (where he is both precise and inventive), and from the slang of intellectual Paris (also the source of his syntax when in polemical vein). The translation, though obviously made with care, is in the long run no less labored than the composer's own prose and often just as hard to follow.

The pieces of high technical interest are among the earliest, from the years of his twenties, when he was building a method and formulating principles. Here we find electronic music and its possibilities (which he does not overestimate) studied from experience and thoughtfully, its Paris Establishment radically debunked. We also find dodecaphonic theory taken apart by an expert. He recognizes that there is nothing about the tempered scale of twelve equal semitones (a tuning adopted by J. S. Bach to facilitate modulation) that renders it indispensable to modern music. True intervals, of which there are at least fifty-two, could as well be employed. Audible octave-spacings are limited to seven. Loudness-levels, though theoretically infinite in number, are surely not practical to distinguish by ear beyond five or six. The shapes of a tone's duration—wedge, pear, teardrop, and their mirror images, including the double wedge—are not many more. And the extent of durations—the raw material of rhythm—is not governed, save for ease of performance, by any numerical necessity at all, though lengths of time, unlike music's other variables, are measurable, hence describable, by numbers. Timbres also are practically infinite; and though they are possible to serialize, few composers have bothered to try.

With all this variability inherent in music's materials, and the number twelve not essential to any of them, it is not surprising that Boulez considers the twelve-tone music of Schönberg to be "a failure," though the idea of serialism itself a boon to music. His admiration for Anton Webern's music, however, is not diminished by the dodecaphonic nonsense; rather he considers it saved by the tension of its intervalic layout and by its creation of forms out of musical materials rather than out of pathos from Old Vienna, which Berg and Schönberg were likely to use. Boulez, like Cage, for all his disillusioned view of dodecaphony, remains convinced that in serialization of some kind lies music's only hope. I must say that virtually all the composers who deny a hierarchy among intervals come sooner or later to substitute for this hierarchy an order of tones arbitrarily chosen for each work and called a row, or series.

At one time or another everything that regards today's music is discussed, always with a furious intensity and generally with penetration. For hazard and its planned use he has only disdain, unless it comes about that his own cerebration (should we read the unconscious?) leads a writer toward unexpected revelation, toward organic form, or toward some vastly valid experiment. In favor of all these he quotes from Mallarmé, "Every thought occasions a cast of the dice."

How to choose a row that will lend itself to development, expression, and intrinsic musical interest is treated in another book by Boulez, published in Germany, 1963, and entitled *Penser la Musique Aujourd'hui.* Here his love of Webern and his own penchant for arithmetic lead him into much eloquence about the hidden symmetries available through subdivisions of the number twelve. Also into a lumpiness of style ever so hard to keep the mind on.

From recent years there are in the present book ten articles written for the *Encyclopédie Fasquelle.* Here the tone is not polemical at all but informative, and the judgments are fair and generally warm, though without conventional compliments. They are entitled "Chord," "Chromaticism," "Concrete (Music)," "Counterpoint, Series," "Béla Bartók," "Alban Berg," "Claude Debussy," "Arnold Schönberg," and "Anton Webern," with an extra one on Schönberg's piano works, written for the jacket of a complete recording of these by Paul Jacobs. The article on Debussy is considered by Jean Roy in *Musique Française* (of the *Présences Contemporaines* series), Debresse, 1962, to be "the most penetrating and complete study [of this composer] ever published." In passing, I should like also to recommend from the same brilliant but erratic musical encyclopedia the understanding article on Richard Wagner by a Boulez pupil, Gilbert Army.

Here, and indeed throughout the book, the Boulez skill in musical analysis and his preoccupation with rhythmic discovery dominate the investigations. He cannot forgive Schönberg and his group for their rhythmic conventionality, as he cannot forgive Stravinsky, who was rhythmically radical, for not really knowing how to write music. He recognizes that a certain impotence in that regard led toward rhythmic construction of the most original kind. All the same, Stravinsky's lack of aptitude for writing in the Western conventional way, with Conservatory solutions always at hand to use or to avoid, he finds deplorable and probably responsible for the neoclassic "decline" into which Stravinsky fell after World War I, when he could not carry forward his rhythmic researches because of poor "writing." By "writing" (*écriture*) Boulez means harmony and counterpoint and the procedures of development (not orchestration, of course, at which Stravinsky was a master).

Beyond the intercourse with a major musical mind which this book offers as a delight throughout, for all the linguistic jambs, its major contribution to musical understanding is a long and detailed examination of Stravinsky's *Rite of Spring.* Every piece of this is given some attention and the two most original ones (hence most resistant to analysis), the Prelude and the Sacrificial Dance, receive depth study such as is rare today and has been since Donald Tovey's now fifty-year-old writings on Beethoven. The fact is mentioned that much of this material, especially the rhythmic analysis of the Sacrificial Dance, is the work of Olivier Messiaen. So be it. The full treatment is there, replete with musical quotations; and its availability now in English makes it an item for every college and music library to own.

The Sacrificial Dance, as examined in 1951, turns out to be exactly the sort of calculation toward collective hysteria that Boulez had declared his faith in three years earlier. The piece represents, as we know, a dancing to death by exhaustion on the part of a young girl chosen for sacrifice. And the collective hysteria that sustains her in the ordeal is not at all a product of rhythmic monotony, so commonly the provoker of group excitement. The rhythms that accompany this event are designed rather to stimulate hysteria in the theater, in the hope that this may induce an illusion of meaning shared, of presence at an ancient savage rite. These rhythms induce hysteria, if they do, by simulating it. The simulation consists of insistence on asymmetrical thumps, tonally and percussively huge. Their hugeness is standard orchestration. Their asymmetry, though novel, is also achieved by method, by a rhythmic calculation seemingly so secret that no amount of rehearsing will reveal to the merely spontaneous ear an identifiable pulse. (Robert Craft, who has heard and conducted the work possibly too often, now finds that "in the last section of the Sacrifical Dance, . . . where the basic meter is three and twos are the exceptions, the effect can sound precariously like a waltz with jumped record grooves.")

What is revealed by Messiaen and Boulez, as rhythmic analysts, is the fact that the continuity is constructed out of small rhythmic cells arranged with a certain symmetry, as structures always are, but with non-symmetrical interruptions by other cells. All are composed of twos and threes, naturally, since the mind breaks down all number groupings into these (plus fast fives, just occasionally possible to hear as units). The whole is a hidden pattern not altogether different from those found in folklore by linguistic students and anthropologists. Not that the Dance was composed by instinct only, though Stravinsky never confessed that it was not; but its asymmetry is so strongly organized that the exposure of a plan behind it is almost as exciting a discovery as that of the symmetries governing marriage customs among Australian aborigines.

Boulez indeed reminds one of the French anthropologist Claude Lévi-Strauss. His language is confusing, but his mind is not confused; it is merely active. Active and very powerful. So powerful that no music resists for long its ability to dismantle a whole engine and put it together again. It is moreover a loyal mind that puts things back right. Darius Milhaud said of him, "He despises my music, but conducts it better than anyone." As an analyst, a critic, and an organizer of musical thought I do not know his equal. As a composer I know none other half so interesting. The personality—in the best French way both tough and tender—has been proved in every musical circumstance and every careerlike stance irresistible. Its toughness is half the charm, its tenderness the source of critical acumen and, in his music, an emotional dynamo wired for power transmission and shielded by mental rigor.

That a European genius type of such clear-to-all authority should give up creative work is unbelievable. That he should be tempted by the Klingsor gardens of orchestral celebrity is not strange at all; but if his heart is pure, as it heretofore has seemed to be, he will possibly make his way through to the Grail. That would mean complete artistic fulfillment—which can only be what he aims toward, and what we hope for. There is precedent for a major artist's resting in his forties. Richard Wagner, Arnold Schönberg, and William Blake are noted examples, seven years the usual period for lying fallow. But Boulez has already been silent, as composer and as critic, for most of eight years; and his orchestral adventure is still on an up-curve. No signs of let-up there. On the contrary, I note a temptation even more dangerous than mere conducting. So far, Boulez has made his career almost entirely out of modern music, a phenomenon not witnessed in bigtime since Mary Garden. And that way, for a conductor, lies missionary madness.

So I am worried. Strauss, Mahler, and Leonard Bernstein are another case. They had always conducted; they needed money; and they wrote music like windmills, at the turn of a leaf. Wagner and Schönberg are better parallels. And they finally came through; that's the best I can say.

Meanwhile, another pungent book has come from France, this one directly—*Sémantique Musicale* by Alain Daniélou (Paris, Hermann, 1967). Subtitled *Essai de Psychophysiologie Auditive*, it examines the musical experience through communications, theory, the physical structure of the ear, and the known, or supposed, facts about auditory memory. In 118 pages, including diagrams, it opens a major matter and offers believable information about it.

Ernest Ansermet's *Les Fondements de la Musique dans la Conscience Humaine* (Neuchâtel, Editions de la Baconnière, 1961) purports to do the same (without information theory but with lots of mathematics and phenomenology) in two large volumes. I shall not discuss the latter work since brevity would be unfair. I merely mention it as another example of Europe's interest in certain musical facts-of-life which before long we shall all be turning our minds to. Musicology is all right, when useful. Analysis and professional judgments are cardinal to the act. But polemical esthetics, commonly referred to as "criticism," are for any purpose but salesmanship, so far as I am concerned, pure lotus-eating. As practiced by Boulez in his twenties, however, they seem a mere incrustation to analysis and judgment and, before the authority with which he already exercised those prerogatives, appear not deeply ingrained, but more like colored lichens on a rock.

P. S. Regarding the difficulties of translation presented by the Boulez super-colloquial style, let me cite a passage from the chapter "Alea," first published in

1957 in the *Nouvelle Revue Française*. Comparing a facile use of chance (the "aleatory") in music-making to the "never very miraculous" dreams described by hashish fanciers, the French text reads: "*Paix à l'âme de ces angéliques! on est assuré qu'ils n'iront point dérober quelque fulguration, puisqu'ils n'en ont que faire.*"

Herbert Weinstock renders this: "Peace to the souls of these angelic beings! One is sure they will never steal any lightning, that not being what they are up to."

In *Perspectives of New Music*, fall-winter 1964, this same passage translated by David Noakes and Paul Jacobs reads: "Peace to these angelic creatures; we can be sure they run absolutely no risk of stealing any thunder, since they wouldn't know what to do with it."

Now using *thunder* instead of *lightning* for *fulguration* is not important. Less exact literally, it is perhaps more apt as image. What arrests me about the sentence is its ending. And here I find the Noakes and Jacobs rendering superior.

I have not counted up or noted down all the suspect items, but here are just a few examples of how tricky this kind of French can be.

[*Debussy*] *est un fameux, un excellent ancêtre*. Now the basic meaning here of *fameux* must be *whopping*, or something like that, for that is the common slangy use of it and far more emphatic in this connection than the literal, the one-dimensional *famous*, used on page 34.

The American localism *tacky* is used on page 331 for *pâteuse* to characterize the parody music in Berg's *Lulu*. *Thick or muddy* would have been closer to the French and more descriptive.

Again of Berg, his propensity for allusions to other music is several times referred to as *citation*, though this word in French means less often that than simply *quotation*.

The year of the *Wozzeck* première is given on page 315 as 1923 (impossible since it was the result of fragments having been heard by Erich Kleiber at a concert conducted by Hermann Scherchen in 1924). The French text gives 1925, which is correct.

For using the word *conduct* to signify the medieval form *conductus* I find among my household dictionaries no precedent. The French word is *conduit*, a past participle like the Latin word, which is standard usage among English-language musicologists. If *conduct* had not been paired on page 294 with *motet*, and both words italicized, I doubt if I should have been able to identify it.

Of Schönberg, "*la suite de ses créations qui commence avec la Sérénade,*" would have been perfectly clear as "the works that followed the Serenade," or better, "the series of works that began with the Serenade." Its rendering on page 271 as "the sequences of Schoenberg's creations that began with the Serenade" is confusing, since sequences, in the plural, are a compositional device and one practically never employed by Schönberg.

Just flyspecks, one may say, on a fine book; and I agree. But there are far too many for easy reading. Time after time one is obliged to consult the original, and that is not easy to read either. But it means what the author wishes it to mean; and with such tightly reasoned trains of thought, his language could not have been simplified much farther. Again a reminder of Lévi-Strauss and of all that exuberant intellection spouting nowadays in France like springs and geysers.

A NOTE REGARDING LOU HARRISON (N.D.)

It was Mozart's boast that he could master any composer's musical style within a week and by the end of that time compose in it adeptly enough to deceive experts.

Lou Harrison has something of that virtuosity himself. The singer Eva Gauthier, who had spent some years in Java, told me that a symphony of Lou's for percussion orchestra was the only Western music she had ever heard that both felt and sounded like Indonesia. There is also a Mass that not only looks Elizabethan on the page but that when performed with Elizabethan tunings takes on a harmoniousness both surprising and convincing. And there are twelve-tone orchestral works which might well be taken for the music of some hitherto unknown contemporary of Arnold Schönberg.

As for the original side of him—early and late his dominant devotion—his work with gamelans and also with instruments of the Korean court tradition (including a jade gong, no less) are not only evocative but, as a result of serious studies undertaken over the last twenty years, authentic.

And he mixes things with infallible imagination. I think of a concerto for pipe-organ and percussion, delicious for the very sound of it, and a work for ten specially-tuned flutes (and they really blend).

As for more deliberate mannerisms, no one could better evoke the bubbly French "pop" style of 1920 than Lou has done in his *Eiffel Tower Wedding Party.* And his restoration of a missing page from Charles Ives's *They Are There!* is famous for its almost note-for-note exactitude when matched against the original, which turned up later.

There is nothing labored about all this. Lou Harrison is not making plastic roses for funeral parlors. He is simply speaking in many personae and many languages. The message itself is pure Harrison. And that message is of joy, dazzling and serene and even at its most intensely serious not without laughter.

I remember several years ago that for a gigantic San Francisco "be-in" regarding the yearned-for ending of war in Viet Nam, when Lou was asked to write a large work involving chorus, orchestra, and soloists, he did exactly that, in three movements. And he called it ever-so-happily *Peace Piece.*

Notes on Composers (1971)

Milton Babbitt

Babbitt's music has the clarity of distilled water and just possibly the sterility. Certainly it leaves in the listener no appreciable deposit of emotion. It is more like an athletic experience, exhilarating, tonic, helps you to breathe. Not the electronic works, which I find gummy and airless, but those for classical instruments, which represent a high degree of both abstraction and distinction. The natural elegance which pervades all his work is most strongly present when the textures are thin.

Samuel Barber

Romantic music, predominantly emotional, embodying sophisticated workmanship and complete care. Barber's aesthetic position may be reactionary, but his melodic line sings and the harmony supports it. His operas are less rewarding than his concert works and ballets.

Arthur Berger

Berger's highly intellectualized compositions, early modeled on Stravinsky's neoclassical period and later influenced by serialism, are often witty and entertaining, with their just-barely-concealed side-walks-of-New-York charm. Nor do they lack nobility in their proportions.

William Bergsma

A striking melodic gift, a cool mastery of the conventional techniques, and a relaxed emotional content all contribute to his music's unquestionable charm. A certain thinness, an understatement in harmony and orchestration, gives it distinction as well.

Leonard Bernstein

A successful composer in both pop and standard fields; as a conductor absolutely top-flight for both concert and opera, with brains, a vast repertory, a store of experience, lots of skill. His own music tends to be derivative—chief sources

Milhaud, Stravinsky, Mahler. Also an accomplished pianist, linguist, musical explicator through books and TV. As a conductor he has programmed U.S. music consistently and played it understandingly.

MARC BLITZSTEIN

A pupil of Rosario Scalero, Nadia Boulanger, and Arnold Schoenberg, Blitzstein was internationally schooled. He also had a strong *sens du théâtre* and a gift for clear prosodic declamation, especially of colloquial American. His operas are strongest when they parody musical styles, underlining character through Marxist satire of class conditionings.

PAUL BOWLES

Bowles's fiction has a worldwide readership, deserved. His songs and chamber music, though less known, are expressive, distinguished, and picturesque, often with an ethnic background (Mexico, Spain, Morocco). His stage music benefits from a strong theatre sense. His songs can be quite delicious.

HENRY BRANT

Henry Brant has a remarkable knowledge of instruments and their possibilities. His far-outness is of the fun-and-games variety—an antiphony of five orchestras playing at once but not without coordination, a symphony for toy instruments from the dime-store, and a surprisingly expressive achievement in the *Concerto for Flute* accompanied by ten other flutes (alto to piccolo). The instrumental virtuosities that his music can mobilize give it high color and a dazzling brilliance.

ELLIOTT CARTER

Music of unusual complexity and refinement at its most striking in chamber works, including the *Double Concerto*. The orchestral works, though punctilious, seem lacking in strength of line; but Carter's chamber music beginning with the *Piano Sonata*, 1945, is in my opinion the most interesting being composed today by anybody anywhere. And I mean intrinsically interesting, not merely attractive to the ear. His genius is to have combined intellectual elaboration and auditory delight with no loss of intensity to either. Researches in instrumental virtuosity commanded by an authentic musical temperament.

DAVID DIAMOND

His string works are idiomatic, his songs melodious, his symphonies romantically inspired. The musical style in general is harmonious, the continuity relaxed. For all its seeming emotional self-indulgence, this is music of artistic integrity and real thought.

LUCIA DLUGOSZEWSKI

Far-out music of great delicacy, originality, and beauty of sound, also ingenious with regard to instrumental virtuosities and of unusually high level in its intellectual and poetic aspects. Typical of Miss Dlugoszewski's practicality and imagination, *Space Is a Diamond*, 1970, is an eleven-minute trumpet solo unaccompanied that seems virtually to exhaust the technical possibilities of the instrument without becoming didactic.

VIVIAN FINE

Miss Fine's music, combining emotional intensity with an intellectualized technique, has from the beginning been atonally oriented, though never serial. No rule-of-thumb, no simplified "method," no easy short-cut to popularity or fame mars the authenticity of its fine hand work.

WILLIAM FLANAGAN

A soaring lyric afflatus and an extreme beauty in the melodic materials give to Flanagan's music a distinction and an authenticity quite unusual.

LUKAS FOSS

A musician of perfect gifts and training, a first-class conductor, as a composer perhaps more accomplished than convincing, but highly ingenious and venturesome all the same.

KENNETH GABURO

Gaburo's orchestral, chamber, and choral music is ravishing in sound on account of its high sensitivity to interval relations. His electronic and partly-electronic music is among the most original that exists. Gaburo is at once far-out and "musical," imaginative and advanced, a strong composer in no way casual. Pierre Boulez has remarked on the originality of his vocal writing.

MORTON GOULD

Among all our recent composers commercially or pop-concert oriented Gould is probably the one most often played by high-prestige conductors. At the same time his *American Salute* and *Cowboy Rhapsody* are virtually classical for bands and high school orchestras, his *Interplay* and *Fall River Legend* repertory dance works.

ALAN HOVHANESS

Hovhaness's music is mostly of Middle East inspiration, especially Armenian; some later works employ Japanese materials. A seemingly inexhaustible composer, his music too goes on and on. As with much music evoking Asia it adds no drama to the structure, but interests through sheer continuity and lovely sound. If like heaven it purports to be eternal, for mortals it can also on occasion seem interminable; but its variety from piece to piece is infinite.

HERSHY KAY

His original compositions may be minor but his contributions as orchestrator and arranger are important. Along with Robert Russel Bennett he represents the highest standard in the world for this kind of workmanship (commercial, of course).

GIAN-CARLO MENOTTI

Menotti, still an Italian citizen, the author of highly effective operas in the *verismo* style with strong librettos written by himself in excellent American. Beneath occasional minor failures of literary taste, his stage sense is impeccable, his dramatic imagination fecund and highly original. His music, though rarely modernistic, is never inelegant or undistinguished.

ERIC SALZMAN

The best critic in America for contemporary and far-out music, his own work, as can happen to critics, is in danger of neglect. It lies chiefly in the "live"-with-electronics realm, involves both speech and song, has imagination and humor.

ELIE SIEGMEISTER

Best known for his use of American folklore materials and populist subjects, Siegmeister has enjoyed considerable success both at home and abroad as a specialist of the backwoods background. His Irish opera *The Plough and the Stars* (after Sean O'Casey) was produced in French at Bordeaux 1970.

VLADIMIR USSACHEVSKY

Ussachevsky is an electronics man, convinced and consecrated. His music for classical instruments is gentle, sweet, and strongly personal. His tape music, whether playful or strong, tends to recall the Romantic masters—charmingly, for such is his nature. His larger works composed with Otto Luening for tape and orchestra have a place in the history of this combo.

CHRISTIAN WOLFF

A Cage disciple so devoted to musical purity that throughout his educative years he avoided all classic musical education. His pieces are quiet, short, and very beautiful.

VII

AUTOBIOGRAPHY

Thomson had two short essays that he often released in slight different forms. One, reprinted here as "Personal Statement," dealt deliciously with ironies in his own life. The second, reprinted in the next section, introduced his single most admired work, Four Saints in Three Acts. "The Music Reviewer and His Assignment" began as a talk to a dinner meeting at the National Institute of Arts and Letters on 17 November 1953. To this audience, Thomson, then 57 and on the verge of retiring from The Paper, felt less constrained. One quality of his memoir of New York culture during the war is his acknowledgment of the role of immigration in introducing not one art but several.

I was born in Kansas City, Missouri (November 25, 1896), grew up there, and went to war from there. That was the other war. Then I was educated some more in Boston and Paris. In composition, I was a pupil of Nadia Boulanger. While I was still young, I taught music at Harvard and played the organ in Boston at King's Chapel. Then I returned to Paris and lived there for many years; till the Germans came, in fact. After that I was for fourteen years music critic of the *New York Herald Tribune*. I still live in New York.

All my life I have written music. There is a great deal of this music. My most famous works are the operas *Four Saints in Three Acts* and *The Mother of Us All* (both to texts by Gertrude Stein), *The Plough that Broke the Plains* and *The River* (films by Pare Lorentz), and *Louisiana Story* (film by Robert Flaherty), though there are also symphonies, concertos, masses, string quartets, and many other works in many forms. I have made over a hundred musical portraits, too, all of them drawn from life, the sitter posing for me as he would for an artist's portrait.

I have appeared as guest-conductor with the New York Philharmonic, the Boston Symphony, the Philadelphia, Denver, San Francisco, Chicago, Minneapolis, Houston, Cincinnati, Indianapolis, Louisville, Pittsburgh, New Orleans, Buffalo, Kansas City, St. Louis, Dallas and many other orchestras in the United States, in Europe and in South America.

I am the author of eight books: *The State of Music* (William Morrow, New York, 1939; and Vintage Books/Random House, New York, 1961); *The Musical Scene* (Knopf, New York, 1945); *The Art of Judging Music* (Knopf, New York, 1948); *Music Right and Left* (Henry Holt and Co., New York, 1951); *Virgil Thomson* by Virgil Thomson (Knopf, New York, 1966); *Music Reviewed: 1940–1954* (Vintage/Random House, New York, 1967); *American Music Since 1910* (Holt, Rinehart and Winston, New York, 1971); and *A Virgil Thomson Reader* (Houghton Mifflin, Boston, 1981).

In 1968 I completed a third opera, *Lord Byron* (libretto by Jack Larson), premiered in New York 1972.

THE MUSIC REVIEWER AND HIS ASSIGNMENT (1953)

Many persons, particularly young persons, hold the romantic idea about music reviewing that it offers a virtually unlimited field for self-expression. They believe it is any critic's delight and privilege to share daily with a vast body of readers his personal tastes and opinions in matters of art. This is not true, of course. No responsible newspaper owner would consider offering the use of his valuable columns for a private pulpit. A newspaper is published for the benefit of its readers, not of its writers.

The sole justifiable purpose of reviewing, in my opinion, is to inform the public; any other is an abuse of confidence. A critic is paid by a periodical to tell the truth about music as he believes that to be; and if he is not expected to advertise himself, neither is he engaged to encourage particular artists toward success, or to discourage them, or to grade them from zero to one hundred, or to help trustees raise money, or to advertise standard repertory, or to form public opinion in any given way, or to uphold standards of execution—how could he?—or to advertise certain schools of composition, or to defend the public against them, or to teach music appreciation in general, or to spread enlightenment. All these things he may do occasionally or incidentally, but his main business is to report the music life of his community truthfully.

This reporting need not be and cannot be entirely factual. It is the reviewer's duty and his privilege to analyze music and its execution, to examine their nature, and to describe them in words. He is a man of letters whose subject is music. Practical knowledge of music gives penetration to his judgment; literary skill may enable him to express it courageously. A certain involvement with music as an art, a personal engagement to it, if he has any such consecration, will prevent him from making irresponsible statements. But he is under no necessity to edify anybody or to improve taste. Musical edification and enlightenment come from music itself, not from descriptions of it; and public taste in music is raised by sound performances of music, not by literary essays on the subject.

A music review, I insist, is a service of information and little else. It is not even a shopping service, like drama or book criticism, because a musical event usually takes place only once and is unavailable by the time the public reads about it. A music review is paid for by a newspaper and addressed to the whole reading public. It is written by an expert and signed with his name or initials. Any reporter is temporarily an expert if the managing editor says he is. If the reading public is not convinced of his knowledge, that is the paper's misfortune. The reporter himself can always go back to the shipping page.

A metropolitan newspaper should trust on the job only writers of sound musical education. They don't have to be right, but they do have to penetrate surfaces. In the criticism of anything, you do not have to be right in your judgment; you have only to use a legitimate means of arriving at it. If there is such a thing as a talent for criticism, it is a talent for judgment. Your loyalty and your workmanship are shown not merely in the way you write but in the intellectual methods by which you defend your intuitive judgment. But any opinion about art is legitimate if it is based on some knowledge and can be expressed in clear language.

I insist upon the informative character of music reviewing, but please note that I hold no brief for informing the public about things that are none of its business, nor do we presume to offer judgment in matters that do not involve us. We do not review musical events which take place in private houses or in clubs, because they are not offered to the public for its judgment. Among matters that are none of our business, let me list student recitals and church services. Student recitals are none of our business because we are not competent to estimate anything that does not take place under professional circumstances or which is not offered to the professional world of music, of which we are members, for professional consideration. It is difficult enough to estimate the qualities of a professional artist; it is even more difficult to estimate those of a student. We leave that to parents and teachers.

As for church services, any religious establishment would welcome reviewing, on condition that all the comments were favorable. Churches love advertising, but they resent criticism. And they have an impregnable position, because the music of religious worship is not offered to the public for its judgment. It is actually not offered to the public at all; it is offered to God. And God does not necessarily judge by professional standards, since sincerity, in His eyes, may make up for many an incompetence. This does not mean that a great deal of excellent music is not performed under religious auspices; of course it is. But judging it is not our business. Besides which, from a purely organizational point of view, it would require a whole separate staff, because most religious music is performed all on the same day and at the same hour.

In offering news and commentary about professional musical events that are open to the public and submitted for its favor, our standards of news coverage are slightly different from those of the city desk. On the news pages, news is classically considered to consist of an extraordinary event happening to anybody, or any kind of an event happening to a famous person. That is to say that if I take a train, it is not news; if Mr. Toscanini takes a train, it is news. If I fall under a train, it is news; if Toscanini falls under a train, then you have a streamer across the front page.

But if we judged the importance of musical events by those standards, we would find ourselves constantly reviewing Toscanini and Marian Anderson. We would be the victims of publicity machinery, because the fame of these artists is not merely a matter of spontaneous public favor; it is also a thing that is worked at by press agents.

We have taken a different attitude on the music pages of the *Herald Tribune*—and this attitude is, I think, shared by most responsible newspapers who give serious attention to music—that intellectual distinction itself is news. It is news on the same basis that my falling under a train might be news, because it is rare. That a famous artist plays a famous piece in public is not news, because it takes place constantly.

The music staffs, if they are musicians—which is largely true in New York City—also find this system of judging the value of news events useful for their private purposes. It makes their work easier, because the performance of a new work, the debut of a new and valid artist, the performance of an old work which is not often heard, or a change in the repertory line of a famous artist—all these things give us a more interesting theme than we could find in constantly reviewing famous people and famous pieces.

All these things we describe for all our readers. We do not write for the artist or for the management or for the backers of concerts or for the trustees of the Metropolitan Opera, and certainly not for our advertisers or their friends. Anybody can understand why you don't write for the advertisers or for trustees. But people do not always remember that your review is not addressed to the artist that you are reviewing. I recall saying to a very experienced singer some years ago, "We don't write for you; we explain you."

She said, "I never thought of that."

I said, "I do not have to mobilize a newspaper in order to make you a personal communication. Besides, correcting you in public would be the kind of rudeness that husbands and wives engage in when they take advantage of a gathering to say things to each other that they haven't quite dared say in private." Personal criticism is an abuse of the public, and the larger the public the greater the abuse.

In writing about an artist's work, I consider the description more important than the estimate of value. The estimate of value has its use, of course, because it enables the reviewer to confess his prejudices and predilections. No reviewer is a perfectly clear glass between the reader and the subject he is writing about; and if the pretends he is, then he is a very dark one indeed. So that an expression of opinion is a perfectly legitimate thing, and it also makes the reviewer feel good; but it is not a very important matter. Whereas the description of what took place, or of the nature of something, can be a quite broad communication. We try to tell the truth as well as we can, and a part of telling the truth is the admission of our prejudice for or against things. Our aim is to describe a musical event truly, as well as we are able.

In order to tell the strict truth, we must observe, of course, strict courtesy. Because if you observe the amenities, you can say much more unfavorable things than if you express them angrily. Actually, musicians do not differ very much about truth of fact; they only differ about opinion. If a vocalist sings off pitch, every musical ear in the house will know it. And any reviewer who states that she did can defend himself by the evidence of other persons present. The analysis of a musical work is subject to similar correction from other expert persons present; and within several months, or sometimes several years, a fairly definitive agreement is usually reached in the musical world about the structural nature of a piece of music.

At the very beginning, of course, many a highly complex work is taken by the naïve reviewer for pure spontaneity. That happened to the work of Arnold Schoenberg; it happened to Debussy; it happened to Beethoven. The ignorant reviewer likes to think that since he is judging hastily, the work was hastily created. And when his lack of preparation makes him unable to understand, he thinks that the work was written as casually as it is being listened to, which is not necessarily the truth at all.

Let me come back to the matter of courtesy in the statement. It enables you to make the really deadly attack, because the specific adjective is practically never actionable, either in court or in public opinion. The noun, yes. Gertrude Stein was right when she said that nouns are the bane of the language, because if you use nouns in talking about somebody, before you know what you have done you have called him a name. But the specific adjective is merely descriptive. Verbs are dangerous, too, because the verbs of motion and the verbs of action all have overtones of approval and disapproval, as the nouns have. But the adjective, the specific adjective, is virtually neutral.

There are adjectives of approval and disapproval, and we try to avoid using them. If you try to make a hierarchy out of "wonderful," "sublime," "splendid," "magnificent" and "outstanding," you weaken your communication, because you are not using those words in any specific meaning. You have turned them into advertising slogans. I tell the boys who work for me and the young people who come to learn the trade that they may use "splendid" only in its correct meaning, which is "shining," and "magnificent" only in the sense of "grandiose." "Splendid" and "magnificent," unless they mean in English what they mean in Latin, are not specific; and they will always sound foolish.

So far I have been talking about a standard operation, which is the reviewing of an artist performing standard repertory. Music reviewing becomes a part of the intellectual life of its time only when it deals with the composition of its time, that is to say, with new music. Now let us observe a little how you make up your mind about a new work.

You can often make up your mind very well from one hearing, from first acquaintance. As a matter of fact, that is what most teachers do with their students' works. And the musical historians, I may say, often make up their minds, or at least express an opinion about a musical work from the far past without any other acquaintance than that of the page.

Similarly, from a first performance, professionally presented in public, one can more often than not form an honest opinion and make an honest description. It is not very many times a year, especially in these days, when there is so little music of an advanced nature in existence at all, that one runs into a work of such complexity as requires preparation ahead of time. When those do come up in the programs we know about them in advance; we provide ourselves with scores; we go to rehearsals. There is no question about it—you always write a better article about something you know something about than about something you are not prepared about.

Let us look a little further into that matter of first acquaintance and what really happens. The very first moment of cognition is extremely important, the way the piece begins and how the first few measures or pages of it taste to the auditory tongue. That tasting is not a final judgment, but it is material for judgment. And as soon as you have got the work's taste, the question arises of whether you go on listening. If your mind wanders, you try to pull it back; but it will not always go; the mind is a very strong organ. The beginning of listening, and the going on of listening should last you through the piece, but there will be some drama about it. The tendency of the mind to wander does not come about because the mind is lazy, but rather because the mind has its own way of judging, the instinctive mind, over and above your intention and your will.

Now as soon as the piece is over, there is another thing that happens comparable to that very first taste when it began, which is an auditory after-image that will last five, sometimes ten and sometimes fifteen seconds, when you can still hear the whole thing—not necessarily as a shape, but as a sound and almost as a shape, in any case as an experience that you are still having. And in that moment of the after-image, of the after-experience, before the applause of the audience or your own fidgeting with your hat, there is a moment of what the French call *recueillement*, for which I do not know the English word, in which one is still absorbed by the work, still tasting it, still feeling it. The intensity of this third experience is important for your final judgment.

Five minutes later, particularly if it is the work of a rival composer, you will find every reason to disapprove of it. If it is the work of a pupil or of a close friend who is not a rival, you will have found reasons for saying you like it. But to find out what you really think you must remember very hard. Your memory of what the piece tasted like when it started to sound, of how vigorously it made you listen to it while it went on, and of what it tasted like after it stopped sounding—these are the data that you have to deal with. You can verify them, test them, prove them. But they are the only reality that you can bear witness to; and you are a fool and a dishonest man if you do not consider them your major evidence.

On the basis of that evidence, you now have to make up your mind. This consists of putting your evidence through the classical procedures of judgment, of testing your reactions for error. You have already asked yourself, "Does it hold my attention?" "Does it remain in my memory?" "Is the taste of it strange and interesting upon the tongue?" You must now try to distinguish between its design and its execution. "Have I heard a good piece or just a very slick performance which deceived me into thinking it a good piece?" "Have I heard a bad piece, or was I so sales-resistant about an over-slick performance that I resisted the piece itself as vigorously as I did the salesmanship of the performance?"

You must also try to separate the expressive power of the work from its formal or structural or textural interest. The world is full of people who think that Sebastian Bach is an extremely expressive composer. All musicians will admit that he is a fascinating composer, because the intrinsic interest of his musical textures is very great. But only heaven knows what they mean! Choose among the whole series of the forty-eight preludes and fugues in *The Well-Tempered Clavier* and describe to me what any of them is about; and I will give you fifty cents. They must be about external things, because they are too varied to be about the composer's interior emotional life. As painters know, no two arms look alike. But the emotional life tends to fall into repeating patterns. So wherever you find a composer whose work is varied in melodic invention, texture and form, you can safely bet that the inspiration for each invention of melody and form was of an exterior nature, because that much variety does not exist inside any one human being. And so you must distinguish, in making up your mind about any piece, whether you are dealing with expression or whether you are dealing with an intrinsic musical interest of form and texture.

If you opine that the expressive power of the work is very great, you must further distinguish between a convincing emotional effect and a meretricious one. I cannot tell you exactly what a meretricious one is; but we all know that composers do have ways, just as theater people do, of making us think pleasurably about our mothers or about sex. Such easy effects are at the disposal of any advertiser, of anybody in show business; but a work of art is something different. It needs to have an objective life, a shape of its own. And if expression is its specialty, it needs to have an expressive power of a much more ample nature than that which merely provokes us to applause or tears.

Let us say that by this time you have heard the piece and that you have taken account of your own spontaneous reactions while hearing the piece, and that you have tested these for errors of judgment and errors of reaction, so far as you are able, and that you are back at your office and about to write your review. You can go farther, if you have time. You can identify the style of the work, answer the question, "What is it like?" You can even sometimes identify its expression, answer "What is it about?" For this you must decide whether it is predominantly a strophic work, imitating speech cadences, or a choric work, imitating body movements, or a spastic one, imitating those anxiety-and-relief patterns that make up our interior life. The great monuments of symphonic music, I may add, are mostly of this latter character.

Now you must start writing. As I said before, you use specific words and try to explain them all. A newspaper man once told me, "Never underestimate the public's intelligence, and never overestimate its information." As evidence of good faith toward the reader, you express your personal opinion of the work. But you mostly try to describe the work by the methods of musical description that are available to you. Never bother about trying to express your enthusiasm or lack of it; that will come through automatically in your choice of words. Just keep your mind on the music and describe it loyally.

When your piece is done, you read it over three times: once for grammar, a second time to see if you have said a little bit of what you meant to say, and a third time—this is the most important of all—to see whether you are willing to mean what you have said. If you are not, you cut out that paragraph of opinion. If you are, you send it down to the printers just as it is.

EUROPE IN AMERICA (1966)

If America in the 1920s exiled its artists, the 1940s, especially their first half, saw a meeting of talent here, both foreign and domestic, that made us for the first time an international center for intellectuals. Central Europeans, notably some brilliant musicologists and art scholars, had been coming throughout the 1930s. In 1940 certain English joined us for the duration. And during that winter and all through '41 those who had reasons (and the means) for leaving France arrived in a steady trickle. The painters Eugene Berman, André Masson, and Yves Tanguy were here already; so was Marcel Duchamp. And the surrealist poet André Breton, arriving after the Occupation had begun, came soon to exercise over poets and painters in New York an authority similar to that which for nearly two decades he had practiced in Paris. He did them good, too, freeing poets from censorship by the hatchet men of T. S. Eliot and setting off a movement in painting that has traveled clean round the world. Also, a scholastic group that included the philosopher Jacques Maritain established here an Ecole de Hautes Etudes Libres, which offered French students in exile university credits valid for after the war.

The standard repertory conductors Toscanini and Bruno Walter had established residence before the war. Wanda Landowska, queen of the harpsichord, arrived on Pearl Harbor day. The composers Arnold Schoenberg, Kurt Weill, and Hanns Eisler had been here since the mid-thirties. Stravinsky in the late thirties kept coming in and out till the war in Europe decided him, like Bruno Walter, to renounce his recently gained French citizenship and opt for ours. A short listing of other composers who joined us in the years around 1940 will recall perhaps the brilliancy of the time.

From Hungary had come to New York Béla Bartók, to the West Coast Miklos Rosza; from Poland Jerzy Fitelberg, Karol Rathaus, and Alexandre Tansman; from Czechoslovakia Bohuslav Martinů. Arriving Russians, via western Europe, were Arthur Lourié and Nikolai Lopatnikoff; Nicolai Berezowsky, Vladimir Dukelsky (Vernon Duke), and Nicolas Nabokov were already here.

From Austria came Jacques de Menasce and Ernst Křenek, from Italy Vittorio Rieti and (to Hollywood) Montemezzi, Castelnuovo-Tedesco, and Amfiteatroff; from Germany via London the pianist Artur Schnabel (also a composer) and via Palestine Stefan Wolpe, via Paris the boy-genius Lukas Foss. Directly from France we had not only Nadia Boulanger, the teacher of us all, but the chief then of all the composing French, Darius Milhaud.

Among my own close friends from France, Yvonne de Casa Fuerte was a welcome helper in the music life. To support herself and her son, aged sixteen, she gave French lessons and violin lessons, also playing in pit orchestras such as that of the New York City Opera and, when this was out of season, in musicals by Kurt Weill and for Billy Rose's Aquacade. She also played in concerts. And in the spring of 1943 we organized together a series of Serenades modeled after her Paris originals.

Our patron was the Marquis de Cuevas, who had given us $5,000. Active with us in the planning were the flute player René Le Roy and the pianist Prince George Chavchavadze. Though the printed prospectus names two more, Carl Van Vechten and Aaron Copland, it is not in my memory that either of these ever sat with us for program making. My membership on the music committee of the Museum of Modern Art helped toward use of its auditorium.

There were five of these Serenades, all involving rare music, much of it presented by artists so remarkable and so new (Leonard Bernstein, for instance, and Robert Shaw) that our evenings offered a refreshing and particular splendor. Thomas Beecham conducted a concert, Vladimir Golschmann another. And one that was devoted to the memory of García Lorca produced both a *cuadro flamenco* with Argentinita and a stage-work by Paul Bowles. Entitled *The Wind Remains*, this was a partial setting to music (in the manner of a *zarzuela*) of a part of a play by García Lorca called *Así que pasen cinco años*, partly in prose and partly in verse, partly spoken and partly sung, partly in English and partly (the verse parts) left in Spanish. It was also partly acted and partly danced. The whole thing was quite beautiful but in an artistic sense only partly successful; largely, I think, because the free form of the *zarzuela* is unacceptable to English-speaking audiences.

Our final concert contained first New York presentations of the Stravinsky *Danses concertantes* and of the Poulenc *Aubade*, the latter with Robert Casadesus as piano soloist. Neither work, however, pleased the press. Olin Downes found the Poulenc "a series of clichés and dull and bad jokes," the Stravinsky "considerably worse." "The pieces were politely received," he said, "and why not? Could a politer set of platitudes be invented? Music guaranteed to upset no one—not even the refugees of the St. Regis." Nevertheless, these concerts were distinguished; and had not my colleague of the *Times* felt moved to crush them, we might have found funds for their continuance. His paper's chronic fear of any take-off toward style came back to mind only the other day, when Howard

Taubman, its drama critic, dismissed a play by the poet Robert Lowell as "a pretentious, arty trifle."

Later, just at the end of the war, I helped to organize more concerts, this time benefitting France Forever. I had become associated with this Free French group through the pianist E. Robert Schmitz, ever a patriot as well as a modern-music defender. And I remember particularly fine performances of a new string quartet by Sauguet and of a work composed in German captivity by Olivier Messiaen, called *Quartet for the End of Time.*

It was in the fall of 1940 that I first encountered, through Suzanne Blum, Hervé Alphand, at that time Economic Secretary to the French Embassy. His wife of the time, Claude, who did not much like Washington and who could not bear at all their Vichy associates, was pressing him to resign, which soon he did, going off to join de Gaulle in London and leaving Claude to stay out the war in New York. Sharing a small flat with her mother, she earned money by singing French chansons in New York night clubs, in Montreal, sometimes in Florida, even in Brazil. She was a 1900-style blonde with commanding beauty, a not large voice, and no knowledge of music at all. Her mother, an excellent musician as well as a first-class cook and hostess, taught her everything; she also ran the house. At public appearances, Rudi Révil, a Parisian song composer, would play for her till toward the close she would sit on the grand piano and sing to her own guitar. Though without the relentless intensity of a Piaf, by nature she had star quality.

Loving both her presence and her singing for making me feel that I was back in France, I helped to start off her career by reviewing its debut. Hervé wrote from London to thank me for that. And Claude sent two bottles of claret, left over from their Embassy days, with a note saying, "*Voici le pot de vin habituel dans l'administration.*" Her light touch and her fearless independence reminded me of Madame Langlois. Women at once so courageous and so beautiful are a sort of masterpiece.

The well-to-do refugees who had so shocked Olin Downes included the American-born Lady Ribblesdale (indeed living at the St. Regis, which was a property of her son, Vincent Astor), the Shakespearean scholar Sir Harley Granville-Barker and his American poet wife (at the simpler Mayfair), and the conductor Sir Thomas Beecham, Bart. (installed at the Ritz Carlton with his longtime Egeria, Lady Cunard). With both these last, my friendship was engaged at first sight. It went on too till their respective deaths, though after 1943 their own tie had been cut by Beecham's marriage.

Born Maud Forbes, in California, and inheriting while still young a quite large fortune, she had married around 1890 Sir Bache Cunard and shortly borne him one child, a daughter. After he had welcomed once her return from an extended absence by building a gate marked "Come into the garden, Maud," she changed her name. Sir Bache himself, with fine estates, was a country man; but

Emerald, as she now became, loved town. So she mostly lived in London, cutting a figure as hostess, becoming the close friend of George Moore and after World War I of Thomas Beecham.

Earlier concerned with letters and politics, she had moved into music after Sir Thomas became owner and impresario of the Covent Garden Opera House, mobilizing society, the arts, and even government to help him fill its boxes. Later, under Edward VIII, she had abetted the king in his marriage plans. Under his successor she fell into disfavor, but not too gravely, one gathered, since Beecham and his career were an occupation and since, with the war, society was largely dispersed to its jobs and regiments.

Beecham had informed the British government at the beginning of this war that he could not, as he had done during the other, support England's four chief orchestras out of his income. And since opera was to be closed down for the duration, he decided in the spring of 1940 to make a gift to Anglo-Saxon solidarity by going off to conduct in Australia, later in Canada and in the United States. Lady Cunard, at the same time, gave up her house in Grosvenor Square and came to America, accompanied by her lady's maid, to spend the summer visiting in Newport. Come fall, as Beecham's guest, she moved to the Ritz in New York, where till 1943 was played out the drama of his impending marriage to a much younger woman, he denying that nothing of the sort was planned and she well knowing that it was.

As who did not, indeed? There had been a press scandal in Seattle about his sharing a house with the pretty pianist. Then she took residence in Idaho for divorcing *in absentia* her English clergyman. And wherever Beecham appeared as guest conductor, Betty Humby was likely to appear as soloist. There was no concealing their constant proximity, though there was enormous effort on the part of Beecham to save face for Lady Cunard in the destruction of their twenty-year bond, even though the friendship, as he said, had been "for the last ten years only that."

And he himself required a divorce, also procured in Sun Valley. And then he was married in New York, later being divorced and married all over again in England, just to make the whole thing stick. But well before the marrying began, Lady Cunard had gone back to London and taken rooms in the Hotel Dorchester, where she went on giving dinner parties, with wine from the Chilean Embassy and with bills paid out of the sale of jewelry and divers *objets d'art* that had remained after a lifetime of expenditure. She was dead by 1950, having never ceased to be an inflammatory hostess, a tonic wit, an Egeria indefatigable. And to the end she had young poets in attendance, attached almost like lovers.

Small, roundish though less than plump, with china-blue eyes and yellow slightly mussed-up hair, Emerald Cunard had always been pretty and remained so. She also passed for being hard of heart, and certainly she was as relentless as any other career-hostess. After her daughter's [Nancy's] communist and Negro frequentations had caused embarrassment, she never spoke to her again, or of her. All the same, she was faithful, with the novelist George Moore and with Beecham, to long friendships deeply engaged. Ever happy with artists, she gave them jolly times, admiration, and money, read their books, hung their pictures, got them posts and publishers, kept them at work, and abetted their love affairs. As an American she could be demanding, even cruel; as a European she was generous and a comrade. For all her preoccupations with grandeur, she was never banal or in friendship dishonest. Nor was she self-indulgent. She merely lived hard every day, reading long into the night; and men of gifts found knowing her a privilege. She once summed up for me a rule, if not of life, of living: "For a good party have beautiful women and intelligent men; for a bad one, intelligent women and beautiful men." Of Beecham she said, "He is deeply sentimental, but also relentless. When he wants a thing, no one can stop him."

Certainly no one stopped him from the marriage he had set his mind on. The young woman, he told Emerald, had awakened in him feelings he "had long thought dead." Betty Humby, on her part, was equally attached and willing to pay with all her strength for the marriage she had long desired. But she wore out that strength in his service. And after she died, fifteen years later, he married again, this time an even younger woman. At eighty, still conducting concerts and recordings and projecting another tour of Germany, he suffered a fatal stroke. For twenty years we had told each other stories, eaten and drunk together, argued and laughed. I know he loved my music, and I think he understood it; I understood, I think, his approach to music making and loved its results. I loved them for resplendent sound and for good sense. He used a shaping hand with Haydn, a warm one with Mozart, a light one for Wagner, and a poetical one (inspired idea!) for Berlioz. And always the sonorities were what musicians call "musical," as if harmoniousness were a virtue, which it is. He once said of his loyal English public, "They have for music little understanding, but they adore the sound it makes."

From our friendship's first beginnings he played my music across the United States, in Canada, in England. No one else has ever made my *Second Symphony* sound so glowing, though I do not think he was comfortable with the work. *Filling Station* and *The River* he played with more abandon. My operas he professed to adore (*Four Saints* was for him "the finest vocal music in English since Elizabethan times"), but he never conducted them. (The BBC refused him *The Mother of Us All* when he proposed to broadcast it for his seventieth birthday.) My *Cello Concerto* he played in Edinburgh, paying for an extra rehearsal to get it right. When I began conducting orchestras myself, he at first made fun of me; but he afterwards invited me to Mexico for preparing and conducting under him Mozart's *The Magic Flute*. I did not go, preferring to compose that summer. And by not grasping the precious opportunity, I proved to both of us the innocence of my conducting ambitions. What I chiefly regretted at not being with him was our conversations. For we stimulated each other; and enlivened by Emerald Cunard's bright presence, we were likely to talk far into the night. She would accuse me of being anti-British and I would reply, "No, only anti-English." Then she would scold me for arrogance, praise both of us intensely, and all the time be guiding us toward themes where we could shine. And he would say afterwards, "Virgil is the only man in the world who can keep me up till four."

Others from England spending the war here were the composers Benjamin Britten, Anthony Arnell, Stanley Bate, and the Australian Peggy Glanville-Hicks. Britten I did not encounter often; but I did review his first opera, *Paul Bunyan*, written to a text by W. H. Auden. By finding its music "eclectic though not without savor," its poetry "flaccid and spineless and without energy," I classified myself as no friend of the Empire.

Arnell would call on me every few months with a brand-new symphony; I found his music mostly pretty thin. Then once there was a different kind, grandly funereal and richly sad; and I think I recommended that piece to Beecham. In any case, he played it. He liked, as I did, its tragical and apocalyptic character, and all the more because the run of British composers was continuing to write as cheerfully as if the Empire called for no lament. Lately Britten has composed a *War Requiem* that makes exception to the general British rule, for though their prose literature has had its angry young ones, and though their older novelists and playwrights have faced society's disaster in the language of Oscar Wilde and Shaw, the basic despair of England seems not yet to have touched deeply either music or poetry.

Stanley Bate wrote optimistic music in a British version of the Boulanger style. He could play the piano poetically, too; and Lady Cunard loved piano concertos. So Beecham presented Bate's; and Emerald found him a paying patron, who bought him a Steinway and set him up in an apartment. But Stanley drank too much and quarreled too much and eventually went back to England. Peggy Glanville-Hicks, his wife, stayed here, supporting herself by writing articles and by copying music, achieved distinction as a composer, and became a citizen. Stanley married a Brazilian consul general, Margareda Guedes Nogueira, who backed him up loyally, just as Peggy had done, in his war against the musical Establishment (chiefly controlled by Britten and his publisher, the latter linked by marriage to the throne). So he wrote less and drank more until eventually, after a heart failure or stroke, he drowned in his bath.

Peggy Glanville-Hicks, thin, passionate, tireless, and insistent (for Australian women can indeed insist), might well have been a burden to us all had she not been so willing to turn her hand to musical odd jobs. She wrote for the *Herald Tribune* and for magazines; she copied music; she mangaged concerts; she ran everybody's errands; she went on lecture tours by bus in the Dakotas; she composed documentary films for UNICEF; she made musicological trips to India for the Rockefeller Foundation; she saw other people's music (particularly that of Paul

Bowles, after his return to Morocco) through the perils of recording. She made her own clothes and dressed charmingly. When alone she did not eat much, but she could be a lively dinner guest. She wrote a great deal of music, got it published and recorded, grew as a composer from modest beginnings (as a none-too-remarkable pupil of Ralph Vaughan Williams) into an opera writer of marked originality, setting first *The Transposed Heads* by Thomas Mann, later collaborating with the poet Robert Graves and with the novelist Lawrence Durrell.

She believed, upon some evidence, that the world was out to crush women composers; and she was convinced (from no evidence) that my music editor, Jay Harrison, actually her protector, was for getting her fired. She complained; she stormed; she telephoned. And with all this she was an indispensable colleague. Even from Greece, where she now lives (still frugally), she continues to fulminate and to be useful. Her generosity is no more to be stopped than her scolding ways. And she remains a memorable composer.

It was also through music that I knew a real French gangster. He had asked for counsel, just at the end of the war, about bringing a French orchestra to America. With perfect discretion, he omitted to mention that his wife, under another name, had sung sizable works of mine in Town Hall. When later I helped her to secure the hall again, he was grateful in the standard gangster way, could never do me favors enough, it seemed.

He lived at the Waldorf-Astoria with his beautiful wife (much younger) and an elderly French maid. Also at the hotel, as his guest throughout the war, was a famous French trial lawyer, to whom he was grateful for having earlier kept him out of prison on charges of white slavery and of trafficking in drugs. He was the eldest of six brothers, Russian Jewish by origin, who had become powerful after World War I in the Marseille underworld. Large assets had been amassed in Alsace and in the Argentine; and he had shipping connections in Jugoslavia. During the Spanish Civil War, with connivance from the French government, I understood, he had run arms into Republican Spain. After World War II he worked directly for his government, he told me, buying coal and steel on the American black market, for these materials were in principle strictly rationed and the French were needing to rebuild their railways quickly.

In addition to his Waldorf-Astoria apartment, he kept one at the Georges V in Paris, and also, to the north, a chateau for weekends. And if he happened not to be in Paris, through the brother who owned a restaurant I always had access to black-market French francs in any amount. No books were kept; I simply paid later in New York. Then the pretty wife got bored with a singing career, spent more and more time with the Cannes high life; and her devoted husband left off coming to New York. By this time his business was mostly in Europe anyway, "working with the American Army in Germany," he called it. What products he procured I never asked. But he grew richer and richer, and more and more wretched at his wife's long absences. I had grown fond of him; and so had others—Oscar Levant, for instance, who had taste in gangsters, and Maurice Grosser, who could introduce the French business associates, if need be, to Negro circles. When a work of Nicolas Nabokov was given in Berlin, our friend arrived with cases of the best champagne, brought by air. And when my landlord requested me to bring him from New York a refrigerator, a blender, and a washing machine, these were all bought at wholesale prices and passed through French customs by the President's secretary. Did he eventually perish of despair? For die he did. And did he leave vast fortunes, open or secret? A few years earlier, tried in Morocco for fraud, found guilty, and assessed three billion francs, he had remarked, "Nobody pays a $6 million fine." All the same, he was forever buying rubies and diamonds for his wife. "You never know," he would say. "Someday she may need money."

I hope she has not come to that; I wish her well. For fifteen years this Waldorf gangster family were my friends; and if with their rubies and diamonds hidden away they were less showy as to bosom than Olin Downes's "refugees of the Saint Regis," their hearts were open and their ways were warm. After all, no law says exiles must be poor.

ALL ROADS LEAD TO PARIS (1966)

The *Herald Tribune* was not alone responsible for my reactivated professional life, for this had put forth buds on my arrival from France. Glenway Wescott had been hopeful that I might compose a ballet with him. Detroit's Pro Musica had offered a lecture and concert. The Metropolitan Opera Guild had engaged me to speak on Mozart, with Frieda Hempel singing arias. And shortly after, Ludwig Bemelmans had sought me out toward collaborating with him on a dance-spectacle about Ecuador. Neither of the ballets came to pass; but after my newspaper debut on October 11, 1940, other proposals started to arrive—for performance and for publication, for lecturing, for composing, for writing articles, and naturally for recommending applicants to the foundations.

It was clear quite early that if I were to lead a practicing musician's life along with that of a reviewer, I should be needing more help than just a secretary. I had to get my music into shape. Also, I needed extra housework. This came to be furnished by one of my Saints, Leonard Franklin, tenor soloist from 1934, a man of impeccable charm and gentle ways. He came to cook and serve, to take care of my clothes, to receive my callers, and to do my errands. And since the Chelsea Hotel did not at that time house colored lodgers, my Saint found a flat near by; and I began to have lots of company.

My musical secretary, Mimi Wallner, a curly-haired athletic blonde just out of Bennington, could copy music, speak French, and play the double bass. She too worked in the apartment, making extra copies of all my unpublished works—which meant virtually all my works—and extracting orchestral parts from my unplayed scores, which meant most of those. With her help my career as a composer could take off.

As long as I had lived abroad, neither conductors nor publishers had shown much interest in my music. Encouraging the composers from near by made better news. And even in the 1930s, when I was a figure in the New York theater, the concert-giving establishments had shown reluctance. My status as an expatriate always going back and forth to France would seem to have dissolved all obligation. They did not even have to read my scores, knowing there would be no pressure here for using them. Then all at once they knew they would be using them. There was no pressure really. But I was in the news; they were aware of me. So they asked which works I wished them to use first and in most cases took them sight unseen. They still, I noted, did not read my scores.

Thus it happened that my works began to travel. And before long I began to travel with them. It was Eugene Ormandy who first found that I could conduct (by letting me show his orchestra how to bounce a rhythm in *Filling Station*). After that, he played a piece almost every year; and I was asked to conduct the Philadelphia Orchestra whenever I liked, in two cases on Columbia recordings. Eventually I conducted almost everywhere, though I was not asked to Boston till after Koussevitsky had retired. I requested no engagement, employed no agent. I merely answered mail and stayed available. Nor did I question any artist's motives. Some may have programed my music to gain good will, though they knew that if they played it in New York, I obviously could not review that concert. Others, taking advice from managements or following private scruples, refrained from seeking favor in this way. Myself, I asked for nothing, held no grudges. But I actually believe that my being alert to a possible conflict of interests kept me more punctilious than most other reviewers about describing each performance truthfully. Certainly my editors found nothing suspect, nor did readers reproach me. When Harl McDonald, manager of the Philadelphia Orchestra, inquired if I thought he should possibly not engage me as guest conductor, I passed his letter on to Geoffrey Parsons; and Geoffrey, after asking at the top, replied that the paper saw no impropriety.

My new works that first winter were theatrical. For a radio program called The Columbia Workshop, John Houseman produced on December 9 *The Trojan Women* of Euripides in a cutting of the Edith Hamilton translation; and I made music after a conception that had not, I think, been ever used before. This was to reverse the usual procedure of putting music between the scenes and sound-effects with them. My scheme of separating the scenes by sound-effect interludes and accompanying them with music was designed to help the listener distinguish one character from another in a play spoken almost entirely by women.

Cassandra, Andromache, and Hecuba were cast for speaking voices of high, middle, and low timbre—Zita Johann, Joanna Roos, and Mildred Natwick, as I recall. And for pointing up this contrast, as well as for aiding identification, I accompanied them respectively on a flute, a clarinet, and an English horn, giving to each of these solo lines the expressive content of the speech. Then for separating the scenes I composed sound-effect passages depicting weather, marching men, whatever was needed for making events seem real. Actually my woodwind obbligati were a variant of the percussive accompaniments that I had learned to do from Orson Welles in the Negro *Macbeth* and later used to build up Leslie Howard's voice in *Hamlet*. They served in *The Trojan Women* for identifying characters, somewhat less for expressivity, since one could not without more rehearsal time train actresses to read less tearfully and leave emotion to the music's line and shading—as when at Cassandra's mention of her child, it took only a tiny tune in the piccolo's low register to evoke the baby's presence and make us weep. I should like to use again this sensitive approach, but with more time to work it out, possibly notating the reading parts for rhythm and for each voice's rise and fall, obtaining in this way a musical elocution suitable both to Greek tragedy and to the English language.

Later that season I did apply it again, this time to choruses intoned in Greek. The play was the *Oedipus Tyrannus* of Sophocles, the locale the library steps at Fordham University, the producer Father William Lynch, S.J., the choreographer Erick Hawkins, himself something of a Greek scholar. Not being a Greek scholar myself, I had to work phonetically. Father Lynch provided me with a word-by-word translation of the choruses, plus a metrical notation of their quantities, cadences, and stresses; and with this help I composed in Greek a monolinear music, accompanied by drums and wind instruments that underlined the modal melodies. It all came off quite well, as I remember; but the really impressive element was Richard Burgi, a boy of seventeen, who played Jocasta with a grand projection. Encountered some years later, he had followed scholarly proclivities; and as I write he is head of the Russian department at Princeton, a constant customer nevertheless at the Metropolitan Opera, where he identifies himself, I am sure, with the singing actors, especially with powerful projectors like Leontyne Price and Maria Callas. I think this because it seems to be roles rather than musical styles that hold his interest.

There was a production of *Four Saints* in the spring of '41, but without staging. Miss Louise Crane, a young woman of means who wished to serve music, had undertaken a series of Coffee Concerts at the Museum of Modern Art, these to include offerings as offbeat as advanced jazz and Yemenite dancing. She esteemed it a cultural service to revive my opera; and in order to broaden the possible audience (since the museum's auditorium could hold only 480), she proposed two performances, one in the museum, to be conducted by me from a piano, and another at Town Hall, with an orchestra conducted by Alexander Smallens. I reassembled my soloists and chorus with the help of my Harlem helper, Leonard de Paur, and prepared the performances. And since it was possible to consider the one at the museum as a rehearsal for the other, the press was asked to skip that and review from Town Hall. It was here that Sir Thomas Beecham, first making acquaintance with the work and identifying it as a child of the Elizabethan masque, came to accept my music as related to his own Britishness. And he loved to tease me about its idiosyncrasies, such as the double bass that would "first play and then not play." The peculiarity he referred to was actually an equivalent of the organist's device for avoiding monotony by now and then taking his feet off the pedals.

Alfred Wallenstein also conducted *Four Saints* in a beautiful performance on station WOR, a broadcast of 1942 aimed at selling war bonds and paid for by the Treasury Department. The original cast was again got together in 1947 and trained by Leonard de Paur for a Columbia broadcast on the Philharmonic hour; and this time I conducted. I also conducted for RCA Victor, with the same cast and orchestra (renamed for the occasion the Victor Symphony Orchestra), a recording of about half the opera. This was the last time the 1934 cast could be used. When the opera was restaged in 1952 for New York and Paris, only Edward Matthews and his wife were still vocally fresh. So a new cast was assembled. But the old one can still be heard, since the 1947 recording, twice reissued, is still in circulation.

Wallenstein had also urged me to excerpt an orchestral suite from *The River;* and it was he, not Beecham, who first played it. The latter became attached to it, however, because of its Protestant hymn content, which carried him back to Lancashire. And Aaron Copland wrote me it was "a lesson in how to treat Americana." Stokowski also took it up, although much later, and gave to its recording a fine buoyancy. I myself have no attachment to it, probably because its pristine inspiration came from an earlier work, the *Symphony on a Hymn Tune,* a piece for me far more original and more evocative of the South.

Beecham had in 1941 asked for a "major" work that he could play that fall in Philadelphia and elsewhere, and I had proposed my *Second Symphony.* On his acceptance, I began to reflect as to whether the piece did not require a bit of adjusting, at least orchestrally. A chance for judging that came in the spring, when the Luxembourg conductor Henri Pensis played some of it in Newark. Hearing it for the first time, though it had been in existence for a decade, I concluded that it wanted higher contrasts and a more striking color—in short, that I must reorchestrate. And this I did during the summer months.

Come June, having caught my periodic grippe-cold, I spent a week being cared for at the Askews'. Then I stayed for a fortnight at Woods Hole, Massachusetts, with Mrs. W. Murray Crane, Louise's mother, a friend and patron from my poverty days. In July I joined Mimi Wallner and her parents in Holderness, New Hampshire, where I began to reorchestrate the symphony from sketches I had made while in Woods Hole; and I went on doing this in pencil while Mimi copied out my score in ink. Meanwhile, for my Sunday column, I had read batches of hefty tomes such as Paul Henry Lang's *Music in Western Civilization* and Gustave Reese's *Music in the Middle Ages*, both of which were new that year. Then Maurice Grosser arrived from Alabama on his motorcycle; and on that we toured New Hampshire, visiting at the end the George Footes in stylish Dublin and my beloved teacher Edward Burlingame Hill in Francestown.

Eventually I visited Jessie Lasell too, at her hunting-and-fishing camp in Maine, where I wrote choral music and composed her portrait. Then I joined Grosser again; and we went to Nantucket, this time to be with the Russian-Armenian painter Inna Garsoian. And there I wrote more Sunday articles, covered the island by motorcycle, swam everywhere, and went bluefishing with my colleague Olin Downes. At some point I had been to New York, where I gave the score to Beecham and talked through two full nights with him and Emerald. And with all those changes in air and altitude and with the satisfaction of having done lots of work, I had restored myself from fatigue to vigor after a successful but vastly tiring year.

In 1939 I had received in Paris a letter from John Cage, requesting of me a new work for percussion, to be performed in Seattle. For company on the program there would be a novelty by Henry Cowell, and Lou Harrison's *5th Simfony* (*sic*). Being occupied just then writing *The State of Music*, I did not join the concert. Two years later, in New York, Cage phoned to ask if he could play for me the records of a broadcast just made in Chicago of works by Harrison and by himself. He could indeed, I said. And here began a long musical friendship, shortly to be complemented by the arrival East of Lou.

Cage, born in southern California, was half of him Tennessee mountaineer. That is to say that his father had come out of Tennessee and that the lanky and freckled red-haired big-boned son was distilling a clear-as-water musical moonshine without the stamp of any Establishment. At this very moment, having been rebuffed by Aaron Copland, who could not admire a music so abstract, he was organizing a concert of his works to be given at the Museum of Modern Art in collaboration with the League of Composers, Copland's own chief arm of patronage. And Copland did not stop this; few persons, indeed, have ever stopped Cage from anything.

His determination has nothing of Tennessee about it; its relentlessness is of southern California, and only barely hidden by a catlike smile. Already thirty, absolutely confident, and without embarrassment in asking for support, he had become by 1941 the designer of a unique product, its manufacturer, and its sole distributor. And if the abstract character of that product made it easier for him to defend than if it had been a more personal outpouring, the self-assurance with which he would explain it was nonetheless breathtaking. In fact, composers of the hand-work-and-inspiration type have never spoken of their own work so convincingly (for whenever Gluck, Wagner, Schoenberg have done so, we tend to freeze) as have Varèse, Boulez, Messiaen, and Cage, all of whom have practiced an objective method.

With all his rigors, Cage has a wit and breadth of thought that make him a priceless companion. For hours, days, and months with him one would probe music's philosophy. And after Lou Harrison, with his larger reading and more demanding ear, had arrived from the West, the three of us provided for one another, with Europe and the Orient cut off by war, a musical academy of theory and practice that supplied us with definitions which have served us well and which, through the highly divergent nature of our musical products, have given our methods of analysis wide distribution.

Lou Harrison, child of the Pacific Northwest and of San Francisco, was plump and round-faced; and though he smiled less than Cage, there was joy inside him, both joy and pain. Both of them had been pupils of Henry Cowell and of Schoenberg. Cage's southern California euphoria turned him eventually to Zen Buddhism and to a mushroom-study form of nature cult. A San Francisco sensitivity had first turned Harrison, it seems, toward the not uncommon worship of Mount Shasta, then to Yoga, to nervous breakdown, to the study of Esperanto, to the hospitalization of animals, to the construction of flutes and harpsichords with special tunings, and eventually to a mastery of classical Korean composition methods. In both, the West Coast cultural freedom is dominant, as in Henry Cowell and in Gertrude Stein and in the Northwestern painters Mark Tobey and Morris Graves. And in both, as also in Graves and Tobey, an Asian attraction has balanced the gravitational pull of Europe to keep them solidly anchored over America, though with no limiting local loyalties of the usual kinds, such as to New England, the Midwest, the New or Old South. Spiritually they are not even anchored to the West Coast.

Both, when I first knew them, had produced percussion music. And when Cage, leaving no doorbell unrung in his searches after support, asked for a Guggenheim Fellowship, I wrote unhesitatingly in his favor. He did not receive this aid till 1949, however, when his music had become better known. Moreover, having by that time looked at postwar Europe, I had even greater confidence in his powers. And so I wrote that I considered him "the most original composer in America, if not in the world, . . . also the most 'advanced,' in the professional sense."

For describing Harrison's music the word "original" would be less applicable than the word "personal," for its meaning is intensely his alone. Nor can the concept of "advanced" describe it, since as often as not it embodies a return to some method long since abandoned. Cage's driving ambition and his monorail view of art, by which quality depends solely on innovation, have brought him fame and followers. Lou's work, though known and widely loved, is without influence. The fault is one of temperament, I think; he lacks not quality, merely pushing ways. He stayed in New York till 1953, also teaching part-time in North Carolina, at Black Mountain College. Then fearing the strains of a no-money Eastern life, he returned to California, settling near his family at Aptos, in the Carmel Valley, from which retreat he sends out compositions or sallies forth to Rome (where he won a festival prize in 1954), to Tokyo (where his Esperanto opened doors), and to Korea (where he studied classical Chinese composition). His letters now are calligraphed, sometimes on parchment, their contents no less savory than ever. "I made a Phrygian aulos the other day & can well understand why Plato mistrusted it; ascending 12/11, 11/10, 10/9, 9/8, 8/7, 7/6; what an allure! I wait to hear the Dorian now."

My own first view of California came in 1943. John Houseman, after more than a year at the Office of War Information, was returning that summer to Hollywood for film producing. He was returning, moreover, by car and with a generous gasoline ration. Going along offered a lovely trip; and the paper welcomed it, Helen Reid filling my hands with introductions. On our way we stopped to visit in Kentucky, where we helped to put up hay, thinned out the hemp (and not remembering it was marijuana, threw it away), fed sugar to the thoroughbreds (when allowed), and drank mint juleps out of silver cups. We also stopped in Kansas City briefly and stayed a week in Colorado Springs. In Los Angeles we took an apartment at the Town House, where I was immobilized all day, there being only one car for the two of us. So I would swim in the pool and write piano études in bed till Houseman would come back and drive me to dinner (with Orson Welles and Rita Hayworth, the Joseph Cottens, Bernard Herrmann) or others would come for me and bring me home (George Antheil, who lived there, Aaron Copland, who was scoring a picture, and the people who ran concerts at the Hollywood Bowl). Also I wrote sometimes a Sunday column.

After a while I went to San Francisco and stayed in the Palace Hotel, where the food was lovely. And it was there I met, through Mrs. Reid's letter to the owners of the *Chronicle*, their music and art critic Alfred Frankenstein, a reviewer far more sympathetic to my aims (and I to his) than any of my colleagues in New York. Perkins had said of him, "He knows what it's all about." Also there were E. Robert Schmitz, his boisterously entertaining wife, Germaine, and gentle learned daughter, Monique; and from Paris the indefatigable Milhauds, both teaching in Oakland at Mills College. And they would come to Schmitz's house for playing me on two pianos Milhaud's just-completed opera *Bolivar*. I met society people too, was lionized. And of a Sunday afternoon in the social hall of Harry Bridges's Seamen's Union, I heard Bunk Johnson play New Orleans jazz.

Coming back by train, as I must have done, since planes were not proof against priorities, I stopped again in Kansas City, where in the spring my father had died of pneumonia at eighty-one. Mother was still in her house, my Aunt Lillie Post staying with her. This had been the arrangement since April, when I had gone there for the funeral. My father's end had been a gentle one. When he had felt it near, he said, "I think you should get me to a hospital." And once there, he had died after saying, "I'm all right now."

Certain Europeans wrote me letters, most touchingly Nadia Boulanger, whose mother I had known in life and whose own life was one long service to the dead, and Igor Stravinsky, whose own father, remembered, had become for him a cult. My personal regret (for my father and I were warmly attached, though without the possibility of much ease) was that now I could never let him know my shame for harsh things said in adolescent years. But he must have known and long since forgiven me, for he was a Christian and a loving one; and though the former I was surely not, he had always understood me and spared reproach.

Back East, I went to stay with Briggs Buchanan, then living with wife and children in upper New Jersey in a large white house. I wrote more piano études there, and Maurice Grosser joined us. Then in September, borrowing a cousin's car, I went off with Grosser to Somesville, Maine, facing Mount Desert, where Inna Garsoian was painting landscapes. He painted still life, I think, while I turned piano portraits into orchestral scores for conducting that fall in Philadelphia.

The Marquis de Cuevas, founding a dance company at that time, had invited several composers along with myself—Menotti and Bowles, I remember—to compose ballets. He had proposed for me a subject about a lonely fisherman and a sea gull which becomes a ballerina—a theme I found not fresh but not quite faded. It might do if I wrote a lovely sea piece. And already I knew how to make the trumpets caw quite realistically. So I went to Southwest Harbor, a fishing town, to pick up other points of atmosphere. There men in yellow-and-black waterproofs were unloading codfish and throwing them choreographically from ship to dock, all to the sound of radio full blast. Moreover, on inquiry I was told that the whole trip is so accompanied and that even simple setters of the lobster pot no longer go to sea or skirt the coast without for company their beloved box.

"Well, well!" I thought. "Each lonely fisherman is wired for sound! That lets me out, and the ballerina too." So I wrote no ballet. But I later used the trumpet's downward-smeared glissando in an orchestral work called *Sea Piece with Birds*.

I was driven again to California two years later, this time by Chick Austin, who had resigned from his Hartford Museum and was being a playboy. With

Houseman I shared a service flat just off The Strip. He was in romance with Joan Fontaine. And once we gave a sumptuous cocktail party, with Lady Mendl and the Stravinskys and naturally the Hollywood social register, for Houseman was important at M-G-M. And we frequented the Cottens and the Herman Mankiewiczes and the Alfred Wallensteins, who lived near, like the Stravinskys. And the surrealist painter Roberto Matta, with an American rich wife, would take us all out to expensive meals.

And we made a two-reel picture for the government, Houseman and I and Nicholas Ray, whom I had worked with in Federal Theatre days. It was an explication for foreign countries (eventually in some forty languages) of how in America we elect our president. Its title was *Tuesday in November*, and though our government's own films, by treaty with the Hollywood government, can almost never be shown publicly in America, it has long been visible to friends and students at the Film Library of the Museum of Modern Art. It is a fine piece of work, though not so dramatic as the Pare Lorentz films that were its model. I used in the score, for expressing a buoyant euphoria, my portrait of Aaron Copland and, for a sidewalks-of-New-York Americanism, my waltz from *Filling Station*. Out of it, I rescued a fugal treatment of *Yankee Doodle*, to make a children's recording, and a Stephen-Foster-like melody that in the two-piano version called *Walking Song* has long served many a duo-team as encore.

It was in San Francisco, again at the Palace, that I received a telegram from the French Embassy awarding me a "mission" to go to France. Since 1944 I had been looking for ways to get there. But the *Herald Tribune*, having only six travel priorities and needing these for its coverage of news, could not afford to waste one just on music. And though I had drunk with friendly colonels through a Washington week end, and they had all promised to "take a crack at it," nobody had yet been able to get me sent abroad. It was Suzanne Blum, back in Paris and knowing I would want to be there too, who had got the invitation out of Emile Laugier, Cultural Secretary at the Foreign Office, for me to spend two weeks in France as guest of the government, for reestablishing contact with French music.

And all the more urgent did going to France seem since Douglas Moore had written me in San Francisco offering to commission an opera for production at Columbia University, and I had wired Gertrude Stein I had an idea for one, and she had written back her delight.

So I called at the French Consulate for my orders, wired Washington for a new passport, asked the paper to pick up a plane passage, and took myself a bedroom on the train called "City of San Francisco" in a car that went through to New York. Nor do I even remember looking any way but East until my plane began to circle round and round over the pale gray stones of Paris, as if to give each passenger a view of the sacred site and to some a glimpse perhaps of house and home.

POSSIBILITIES: V.T. QUESTIONED BY 8 COMPOSERS (1947)

Possibilities was an arts magazine co-edited by John Cage (1912–1992), who later co-authored the first monograph on Thomson (1959). The eight interrogators were all contemporaries and successors, some of whom are still alive.

1. STEFAN WOLPE

Today, values are continuously shifting in the direction of the practical needs of the moment due to the complexity of the struggle in our social organization. How can we, who wish to express in a high state of organization the most positive and sensitive aspects of life, justify the function of our music?

The functions of music in any society are many. The social ones are like folklore patterns and not under our control. The expressive ones need no justification, either, though we sometimes have to fight for the dignity of our sentiments.

2. WALLINGFORD RIEGGER

Do you consider present-day music as deriving more logically from the pre-classical period or from the 19th century?

Everything we have in music, I should think, comes from the nineteenth century, either by reaction or by direct inheritance. Pre-classical revivalism is itself a nineteenth century formula. I need only cite Mendelssohn, who copied Bach, Brahms, who aped Handel and edited Couperin, and Wagner, who rewrote Gluck. Beethoven revived the fugal style, too. And the Benedictine monks brought medieval plainsong back to life.

3. PAUL BOWLES

Which of the three do you consider most vital to civilization today: painting, music, or literature? Why? And to what extent do you believe the subconscious should be allowed free rein during the process of musical composition? Why?

I can't get anywhere with the first question. It sounds artificial to me. The subconscious is our wellspring of inspiration. Some need to use a pump. Others have only to cap a gusher.

4. ELLIOTT CARTER

To be simple, unadorned, natural, to use the humblest musical devices in a new way has been the valuable lesson your music has taught us. Coupled with this is a tendency toward automatic writing which probably comes from a very understandable love of the spontaneous. It is about automatic musical writing that I would like to question you. For I remember you used to advise composers to write, as you sometimes may have done, whatever came into their heads and to stop when inspiration ran out even if it were in the middle of a phrase. You advised them not to torture their ideas with invented developments and continuations but to start afresh every time a new idea arose from the subconscious, from a "semi-euphoric state of automatism" as you phrased it in one of your recent columns.

But the puzzle is this: How can you expect the active listener to keep his mind on his work if the composer didn't keep his mind on his? Attention seems to parallel attention in ascending degrees until you get to the extreme case where the listener is worn down before the music gets very far. But at the other end of the scale, in automatic writing doesn't everybody's mind wander? (Except, of course, for the fellow-composer always on the lookout for surprises to remember.) Or doesn't this make any difference?

Don't confuse a disciplined spontaneity with the laziness of a loose tongue. Of course, music that bores the author will bore everybody. So will lots of music that interests the author. I do think that most of our best work, by anybody's judgment, is the product of a concentrated mental state in which one lets things happen. When concentration leaves and won't come back, it is better to knock off for the day. You save time that way. Concentrated work can always be polished up later, if there is time. Half-hearted work is the very devil to revise.

5. CARTER HARMAN

Explain your conception of the overtone theory of orchestration.

I am not aware of holding any such theory. Obviously, a well-written orchestral *tutti*, like a well-designed pipe-organ, respects acoustical phenomena. One uses everywhere acoustical compensation, doubling at the octave for brilliancy, adding plucked sounds for rhythmic definition, and so forth. But I am not aware that any good orchestrator uses mathematical acoustics in his calculations. So far, composers seem to be satisfied with ancient rules of thumb and with a trial-and-error procedure based on the instinctive or "musical" ear. Anyway, we write for halls and studios, no two of which are acoustically identical.

6. ARTHUR BERGER

What is the present status and character of the French movement that passes under the slogan, neo-Romanticism? I do not recall your having used the term more recently. In any case, you seem to use it less frequently than you once did. What significance, if any, attaches to this? Where do you, as one of the founders of the movement, now stand with regard to it? How has it been affected, if at all, by the war-time reversion of Jeune France to a kind of mysticism which, it seems to me, is a "post-" rather than "neo-" Romanticism—a Romanticism almost without alloy? What prognosis is there for neo-Romanticism?

Neo-Romanticism remains the esthetic of Poulenc and Sauguet, to name two successful French composers now in their middle forties. It has also tempered the formerly more ironic and severe neo-Classicism of Milhaud, Honneger and Barraud. La Jeune France I should call neo-Impressionist; and I include Rosenthal under that heading. An addiction to religious subject matter, common all over post-war Europe, is no more significant in Messiaen than is orientalism with Jolivet or the classical humanism of Rosenthal (and Malipiero).

Neo-Romanticism involves rounded melodic material (the neo-Classicists affected angular themes) and the frank expression of personal sentiments. I remain its most easily-labeled practitioner in America, though Paul Bowles, Nicholas Nabokov and possibly Douglas Moore, can be included among the neo-Romantics. Merton Brown, Lou Harrison and the other neo-contrapuntalists who derive from Ruggles are involved deeply with rounded material, not so deeply with personalized sentiment. Prokofiev's *Fifth Symphony* employs both in its first movement, before reverting to more familiar matters. The twelve-toners have never adopted an esthetic; they are eclectic in expression. Of late, some of them have been experimenting with neo-Romantic grace and intimacy; but the majority still write melodies that jump about. Everybody, I think, has been a little bit influenced by us.

I do not wish here to defend the neo-Romantic position, merely to assure you that it is still both reputable and influential. That position is an esthetic one purely, because technically we are eclectic. Our contribution to contemporary esthetics has been to pose the problem of sincerity in what is for our century a new way. We are not out to impress, and we dislike inflated emotions. The feelings we really have are the only ones we think worthy of expression. The resemblance of this code to that of Schumann is why we are called neo-Romantics. The term is not a very good one, because it does not express our almost exclusive attachment to the intimate side of Romanticism. The grandiose objective depictions of Berlioz and Wagner and Liszt, equally Romantic, are the heritage rather of the neo-Impressionists, of Messiaen and Rosenthal and of our own Bernard

Rogers. Sentiment is our subject, and sometimes also landscape, but preferably the landscape with figures.

7. LOU HARRISON

What, if any, is the relation of your doctrine specific expressivity (or music-meanings) to the Baroque doctrine of the affections?

The *affetto* is basically a style of execution, only incidentally a device of composition. It survives today chiefly in night clubs. In higher musical circumstances the *affettuoso* style seems to us affected rather than affecting. A good jazz-player does something closer to the *affetto* than anything we long-hairs care to ask for, to write for or to hope for out of standard players. When I speak of music's meaning, I mean something inherent in the design that makes a specific communication, if not inevitable, at least possible, no matter how you play it.

8. MERTON BROWN

What do you think is the relation of human character or personality to a composer's music exclusive of musical training? Can you illustrate this connection if you find one by specific examples?

Every composer, if he writes enough to achieve freedom and if he works hard at being honest, can look forward, I think, to complete self-expression through his art. Since Wagner's time many a composer has believed firmly that one could be a low moral character at the same time. Perhaps one can. I should not wish to judge my fellowman by thinking otherwise. But I doubt if any artist ever remains long unpunished by his muse for insincerity. The bourgeois "virtues" (and the socialist ones) are another matter. No artist has to do anything about those unless he wants to.

VIII

HIS OWN WORKS

Thomson wrote so well about his own works—incisively and yet modestly—that it is regrettable that such texts are so few.

The making of musical portraits dates from at least the eighteenth century, when François Couperin drew hundreds of them for harpischord, chiefly of ladies denominated *L'Audacieuse*, *L'Aimable Thérèse*, and the like. Robert Schumann in his *Carnaval* for piano (1837) lightly sketched the composer Frédéric Chopin, and maybe others. Later in the century Anton Rubinstein made twenty-three piano portraits of the guests at an island house-party, toward the end of these adding a picture of the locale itself, Kamennoi-Ostrow. The best known twentieth-century group is Edward Elgar's "Enigma" Variations for orchestra, each of which, though not identified, is the likeness of some friend.

When I began to make musical portraits, back in 1927, I worked, as the others had mostly done, from memory. But shortly I found, as had many visual artists centuries before, that one gets a more living likeness in the presence of a sitter. Consequently, since that time, I have not done them otherwise.

As to what is a likeness in music, resemblance there, like characterization in opera writing, can come from divers directions. Music can imitate a gesture or typical way of moving, render a complexity or simplicity of feeling, evoke a style or period, recall the sound of a voice, or of birds or trumpets or hunting horns or marching armies.

It was Pablo Picasso, inquiring about my method, who found an explanation of it in the mere fact of proximity. To my answer that I sketched very much as he did, which is to say, by first looking a bit and then letting my pencil put down what came to my mind, he replied, "Ah, yes, of course! If I am working and you are in the room, anything I draw is automatically your portrait."

There are by now a hundred and more of such portraits, all but the first six drawn from life, and each one bearing, in the judgment of persons acquainted with the sitter, some resemblance to its model. All have been sketched in silence too, usually at one sitting, save for those that comprise several sections, in which case each movement has been composed without interruption. And I do not stop to try out on a piano, to hear, correct, or criticize what I have done. Such adjustments are left for later, as is orchestral elaboration should this occur. Descriptive subtitles, such as Lullaby or Hunting Song, are also subsequent additions. My effort while at work is to write down whatever comes to me in the sitter's presence, hoping as I transcribe my experience that it will, as the painters say, "make a composition."

The result of this disciplined spontaneity, for I do think one may call it that, has been in all cases an instrumental piece. Instrumental also is likely to be any musical characterization for choreography, since singing is rare in the dance theater. In the opera, however, where singing is the basic operation, that without which there is no opera, characterization has from opera's beginnings, and emphatically so since Mozart, been a chief duty of the vocal line. Even in Richard

Wagner, where themes and motives are passed from voice to voice and back and forth from orchestra to voice, Siegfried does not sing quite like Fafner, nor Ortud like Elisabeth. Each works in character and vocally paints his own portrait, this portrait remaining strongly marked even in the ensemble pieces. It is noticeably so, for example, in the quartets from Mozart's *Don Giovanni* and from Verdi's *Rigoletto*. Also in the *Lucia di Lammermoor* sextet, where the heroine proclaims frustration by singing in syncopation against the others.

Instrumental illustration also can exist in stage works, from some villain's heavy-footed entrance to the threatening trumpet-calls of Cherubino's impending military service. But these are likely to have more to do with the drama—as description of a locale or the kinetics of a situation—than with the immediacy of a character's nature and presence.

Nevertheless, orchestral style and color are not excluded from characterization. I tend in my own practice to use them as extensions of the vocal self-portrait, as when, in *The Mother of Us All*, the shining militancy of Susan B. Anthony is constantly pointed out by a blend of trumpets and strings; and whenever Lord Byron, in the opera that bears his name, takes on a bardic pose, the harp and its idiomatic ways are clearly indicated.

In the vocal line itself, a florid, or coloratura, style, so often judged to be meaningless, can actually express many things—cruelty, for instance, or lightness of heart, or cold anger, or (for contraltos) villainy, or (for basses) pomposity, for tenors either insincerity, as in *Rigoletto*, or, as in *Don Giovanni*, the suavities of true love and joy in faithfulness.

My first portrait was of a Spanish girl who was staying with her mother in a small hotel near St.-Jean-de-Luz, where I was also staying, having just completed there my first opera, *Four Saints in Three Acts*. She had a grand and very Spanish way of walking, like a dancer coming out on stage, as she would enter our dining-garden, her mother, as is the Spanish way (the American too, for that matter), following just one step behind. She also played the violin. So, wishing to offer a gift that she could play, I made a musical portrait of her walk and gestures for unaccompanied violin, which I entitled *A Portrait of Señorita Juanita de Medina Accompanied by Her Mother*, for that was exactly what I had essayed to depict. But the mother, who was also a musician, asked thereupon my permission to compose an accompaniment for it. So that the piece became, in their version, a portrait of the señorita accompanied by her mother on the pianoforte.

The last of my early portraits for violin alone, of which there are seven, was of the composer Henri Sauguet, which I entitled *Sauguet, from Life*. And the next hundred or more were all so drawn.

A portrait usually takes me an hour or an hour and a quarter. That seems to be about the limit in time of my ability to keep my mind on the subject, to work rapidly, and to bring the piece to a close. Later I may correct, if need be, fill in the sketched patterns of some complex harmonic texture, or, if I have been garrulous, cut out measures. I have no principles against reworking an inspiration to improve detail. But unless the piece turns out to be a whole piece and embodies what I esteem on later examination to be a good musical idea, I treat it as a painter would an unsuccessful effort. I discard it.

FOUR SAINTS IN THREE ACTS (N.D.)

Why did Gertrude Stein and Virgil Thomson, in 1927, choose saints as their theme for an opera? Because they viewed the lives of the saints as parallel to theirs. In all times the artist has tended to live surrounded by younger artists, and by his own example to guide them toward discipline and spontaneity. Indeed, for anyone so to channel his gift is surely to invite "inspiration," and hopefully, through his work, create "miracles." Just like the saints.

Gertrude Stein liked rhymes and jingles, and she had no fear of the commonplace. Her communion hymn for all the saints is "When this you see remember me." And when Saint Ignatius sees the Holy Ghost, she describes his vision as "Pigeons on the grass alas and a magpie in the sky." Also she loved to write vast finales like Beethoven's great codas, full of emphasis, insistence, and repetition. She wrote poetry, in fact, very much as a composer works. She chose a theme and developed it; or rather, she let the words of it develop themselves through free expansion of sound and sense.

Putting to music poetry so musically conceived as Gertrude Stein's has long been a pleasure to me. The spontaneity of it, its easy flow, and its deep sincerity have always seemed to me just right for music. Whether my music is just right for it is not for me to say. But happiness was ours working together, and a strong friendship grew up between us. This friendship lasted twenty years, till her death.

Her last completed work was another libretto written for me, *The Mother of Us All.* That too became an opera and was produced, but Gertrude Stein never saw it. I am sorry now that I did not write an opera with her every year. It had not occurred to me that both of us would not always be living.

Synopsis

Four Saints in Three Acts is something between an opera and an oratorio. Its subject is the religious life, its leading characters Saint Teresa of Avila and Saint Ignatius Loyola. These personages are shown in characteristic scenes from their saintly lives, both of them surrounded by younger saints who are their pupils and apprentices, so to speak. There are also a commère and a compère, a lady and gentleman in modern dress who converse with the chorus, with the leading characters, and with each other about the action and progress of the play. They also speak directly to the audience from time to time.

Act One takes place on the steps of the cathedral at Avila, where Saint Teresa and her ladies are showing to assembled visitors, by means of a play or pageant, characteristic incidents from her busy life as a religious organizer.

Act Two is wholly pastoral. It represents a picnic in the country, where the saints are seen enjoying sociability and recreation.

Act Three shows Saint Ignatius and his disciples in the garden of a monastery near Barcelona. Study, exercise, and military discipline are their occupations; visions of the Holy Ghost and of the Last Judgment are their reward. This act ends with a procession, during which all the saints join in the singing of hymns about the future life.

Act Four is a sort of epilogue. It shows the saints in glory. The final chorus is a communion hymn, "When this you see remember me."

The opera begins with a choral introduction to all the saints, actually about thirty in number. There are four principal ones, including Saint Settlement, confidante of Teresa, and Saint Chavez, aide-de-camp to Ignatius Loyola. There are three principal acts, with a short Act Four rounding them off like a postlude.

Act One represents a religious entertainment on the steps of Avila Cathedral. This depicts Saint Teresa and her women in their daily practices. They sing, they pray, they receive callers, and they take trips to found convents ("half indoors and half out of doors").

Act Two gives us a garden party or picnic in the country Saint Teresa and Saint Ignatius are present with their helpers, who play light-hearted games and eventually see in a vision the Celestial Mansions ("How many doors and floors are there in it").

Act Three shows Saint Ignatius with his Jesuits near Barcelona. They mend fish nets, do military drill, and witness a miraculous vision of the Holy Ghost ("Pigeons on the grass alas and a magpie in the sky"). Saint Teresa and her women, visiting the establishment, are overtaken by a storm, which Saint Ignatius quiets, and in which all see in a sunburst which comes through the clouds a preview of the Last Judgment. At this point they line up for the expiatory procession, chanting ("led wed dead") and singing hymns about the future life ("There be vine time there all their time there").

After a short argument between the Compère and the Commère, it is decided that there is to be after all an Act Four. This gives us briefly all the saints in heaven, remembering with pleasure scenes from their earthly life ("May follows June and June follows moon and moon follows soon and it is very nearly ended with bread"). Whereupon all join in the communion hymn ("When this you see remember me") and to the announcement "Last Act" joyously shout "Which is a fact."

Why did it occur to Gertrude Stein and myself to write an opera about saints? Simply because we saw among the religious a parallel to the life we were leading, in which consecrated artists were practicing their art surrounded by younger artists who were no less consecrated, and who were trying to learn and needing to learn the terrible disciplines of truth and spontaneity, of channeling their skills without loss of inspiration. That was our theme; certainly that was our theme. That the daily life of saints could be, as regards their work and their preparation for it, a model to ours.

The opera takes place among Spanish saints and in Spain because Gertrude Stein had lived in Spain and loved its landscape, its intensity.

I had never been to Spain, and I refrained from going there till I had finished my score. I did not wish to encounter 20th-century Spain, so thickly overlaid musically with 19th-century gypsy ways, while trying to evoke an earlier time. Nor dared I attempt musically a historical reconstruction when my librettist had assumed no such obligation. So I took my musical freedom following her poetic freedom, and what came out was a virtually total recall of my Southern Baptist childhood in Missouri.

So do not try to understand the words of this opera literally nor seek in the music of it undue reference to modern Spain. If, through the poet's liberties with logic and the composer's constant use of the plainest musical language, something is evoked of the inner gayety and the strength of lives consecrated to a nonmaterial end, the authors will consider their labors rewarded.

SEA PIECE WITH BIRDS (1952)

My *Sea Piece with Birds* is an attempt to portray the undertow of the sea, the surface tension of waves, and the flight of birds as they sail back and forth above the sea. Toward the end trumpets imitate also their sound, the cry of sea gulls. The musical texture is that of double, and sometimes triple, chromatic harmonies. The form, which is free, contains no thematic repetition. [Program Note, Dallas Symphony (1952)]

THE SEINE AT NIGHT (1948)

The *Seine at Night* is a landscape piece, a memory of Paris and its river, as viewed nocturnally from one of the bridges to the Louvre—The Pont des Saints-Peres, the Pont des Arts or the Pont Royal. The stream is so deep and its face so quiet that it scarcely seems to flow. Unexpectedly, inexplicably a ripple will lap at the masonry of its banks. In the distance, over Notre Dame or from the top of far-away Montmartre, fireworks, casual rockets flare and expire. Later in the night, between a furry sky and the Seine's watery surface, fine rain hangs in the air.

The form of the piece is a simple AABA. The melody that represents the river is heard in three different orchestra colorations. Between the second and third hearings there are surface ripples and distant fireworks. At the very end there is a beginning of quiet rain. If my picture is resembling, it will need no further explanation, and if it is not, no amount of harmonic or other analysis will make it so. Let us admit, however, for sake of the record, that the melodic contours are deliberately archaic, with memories of Gregorian chant in them; that the harmony, for purposes of perspective, is bitonal and moments polytonal; that the rocket effect involve invented scales and different sets of four mutually exclusive triads as well as four sets of three mutually exclusive four-note chords, and that there are several references to organ sonorities.

THE FEAST OF LOVE (1964)

Virgil Thomson's *The Feast of Love*, for barytone and orchestra, was commissioned by the Library of Congress and first performed there at the Elizabeth Sprague Coolidge Birthday Festival on November 1, 1964. The soloist was David Clatworthy and the conductor Walter Hendl.

The work is a setting in the composer's free translation of the *Pervigilium Veneris*, a collection of rhymed Latin stanzas from the second or fourth century A.D. celebrating the three-day festival of Venus.

The beginning stanzas, repeated at the end, intone over a rhythmic insistency of plucked strings the declaration that "tomorrow all shall know love."

A more lyrical section, "in west wind's warmth," describes the opening of buds by night till in the dawn "the shameless rose reveals her hidden splendor."

Diana is besought to refrain from the cruel hunt of beasts and to absent herself from the woods for these nights of love-asking.

And Venus, as Dione the earth-mother, is invoked as the source of fecundity, till the poet himself laments to Apollo that only he among all those birds and married beasts shall never sing again.

Tomorrow all know love;
Love knows all tomorrow.
O, spring, singing spring!
Singing in spring, lovers love and all birds mate;
Under spring's warm rain Diana's woods unbind their hair.
Tomorrow shall all know love;
The unknowing shall know as well as the knowing.
She who loves coupling lovers has made them myrtle tents
And under bird-filled trees leads dance with song;
Tomorrow all shall love; Venus commands.
All shall love tomorrow,
All who have never loved.
In west wind's warmth, cluster's blush and swelling buds burst open;
Star-lit globes of heavenly moisture tremble, hesitate, explode;
By dawn the virgin vests are all undone.
As Venus tears their robes away
And purple flowers burst into flame,
The shameless rose, glowing like gems and fire,
From out its moistened sheath reveals her hidden splendor.
All shall know love tomorrow;
Tomorrow even the unknowing shall know love.
Holy Diana, Venus brings to thy wood
Maidens of no less modesty than thine;
Absent thyself tonight; shed no beast's blood.
She would invite thee, wert thou less chaste;
For three nights wouldst thou hear their festive sound,
As joyful companies traverse thy glades.
All night they dance to celebrate the spring
With braided garlands and with myrtle boughs;
With Ceres and with Bacchus, god of song,
Venus triumphs in Diana's wood.
Love is for all tomorrow;
Tomorrow the unknowing and the knowing know love.
Tomorrow remembers the union primeval,
When fluid from Zeus shot through the foam
To beget among rearing sea horses
Dione¹ out of the sea.
Love shall find all tomorrow;
Tomorrow the unknowing and knowing all shall love.
And now from out the clouds of spring,
Reins fill the lap of our mother-earth,
Then move through sea and sky back to the land for feeding all.

Venus, who governs all on land or sea,
Has given each living thing a fecund seed,
Commanding all to love and to give birth.
Venus's voluptuous ways people the countryside,
Where Love was born, a country boy.
There love doth multiply the herds;
Bulls rest with cows on yellow broom
Ewes lie in the shade with rams,
And singing is neglected by no bird.
Where swans call raucously from pool to pool,
Tireus's daughter, by the poplar, sings
As if her passionate sweet tune
Were all of love, not of her sister's death.
She sings, not I; my voice is lost.
When shall the soaring swallow mount again?
O, glance at me, Apollo, lest I remain
Forever mute, a ruin on the plain!
Tomorrow all know love;
Love knows all tomorrow.
O, spring, singing spring!
Singing in spring, lovers love and all birds mate;
Under spring's warm rain Diana's woods unbind their hair.
Tomorrow shall all know love;
The unknowing shall know as well as the knowing.
She who loves coupling lovers has made them myrtle tents
And under bird-filled trees leads dance with song;
Tomorrow all shall love; Venus commands.
All shall love tomorrow,
All who have never loved.

(from the *Pervigilium Venerts,* anonymous Latin stanzas of the 2nd or 4th century A.D.)

Translated by Virgil Thomson.

Notes
   1. Venus the earth-mother.

BIBLIOGRAPHY — WORKS BY VIRGIL THOMSON

American Music Since 1910. New York: Holt, Rinehart and Winston; London: Weidenfeld and Nicolson, 1971. Reprinted in paperback by Holt (1972).

The Art of Judging Music. New York: Alfred A. Knopf, 1959. Reprinted by Greenwood (Westport, CT), 1969.

Everbest Ever: Correspondence with Bay Area Friends. Gathered and annotated by Charles Shere with Margery Tede. Berkeley, CA: Fallen Leaf, 1996.

Music Reviews, 1940–1954. New York: Random House, 1967. [This collects *New York Herald-Tribune* reviews previously collected in *The Musical Scene, The Art of Judging Music, and Music Right and Left*, and so represents an abridgment of those three books.]

Music Right and Left. New York: Henry Holt, 1951. Reprinted by Greenwood (Westport, CT), 1969.

Music with Words: A Composer's View. New Haven, CT: Yale UP, 1989.

The Musical Scene. New York: Alfred A. Knopf, 1945. Reprinted by Greenwood (Westport, CT), 1968.

The Selected Letters of Virgil Thomson. Ed. Tim Page and Vanessa Weeks Page. New York: Summit, 1988.

The State of Music. New York: William Morrow, 1939. Reprinted by Greenwood (Westport, CT), 1974. Second ed., revised, with a new preface: New York: Random House, 1962.

Virgil Thomson. New York: Alfred A. Knopf, 1966; London: Weidenfeld & Nicolson, 1967. Reprinted by Da Capo (New York), 1977; Dutton (New York), 1985.

A Virgil Thomson Reader. Boston, MA: Houghton Mifflin, 1981. Reprinted by Dutton (New York), 1984.

[The Music Library at Yale University has a detailed list of Thomson's papers in its possession divided into these categories: "Books and Articles," "Lectures, Speeches, and Eulogies," "Program and Linear Notes," "Interviews," "Broadcasts, Panel Discussions, and Film Scripts," "Miscellaneous."]

INDEX OF PROPER NAMES

COMPILED BY STEPHEN DEKOVICH